BLACK SAN FRANCISCO

BLACK SAN FRANCISCO

The Struggle for Racial Equality in the West, 1900–1954

ALBERT S. BROUSSARD

UNIVERSITY PRESS OF KANSAS

© 1993 by the University Press of Kansas

Published by the University Press of Kansas (Lawrence, Kansas 66049),
which was organized by the Kansas Board of Regents
and is operated and funded by Emporia State University, Fort Hays State
University, Kansas State University, Pittsburg State
University, the University of Kansas, and Wichita State University

Library of Congress Cataloging-in-Publication Data

Broussard, Albert S.
Black San Francisco : the struggle for racial equality in the
West, 1900–1954 / Albert S. Broussard.
p.   cm.
Includes index.
ISBN 0-7006-0577-0
1. Afro-Americans—California—San Francisco—History—20th
century.   2. San Francisco (Calif.)—Race Relations.   I. Title.
F869.S39N424   1993
305.896'073079461'09045—dc20   92-30597

British Library Cataloguing in Publication Data is available.

Printed in the United States of America

10 9 8 7 6 5 4 3 2 1

The paper used in this publication meets the minimum requirements
of the American National Standard for Permanence of Paper
for Printed Library Materials Z39.48–1984.

To Mary L. Broussard

CONTENTS

ACKNOWLEDGMENTS

In the course of writing this book I have incurred many debts. My greatest intellectual debts are to the late B. Joyce Ross, who introduced me to Afro-American history as an undergraduate at Stanford University, and to Raymond Gavins, who supervised the Duke University dissertation on which this book is based. Ray Gavins embraced me as a student as well as a friend and I hope that this book meets his exacting standards. Richard L. Watson, Sidney Nathans, and Peter Decker also helped see the dissertation through to completion and encouraged me to expand the study to cover the postwar years. George C. Wright read every draft and helped to improve this book immeasurably through his incisive comments. The late James de T. Abajian not only shared my zeal in writing this book, but also permitted me to use his personal collection on Afro-Americans in the West. Others who read all or part of the manuscript and offered valuable suggestions were Eugene Berwanger, Robert Calvert, Donald Pisani, Lawrence B. de Graaf, Darlene Clark Hine, August Meier, Steven Channing, Joe William Trotter, Ronald G. Coleman, and Alphine W. Jefferson.

Many librarians also contributed to the publication of this book. Esme E. Bhan at the Moorland-Spingarn Research Center was especially helpful in providing me access to material. Irene Moran at the Bancroft Library always answered my inquiries on material regarding blacks in the West. Ethel Ray Nance at the Afro-American Historical and Cultural Society in San Francisco was especially generous with her time and knowledge about black San Francisco. The staffs of the Library of Congress Manuscripts Division, California Historical Society, San Francisco Public Library's department of Special Collections, and the San Francisco City Archives assisted me at various phases of this study. I am especially indebted to Cynthia Miller and Susan McRory, my editors at the University Press of Kansas, Carol Estes, whose meticulous copy-editing was indispensable, and Daisy Jones, who typed the final version.

This study was expedited by a Fellowship for College Teachers, a Summer Research Stipend, and a Travel to Collections Award from the National Endowment for the Humanities, a Grant-in-Aid from the American Philosophical Society, and a Summer Research Stipend and a Mini-Grant from Texas A&M University.

Finally, I wish to thank my family for their support during the years that I wrote this book. My mother, Margaret Broussard, has always been a source of strength and inspiration, and the publication of this book is only a small reward for her support. My brothers, Michael and John, and my sister, Sharon, have also waited patiently for this project to reach its final form. My wife, Mary L. Broussard, to whom this book is dedicated, has served as a catalyst, critic, supporter, and companion. Her inexhaustible patience may be unrivaled. This book could not have been written without her loving support.

BLACK SAN FRANCISCO

Map 1. San Francisco's Neighborhoods, 1900–1940.

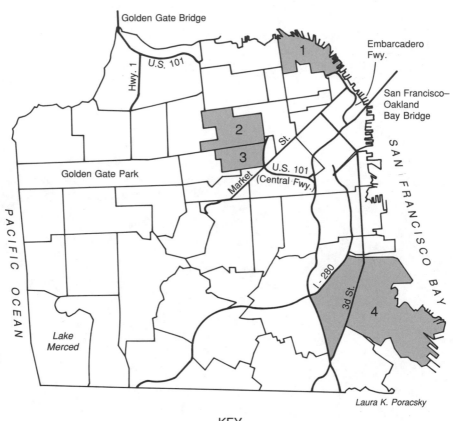

Golden Gate Bridge

Embarcadero Fwy.

San Francisco–Oakland Bay Bridge

U.S. 101

Hwy. 1

Golden Gate Park

Market St.

U.S. 101 (Central Fwy.)

SAN FRANCISCO BAY

PACIFIC OCEAN

I-280

3d St.

Lake Merced

Laura K. Poracsky

KEY

1. Telegraph–North Beach
2. Western Addition
3. Hayes Valley
4. Bayview–Hunter's Point

INTRODUCTION

Within the past two decades, our understanding of black urban life has increased significantly. Books have appeared on blacks in numerous northern, southern, and border cities.[1] Despite this breadth of scholarship, the majority of which is of exceedingly high quality, the history of blacks in the twentieth-century urban West has been largely neglected. Indeed, as the historian Lawrence B. de Graaf observed in 1975, it is "the greatest vacuum in western history." Little has been done in the past decade and a half to fill this vacuum, as scholars have concentrated on cities with large black populations and focused largely on the process of ghettoization that occurred during the era of the First World War. Thus, as Gerald D. Nash wrote in 1973, the "story of black Americans in the West [in the twentieth century] still needs to be told."[2]

In this book I attempt to tell part of that story by focusing on San Francisco's black community between 1900 and 1954. San Francisco's image as a liberal and progressive city provides an opportunity to study the black experience in a western city and to compare that experience with those of black communities in northern and eastern cities. Did blacks find greater social, political, and economic opportunity in San Francisco? Were black migration patterns to western cities like San Francisco like those to midwestern and eastern cities? How did San Francisco's black leadership, protest organizations, and race relations differ from other cities? Were white racial attitudes similar in San Francisco to those in other sectors of the nation during the twentieth century? Were they similar even to the attitudes found in other western cities?[3] What impact did World War I, the Great Depression, the New Deal, and World War II have on black San Franciscans? And did black San Franciscans improve their status during the post–World War II era, as their counterparts throughout the nation were struggling for civil rights and racial equality?

These questions, to be sure, can also be raised about other West Coast cities such as Los Angeles, Oakland, Seattle, and Portland. But San Francisco represents a particularly intriguing case for many reasons. It was the "preeminent" Pacific Coast city in 1865 and maintained that distinction throughout the nineteenth century. One scholar called San Francisco the "Rome of the Pacific Coast; all roads led to it."[4] It was the eighth largest city in the nation by 1900, containing 21 percent of the total population of California, Oregon, and Washington. San Francisco also played a pivotal role in the economic growth of the Pacific Coast. It was a center of banking and finance; its manufacturers produced 60 percent of the region's goods. San Francisco also controlled much of the coastal trade and provided a wide range of economic opportunities to its ethnically and racially diverse labor force. As William Issel and Robert W. Cherny wrote in a recent study of San Francisco, three decades after the discovery of gold San Francisco "stood virtually unchallenged as the economic capital of the Pacific Slope."[5]

San Francisco was also the leading social, cultural, political, and economic center for blacks throughout California during the nineteenth century. It contained the largest black population in the state until 1900, when it was surpassed by Los Angeles. Black San Franciscans established the state's earliest black schools, press, churches, political conventions, protest organizations, and benevolent societies. They were also the most prominent figures in the struggle for civil rights throughout the state during the nineteenth and early twentieth centuries.[6]

In addition, San Francisco, rather than Oakland, Los Angeles, Portland, or Seattle, possessed a mystique as a racially tolerant and progressive city toward blacks. Few white San Franciscans admitted that any form of racial discrimination existed in their city before 1940. Former president William Howard Taft had described San Francisco, famed as an international city and renowned for its beauty around the world, as "the city that knows how," and most whites believed that this appellation applied to race relations as well. Unlike many midwestern and eastern cities, San Francisco whites did not restrict blacks to well-defined communities as they did in many cities, including Los Angeles.[7] The majority of San Francisco's segregation laws were abolished by 1900, and blacks were permitted to frequent most places of public accommodation, ride public transportation, and attend the public schools on an integrated basis. Not one black was ever lynched in San Francisco, and there are few recorded instances of interracial violence between blacks and whites. Nor did San Francisco ever experience race riots before the 1960s, like

many northern and southern cities that exploded during the World War
I era and in the early 1920s. Thus San Francisco's race relations did not
conform to the rigid pattern that developed in many twentieth-century
urban centers.[8]

San Francisco is an important city to study for several other reasons.
Prior to the 1940s, it did not contain a large industrial black working
class like Chicago, Cleveland, Detroit, Pittsburgh, or Milwaukee, although the number of blacks in industrial jobs did increase steadily after
1910. Black workers were slower to gain industrial jobs in San Francisco
than their counterparts in other cities, however, and the vast majority of
black workers remained outside organized labor until the 1940s. San
Francisco's black population also remained relatively small between
1900 and 1940, at a time when many northern and southern cities experienced sizable increases in their black communities. Thus San Francisco
offers not only an opportunity to examine a relatively stable black community over four decades (1900–1940), during a period of rapid demographic changes in many black communities, but also a chance to examine a western city during a period of cataclysmic economic, social, and
demographic change (1940–1954).

Many aspects of San Francisco's black community have been ignored
by scholars.[9] Douglas H. Daniels's study of black San Francisco is valuable in illustrating the struggles of blacks throughout the nineteenth and
early twentieth centuries to come to grips with racial discrimination and
the illusion of San Francisco as an open, egalitarian city. His book is
particularly strong in describing cultural characteristics, social life, and
the wide variations in black life-styles that permitted blacks to adapt to
the urban milieu. The study, however, gives little attention to black leadership, racial ideologies, protest organizations, politics, and interracial
societies. Nor does Daniels examine in detail the impact of the Great
Depression and the New Deal, World War II, or the postwar era on San
Francisco's black community.

The major focus of my study is the twentieth century, particularly the
years from 1900 to 1954. The turn of the twentieth century marked
much more than just a logical place to begin this study. It also signaled
a new era in San Francisco's black community, which had struggled between 1850 and 1900 to gain many civil and political rights, including
the right to vote, serve on juries, ride public transportation, testify in
court against whites, and attend the public schools on an integrated
basis. In Part One I examine patterns of black migration, family life,
employment, housing, social life, politics, protest activities, and the status of blacks during the Great Depression and New Deal. During these

years, San Francisco's relatively small black community struggled to find decent jobs and adequate housing and to maintain their dignity. They also attempted to eliminate any racial barrier that restricted their social, economic, and political progress, through protest organizations like the National Association for the Advancement of Colored People (NAACP). Black San Franciscans were not altogether successful in eradicating racial discrimination before 1940, for they possessed virtually no political power and could never influence most of the powerful trade unions to accept black workers. Although black workers made progress in some occupations before 1940, they lagged behind white and Asian workers in most job categories, and they were overrepresented in unskilled labor and the service sector. Here, black San Franciscans paralleled the struggles and travails of black Bostonians, who also lagged far behind both native white workers and white immigrants and made little occupational progress relative to white workers before 1940.[10]

The impact of World War II and the postwar era on San Francisco's black community is the subject of Part Two. The Second World War was a watershed for black San Franciscans, because it provided, for the first time, jobs in semiskilled, skilled, and white-collar occupations in sizable numbers. The war also shifted the major patterns of black and white migration from the North to the Sunbelt states. Black migration, in particular, increased dramatically throughout the entire San Francisco Bay Area, as high-paying industrial jobs became available in Bay Area shipyards and defense industries. San Francisco's black population increased more than 600 percent between 1940 and 1945 alone, as black southern migrants sought economic opportunity, better schools for their children, and freedom from racial violence. The war also accelerated the campaign for racial equality that black San Franciscans had been waging for more than four decades. As black leaders joined with white leaders to form interracial organizations, racial discrimination was under greater assault than ever before, and by 1954, blacks faced fewer barriers in their quest for full equality. I concluded my study in 1954, because blacks throughout California and the nation would push even more vigorously for civil rights and racial equality during the mid-1950s and 1960s. Thus the period after 1954, which some scholars have called the "Second Reconstruction," launched a new era in San Francisco's racial history and is beyond the scope of this study.

My research on San Francisco's black community and on other black urban communities in the West reveals that western black communities developed differently in some respects from those in the East and Midwest. Before 1940, one of the characteristics that set black communities in the West apart from those in other regions was their relatively small size. With the exception of Los Angeles, which had a black population of 63,774 in 1940, black urban communities along the Pacific coast and in the interior grew at a much slower rate than those in the North.[11] Migrating to a West Coast city like San Francisco was more difficult because of the distance and the expense, but many blacks also considered it impractical because fewer industrial jobs were available there. And although blacks in some midwestern cities were organized by the Congress of Industrial Organizations (CIO) during the 1930s and 1940s to work in the automobile industry, most black westerners were excluded from organized labor until after World War II. Only as longshoremen were numbers of black San Franciscans welcomed on an integrated basis and permitted to join a white union.[12]

Another characteristic that distinguished San Francisco and most western black communities was the absence of black ghettos before World War II. True, Los Angeles had formed a black ghetto as early as 1930, but Los Angeles was exceptional because it contained nearly as many blacks as every other western city combined. No black ghetto developed before 1940 in San Francisco, Oakland, Portland, or Seattle. Blacks in these cities generally lived in integrated neighborhoods and attended integrated schools, although small black enclaves had developed in some cities before their black communities became sizable. The process of ghettoization that developed in eastern and midwestern cities between 1916 and 1920 was delayed between twenty-five and thirty years in western cities like San Francisco.[13]

San Francisco, Seattle, and Los Angeles, unlike midwestern and eastern urban centers, also had large communities of Asians, particularly Chinese and Japanese. San Francisco, in fact, had the largest Chinese community in the nation during the nineteenth and early twentieth centuries. During the nineteenth century, black and Chinese migrants arrived in San Francisco at roughly the same time, lived in proximity to one another, shared similar aspirations to better their economic and social position, and occasionally even shared the same recreation facilities. Yet San Francisco's Chinese community was more than ten times larger than its black population in some years and constituted a significant percentage of the city's labor force. Elsewhere I have compared some aspects of the black and Chinese communities in San Francisco, including migration patterns, employment, housing, education, and white attitudes toward both groups, as Quintard Taylor has done for the black and Japanese communities in Seattle.[14] The Chinese, despite also being portrayed by whites as an undesirable and inferior race, made significantly

more progress than blacks in employment and dominated some occupations, such as laundry work and cigarmaking, during the nineteenth and
twentieth centuries. Yet they lagged behind blacks in education, housing,
and health care and were occasionally the targets of mob violence. In this
respect, the Chinese served as a buffer between the white and black
communities, for they, rather than blacks, were perceived by white workers as a threat to their wages and working conditions.[15]

In this book I also explore the impact of the Great Depression and the
New Deal, World War II, and the postwar era on San Francisco's black
community. Only two studies of urban black communities, Joe William
Trotter, Jr., *Black Milwaukee: The Making of an Industrial Proletariat,
1915–1945*, and Darrel E. Bigham, *We Ask Only a Fair Trial: A History
of the Black Community of Evansville, Indiana*, evaluate the impact of
the Great Depression, New Deal, and Second World War on blacks.[16] No
scholar has examined the postwar era and its impact on a black urban
community to date, although Arnold R. Hirsch's *Making the Second
Ghetto: Race and Housing in Chicago, 1940–1960* explores the black
struggle for decent housing in a northern metropolis between 1940 and
1960, and Nicholas Lemann's *The Promised Land: The Great Black Migration and How It Changed America* examines how the migration of
southern rural black migrants from Clarksdale, Mississippi, to Chicago
during the 1940s and 1950s affected family relations, housing patterns,
employment, and race relations in a northern city.[17] My research sup-
ports Gerald D. Nash's conclusion that World War II had a "transforming
effect" on race relations in the West[18] and shows that an active civil
rights movement existed in San Francisco during the 1940s and 1950s,
the product of a committed interracial leadership and a new black leadership class that had migrated to San Francisco during World War II.

Black San Francisco, then, is about how blacks attempted to gain
social, political, and economic equality in a western city with a progressive image, few segregation laws, and a liberal reputation. Despite the
small size of San Francisco's black population between 1900 and 1940
and the nominal economic competition between black and white workers,
most whites perceived blacks as an inferior racial caste and restricted
their progress socially, politically, and economically. Although black San
Franciscans fought to eradicate these attitudes between 1900 and 1940,
largely through protest organizations and the black press, they did not
have the power to significantly alter their status. As the black population
increased dramatically between 1940 and 1954, white prejudices became
even more virulent. During the 1940s and 1950s, many blacks still found
it difficult to rent or purchase decent housing in integrated communities

and to find employment other than unskilled, menial jobs. This racial caste system dictated, as David M. Katzman showed in his study of Detroit's black community, that blacks and whites, irrespective of class or qualifications, rarely interacted on an equal footing. This was true both socially and politically but was especially evident in the employment sector. Black San Franciscans were generally denied access to trade unions before 1945 and barred from many skilled, white-collar, and professional jobs. Black women fared even worse. In San Francisco and most of the West, black women were overwhelmingly relegated to domestic and personal service jobs or "black women's work."[19]

Understanding the texture of this racial caste system is critical to understanding why blacks made so little progress in areas like employment and housing, despite the absence of segregation laws. Many whites resented the presence of blacks unless they occupied subservient or menial roles. Yet white San Franciscans were also conscious of San Francisco's national image as a tolerant and progressive city, and some worked diligently to maintain that reputation. Most whites were civil in their contacts with blacks, irrespective of their personal prejudices, and displayed what one historian has called "polite racism." Yet civility only masked the antipathy, disdain, and hostility that many whites felt toward black San Franciscans. So although I agree with the contention of historian William H. Chafe that "civility is the cornerstone of the progressive mystique, signifying courtesy, concern about an associate's family, children, and health, a personal grace that smooths contact with strangers and obscures conflict with foes," I believe that the racial caste model adopted by David Katzman has far greater applicability to San Francisco.[20]

On the eve of the historic *Brown v. the Board of Education, Topeka* decision in 1954, which outlawed segregation in public schools, blacks still faced many of the same problems they had confronted more than a decade earlier. To be sure, progress had been made in many areas, but black San Franciscans continued to be excluded from many areas of employment because of their race, and they occupied some of San Francisco's worst housing. In spite of San Francisco's civility and its liberal reputation, racial discrimination and the white perception that blacks constituted an inferior racial caste limited black progress and advancement in many areas. Thus W. E. B. Du Bois's prophecy that "the problem of the twentieth century is the problem of the color line" also included a "politely racist" western city like San Francisco.[21]

PART ONE

THE EVOLUTION AND SHAPING OF SAN FRANCISCO'S BLACK COMMUNITY, 1900–1940

1

THE GROWTH AND DEVELOPMENT OF SAN FRANCISCO'S BLACK COMMUNITY, 1900–1930

Few American cities had undergone the rapid demographic and economic transformations that San Francisco experienced during the nineteenth century. By 1900, San Francisco had become the leading West Coast metropolis and one of the fastest-growing cities in the nation. The discovery of gold at Sutter's Fort in 1848 had sparked an international movement of fortune seekers to northern California, and San Francisco's population grew at an astonishing rate for the next three decades.[1] In 1848, San Francisco recorded a population of only 1,000 people. Four years later the city's population had swelled to 30,000, and in 1860, 56,803 people resided in this once tiny hamlet—an increase of 89 percent from the 1850 census.[2] This rate of growth is impressive by any standard; it is even more remarkable when measured by the standards of East Coast cities like New York and Philadelphia, which took nearly two centuries to achieve this rate of growth. "Despite its inauspicious location," wrote Roger W. Lotchin, "a great city had grown up on the north end of San Francisco Peninsula."[3]

San Francisco's growth was equally impressive between 1860 and 1900. In 1870 its population had grown to 149,473, an increase of 163 percent from the previous census. And although San Francisco's population growth had slowed to 57 percent between 1870 and 1880 and 28 percent between 1880 and 1890, these were nonetheless significant increases. By 1900, 342,782 people lived in San Francisco, making it the largest city on the West Coast.[4]

San Francisco's rapid population growth was accompanied by a parallel boom in business and economic development, and by 1880 San Francisco led the entire West Coast as a center of finance. "The city had more manufacturing establishments, more employees in workshops, greater capitalization, larger value of materials, and higher value of products than all the other twenty-four western cities combined." San Francisco's foreign imports ranked fourth in the nation in 1890, trailing only those of New York, Boston, and Philadelphia. Equally impressive was San Francisco's export trade, which ranked fifth in the nation and was fueled largely by the shipping of wheat and flour.[5]

Manufacturing grew rapidly in San Francisco during these years, and by 1880 the city had the most broadly based, diversified manufacturing sector in the state. The value of San Francisco's manufactured goods had risen to $118 million by 1890, an increase of $81 million dollars in the space of two decades. Although the majority of employers hired fewer than five employees in 1880, both small and large companies grew rapidly during the decade, producing a variety of goods, including foodstuffs, cigars, clothing, textiles, lumber, and leather goods. San Francisco's food-processing industry alone earned $50 million dollars in 1890, and the sugar-refining industry, largely under the domination of Claus Spreckels, emerged as one of the largest sugar refineries in the nation. This industry earned $17 million in 1890, making it the dominant manufacturing industry in San Francisco and in the western region.[6]

In the wake of the gold rush, the city had no shortage of banks, and several of these institutions, such as the Nevada Bank and the Bank of California, also brought large profits from Nevada silver to San Francisco. This capital stimulated the growth of commerce, industry, and real estate development. The Nevada Bank, located at Montgomery and Pine streets, was capitalized at $10 million and had over $20 million in additional reserves. Prominent bankers, such as James Phelan and Charles Croker, were among San Francisco's economic elite during the late nineteenth century. They shaped the city's economic life for more than five decades[7] and, along with their fellow bankers and industrialists, organized and led some of the most important financial institutions in San Francisco. They also invested heavily in numerous local and state enterprises, including insurance, shipping, railroad, real estate, and utility companies. By virtue of their economic influence they also dominated the political arena in San Francisco throughout the nineteenth century.[8]

As in many American cities, San Francisco's economic elite also served as the city's social and cultural leaders. Former San Francisco Mayor James Phelan, for example, served as president of the San Francisco Art Association, the Pacific Union Club, and the Bohemian Club, and the membership of these organizations read like the city's social register. Phelan used his influence in social, political, and economic circles to bring the City Beautiful movement to San Francisco. Under the auspices of the Association for the Improvement and Adornment of San Francisco, Phelan commissioned Daniel H. Burnham, recognized as the leading city planner in the nation, to provide a comprehensive design for an "Imperial San Francisco" that would rival the great cities of the world. Although the Burnham Plan was never adopted, it illustrated the influence that San Francisco's economic elite had in cultural affairs.[9]

The rise and proliferation of labor unions between 1849 and 1890 was a significant factor in San Francisco's economic growth and contributed, in large measure, to the relatively high wages workers received. Labor agitation was a conspicuous feature of San Francisco's history during the late nineteenth and early twentieth centuries, as labor unions used the favorable business climate to press for higher wages and better working conditions.[10] Some of these early unions, such as the Trades Assembly, the Knights of Labor, and the International Workingman's Association, enjoyed limited success but were short-lived. Others, such as the San Francisco Labor Council, established in 1891, and the Building Trades Council (BTC), created in 1896, were extremely influential and a boon to organized labor. The BTC "became perhaps the most powerful labor organization in the country."[11] Because of its domination of San Francisco's construction industry, the BTC could require union membership as a prerequisite for employment. The BTC's reliance on the closed shop gave it tremendous leverage in negotiating wages and working conditions. Moreover, its organizational structure, which consisted of autonomous locals of different trades that were affiliated with national unions, ensured that "undesirable" workers such as blacks and Asians would not easily obtain membership.[12] Consequently, black San Franciscans, as well as their Asian counterparts, remained virtually excluded from organized labor until after World War II.[13]

While most San Franciscans believed that ample opportunity to excel existed throughout the nineteenth century, social mobility had slowed considerably by 1880. As Peter R. Decker showed in his study of white-collar mobility in nineteenth-century San Francisco, "class social boundaries were more closely drawn" by the 1880s, and it had become increasingly difficult for blue-collar workers to rise into white-collar occupations. Only 5 percent of the 1880 elite, for example, "had worn a blue collar in their first San Francisco job, a smaller group than the 16 percent of the first merchant generation (the elite of the 1850s) who emerged from the ranks of workingmen," Decker noted.[14] The average worker found that opportunities to move up the occupational ladder were more rather than less restricted as time progressed, and San Francisco's social structure began to replicate that of many northern and eastern cities during the late nineteenth century. Fortunes could still be made and white-collar mobility was a conspicuous feature of the middle class, but San Francisco's social structure was not as open or fluid as it had been during the city's formative decades. Most occupational mobility was limited to the white-collar sector by 1880, and this new elite dominated San Francisco economically and politically well into the twentieth century.[15]

Against this backdrop of a city that had grown from a commercial village to an urban metropolis in the space of a few decades stood a small black community that aspired to improve its social, political, and economic status. For black leaders like Peter Cole, who delivered an address in 1865 before the black state convention in Sacramento, California was the site where "the work of black liberation was destined to begin."[16] These early black migrants were as optimistic as white immigrants that San Francisco offered them a fresh start, hope, and myriad economic opportunities. One black migrant was so impressed with San Francisco's economic promise that he called the city the "New York of the Pacific."[17] Indeed, work was plentiful during the city's formative years. A few black migrants ran small businesses or were employed as artisans or semi-skilled workers, but the majority did not fare so well. Eighty percent worked in unskilled, service-oriented positions in 1860. Several luxury hotels, such as the Palace Hotel, employed black work crews, and 20 percent of black workers were employed as cooks. Most black working women were employed in domestic service, a pattern they would not break until World War II.

Despite restricted employment opportunities, a minuscule number of black San Franciscans, such as Mifflin W. Gibbs, however, were relatively successful. Born a free black in Philadelphia in 1823, Gibbs was lured to San Francisco by gold. He found employment as a carpenter, but was dismissed after white employees threatened to strike rather than tolerate a black co-worker. Although he was discouraged by this experience, Gibbs went on to establish a small business, the Pioneer Boot and Shoe Emporium, which specialized in the sale of "fine boots and shoes." According to Gibbs, "The business, wholesale and retail, was profitable and maintained for a number of years."[18] Gibbs's success as a black merchant was unusual: he was one of only three blacks listed among 3,100 merchants in the 1852 census for San Francisco. Gibbs acknowledged that he was an exception and that most blacks worked "in the lower and less remunerative pursuits."[19] With the rise of white unions in the service trades during the 1880s and the continuing competition with Chinese workers, who outnumbered blacks significantly during the nineteenth century, black workers were challenged and displaced, even in unskilled positions.[20]

The earliest black migrants also discovered that San Francisco's racial patterns, though never as rigid or oppressive as the conditions black Southerners endured, were similar to those in many northern and western cities. They also found that they were denied many civil and political rights. San Francisco's small black population, which grew from less than five hundred in 1852 to 1,847 in 1890, struggled to gain the vote, to attend integrated schools, to testify in court in cases involving whites, and to use public accommodations on an equal basis.[21] True, these types of racial restrictions characterized most western cities during the nineteenth century, as well as northern and midwestern urban centers such as Cleveland, Detroit, and Evansville, Indiana. But black migrants had hoped San Francisco would become a more open and egalitarian society. Instead, the world of black San Franciscans contrasted sharply with that of their white counterparts, who did not have to wage a protracted struggle to gain civil and political rights, to attend integrated schools, to ride public transportation, and to join labor unions on an equal basis. The experience of blacks resembled more closely the plight of the Chinese, who also fought for political and civil rights, and who were often the targets of mob violence by white workers. Thus, even though life may have been difficult for the majority of nineteenth-century San Franciscans and particularly harsh for some groups such as the Irish and the Chinese, the attitude of most whites toward blacks was one of contempt throughout the nineteenth century. As Lotchin concluded, "San Franciscans shared the general white American prejudice against Negroes."[22] White San Franciscans were reluctant integrationists, and they did not extend equal rights to blacks until they were pressed to do so. In his study of Detroit's black community, David Katzman observed that whites perceived blacks as an inferior caste unfit to interact with them under most circumstances. White San Franciscans, in many instances, shared these views. The term "caste" seems appropriate to explain whites' antipathy and contempt toward blacks of all social and economic classes. These attitudes contrasted sharply with San Francisco's image as a liberal and racially progressive city. The incongruity of the small black caste struggling for dignity and civil rights in the midst of an avowed liberal and racially tolerant white community would characterize San Francisco's race relations throughout the nineteenth and early twentieth centuries.[23]

Blacks responded to economic restrictions and racial inequality in a number of ways. Some migrated to other California cities, such as Oakland or Los Angeles. Others returned to their home states. The *San Francisco Elevator*, a black newspaper, wrote in 1868 that the "tide of travel [to San Francisco] is reversed. Our representative men are leaving us, going East, some never to return. California does not hold out sufficient inducements for able colored men to come here and waste their time and bury their talents where they are not appreciated."[24] Limited employment opportunities created a class of idle blacks who frequented street corners and occasionally proved to be public nuisances. A black barber complained about the "great number of idle Negroes lounging around the bootstands, discussing politics; often drunkenness, profanity and quarreling among them is a great detriment to my business and disgusting to the public."[25]

Although black leaders knew that racial discrimination was in part responsible for the diminished employment opportunities available in San Francisco, they also argued that unless more blacks learned trades, the race would never overcome its lowly occupational status. The *Pacific Appeal*, a black weekly, asked its readers, "How can you ever expect to occupy any other position, than that of menials, if you educate your children for no others?" Trades, the paper argued, would make blacks "independent of the whitewash brush and the shop bucket." Similarly, black editor Philip A. Bell believed that the succeeding generation should strive to be more than "waiters, bootblacks, white-washers, and barbers." As late as 1890, the black press continued to extol the virtues of learning trades as an important precondition for social mobility and economic progress. Yet blacks made only marginal progress in skilled and semi-skilled jobs before the 1940s.[26]

The vast majority of black San Franciscans chose not to leave for other cities. Instead, like the thousands of white ethnic immigrants who preceded them to the Bay Area, they remained and strove to improve their status. Much of their struggle would be channeled through an array of committees, protest organizations, and institutions (such as churches, lodges, literary societies, political leagues, and black newspapers) established between 1850 and 1870. Thus organized black protest was an integral part of San Francisco's heritage. As early as 1851, black leaders, led by Mifflin Gibbs and J. H. Townsend, printed a list of resolutions in the *Alta California* protesting the denial of the franchise and the right of blacks to testify in court cases involving whites. The right of testimony and the franchise, both integral parts of the democratic process, were two of the most important issues for black leaders. Jeremiah Burke Sanderson, a black minister and activist, wrote that the denial of the right to testify was the catalyst for the 1855 black state convention, in which black San Franciscans played a pivotal role. Blacks also associated the testimony right with the right of self-defense. The *Pacific Appeal* wrote that the denial of the right to testify against whites would leave the black populace in an untenable position, "victims of every lawless ruffian who chose to murder, rob and oppress us." It described the restrictions as "relics of barbarism and slavery," and lobbied to remove them. Black leaders also conducted petition drives, which were supported by some whites throughout the state, but twelve years transpired before the state legislature granted blacks the right to testify against whites in 1863.[27]

Black San Franciscans, like their counterparts in Cleveland and New York, also struggled during the 1850s and 1860s to gain the franchise. Black suffrage associations were established in San Francisco as early as 1852, when the Franchise League was founded, although the campaign to obtain the vote did not intensify until the 1860s. Philip A. Bell, the editor of the *San Francisco Elevator*, a weekly black newspaper, provided the spark and impetus behind the drive. "Let the entire state be canvassed," Bell wrote in 1865. Realizing the role that public opinion would play in this campaign, Bell continued, "It is not legislation alone to whom we must look to extend us that right. We must educate the people." Bell also maintained that black voters would be as sophisticated in their use of the franchise as white voters and that it would not "require a generation to educate them [blacks] to an intelligent use of the ballot," as some critics had charged.[28]

Black San Franciscans formally petitioned the state legislature in 1867, two years after that body had defeated an 1865 amendment to repeal the racially restrictive franchise law. Once again, however, the legislature ignored the pressure by black leaders to grant them the right to vote. Thus blacks were unable to vote in California until the passage of the Fifteenth Amendment in 1869.[29]

The issue of integrated education was also as volatile in San Francisco as in most northern communities. Although California's earliest school laws made no specific mention of race, black children were required to attend segregated schools as early as 1854. Black leaders made impromptu inspections of the Jim Crow school, located near the corner of Jackson and Virginia streets, and often found the conditions deplorable. Housed in the basement of a black church, the colored school was "dark, damp, with only one small yard as a playground."[30]

Black parents also protested the Jim Crow school's location. They argued that their children were forced to walk several miles to school,

often in poor weather, and that this had an adverse effect on black attendance. Indeed, by the late 1860s, a higher proportion of blacks than
whites failed to attend school. Between 1869 and 1870, 145 black children were enrolled in school, but the average daily attendance was seventy-six pupils. Since most black parents could not afford to send their
children to private schools, and since Catholic schools were also expensive and discriminated on the basis of race, many black children simply
stayed home. The precise number of black children who did not attend
the colored school cannot be determined. However, during the 1859-1860
school year, one hundred black students were enrolled in the colored
school, but the average daily attendance was only thirty-nine students.[31]

As in their earlier struggles for the right to testify and the right to vote,
black San Franciscans used the meager resources within their community to protest segregated schools for black children. Indeed, the school
issue dominated the black press in the 1870s, and the concern by local
blacks was echoed statewide. "The proper education of our children is
paramount to all other considerations," wrote the *Pacific Appeal*. Black
leaders organized a district educational convention in Stockton in 1871
to discuss this issue and devise a strategy, and the 1873 California
black state convention passed several resolutions denouncing segregated
schools.[32]

Black San Franciscans finally appealed to the courts. In 1872, the
parents of Mary Frances Ward sued Noah Flood, the principal of the
Broadway Grammar School, and the San Francisco school district when
their daughter was refused admission because of her race. John W.
Dwinelle, a prominent white local attorney, agreed to serve as Ward's
counsel and to test the legality of the de facto policy that prohibited black
children from attending school with white children. Dwinelle argued that
the existing school code violated the Fourteenth and Fifteenth amend-
ments and the Civil Rights Act of 1866. Even though he knew that two
bills designed to admit black children to the public schools had been
defeated by the legislature in 1872, Dwinelle was optimistic that the
state supreme court would rule in his client's favor. Less than two years
after the case had been filed, the California State Supreme Court ruled
that unless separate schools for blacks were maintained, blacks could not
be legally excluded from white schools. This decision "established the
principle of 'separate but equal' in California law—twenty-two years
before the United States Supreme Court adopted it in the case of *Plessy
v. Ferguson*." Black leaders called the decision a compromise, rather than
a victory, for it avoided the real question of equality before the law. The
"old barn, called a colored school stands upon Russian Hill with no more

additional improvements or facilities than before the decision was given," wrote the *Pacific Appeal*. The San Francisco Board of Education finally voted to end segregated public schools for blacks in 1875, after a committee of the board "recommended that 'colored children' be allowed to attend any public school and that separate schools be abolished."[33]

The board's decision to abolish segregated schools was the result of public pressure by local leaders, both black and white, and a declining economy. San Francisco's black leadership had pushed for the abolition of the Jim Crow school for two decades without success, but their struggle drew attention to the colored school's deplorable condition. Several influential whites, including John W. Dwinelle and J. F. Cowdery of San Francisco, a local assemblyman, opposed the Jim Crow school. The state's declining economy during the 1870s also contributed to the board's decision. The city's colored school was more expensive to operate on a per pupil basis than were the larger white institutions, according to Charles Wollenberg, and many voters balked at paying taxes to support it during a depression. The expediency of the board's decision was not lost on the *Pacific Appeal*, which wrote that board members favored ending the Jim Crow school because of "retrenchment and economy rather than a really spontaneous desire at this time to do justice to colored children." Regardless of whether the board's motivation was ideological or merely pragmatic, this was an important decision. It signaled the crumbling of another caste barrier in San Francisco. Five years later, segregated school facilities for blacks were outlawed throughout California.[34]

Black San Franciscans were generally permitted access to public accommodations, but they were occasionally barred from public transportation and restricted in certain establishments. One proprietor reported that a Negro was free to patronize his tavern, "provided he did not come too often." At least four blacks filed suit against public transportation companies in San Francisco and collected damages, an indication that this problem was more widespread during the 1860s than many people believed.[35] After 1867, blacks apparently rode local transportation without harassment, but were not as fortunate in other areas. Charles Green, a twenty-four-year-old black man, sued T. R. Jackson in 1876 after he was denied access to the dress circle during a performance of the Jubilee Singers. Jackson, who managed Maguire's New Theatre, a popular local establishment, was acquitted in the U. S. Circuit Court, on the grounds that the owner of a private establishment had the right to determine his own procedure for seating. Green appealed the decision but lost his appeal. As historian Roger W. Lotchin concluded about San Francisco's race relations, "the hostility was always ambiguous, and respect and support coexisted with antipathy." So although blacks were allowed to frequent most restaurants and theaters, albeit in restricted seating areas, they could not attend San Francisco's public baths and were required to sit in the balcony in some theaters. Thus caste barriers were eradicated in education, voting, and the right to testify in court by the 1870s, but they remained intact in other areas, such as public accommodations.[36]

The difference in black access to education and transportation, on the one hand, and to places of public accommodation, on the other, was a matter of degree. True, blacks did not have to wage extensive public or legal campaigns in order to frequent public establishments, but then black patrons had more alternatives in selecting places of public accommodation than they did in choosing schools and transportation. When black patrons received poor service or were offended by racial slurs at one restaurant or tavern, they simply chose another establishment where they felt more comfortable. When it came to schools or local transportation, however, their options were few and the stakes were higher, which may explain why blacks chose to wage more intensive campaigns in these areas.

By 1900, San Francisco's small but cohesive black community had made significant progress in breaking down the racial caste system in many areas. Black leaders had secured a number of rights: the right to vote, to attend integrated schools, to ride public transportation, to testify against whites, and to frequent most public accommodations. Moreover, blacks could live anywhere they could afford to live. These were impressive achievements for a black community that did not reach 2,000 during the nineteenth century and was never more than one percent of the city's total population. Black leaders were less successful, however, in opening up employment opportunities for black workers and breaking down discriminatory barriers in white trade unions. In fact, by the closing decades of the nineteenth century, black San Franciscans began to lose ground, even in the service trades, as emerging white trade unions barred black workers.[37] The limitations on black advancement in these areas would carry over into the twentieth century. Yet black San Franciscans never gave up. They had not forgotten that conditions were much worse when the first black migrants arrived during the 1850s, but they also realized that they could not rely solely on white San Franciscans to set the agenda for racial progress. Like their counterparts in other northern and southern cities, local black leaders advocated self-help, racial solidarity, business enterprise, and the efforts of their own community institutions to bring about change and to mold San Francisco into a racially progressive city.

San Francisco's blacks had established patterns and characteristics by 1900 that shaped the black community for several decades and distinguished it, in some respects, from black communities in other parts of the nation. The small size of the black population, which had grown slowly throughout the nineteenth century, was one of San Francisco's most striking features. Like most far western cities, San Francisco contained only a nominal percentage of blacks by 1900 and never approached the percentage that characterized northern industrial centers like Chicago, Cleveland, Pittsburgh, or northeastern cities like New York and Boston. Excluded from labor unions and most skilled occupations throughout the Bay Area, blacks struggled and scratched to make a living. It is hardly surprising that San Francisco's black community never exceeded one percent of the city's total population. This was in stark contrast to San Francisco's large Chinese population, which had grown to almost 14,000 by the turn of the century and comprised the largest racial minority group in San Francisco. The Chinese community was eight times larger than the black population in 1900, and its work force had attained a greater foothold than blacks in industrial and skilled jobs. But if blacks faced restrictions in some areas compared to the Chinese, they also enjoyed some advantages. Because San Francisco had integrated its public schools in 1875, virtually the entire black community was literate by 1930. Finally, San Francisco was relatively free of the violence and racial harassment that blacks faced in other parts of the nation, although these problems did afflict the much larger Chinese population.[38]

Blacks were not attracted to San Francisco in large numbers between 1900 and 1940, because of limited economic opportunities and competition with other nonwhite groups for unskilled jobs. Furthermore, the distance of San Francisco from the South made it more difficult city to migrate to than many northern or midwestern cities. Only 1,654 blacks lived in San Francisco at the turn of the century, a decline of 10.4 percent from the previous census. Some of these individuals probably moved to Oakland, which almost doubled its black population between 1890 and 1900 and was considered more hospitable to blacks seeking industrial employment. A decade later, San Francisco's black community experienced another population decline, reporting 1,642 residents, twelve fewer than the previous census. Although it was no precipitous skid, the

decline indicated that San Francisco was not a magnet for black migrants even though black populations in many other western and northern cities were growing. Oakland, for example, almost tripled its black
population between 1900 and 1910, as more black migrants and some
black San Franciscans selected San Francisco's east bay rival as their
preferred residence. In 1920, San Francisco's black population recorded
its first growth since 1890, when it reached 2,414. In 1930, the black
population of San Francisco reached 3,803, approximately one-tenth the
size of Los Angeles' black population, and half the size of Oakland's. On
the eve of World War II, 4,806 blacks lived in San Francisco out of a total
population of 634,536.[39]

Although the black community of San Francisco is small when measured against those of northern urban centers, it increased over two
successive decades. This increase is important, because it reveals that
San Francisco's black population was not static between 1910 and 1940.
In fact, in some respects, its growth was impressive. Although the number of blacks who migrated to San Francisco was not as great as the
number that migrated elsewhere, the black population of San Francisco
increased 131 percent between 1910 and 1930, and 193 percent between
1910 and 1940. These gains would be impressive for any black urban
population, and they indicate that San Francisco did offer some economic
inducements to black migrants between 1910 and 1940. This growth also
reveals that many blacks began to perceive San Francisco differently
after 1910. As fewer employment restrictions hampered black workers,
more were willing to make the long westward trek.[40]

The distance between the West Coast and many southern rural communities probably discouraged blacks from migrating to San Francisco
and neighboring cities during the Great Migration and the 1920s. The
vast majority of these migrants were southern rural blacks, who migrated
to northern and midwestern cities primarily in search of better-paying
jobs. Rail and water transportation to northern cities was not cheap, but
through ingenuity, frugality, and the occasional assistance of white industrialists, many impoverished blacks obtained enough money to make the
trip. San Francisco, however, was almost twice as far from Florida, Georgia, Alabama, and Mississippi as most northern industrial cities. The trip
was not only longer, but also less direct and more expensive, as regular
railroad passage was computed per mile. Moreover, it was unlikely that
many southern migrants had either friends or relatives in San Francisco,
given the small size of its black community. Thus the vital network
of friends and family members that propelled so many southern blacks
northward was not a significant factor in San Francisco's black com-

munity before World War II. Similarly, there is no evidence that rail-roads attempted to lure southern black migrants to western cities as cheap laborers before World War II, for Bay Area industrialists did not experience the critical labor shortage that their counterparts faced in the North. Nor did San Francisco contain a militant black newspaper com-parable to the *Chicago Defender*, which urged blacks to leave the South and migrate North. Hence, many black southern migrants probably never considered going to San Francisco, viewing such a move as difficult, impractical, and undesirable, given the paucity of industrial jobs.[41]

The impact of the 1906 earthquake and fire also had a devastating effect on the city's black community and retarded its population growth. Many of the residential hotels and apartments that black workers occu-pied in the central district (south of Market Street and near the Embar-cadero) were destroyed. Once the city lay in virtual ruins, housing of any type became difficult to find, and the lowly economic status of blacks made their search even more difficult.[42] Restricted economic opportunity, however, was the major factor explaining the slower growth of San Fran-cisco's black community relative to other cities before World War II. Unlike northern industrial cities, which experienced substantial increas-es in their black populations during the Great Migration (1916–1919), San Francisco's black population grew at a rate of 47 percent between 1910 and 1920, when it added approximately 800 black residents. True, this number seems insignificant in comparison with the 65,355 blacks who migrated to Chicago between 1910 and 1920; however, it is compa-rable to the 2.0 percent increase in Evansville, Indiana's black com-munity between 1910 and 1920. Moreover, San Francisco's black popu-lation in 1920 was slightly larger than that of some industrial cities, such as Milwaukee,[43] yet San Francisco offered fewer high-paying industrial jobs to southern black migrants. Black migrants were generally at-tracted to cities that were more oriented toward manufacturing, which explains in part the attraction of both Oakland and Los Angeles, whose black communities grew at a much faster rate than San Francisco's after 1910. These two cities also offered a warmer climate and the opportunity for more blacks to become homeowners. However, the fact that San Fran-cisco provided limited opportunities for black workers in industry and manufacturing proved the most significant reason explaining its small black population.[44]

As blacks settled in San Francisco, they attempted to form stable, two-parent families and, to a large extent, they succeeded.[45] Indeed, by 1900, 81.9 percent of black households were headed by men. Black women headed only 18 percent of all households, and three-fourths of these

Table 1.1. Black Population in San Francisco, Oakland
and Los Angeles, 1900–1950

Year	San Francisco	Oakland	Los Angeles
1900	1,654	1,026	2,131
1910	1,642	3,055	7,599
1920	2,414	5,489	15,579
1930	3,803	7,503	38,894
1940	4,806	8,462	63,774
1945	32,001	37,327	133,082
1950	43,460	47,562	171,209

Source: United States Bureau of the Census, Population, 1900–1950: Special Census of San Francisco, Oakland, and Los Angeles, United States Bureau of the Census, 1945 and 1946.

women were widowed. Although the number of male heads of households had declined to 74.5 percent by 1930, these figures illustrated a high degree of family stability and were similar to the high percentage of male-headed black families that historian Herbert Gutman found in New York.[46]

San Francisco's black families were also smaller than white families. Nearly a third of black families in 1900 had no children and 22 percent had only one child. By 1930, the median size of black families was only 1.98, compared with a median of 2.85 for foreign-born white families and 2.39 for native white families.[47] Approximately a third of all black families in 1930 consisted of a single person. Another third had only two members. Families with three members composed only 14.5 percent of black family units, and black households with four or more members constituted 16.5 percent of black households.[48] White families, in contrast, were slightly larger than black households. Only 17.9 percent of native white families and 14.9 percent of foreign-born white families contained only one family member in 1930. Two-person families made up 35.9 percent of all native white households, similar to the black percentage. Foreign-born whites also had larger families than blacks; two-person families were 25.5 percent of the total. The percentage of families with three or more members was also larger among both native whites and foreign-born whites than among blacks.[49]

The large percentage of one-person black families in 1930 marked a sharp break with the figures of earlier years and reflected, in part, an influx of single males between 1910 and 1930. The black population increased 131 percent during these two decades, and many of these migrants apparently settled in San Francisco as single family units. The reasons for black San Franciscan's reluctance to have children cannot be ascertained easily. Hardly a youthful population, 90 percent of black residents were at least twenty-five years old by 1930. The median age for blacks was higher than for native whites, but significantly lower than for foreign-born whites. Since foreign-born whites possessed the largest median family size of all groups, age was not apparently the most serious obstacle in having children, as Lawrence B. de Graaf speculated about black women in the West. The decision to have small families or no children at all cut across the entire spectrum of black society and was not limited to one social class or economic group. Often members of the black working class, such as Alfred Butler, as well as members of the black middle class, such as Katherine Stewart Flippin, chose not to have children. This preference was also evident in other urban communities throughout the West. It reflected the beliefs of many black westerners that their tenuous position in the labor market and the resulting economic hardships made the prospect of large families undesirable.[50]

As in many northern cities and throughout the West, the ratio of males-to-females was disproportionate in the San Francisco black community. Black men had migrated to San Francisco since the 1849 Gold Rush, expecting to improve their economic status. Many eventually sent for their families, but there was still a shortage of black women to date or marry. Although this problem was not unique to blacks, it was exacerbated by the strict social and legal etiquette governing interracial dating and marriages. Black men were less likely to marry than either native whites or foreign-born whites, which explains, in part, the relatively small number of children in the city's black population. The black male-to-female ratio remained imbalanced in San Francisco until 1940, when it became virtually equal. A larger number of single black females migrated to San Francisco between 1920 and 1940, and fewer single black males migrated to San Francisco during the 1930s, a reflection of the economic hardships that blacks faced during the Great Depression. Not until 1945, with the large influx of black migrants to San Francisco, did black females outnumber black males.[51]

Table 1.2. Males per 100 Females by Race, San Francisco, 1910–1950

	Negroes	Native whites	Foreign-born whites
1910	166.1	125.8	162.4
1920	129.5	113.9	114.8
1930	135.8	109.5	138.7
1940	103.2	94.9	122.4
1950	94.9	96.6	108.4

Source: United States censuses, 1910–1950.

Table 1.3. Illiteracy by Race, San Francisco, 1910–1930 (in percentage)

	Negro	Native white	Foreign-born white
1910	5.2	0.2	4.7
1920	3.1	0.2	4.8
1930	1.6	0.2	3.7

Source: United States Bureau of the Census, Fifteenth Census of the United States, 1930: Reports by States, vol. 3, pt. 1 (Washington, D.C.: Government Printing Office, 1933), p. 69.

If black San Franciscans placed a high premium on family stability, they placed an equally high value on education. Accordingly, blacks took advantage of San Francisco's commitment to eliminate illiteracy and to educate its entire school age population. The black illiteracy rate in San Francisco was always fairly low and gradually improved until it approximated the rate for the city as a whole. In 1910, 5.2 percent of blacks were classified as illiterate compared to a city-wide percentage of 2 percent. By 1920, the black illiteracy rate had declined to 3.1 percent, while the city-wide figure stood at 1.9 percent. Within a decade, the black illiteracy rate was cut in half to 1.6 percent, equalling the city-wide percentage (see Table 1.3). Even though illiteracy rates were much lower in far western cities than in the urban South, San Francisco had made exceptional progress in educating virtually its entire school age population within two decades, and the city possessed one of the most literate black communities in the nation. The low black illiteracy rate in San Francisco is also impressive when measured against a northern city like Cleveland, which reported a black illiteracy rate of 15.7 percent as late as 1930.[52]

The commitment of San Francisco blacks to education was also reflected in the percentage of children who attended high school and college. Almost 16 percent of the city's blacks had completed between one and three years of high school by 1940, compared to 19.2 percent of native whites. Yet 30.2 percent of blacks had completed four years of high school in 1940, compared to 46.5 percent of native whites and 23.5 percent of foreign-born whites. The percentage of blacks who completed between one and three years of college was also higher than that of foreign-born whites, but only half the percentage of native whites. The percentage of blacks who completed four years or more of college lagged behind that of both native whites and foreign-born whites. The median number of school years that blacks completed was higher than the median for either foreign-born whites or members of other nonwhite races, but lower than the median for native whites. San Franciscans could

Table 1.4. Years of School Completed by Ethnic Group,
San Francisco, 1940 (in percentage)

	Other races	Negro	Native white	Foreign-born white
No school completed	10.5	2.7	0.4	4.9
1–4 years	19.1	12.0	2.2	12.0
5–6 years	13.6	15.0	4.3	11.1
7–8 years	21.9	31.7	29.0	29.7
High school: 1–3 years	12.4	15.6	19.3	9.1
High school: 4 or more	14.0	14.6	27.2	14.4
College: 1–3 years	2.4	3.9	8.5	3.2
College: 4 or more	3.6	2.1	7.9	3.6
Median school years	7.7	8.2	11.4	8.0

Source: United States Bureau of the Census, Sixteenth Census of the United States, 1940: Characteristics of the Population, Reports by states (Washington, D.C. Government Printing Office, 1943), 2:621, 660.

boast that their small black community was as literate and educated as most whites and that blacks shared a strong commitment to educate their children[53] (see Table 1.4).

Family stability among black households was also reflected in adequate health care, low juvenile delinquency levels, and low crime rates. Public health care for black San Franciscans, though superior to the health care blacks received throughout the South and in some northern cities, still lagged behind white health care in several areas. In some years blacks suffered a significantly higher mortality rate than whites as well as a higher incidence of some diseases. Between 1937 and 1941, according to the San Francisco Department of Public Health, the black mortality rate was 50 percent higher than the white rate. Blacks died from syphilis at a rate seven times higher than whites, from nephritis five times more frequently than whites, and from respiratory diseases, such as pneumonia and influenza, between two and three times more often than whites. Whites died at comparable rates from many diseases, however, and outstripped the black death rate in several others. The death rate from diabetes was almost equal for both races, and white mortality rates from cerebral hemorrhage and heart disease exceeded those of blacks. By and large, blacks benefited from San Francisco's health care facilities and acquired few of the chronic health symptoms that characterized blacks in northern ghettos, such as disproportionately high rates of infant mortality and infectious diseases.[54] Moreover, black patients, though not black physicians, were permitted to use San Francisco's clinics and hospitals and the full range of the city's health facilities on an integrated basis.

The options for black families in caring for their old, sick, and destitute were limited by their low economic status. Lacking the financial resources to commit their family members to private nursing homes, most blacks simply let their parents live out their remaining years under their own roofs. Since black families were generally small and the number of elderly blacks was never very large, aging blacks often spent their final years in the company of a charitable person, in one of the city's almshouses, or in the public relief home. For instance, the black editor Philip A. Bell was supported by a charitable "society of ladies" during his final years. Similarly, the black boardinghouse keeper Mary Ellen "Mammy" Pleasant spent her final year in the company of friends in San Francisco. Black physician Stuart T. Davison, however, lived his final year in Laguna Honda, the city's public relief home. Oakland's black community, which had almost twice the number of blacks as San Francisco by 1930, attempted to solve this problem, at least in part, by establishing a home for their aged and infirm. Black San Franciscans, however, relied upon the support of family and friends, charity, and public institutions.[55]

It appears that the crime rate was low in San Francisco's black community. Since annual police reports did not list the race of offenders before 1940, it is difficult to ascertain the crime rate among any race or ethnic group, but neither the white press nor public officials labeled blacks a crime ridden population. The Chinese community, on the other hand, was repeatedly portrayed by the press as a cesspool of vice, prostitution, gambling, and drugs, particularly opium. In only one category, prostitution, were blacks arrested at a higher percentage than whites, which was true throughout the West. The economic pressures on black women, coupled with the meagerness of the incomes they earned from domestic and menial service, made them more likely to resort to prostitution than white women.[56]

Juvenile delinquency was never a serious concern for black leaders or San Francisco's city fathers. The black juvenile case load was small in most years and the offenses were generally minor. In 1928–1929, for example, black teens were only three of 463 juvenile delinquency cases, and four years later, only six of 563. By 1938, blacks made up only 30 cases, although the city-wide case load had grown to 1571.[57] In San Francisco, unlike many large cities, there was no evidence of black street gangs or of large groups of black children lounging on street corners creating a public nuisance. On the contrary, newspapers, public records, and personal interviews reveal that black children in San Francisco were orderly and well behaved and that the majority of their social and recreational activities were structured and organized through schools, churches, and community centers.

It is difficult to explain the low black delinquency rate in San Francisco, given the magnitude of the problem in other urban areas. Mary White Ovington and W. E. B. Du Bois believed that the high incidence of working black mothers in New York and Philadelphia contributed to the high delinquency rate in those cities, for their children were left unsupervised and without structured activities to occupy their time. Black women in San Francisco, however, were employed in equal proportion to black women in most northern cities, so employment alone would not explain this problem. The well-coordinated recreation and social service programs available for black San Franciscans provide a partial answer. The Madame C. J. Walker Home for Motherless Girls and the Booker T. Washington Community Service Center offered diverse programs, including lodging, recreation, and community activities. Du Bois wrote in his classic study, *The Philadelphia Negro*, that these services were absent in Philadelphia's seventh ward, where most blacks resided, and that a community center or YMCA "might meet the wants of the young man."[58] Additionally, the small number of black children in San Francisco may have curtailed some antisocial behavior, such as the formation of street gangs, which were more common in larger black and Hispanic communities. Several black San Franciscans, including Alfred Butler and F. L. Ritchardson, argued that black children were more respectful of adults when the black community was small, and that children who misbehaved in public would be more likely to encounter reprisals from their parents in a community where everyone knew each other. In San Francisco's tightly knit black community, adults were not only expected to maintain authority over their own children, but also to exert influence over black children in the larger community.[59]

San Francisco's racial ambivalence was most clearly evident over the issue of housing for blacks. Black families had faced a relatively flexible housing market before 1900, and between 1900 and 1930 they were restricted neither by statute nor by restrictive covenants from residing in almost any residential area. Like Milwaukee, which also had a small black population, San Francisco never created a black ghetto. Blacks were dispersed throughout the city in integrated neighborhoods, intermingled with an array of other ethnic and racial groups. Although small black enclaves did spring up in the Central district, the downtown sector, North Beach, South of Market, and the Western Addition, the incidence of residential segregation was low—a fairly typical pattern in western communities. (Many western cities did not designate segregated neighborhood boundaries during their formative decades, but would adopt more restrictive housing laws as the black populations increased in the twentieth century.) Although restrictive housing statutes had been directed at San Francisco's large Chinese population during the late nineteenth century, those statutes had no impact on the residential patterns of blacks. In fact, the absence of housing segregation laws directed against blacks would set San Francisco apart from many northern cities, such as Chicago and Cleveland. Because San Francisco's black population remained small between 1900 and 1940, in contrast to its larger Chinese population, most whites never feared an "invasion" of blacks into their neighborhoods that would lower their property values and disrupt their way of life—a fear that Allan H. Spear and Kenneth L. Kusmer documented in Chicago and Cleveland. Nor did white San Franciscans seem to share the fear that polarized Detroit during the 1940s—that if blacks lived in white neighborhoods they would either molest white women or marry them. Consequently, neither the social unrest nor the racial violence that plagued many American cities between 1917 and 1940, when blacks attempted to rent or purchase homes in white communities, occurred in San Francisco.[60]

Between 1920 and 1930, however, as San Francisco's black population began to increase, a greater proportion of blacks began moving into the Western Addition. By 1930 almost half of San Francisco's blacks resided in this area. Assembly district thirty alone contained 38.1 percent of all blacks. Another 14.6 percent resided in assembly district twenty-two, 15.8 percent occupied assembly district thirty-one, and 10 percent lived in Assembly district thirty-three. These four assembly districts contained 78.5 percent of all black residents in 1930, an indication that blacks had become more likely to cluster in the wake of an expanding black population.[61]

The Western Addition, an area approximately one square mile in size, became the hub of black life by 1930 and the preferred residential area for black residents. The narrow strip along Fillmore Street from McAllister to Sutter, bordered by Divisadero Street and Webster Street, in particular, became the focal point of black activity. By 1933, the *San Francisco Spokesman*, a black newspaper, labeled the Fillmore district "densely populated with Negroes."[62] The majority of black businesses and institutions were located in this section, roughly eight blocks by six blocks, and blacks frequently gathered alongside the shops and business establishments to converse and intermingle. Small settlements of blacks could be found as far north as California Street, but the further north one ventured, the less integrated the neighborhoods became. The thirty-first assembly district, an area running north to south from Pine Street to the Marina district, and bordered by Van Ness Avenue on the east and Parker Street on the west, also contained a large settlement of blacks. Additionally, an enclave of blacks emerged south of the downtown sector, from Market Street to Bryant Street, and continued along the Embarcadero.[63]

San Franciscans of all races were more inclined to rent than to own property, and blacks were no different. Yet blacks were far less likely to own property than foreign-born or native whites. By 1900, 92 percent of black San Franciscans rented their dwellings, which approximated the percentage of black renters in a northern industrial city like Pittsburgh. By 1930, only 13.6 percent of black families owned their dwellings, compared with 35.1 percent of native white families and 41.6 percent of foreign-born whites. Moreover, blacks paid substantially less for their homes than white property owners. The median value of native whites' homes was 24 percent higher than that of the homes of blacks. Although less striking, the median value of the homes of foreign-born whites was 10 percent higher than that of homes owned by blacks. The higher property values of whites reflected their more secure economic footing, particularly their domination of the professions and the skilled trades, but also their virtual monopoly of white collar jobs.[64]

Blacks also occupied a disproportionate amount of substandard housing. True, San Francisco faced a "housing problem," but blacks were far more likely to occupy inferior housing than whites. The *1939 Real Property Survey*, a comprehensive report of housing conditions in San Francisco, noted that almost all blacks lived in the Central, Western Addition, or South of Market districts, and that black households were "in poor condition and more congested than homes occupied by white families." The principal black district (census tract J, which included the Western Addition), concluded the report, was a "blighted community," for it contained over a third of the city's substandard housing.[65]

The housing conditions of blacks, however, must be viewed in the total context of San Francisco's residential conditions, because a significant percentage of San Francisco's housing was of poor quality. But if housing was bad for most San Franciscans, blacks were several notches down the ladder, and the Chinese occupied the bottom rung.[66] Although the substandard residential hotels housed almost exclusively white renters, the Chinese perhaps suffered most in their pitifully overcrowded conditions. The housing situation for the Chinese offers a stark contrast with the

opportunities for blacks to secure decent housing. San Francisco's Chinatown was a segregated community, "as thoroughly segregated as black
districts of the South during the same time period."[67] And whereas blacks
had gained the right to live in any neighborhood that they could afford,
the Chinese, with few exceptions, were trapped in some of the worst
housing in San Francisco. A San Francisco Board of Supervisor's report
noted that some of Chinatown's places of business and places of amuse-
ment were "the filthiest spot[s] inhabited by men, women and children
on the American continent." The investigators discovered that overcrowded conditions were the rule: in one instance ninety-four occupants
lived in ten rooms designed to accommodate thirty-one people. The fact
that the Chinese composed approximately 8 percent of San Francisco's
population in 1870 and 4.6 percent in 1900 (in contrast to 0.9 percent and
0.5 percent for blacks during the same years) meant that their housing
needs were considerably greater than blacks. This may explain why
whites were willing to integrate a small black community into their
neighborhoods, but unwilling to integrate the Chinese.[68]

Housing discrimination, although evident and assailed by black leaders in their press and their protest organizations, was not a conspicuous
feature of San Francisco's race relations before 1940. This fact set San
Francisco apart from many cities that segregated blacks residentially.
Black San Franciscans lived in virtually every neighborhood, and members of the black middle class, such as Joseph Foreman, Emma Scott,
Mary McCants Stewart, and Irene Bell Ruggles, purchased homes in the
predominantly white Richmond and Sunset districts without difficulty.
These individuals, all solid members of the black middle class, were
widely respected in both the white and black communities. There were
no restrictive covenants in these neighborhoods prohibiting the sale of
property to blacks and little evidence of community-wide opposition
when blacks bought homes in predominantly white neighborhoods. The
number of blacks who purchased homes in white communities was never
very large and apparently did not pose a threat to middle-class whites.
Consequently, most white San Franciscans neither responded with racial
violence nor frantically attempted to sell their homes when blacks moved
into their neighborhoods. Nor did unscrupulous black businessmen engage in "blockbusting," the practice of deliberately alarming whites and
convincing them to sell their homes below market value in anticipation
of a black "invasion."[69]

Overt residential segregation did surface sporadically in San Francisco. Shortly after the 1906 earthquake, the Oakland *Sunshine* wrote
that "real estate agents do not care to rent to blacks in San Francisco."

The San Francisco NAACP defended a black family in court who had been denied the opportunity to rent a house in a predominantly white neighborhood. The exclusive white Nob Hill community also attempted to keep blacks out of their neighborhood when they petitioned the court to "enjoin one of their neighbors from leasing property to other than white persons." Similarly, the *San Francisco Spokesman* opined in an editorial: "Residential segregation is as real in California as in Mississippi. A mob is unnecessary. All that's needed is a neighbor[hood] meeting and agreement in writing not to rent, lease, or sell to blacks and the Courts will do the rest." The *Spokesman's* editorial is instructive, because it illustrates that white fears had increased as the black community expanded between 1920 and 1930. It also reveals that restrictive covenants were present in some areas of San Francisco, although the paper never clarified which neighborhoods barred blacks.[70]

Neighborhood improvement associations were also established to keep blacks out of traditionally white neighborhoods. These organizations began to surface during the 1920s as a reaction to the increasing number of blacks who moved into the Western Addition between 1920 and 1930. The most active organization, the Western Addition Improvement and Protective Association, operated in an area of the Western Addition where many blacks lived during the 1920s. The Improvement Association fought to keep blacks out of certain neighborhoods in the Western Addition. In one case it attempted to prevent a black woman from obtaining a permit to remodel an old building for the purpose of establishing a church. It also opposed the sale of property in the Western Addition to the Booker T. Washington Community Center.[71]

Named in honor of the great Tuskegee leader, the Booker T. Washington Community Center originally operated from a Geary Street basement with a low ceiling. The former director of boys programs, F. L. Ritchardson, stated that conditions were so cramped and awkward that tumbling was virtually the only activity that boys could engage in. Through diligent fund raising and careful planning, the Community Center purchased a building on Divisadero Street in the Western Addition.[72] The Improvement Association contested the purchase and organized strategy meetings in an attempt to nullify the sale, arguing that blacks and Asians depreciated property values. It vowed to halt the growth of both groups in the Western Addition. "It is now high time for the white residents and property owners to get together and protect themselves from this rapid invasion," said one official. An Improvement Association spokesman cautioned that if white residents ignored his warning "you may wake up any morning to find that you have some new

colored neighbors who have moved into the house next door to you."[73]
These charges united the Improvement Association's white supporters.
They hired an attorney, who pledged to inform residents how they could
"protect property by law upheld in [the] Supreme Court." In the end, the
association was not successful in preventing the sale of the property to
the Community Center, but it kept abreast of the financial status of the
new center. When it learned that the Community Center had missed a
single payment, it bought the mortgage and demanded the entire payment at once. "We have been having quite a fight here in San Francisco
for the past month," wrote local black attorney Edward Mabson to Robert
Bagnall, director of branches of the NAACP's national office.[74]

Although shaken, the small black community regrouped and attempted to raise the necessary funds. Black ministers held special services and collections and emphasized the necessity of community-wide
unity. Black women's clubs organized fund raising activities—dances,
bazaars, and teas. Black and white volunteers went door-to-door solicit-
ing small contributions. Alice Butler, the wife of San Francisco's only
black funeral director, organized a committee that raised several thousand dollars. In a matter of weeks, the necessary funds were raised and
the potential crisis averted. "In spite of their determination, we have been
successful in stamping out the movement," noted Edward Mabson.[75]

The episode unified the black community. The Improvement Association's opposition also illustrated that black institutions like the Booker T.
Washington Community Center could exist in proximity to white residential areas during the 1920s, provided they were willing to fight. The
Improvement Association's opposition to the Community Center revealed
that some white organizations feared a potential black influx into their
communities and were willing to organize to maintain the status quo.

The extent of San Francisco's residential segregation between 1900
and 1940 is difficult to measure for several reasons. Realtors and property owners were reluctant to admit their bias in renting or selling property to blacks, blacks did not always report housing discrimination, and
improvement associations left few records of their activities. No single
agency served as a watchdog to report housing discrimination, although
the NAACP did report and investigate cases that were brought to their
attention. Nor did local or state laws prohibit housing discrimination in
San Francisco. Most of the evidence regarding housing discrimination is
drawn from the black press or the files of the San Francisco NAACP. On
the face of it, these sources indicate that housing discrimination against
blacks was infrequent between 1900 and 1930, and that it was practiced
primarily by individual property owners, rather than orchestrated by

powerful interest groups. When whites did organize to ban blacks from their neighborhoods, as the Western Addition Improvement and Protective Association had attempted to do, they did not always succeed.

Between 1930 and 1940, as some whites had feared, more and more blacks moved into census tract J in the Western Addition. It is difficult to explain why. Perhaps the onset of the Great Depression forced some black families to move into this area, but the rents there were not cheaper. The *1939 Real Property Survey* reported that black tenant families had the highest median gross monthly rental at $25.89 of all groups in San Francisco. The Chinese reported the lowest rate at $18.97, followed by whites at $23.89. Black tenant families also paid a higher percentage of their income than either the Chinese or white San Franciscans for shelter. Black families with an annual income of $400 to $599, for example, paid 55.5 percent of their income for housing, compared to 39.6 percent for Chinese families and 49.1 percent for white families with comparable incomes. Similarly, black families that earned between $1200 and $1399 annually, the highest category reported, paid 26.8 percent of their income for housing, compared to 20.3 percent for Chinese families and 23.0 percent for white families. These figures are striking for several reasons. First, they reveal that despite living in substandard housing, blacks still paid higher rents than whites, while the Chinese paid the lowest rents of any race for substandard housing. Neither the income level nor the social class of blacks made any difference in the percentage of their annual income that was paid for rental housing. Black renters paid a higher percentage of their incomes than either the Chinese or whites at every level for which annual incomes were reported.[76]

Although higher rents for blacks in substandard housing indicate that blacks were treated differently than whites in the rental market, it is a poor barometer of the extent of housing discrimination. Alma and Karl Taeuber concluded, however, in their broad study of residential segregation, *Negroes in Cities*, that San Francisco's residential segregation index in 1940 was higher than the index in any major city in northern California. Morcover, the average residential segregation index for ten cities in the West was 82.7 compared to an average index of 85.2 for all regions of the country. Hence, the small black populations in western cities like San Francisco, Oakland, Portland, Seattle, and Denver, did not necessarily facilitate integrated housing patterns. Rather, by 1940, black San Franciscans were concentrated in a handful of well-defined neighborhoods, much like their counterparts in medium-sized cities like Evansville and Milwaukee as well as larger urban communities throughout the nation.[77]

Table 1.5. Indexes of Residential Segregation for
Selected Western and Northern Cities, 1940

Berkeley, Calif.	81.2	Philadelphia, Pa.	88.0
Boston, Mass.	86.3	Pittsburgh, Pa.	82.0
Chicago, Ill.	95.0	Pasadena, Calif.	84.2
Cleveland, Ohio	92.0	Portland, Oreg.	83.8
Denver, Colo.	87.9	Sacramento, Calif.	77.8
Detroit, Mich.	89.9	San Diego, Calif.	84.4
Los Angeles, Calif.	84.2	San Francisco, Calif.	82.9
Milwaukee, Wis.	92.9	Seattle, Wash.	82.2
New York, N.Y.	86.8	Topeka, Kans.	80.8
Oakland, Calif.	78.4	Mean	82.7
Omaha, Neb.	89.5		

Source: Karl E. Taeuber and Alma F. Taeuber, Negroes in Cities: Residential Segregation and Neighborhood Change (Chicago: Aldine Publishing, 1965), pp. 39–41.

San Francisco's residential segregation index in 1940 illustrated that housing discrimination had intensified in the space of a decade, although no ghetto had developed by 1940. The large concentration of black San Franciscans in fewer assembly districts in 1940 reveals that the majority of blacks had moved into a narrow belt of the Western Addition by this time. Although blacks were not forced by statute to reside in a well-defined neighborhood, the Western Addition had become the black section of San Francisco, the geographical area that most whites associated with black settlement. The Western Addition contained most of the substandard housing in San Francisco, and more than half of all black families were housed in these dwellings. The firm belief that future black migrants should continue to settle primarily in the Western Addition, rather than disperse throughout the city, was also established by 1940. This idea shaped San Francisco's housing policy during the Second World War and became a critical factor in the creation of a black ghetto during the postwar period.[78]

In spite of its relatively small numbers, between 1900 and 1940, San Francisco's black community was not static in any sense of the word. Quite the contrary, it possessed the same energy and dynamic qualities of more sizable black communities. The expanding black population between 1910 and 1940 would affect the pace of black protest, encourage the growth of black institutions, and influence the quest for better housing and greater employment opportunities. Many black migrants who came to San Francisco between 1910 and 1940 also pressured white employers to hire them in business, industry, the professions, and the service sector, and accordingly, the black industrial class grew rapidly during these years. Similarly, the demographic growth of the black community between 1910 and 1940 placed increasing pressure on San Francisco's housing market and would result in an increase in housing segregation by 1940. Thus the growth of San Francisco's black community was intimately related to a host of larger issues, including black protest, the growth of the black industrial working class, and increasing ghettoization. Each of these issues had important roots in the demographic changes that the black population underwent before 1940. On the eve of World War II, San Francisco blacks had made considerably more progress in education, health care, and housing than their black counterparts in many other cities. They had also succeeded in breaking down almost every caste barrier that had been erected during the nineteenth century. So, although black San Franciscans were almost equal by 1940, they still lagged behind whites, both natives and foreign-born, in employment opportunities. Politically they exerted no power whatsoever. The degree to which blacks would be permitted to improve their status in these areas would serve as a crucial test for San Francisco's liberalism and challenge the city's image as a racially progressive city. It would also reveal much about San Francisco's civility, its commitment to an egalitarian community, and the strength and vitality of its black leadership and their community institutions.

2

EMPLOYMENT AND ENTERPRISE, 1900–1930

By 1900, San Francisco was clearly the leading financial and commercial center on the West Coast, offering numerous economic opportunities to its diverse labor force. Labor unions boasted that San Francisco was a strong union town, and at its peak, union membership was estimated at 100,000. Accordingly, wages were relatively high. Rapid expansion in the manufacturing, trade, transportation, and communications sectors provided jobs for more than two-thirds of all male workers in 1900. By 1930, more than two thousand industries were established within the city.[1]

Working women also found considerable economic opportunity in San Francisco. Even though a higher percentage of women than men engaged in domestic and service work, women were also employed in clerical and sales jobs, as semiskilled operatives, and to a lesser degree, as proprietors, managers, and officials. A broad spectrum of jobs were open to workers of both sexes, though women, admittedly, had far less opportunity than men.[2]

Despite the wide range of jobs for other San Franciscans, economic opportunities for black workers were restricted because of racial discrimination, social custom, and the reluctance of many whites to work with blacks. Blacks were relegated to the bottom of San Francisco's labor force and made only marginal gains in the professions, skilled and semiskilled trades, clerical work, or white collar jobs between 1900 and 1930. Only in manufacturing did the percentage of black workers rise sharply, but black San Franciscans were far less likely to secure the better-paying skilled factory jobs than either native-born whites or foreign-born whites. Blacks in San Francisco did not have the benefit of large-scale factory work and industry as they did in cities like Milwaukee and Pittsburgh, where blacks could readily find jobs and a limited number had the opportunity to work in semiskilled and skilled areas.[3] Black laborers in San Francisco were almost totally excluded from positions as supervisors and foremen before 1930.

Because black workers often experienced difficulty obtaining work in San Francisco, the city gained a reputation as an urban center for blacks to avoid. Although the notable increase in the black population of Cleveland, Detroit, and Chicago had been encouraged by black leadership, San Francisco's black leaders did not encourage migration to the city during the World War I era.

The belief that San Francisco was unfriendly to blacks had gained wide currency by 1915, when the Panama-Pacific International Exposition was held there. "We hope members of our race will not come here expecting to find employment, as the conditions are not favorable," wrote one black weekly. Instead, blacks found themselves being challenged and even displaced in long-standing positions as cooks, domestics, and menial laborers. In one instance, a white work crew replaced the black workers in the baggage department at the posh Palace Hotel, which had served as an important source of employment for blacks from its opening in 1875. Similarly, a San Francisco restaurant discharged its entire black

Table 2.1. Occupations by Race, Sex, and Ethnic Group, San Francisco, 1900 (in percentage)

	Negro	Other nonwhite	Foreign-born white	Native white, white parentage	Native white, foreign parentage
Males					
Professional	5.5	2.6	4.3	11.4	6.5
Domestic, personal service	62.8	51.4	25.7	17.0	14.9
Trade and transportation	24.9	19.0	35.3	43.2	41.5
Manufacturing	6.6	24.8	32.1	27.4	36.2
Agricultural	.3	2.2	2.7	1.0	.8
Females					
Professional	2.4	1.2	4.6	17.4	11.5
Domestic, personal service	79.3	49.8	65.0	31.2	25.7
Trade and transportation	2.7	2.2	9.0	22.4	23.8
Manufacturing	15.5	46.6	21.0	28.9	38.9

Source: United States Bureau of the Census, Twelfth Census of the United States, 1900: Occupations (Washington, D.C.: Government Printing Office, 1904), pp. 720-24.

crew and replaced it with whites. An employment bureau for domestics even ordered black women to "stay away." The tenuous status of black workers in the Bay Area prompted the *San Francisco Spokesman* to lament, "Perhaps nowhere in the United States is work for Negroes so difficult to obtain than in Northern California."[4]

Unlike rival ethnic groups, black workers did not monopolize any sector of the labor market. They were unable to gain a firm foothold in barbering, catering, or even in the menial service areas. Economic competition from Chinese, Japanese, and foreign-born white workers heightened the competition for jobs. Appalled at the dismal plight of black workers, particularly at their inability to secure semiskilled and skilled jobs in large numbers, C. L. Dellums stated shortly after his arrival in the Bay Area, "I had been around here long enough then to realize that there wasn't very much work Negroes could get." Black workers, he continued, could either "go down to the sea in ships or work on the railroads." Similarly, F. L. Ritchardson, a black postal official, recalled that upon his arrival in San Francisco in 1919 "there wasn't many tasks that Negroes could perform except as doormen, elevator operators, redcaps, or domestic work." Beatrice Greene, a black domestic, confirmed that there was considerable employment discrimination in San Francisco before World War II. Although Greene graduated from Commerce High School with an accounting major, she could not find employment in that field. "The only thing that was open to us [black women] was housework," she reported. Revels Cayton, a prominent black labor leader, affirmed that the black workers were not only excluded from many jobs, but from San Francisco's labor unions as well.[5]

The federal census enumerations of occupations between 1900 and 1930 confirm the reports of Dellums, Ritchardson, Greene, and Cayton: even though the San Francisco economy was expanding at a rapid pace, black workers did not share proportionately in its growth. By 1900, the majority of black males worked as unskilled and semiskilled laborers, janitors, servants, waiters, and porters. The 1900 census reported that 62.8 percent of black males and 79.3 percent of black females were employed as domestics and personal servants, yet only 25.7 percent of foreign-born white males and 65.0 percent of females worked in these jobs. Black males were sparsely represented in the manufacturing sector, at 6.6 percent and as professionals, at 5.5 percent. However, manufacturing jobs provided work for 32.1 percent of foreign-born white males, 27.4 percent of native whites with native parents, 36.2 percent of gainfully occupied native white males with foreign-born parents, and 25.7 percent of other races. Professionals constituted a small proportion of all workers

Table 2.2. Occupations by Race, Sex, and Ethnic Group, San Francisco, 1910 (in percentage)

	Negro	Native-white, native parents	Native-white, foreign & mixed parents	Foreign-born white	Other Nonwhite
Males					
Agriculture	1.0	0.6	0.4	2.7	3.9
Manufacturing	10.9	23.0	10.9	25.7	12.7
Transportation	10.8	9.2	8.2	17.1	1.7
Trade	4.9	13.9	21.1	13.7	20.9
Public service	3.7	10.6	5.5	3.1	0.3
Professional	2.1	3.5	2.4	1.1	0.5
Domestic, personal service	47.5	6.6	5.7	13.9	38.4
Clerical	3.1	10.6	10.9	3.4	2.6
Females					
Manufacturing	10.0	14.7	17.6	15.3	30.4
Transportation		2.8	3.0	0.5	0.9
Trade	1.1	10.4	11.9	6.7	2.5
Professional	3.5	14.3	10.9	5.8	2.5
Domestic, personal service	70.4	22.6	18.3	55.5	56.1
Clerical	3.1	22.9	25.5	4.9	0.2

Source: United States Bureau of the Census, *Thirteenth Census of the United States*, 1910, vol. 4, *Occupations* (Washington, D.C., 1914), pp. 600–601.

in 1900, but a large percentage of black male professionals were actors, entertainers, and music teachers. Only forty-one blacks were listed as professionals, of whom twenty-three, or 60 percent, were actors, musicians, or music teachers—a considerably higher percentage than for any other race or nationality in San Francisco. Moreover, thirty-five of these forty-one professionals were males, an indication that black females had greater difficulty than black males in obtaining professional employment.[6]

Although black females were employed in greater percentages than white females in San Francisco and in most other western cities, they were generally relegated to domestic and personal service employment, a situation they were unable to change before 1940. In 1900, few black women worked in the professions or at skilled trades, clerical work, or white collar jobs. Black females had made some breakthroughs in manufacturing (15.5 percent) and the semiskilled trades (2.7 percent), though principally as dressmakers and seamstresses. White women made greater inroads into clerical work, manufacturing, and semiskilled jobs than black women, and these occupations earned considerably higher wages, had more employment stability, status, and opportunities for promotion. Only six black women were employed in clerical positions in 1900; almost two hundred were employed in domestic and personal service jobs. Although domestic service was the single largest category of employment for all women in 1900, black females far outstripped native whites, foreign-born whites, and members of other nonwhite races in that category. Seventy-nine percent of black women worked in domestic service in 1900 compared with 49.8 percent for other nonwhite races, 65 percent for foreign-born whites, and 31.2 percent for native-born whites with white parentage. San Francisco's labor force provided limited entry for skilled black female workers, for thirty-four were employed as dressmakers and seamstresses, shirtmakers, and printers, and one was a confectioner (see Table 2.1).[7]

Several changes in the workplace that were significant for black males occurred between 1900 and 1920, indicating that the occupational structure was not stagnant. The percentage of black males engaged in domestic and personal service jobs had declined from 62.8 percent in 1900 to 47.5 percent in 1910. By 1920, it had declined to 40.2 percent, a significant decrease in the space of two decades. During the same period, the percentage of black males employed in manufacturing increased—from 6.6 percent in 1900 to 10.9 percent in 1910, and to 27.5 percent in 1920. This increase represented a notable improvement over the course of two decades and a rapid expansion of the black industrial working class. Although 25 percent of all black male workers held jobs in these two categories in 1900, the percentage had declined to 15.9 percent by 1920, an indication that black males had lost ground to both foreign-born and native white workers. The number of black professional males also declined during these years, although the black professional class in San Francisco had always been small and would remain so until World War II.

The most common occupations in the black professional class were actors, showmen, and musicians. (Eighteen of the nineteen black male professionals reported in 1910, for example, were listed as musicians.) These occupations were transient, which probably explains part of the decline in this category. The devastating earthquake and fire in 1906 may also have affected the availability of work for black musicians and actors in San Francisco, as the city was literally digging out from under ashes and ruins. It is equally evident that black professionals did not migrate to San Francisco in large numbers before 1940. Several who did, such as McCants Stewart and William L. Patterson, both attorneys, complained that racial discrimination and the small size of the black community made it difficult to earn a livelihood. The low number of black professionals in San Francisco was not unusual. Industrial cities like Milwaukee and Evansville, Indiana, as well as western cities like Portland and Seattle, also had small classes of black professionals. In Cleveland, though, the black professional class was proportionate in size to that of other racial and ethnic groups. Yet the number of black male professionals in San Francisco declined still further, from thirty-five in 1900 to eighteen in 1910, a decline of more than 50 percent.[8]

Black female professionals, on the other hand, increased from six in 1900 to nine a decade later and twenty by 1920—more than a threefold rise. The breakthrough in nursing was particularly important, as no black women had been listed in this category in 1900. Two black nurses were reported in 1910 and six by 1920. The increase in black nurses in San Francisco coincided, as Darlene Clark Hine noted in her important study of black women in the nursing profession, with the professionalization of nursing in the United States between 1890 and 1925. It appears that black females in San Francisco were beginning to take advantage of these new opportunities. Moreover, sixteen black women were listed as midwives in 1910, a surprisingly large number given the small population of black women in San Francisco.

Actors, musicians, and music teachers still constituted the majority of San Francisco's black professionals in 1910 and 1920, irrespective of gender, and no blacks were permitted to teach in the San Francisco Unified School District before the 1940s. However, several black females reported their occupations as teachers between 1900 and 1920. These women, few in number, probably operated private schools out of their homes or tutored black children, a practice that had prevailed since the antebellum era, when black teachers had difficulty obtaining employment in predominantly white school districts[9] (see Tables 2.1 and 2.2).

In sharp contrast to the new opportunities for black males, job opportunities for black women did not improve in either manufacturing or the trade and transportation sectors between 1900 and 1920. In several areas black females fell even further behind their white female counterparts. Seventy percent of black women were employed as domestics and personal servants in 1910, as contrasted with 22.6 percent of native-born white women with native parents, 18.3 percent of native-born white women with foreign-born or mixed parents, 55.5 percent of foreign-born white women, and 56.1 percent of women from other nonwhite races. A decade later, 80 percent of black females worked as domestics and personal servants compared to 43.7 percent of foreign-born white females, 16 percent of native whites with native parents, and 14.7 percent of native whites with foreign-born or mixed parents. While domestic service employment declined among white women between 1900 and 1920, as they began to move increasingly into clerical and semiskilled jobs, the percentage of black women in these menial jobs increased by one percent (see Tables 2.2 and 2.3).

Black females also lost ground in the manufacturing sector, as the percentage of black females engaged in manufacturing jobs declined from 15.5 percent in 1900 to 10 percent in 1910 and 9.2 percent in 1920. However, manufacturing jobs had declined among several other groups of female workers in San Francisco between 1900 and 1920. The most striking decrease occurred among women from other nonwhite races, whose percentage of manufacturing jobs declined from 46.6 percent in 1900 to 30.4 percent in 1910 to 26.9 percent in 1920. Similarly, the percentage of manufacturing jobs held by native-born white females with native parents also declined sharply, from 28.9 to 13.1 percent between 1900 and 1920. Native-born white females with foreign-born or mixed parentage

Table 2.3. Occupations by Race, Sex, and Ethnic Group, San Francisco, 1920 (in percentage)

	Negro	Native white, native parents	Native white, foreign or mixed parents	Foreign-born white	Other nonwhite
Males					
Manufacturing	27.5	29.4	35.1	41.0	14.1
Transportation	11.9	12.1	11.1	13.5	2.0
Trade	4.0	17.2	20.4	14.7	25.4
Public service	7.3	12.9	7.1	3.8	3.1
Professional	3.4	7.7	6.5	3.5	2.9
Domestic, personal service	40.2	5.9	4.8	14.9	44.4
Clerical	4.8	13.3	13.7	4.9	4.4
Females					
Manufacturing	9.2	13.1	17.6	26.3	26.9
Transportation	.4	4.5	4.9	1.2	0.8
Trade	2.0	14.1	13.0	9.9	9.6
Professional	4.1	17.8	14.0	8.7	4.2
Domestic, personal service	80.4	16.0	14.7	43.7	54.2
Clerical	3.5	34.2	35.6	10.0	3.3

Source: United States Bureau of the Census, Fourteenth Census of the United States, 1920, vol. 2, Population (Washington, D.C., 1922), pp. 1226–30.

also worked fewer manufacturing jobs, for their percentage in this category fell from 38.9 percent in 1900 to 17.6 percent in 1920, a decline of almost 60 percent. White foreign-born females, on the other hand, were able to hold their ground in manufacturing jobs between 1900 and 1920, after also losing some semiskilled and unskilled jobs in 1910. Their percentage of manufacturing jobs had fallen from 21 percent in 1900 to 15.3 percent in 1910, but increased sharply to 26.3 percent in 1920.

Black women made almost no progress in any other area of the labor force between 1910 and 1930. For them, virtually no change had occurred in the trade and transportation sectors, professional, or clerical jobs between 1900 and 1920. There was not a single black female telephone operator employed in San Francisco in 1910 and only two by 1920, although almost two thousand women worked in these jobs by 1920. The number of black female clerical workers had risen to only eleven by 1910 and seventeen by 1920. Black women like Mary McCants Stewart, who worked as a clerk in a pharmaceutical company, were only slowly beginning to make inroads into white-collar jobs as clerks, typists, and stenographers. On the other hand, fewer black women than ever before succeeded in obtaining employment in either skilled or semiskilled manufacturing positions, for only thirty-five black women worked as semiskilled operatives in 1920, of whom twenty-four were dressmakers, and only a single black female (a tailor) reported working in a skilled trade. The overwhelming majority of black female workers remained entrenched in domestic and personal service jobs.[10]

By 1930, the onset of the Great Depression had had a major influence on the occupational status of black women, and it began to slide even further. Almost 89 percent were employed in domestic and personal service jobs, an increase of 9 percent from the previous census. The percentage of white females and women from other nonwhite races who were employed in domestic jobs had declined by 1930, an indication that those groups had continued to make occupational gains between 1920 and 1930. A smaller percentage of black women were also employed in clerical work, manufacturing, and the trade and transportation sectors by 1930 than in the previous census, and the number of black female professionals increased by only one between 1920 and 1930. Thus, as job opportunities for white women gradually improved in San Francisco between 1920 and 1930, black women occupied the lowest strata of the job sector and continued to lose ground. For them, San Francisco's promise of greater economic opportunity was flawed. Even women in other nonwhite races, particularly the Chinese and Japanese, who often faced pervasive employment restrictions, made far greater progress than black women as semiskilled and skilled workers. Asian women entered the labor market earlier and in larger numbers than black women as factory operatives, dressmakers, seamstresses, and tailors, and held this advantage into the twentieth century. Black females, on the other hand, never gained a firm foothold in these areas and thus never represented a serious challenge to the gains that either Asian or foreign-born white women made in these occupations. Black females were also plagued by greater job competition as a result of the Great Depression, by the stigma of working almost exclusively in menial jobs, and by the reluctance of white employers in both the public and the private sector to hire them in clerical and white-collar jobs. A mere seventeen black females were employed as clerical workers in 1930, and only six as skilled workers. The number of black female semiskilled workers remained stagnant also, as twenty-two dressmakers and twenty-one operatives were reported in the 1930 census.

The predominance of black females in unskilled and menial jobs almost guaranteed that they, regardless of their marital status, would be employed in higher percentages than white females or women from other nonwhite races. Indeed, the percentage of working black women who were either married or widowed and divorced exceeded the rate for every other group in San Francisco. The number of single black women who were employed (68.1 percent) was exceeded only by the number of foreign-born white women (75.3 percent). Yet nearly three times as many married black females worked as foreign-born white women, and married black women were more than twice as likely to work as married native white women or married women from other nonwhite races (see Tables 2.4 and 2.5).

The expansion of opportunities for black males between 1910 and 1930 explains in part the significant increase in the black population during these years (131 percent) as well as the disproportionate male-to-female ratio before 1940. Employment opportunities were improving for black males in unskilled manufacturing jobs, and these positions had traditionally encouraged blacks to migrate to northern and midwestern cities. For the first time, San Francisco's industrial and manufacturing sectors were beginning to open their doors to black male workers in larger numbers. Yet black workers were still prohibited from joining most trade unions before the 1930s, and the jobs available to them were at the lowest level. It was during the 1920s that Thomas C. Fleming, who later became managing editor of the *Sun-Reporter*, a black weekly, migrated to San Francisco from New York. Fleming and his mother had originally settled in Chico, a small agricultural community, but they decided to

Table 2.4. Occupation by Race, Sex, and Ethnic Group,
San Francisco, 1930 (in percentage)

	Negro	Native white	Foreign-born white	Other nonwhite
Males				
Manufacturing	16.5	29.5	38.8	21.6
Transportation	13.5	12.8	13.0	10.7
Trade	3.8	23.2	17.4	15.2
Public service	1.7	5.2	3.0	.6
Professional	2.7	7.6	3.9	3.1
Domestic, personal service	58.0	6.3	16.8	42.3
Clerical	3.5	14.4	5.4	3.8
Females				
Manufacturing	5.6	10.1	21.3	42.4
Transportation	.1	5.0	1.6	1.3
Trade	1.0	13.9	11.0	7.4
Clerical	1.4	38.1	13.8	7.5
Professional	2.7	16.4	10.2	6.6
Domestic, personal service	88.9	16.4	41.8	34.6

Source: United States Bureau of the Census, *Fifteenth Census of the United States, 1930, Occupations: Reports by States*, vol. 3, pt. 2 (Washington, D.C.: Government Printing Office, 1933), pp. 208-10.

Table 2.5. Employed Women by Marital Status, San Francisco, 1930
(percentage of total female population)

Ethnic group	Single	Married	Widowed & divorced
Native white	61.5	18.7	47.5
Foreign-born white	75.3	14.5	29.6
Negro	68.1	41.9	73.6
Other races	47.2	18.5	40.6

Source: United States Bureau of the Census, *Fifteenth Census of the United States*, vol. 4, *Occupations* (Washington, D.C.: Government Printing Office, 1933), 82.

Note: Includes women fifteen years of age and older.

move to San Francisco in 1926 because they believed that the job market had become more fluid for black workers. The 26-percent increase in San Francisco's black population between 1930 and 1940 indicates that not all of these employment gains were erased by the economic downturn of the 1930s.[11]

A small percentage of black males performed skilled and semiskilled tasks in San Francisco's factories during the 1920s, although without an Urban League branch to conduct systematic studies on the employment conditions of black workers in the Bay Area, only a few accounts of their

activities have survived. Valenti Angelo, the prominent Bay Area artist
and book illustrator, recalled that black men worked at the Illinois-
Pacific Glass Company in San Francisco's Mission District, where
Valenti himself had worked briefly. "The operation was performed by
deep-chested men, mostly Negroes, who used a metal staff which was
placed through an opening in the Kiln—twirled to contain a lump of
molten glass, withdrawn red-hot and quickly placed in a mold, then
blown into shape." Although these positions paid high wages, the work
was dangerous, difficult, and unpleasant. "The place was as hot as I
imagine Hades might be," reported Valenti. Industrial cities such as
Milwaukee, Pittsburgh, and Louisville had traditionally used blacks in
"low-paying, dirty, difficult, unpleasant, and dangerous tasks that whites
often refused to perform." The practice of employing blacks in dangerous
positions that whites did not want, noted Howard Rabinowitz, was also
a conspicuous feature of the urban South following emancipation. San
Francisco fit this common pattern.

Although San Francisco's black industrial class was expanding, it remained small compared to northern, midwestern, and eastern black communities. Only eighty-one black workers were employed in manufacturing jobs in 1900. By 1920, however, that number had risen to 374.
Seventy-two of these workers were employed in the building trades
alone, an indication that black workers were beginning to share some of
the rapid growth of this industry during the 1920s. However, industrial
work remained the exception for San Francisco's black workers before
1940, a major departure from the employment patterns of the black
working class in almost every midwestern, eastern, or northern city.[12]

The discriminatory constitutions and bylaws of organized labor were a
major factor in the inability of many blacks to improve their occupational
status. San Francisco was a closed-shop city, and most unions prohibited
blacks as well as Asians. A few unions, such as the Seamen's Union and
the International Brotherhood of Boilermakers, formed segregated auxiliary unions for black workers. "With but few exceptions, all the avenues
of trade are closed to the Negro workman through the powerful influences of the trade unions who rule San Francisco," wrote Delilah L.
Beasley in 1919. By the early 1930s, the San Francisco NAACP's president, Leland Hawkins, wrote that "labor unionism had frozen the Negro
out of all work in this section of the country." Similarly, the *Spokesman's*
editor, John Pittman wrote: "For Aframerican workers in the Bay cities,
union labor has been and still is the chief obstacle to employment." Discriminatory policies in white trade unions hurt the progress of black
workers along the entire Pacific Coast. In Detroit, approximately a quar-

William Byron Rumford applied for a job at the Highland County Hospital in Alameda. Rumford passed the written exam with little difficulty, but the oral examiners made a mockery of the civil service proceedings and failed Rumford three consecutive times. Rumford stated that on one occasion the examining board came into the room, looked him over carefully, and asked him if he thought Joe Louis was a good fighter. When he said, "yes," he was informed that the oral exam had terminated and that he had flunked. The black press concurred with Rumford that the Civil Service Commission's policy of conducting oral interviews worked against the interest of Afro-Americans.[23]

San Francisco, like many West Coast and midwestern cities, contained a small black professional class composed of ministers, musicians, music teachers, attorneys, doctors, and nurses. These black professionals were generally college-educated males who possessed status within San Francisco's black community, though not necessarily lucrative jobs. Widely known throughout the community, black professionals were active in black institutions, such as the NAACP, black churches, and the Booker T. Washington Community Center. As Willard B. Gatewood observed in his study of the black elite, these individuals also felt that it was their duty and obligation to interact with prominent white San Franciscans, when they represented the black community, and to be in the vanguard of every black protest campaign. Most resided in the black community and geared their services or expertise primarily to blacks.[24]

The careers of San Francisco's black attorneys epitomized the inherent hardships of many black professionals. Although they had attended some of the country's finest law schools, many struggled financially in the same manner as the black working class. The early career of William L. Patterson was typical. As a promising senior law student at Hastings Law School in San Francisco, Patterson was instructed to report as a clerk to the office of Samuel Shortridge, who later became a United States Senator. Shortridge expressed apprehension at the idea of a black working in his law firm and denied Patterson the appointment. Voicing a common complaint, Shortridge exclaimed that his white clients "would find it difficult to adjust themselves to talking business and personal matters with a Negro." Patterson eventually went to work for McCants Stewart, a local black attorney.[25]

McCants Stewart also struggled financially throughout his legal career. The son of the distinguished southern black leader, T. McCants Stewart, the younger Stewart, who received his law degree from the University of Minnesota Law School in 1899, relocated from Portland, Oregon, to San Francisco in 1917 because of the difficulty of earning a

ter of blacks were employed in the automobile industry and organized by the United Auto Workers. San Francisco had no comparable industry or union that employed or organized black laborers.[13]

Neither the San Francisco Labor Council's leadership nor its rank and file permitted blacks to join most unions on parity with white workers. Daniel C. Murphy, president of the Labor Council and later, head of the State Federation of Labor, expressed the ambiguity of labor's attitude toward black workers. As a delegate to the 1917 American Federation of Labor's annual convention, Murphy introduced a resolution supporting the interests of black laborers. When pressed by a southern delegate to explain his motives, Murphy stated that "neither he nor the San Francisco Labor Council had any particular interest in the Negro worker," but his actions stemmed from support that black workers had given organized labor in a recent strike. San Francisco's mayor, James Rolph, Jr., because of his solid labor backing, never pressed for the integration of blacks into organized labor during his five terms in office, and few within the ranks of labor pushed for the inclusion of blacks in craft unions. Most black workers, therefore, remained outside organized labor before 1940, which made their attempt to obtain skilled and semiskilled employment exceedingly difficult.[14]

The plight of black longshoremen illustrates, on the one hand, the discriminatory policies of organized labor in San Francisco, and on the other, the opportunities that were becoming available to black workers between 1910 and 1930. During the 1920s, local shippers provided an increasing number of jobs on San Francisco's docks for young blacks attending school, such as Stuart T. Davison, a black medical student, as well as for experienced black workers. One company, according to Thomas C. Fleming, reportedly employed over 250 Bay Area black workers, a figure that is not supported by the federal census enumerations. Yet black longshoremen, as one astute scholar noted, "had a strong balancing lever on the waterfront," despite their relatively small numbers. Since they were not welcomed into the unions on an equal basis, there was always the threat that they could be used as strikebreakers to settle labor disputes. If black workers were courted too heavily, management charged, white employees would refuse to work with them. "If they work, they are traitors to labor, but if they remain idle, they are traitors to their stomachs," wrote the *Spokesman*.[15]

Before 1934, black longshoremen were not only prohibited from joining the parent union, but also required to labor in segregated work gangs. Since they were nonunion, blacks were occasionally utilized by management as strikebreakers. As early as 1901, black workers were brought in from southern California and the Midwest to break a strike along the waterfront. Similarly, black workers were used as strikebreakers during the longshoremen's strikes of 1916 and 1919, although in neither case did they obtain permanent employment after the strikes were settled. Yet the fact that blacks were employed in larger numbers as longshoremen after 1920 reveals that in spite of segregation, some new areas of employment were opening up to black workers. Black workers, however, would make their greatest gains as longshoremen during the 1930s and 1940s as a result of the emerging CIO unions, which broke down many racial barriers in organized labor for the first time.[16]

The Bay Area railroads also attracted blacks, largely because of the relative ease in obtaining employment there and the railroads' long-standing practice of hiring black laborers. With Oakland as a terminus for the Southern Pacific Railroad, blacks were in demand as Pullman porters, waiters, and laborers. Indeed, some blacks migrated to West Coast cities, such as San Francisco, Oakland, Los Angeles, Portland, and Seattle, specifically to work on the railroads, for the black populations were considerably smaller in these cities and there was less competition for unskilled jobs. C. L. Dellums wrote that he merely "stood around the Southern Pacific station trying to get on as a waiter" when he arrived in the Bay Area. Similarly, Thomas Fleming worked as a waiter aboard a dining car shortly after his arrival in San Francisco. The National Urban League's secretary, T. Arnold Hill, estimated that the Southern Pacific Railroad employed one thousand black workers throughout the Bay Area in the 1930s, a figure that is clearly inflated but nonetheless illustrates the importance of railroad employment to the Bay Area black communities. Because large-scale factory employment was unavailable and blacks were virtually locked out of the skilled trades, the railroads would continue to serve as an important source of employment for West Coast blacks until World War II.[17]

Black railroad workers performed numerous functions, not all of which were menial. They served as cooks, waiters, Pullman porters, redcaps, locomotive firemen, and laborers. Some of these workers, like their counterparts in Chicago's black community during the Great Migration, bought homes and became part of the city's small black middle class. Orval Anderson, a redcap, purchased a modest home in San Francisco and educated his children at Lowell High, the city's finest public school. Walter Maddox, a black railroad worker who also served briefly as president of the San Francisco NAACP, attained a prominent position as a timetable expert for the Southern Pacific. His substantial income enabled him to purchase a large farm in Orland, California.[18]

The majority of black railroad workers were porters, and their wages and working conditions varied considerably. A porter's average annual pay in 1925 was $810 plus tips, placing his income in the same category as some black professionals. Yet porters worked a minimum of 300 hours a month and, in some cases, 400. Their responsibilities began with preparations several hours before the train departed, for which they did not get paid. Their pay terminated when the train arrived at its destination, even though they continued to work. "We put in twenty hours out of twenty-four," lamented C. L. Dellums, who worked as a Pullman porter and later rose to become International President of the Brotherhood of Sleeping Car Porters.[19]

Racial barriers also existed in white-collar jobs and the civil service. Few establishments employed blacks as office managers, supervisors, clerks, and secretaries, regardless of their education or previous experience. Before 1930, San Francisco did not have a single black bank teller, public school teacher, policeman, fireman, bus driver, or cab driver who worked for a predominantly white company. In at least one instance, a black female, Carlotta Stewart Lai, decided to remain in the territory of Hawaii, where she taught in the public schools, rather than move to San Francisco, where she faced the possibility of being barred from her profession because of her race.[20] While blacks succeeded in gaining employment with the U.S. Postal service, they were frequently hired as temporary workers, and thus rarely able to gain permanent status or seniority. The number of black mail carriers did not exceed three before 1940. The black press reported in one instance that three black women were denied employment at the post office because white women refused to work with them.[21] Richard Williamson, a respected member of San Francisco's black middle class, filed a complaint after he passed the junior stenographers and typist examination but failed to get placed. Williamson, an employee in government services for thirteen years, passed second on the federal civil service list. He was "certified to twelve different places," but rejected each time. Black protests prompted the Civil Service Commission to conduct an inquiry. The commission stated that the "civil service rules do not permit discrimination because of color," but that "an appointing office may consider as many as three names for each vacancy and he is not required to select any one eligible person certified." Nor was the appointing officer required to explain his selection.[22]

East Bay blacks also experienced many of the same problems in their quest to obtain white-collar and professional jobs, particularly in those areas where blacks had not broken the color barrier. After graduating from the University of California School of Pharmacy in San Francisco

living in the Pacific Northwest. Stewart settled in San Francisco and joined the practice of the prominent black attorney and businessman Oscar Hudson, and together they shared an office in the city's financial district. Stewart hoped that the larger black communities of San Francisco and Oakland would provide new challenges and opportunities, and most importantly, support his fledgling legal practice. Much to his dismay, Stewart found that San Francisco was no better than Portland. His practice struggled and his earnings were "not sufficient to meet the demands of his household." He wrote his daughter Katherine in 1917 that his savings account contained only $5 and that he had no steady source of income. Moreover, Stewart instructed his wife, who had remained in Portland, to sell some of the household items in their Portland home to raise money. Gradually Stewart began to lose his eyesight, after having lost a leg in a streetcar accident several years earlier. The combination of his failing vision, the loss of his leg, and the numerous economic burdens were too much for him to bear. In 1919, at the age of forty-two, Stewart committed suicide, leaving behind a wife, daughter, and "many debts."[26]

Although the number of black attorneys in San Francisco was small before 1930 (two in 1920 and four in 1930), they found it difficult to earn a living. William L. Patterson avoided the pervasive discrimination against black attorneys by leaving the state and joining the Communist party, where he became executive secretary of the International Labor Defense. Tabytha Anderson, San Francisco's first black female attorney, practiced out of her home, unable to find employment with a San Francisco law firm. Even the two most prominent black attorneys, Edward Mabson and Leland Hawkins, though widely respected by white attorneys and jurists, never had the large clientele or the financial security of San Francisco's most prestigious white lawyers.[27]

Black physicians and nurses, typically few in number, also encountered discrimination in the health profession. Black nurses, for example, complained that despite their qualifications, they had trouble gaining admittance to nursing programs and finding living facilities. Because San Francisco did not have a segregated hospital exclusively for black patients, unlike many southern and some northern cities, black nursing students interacted with white nurses in the classroom, in hospitals, and occasionally in their living quarters. Whether white nurses, white physicians, or white hospital administrators objected to the presence of black nurses in San Francisco, as they did in Cleveland and elsewhere, is unclear. As Darlene Clark Hine wrote, "Most of the hospital nursing schools in the North imposed racial quotas, while institutions in the South excluded black women." These problems apparently did not discourage black females from entering nurse training programs in San Francisco, for the number of black nurses increased slowly between 1910 and 1930.[28]

Most San Francisco hospitals also prohibited black physicians from working within their domain. Black physicians were allowed to admit patients to the city's hospitals, but lost control of their patients to white doctors immediately after admittance. In effect, San Francisco's black physicians were denied the same staff and consulting privileges as white physicians solely because of their race. This policy was not unique to San Francisco. In Cleveland, "white physicians and hospital administrators were united in their opposition to the admission of black doctors and nurses to hospital staffs." Cleveland's black physicians finally succeeded in joining the staffs of white hospitals in 1919, considerably earlier than black doctors in San Francisco. Chicago's white hospitals granted staff privileges to only one black physician, Daniel Hale Williams, but excluded other black physicians. Despite protests from both black and white leaders, San Francisco hospitals continued to bar black physicians until 1950.[29]

This policy reflected the disdain whites felt toward black professionals in general; it also illustrated whites' disregard for the qualifications and skills of black doctors. Even though there were never more than three black physicians and surgeons in San Francisco between 1900 and 1930, whites refused to acknowledge that they were capable of performing the same functions as white physicians. Despite their education, training, and expertise, black doctors were relegated to a subservient caste status that was similar in many respects to that of their nonprofessional black brethren.

A few black professionals succeeded in spite of racial restrictions, but they were the exception, rather than the rule. Dr. Earl T. Leaner and his father, a barber, established the California College of Chiropodists in San Francisco. After several years, Leaner left the school to take an office adjacent to San Francisco's prestigious Olympic Club on Post Street, where he maintained his practice for over fifty years. Although the club had no black members, Leaner used the club's facilities and became acquainted with some of the most powerful white leaders in San Francisco. Unlike most black professionals, Leaner earned a lucrative income and owned property in both San Francisco and the East Bay. He also had the support of influential whites, apparently an important determinant in the material success of black professionals before 1940.[30]

Ministers were among the most successful and respected members of the black professional class. Most black ministers were educated male migrants and all had begun their ministerial careers before coming to San Francisco. Reverend E. J. Magruder, for example, migrated to San Francisco from New Orleans in 1909. After serving as pastor of the First African Methodist Episcopal (A.M.E.) Zion Church in Oakland for several years, Magruder was appointed pastor of San Francisco's First A.M.E. Zion Church in 1926, where he remained until his death in 1941. Similarly, Reverend F. D. Haynes migrated to San Francisco in 1932 and served as pastor of the influential Third Baptist Church for nearly four decades. Mother C. Jones Robinson, the only prominent female minister in San Francisco's black community before 1940, led the Emanuel Pentecostal Church, a smaller black congregation than either First A.M.E. Zion or Third Baptist. On the whole, however, San Francisco's black churches were typical of black churches in northern cities—led primarily by male pastors.[31]

Unlike black attorneys, who sought entree into predominantly white law firms and a racially mixed clientele, black ministers segregated themselves. They depended almost exclusively on the black community to support their salaries, churches, and church-related activities. Although white politicians and civic leaders attended black churches occasionally, few of these churches ever achieved more than token integration. Black ministers were also relatively secure financially. The majority owned their homes, provided a college education for their children, and were members of San Francisco's black elite. Black ministers were not perceived as a threat, for they never competed openly with white ministers for parishioners, and only three black churches existed in San Francisco by 1926—hardly a cause of concern among white ministers. On the other hand, white ministers and priests succeeded in attracting a small number of black Catholics, Episcopalians, Presbyterians, and Congregationalists to their churches. The relatively small number of black ministers in San Francisco before 1930 and the absence of storefront churches, which had typically served a large number of rural black southerners in the wake of the Great Migration, also worked in favor of the white churches. By 1930 however, the number of black ministers had soared to ten, a significant increase for a black community the size of San Francisco's. Indeed, by 1930 San Francisco's black professional class reflected greater diversity than ever before, and the number of ministers was exceeded only by the number of musicians, still the largest professional group in San Francisco's black community.[32]

Compared to successful black businesses in many northern and southern cities, such as Chicago, Cleveland, Durham, and Louisville, where blacks established banks and insurance companies, the vast majority of business enterprises in San Francisco were small, single-owner, service-oriented establishments. Despite San Francisco's relatively small black population, most black businesses were located in the black community, or in close proximity to a concentration of blacks (an arrangement that approximated the institutional ghetto in many northern and southern urban centers). The majority were started with a capital outlay of between $1000 and $2000 and did not expand significantly. Since they catered primarily to a black clientele, black businesses rarely competed with white or Asian businessmen for the larger, more lucrative white and Asian markets. Here, black San Franciscans faced the same difficulties as their black counterparts in Seattle, who found it almost impossible to penetrate the Asian market. Nor did black San Franciscans succeed to the same degree as Asians in establishing business enterprises that took advantage of the expanding economy in either Seattle or San Francisco. Small services industries, such as barber shops and beauty parlors, were the most numerous black enterprises, but blacks also established billiard parlors, candy stores, smoke shops, real estate offices, newspapers, and a funeral home.[33]

The Butler Funeral Home, located at Sutter and Fillmore streets in San Francisco, was the most lucrative black enterprise before 1930. The business was owned and operated by the black activist, John Howard Butler. "Tod" Butler, as he was known in the Bay Area black communities, migrated to California with his father in the early 1900s. The family settled in Oakland, where the older Butler worked for the Southern Pacific Railroad, a job he held for fifty-two years. Meanwhile, Tod Butler entered into a partnership with Luther Hudson, an East Bay black businessman, and established the Hudson and Butler Funeral Home in Oakland. After two years, Hudson encouraged Butler to start his own funeral home in San Francisco to serve the city's expanding black community. Butler agreed and established the Butler Funeral Home in 1923, San Francisco's only black mortuary. Butler's business, according to his brother, Alfred Butler, was "very profitable." Butler also served San Francisco's large Asian population, particularly the Chinese community, an anomaly that was not evident in any other Pacific Coast city. The Butler Funeral Home was one of the few cases where a black businessman succeeded in making an inroad into the Asian community. This was admittedly a difficult task, as Quintard Taylor noted in his study of blacks and Asians in Seattle, given the cultural barrier that separated these two groups and the economic competition between them. Unlike most black businesses, which failed to survive the death of their owners, the Butler Funeral Home continued to prosper long after John Howard

Butler's death. The business was managed by Butler's wife, Alice, until it was ultimately sold to Cecil Finley, a black mortician.[34]

San Francisco's black business class differed from those in other cities in still another important respect. Unlike blacks in Cleveland or New York, who profited from the booming real estate market, only a few black San Franciscans appeared to have tapped the lucrative real estate market, and none to the extent of Philip A. Payton in New York's Harlem. Walter Sanford, who worked as an aide and messenger for three mayors, invested his earnings in real estate and was reportedly a millionaire at the time of his death. Black businessman Hannibal T. Sheppard, who later served as president of the San Francisco branch of the NAACP, owned a realty company in the Western Addition. M. B. Witten, a black realty broker, also owned the Inter-City Finance Company, but unlike Sanford and Sheppard, was not active in the black community. Most blacks possessed little capital, however, and the restricted economic opportunities open to them meant that few would even own their homes. It was the existence of a black ghetto that had allowed black businessmen to make large profits in many northern and midwestern cities, as housing was in short supply and blacks were restricted to specified neighborhoods. There was no black ghetto in San Francisco. Thus the opportunity to invest in real estate, in the absence of a substantially larger black community, was nonexistent for most black businessmen before 1940.[35]

Racial restrictions were not the sole barriers to opportunities for black businessmen. San Francisco's black community was not large enough to support a class of black entrepreneurs. Unlike black businessmen in many northern cities, which increased the size of their black business class substantially after the Great Migration, San Francisco's black entrepreneurs did not have the benefit of an expanded black population like Chicago's south side or New York's Harlem. Moreover, their small, service-oriented businesses were competing against a substantially larger pool of white and Asian businesses with more capital, more credit, more business experience, and a substantially larger pool of customers. Consequently, black capitalism remained more shadow than substance until the black population increased significantly during the 1940s.[36]

In summary, racial discrimination and white hostility hampered blacks in virtually every sector of the labor force, and employment opportunities for most blacks between 1900 and 1930 were limited largely to unskilled, domestic, and service jobs. Yet some blacks made significant progress in manufacturing jobs between 1910 and 1930, in spite of racial discrimination and opposition by white trade unions. Black workers also made limited progress in the skilled trades, but they were prohibited from joining most labor unions by discriminatory constitutions and bylaws. White-collar jobs in both the public and private sectors were also difficult for black workers to obtain, irrespective of gender, and many blacks found that cracking the color line in the Civil Service was virtually impossible. San Francisco's small black professional class also declined after 1920, as few opportunities were open to college educated blacks, and neither San Francisco's public nor private schools employed black teachers before 1940. In the employment of black teachers, San Francisco lagged behind eastern and midwestern cities like Chicago and New York, which had employed black teachers since the nineteenth century, or Oakland, which had hired its first black teacher in 1926.[37] Similarly, black physicians were shut out of San Francisco's hospitals, a pattern that surfaced in at least two midwestern cities.[38]

Even though occupational progress for blacks lagged behind that of San Francisco's white workers in almost every category, the black industrial working class grew rapidly between 1900 and 1930, evidence of increasing proletarianization. Here San Francisco's black community was slowly beginning to resemble that of a northern city like Milwaukee, although black San Franciscans never established the foothold that black Milwaukeeans secured in factory jobs between 1915 and 1930.[39] The black San Franciscans' collective struggle against underemployment and racial discrimination in the labor sector underscores the hostility and disdain that most white San Franciscans felt toward blacks in all classes. In the opinion of white workers, their black counterparts represented an inferior caste who should be denied the opportunity to advance in the labor force alongside whites. This "consensus in favor of white supremacy," as George M. Fredrickson refers to it, affected black workers in all classes, regardless of their education or qualifications.[40] For many black workers, San Francisco offered less employment opportunity than most northern cities and several other California urban centers, such as Oakland and Los Angeles. On the other hand, the employment restrictions that blacks faced in San Francisco were virtually identical to those faced by their counterparts in Seattle, which had approximately the same number of blacks as San Francisco and a large Asian population, and Boston, where Stephan Thernstrom illustrated that black Bostonians lagged far behind even first-generation white immigrants between 1890 and 1930.[41] The slower growth in San Francisco's black population between 1915 and 1930, at a time when most northern black communities were expanding at a rapid rate, was a rejection of its liberal employment facade.

3

CLASS, STATUS, AND SOCIAL LIFE

Class distinctions were important in San Francisco's black community. Despite the tendency of white journalists and observers to characterize them as one homogeneous mass, blacks did not think of themselves as a single, static, all-encompassing unit. Class distinctions were expressed in occupation, residence, education, and social and cultural life. Class status and social hierarchy were also manifested through long-standing family names and association with prominent white San Franciscans.

Milton Gordon noted that the black community's class structure "is a social order of its own (with somewhat different dividing lines from the white class structure) within the Negro social system."[1] Unlike social ranking in white society, income and occupation were not always crucial determinants in black class structure. Blacks attached equal importance to attitudes, values, behavior, lifestyle, popularity, and image in the larger society. A prominent black leader like Walter Butler, president of the Northern California branch of the NAACP, was considered a member of the black elite, even though he never moved beyond the position of insurance clerk. Black San Franciscans themselves decided who should be accorded elite status, and their subjective criteria in assigning class labels often took precedence over the larger society's traditional distinctions of wealth, power, and good breeding. Thus blacks had a broader and more fluid definition of class standing than whites, and even though middle-class white mores overlapped with the behavior and values of elite blacks, black class ranking was not defined solely by white norms.[2]

Black San Franciscans never developed an upper class comparable to the white upper class. Instead, black elites constituted the upper strata of the black middle class, and they resembled the white middle class in their occupations, values, and life-style. "In many respects the older Negro elite sought to emulate the lifestyle of more affluent members of the white middle class," argued Kenneth Kusmer. Black elites in San Francisco sought to distinguish themselves from the larger black middle and lower classes in several respects. Socially, they mimicked the mannerisms of polite white society. Their insistence on proper moral behavior, sound character, and good breeding set them apart from most blacks, as did their formal dances, literary societies, elaborate teas, and exclusive social clubs.[3]

Elite blacks typically married within their social group and selected spouses of comparable education and family background. Education was an important factor in social ranking, so most elite blacks completed high school and, in some cases, obtained a college education or professional training. Members of this upper strata of the black community took considerable pride in their family names, especially if their families were second or third generation San Franciscans or if they were descendants of pioneer families. In many cases, they owned property, though less frequently than San Francisco's white elite. The black elite traveled much more than lower-class blacks, and several individuals, such as Berlinda Davison and Josephine Cole, traveled abroad. As Kusmer noted in Cleveland's black community, travel became an important badge of prestige among elite black San Franciscans, a signal to both blacks and whites that not only were these individuals cultured, but they also possessed the financial wherewithal to enjoy their status. Elite blacks were also more inclined to mingle socially with prominent whites, and they often attended formal receptions and important political functions. Elite blacks perceived themselves as leaders or, as Willard B. Gatewood wrote, "aristocrats of color" with a sense of noblesse oblige and the moral imperative to help blacks less fortunate than themselves. They generally occupied leadership roles in both black and interracial organizations like the NAACP, League of Women Voters, YWCA, black press, and colored women's clubs. Because they saw themselves as leaders, they aggressively sought to maintain their privileged position and were cautious about who they admitted to their exclusive social circle.[4]

The black professional was the backbone of the small black elite class. Physician Stuart T. Davison and his sister Berlinda reflected the lifestyle and attitudes of this group. As residents of San Francisco from the turn of the century, both Davisons had attended the University of California, Berkeley, which had admitted black students as early as 1881. Berlinda earned a master's degree in education in 1922. Stuart entered the University of California medical school at the onset of the First World War, after briefly delaying his medical education in order to enlist in the army as a medical officer.[5]

Several factors set the Davisons apart from most blacks. They were educated, owned their homes, participated in exclusive social activities, and enjoyed extensive leisure time. Berlinda married a black of comparable wealth and status. Unlike most San Franciscans, black or white, Berlinda traveled extensively before her marriage. She took a two-and-a-half-year trip around the world, stopping in Helsinki, London, Madrid, Rome, Brussels, Norway, Geneva, Germany, Paris, Holland, and Ceylon. After working as a professor of languages at Virginia Normal and Industrial Institute, she returned to San Francisco in the early 1930s and married an influential black attorney, Edward D. Mabson, himself a member of the city's black elite.[6]

Stuart and Berlinda Davison's family exhibited a keen concern for good breeding and proper moral behavior and limited their associations to blacks of comparable status. The family's residence contained a library, reading room, piano, and even a parrot, all signs of middle-class stability. None of the young women in the Davison family worked, although most young black females in San Francisco were employed. The Davison girls, Berlinda and Ophelia, took piano lessons, embroidered, read widely, participated in a sewing circle, wrote letters, and were active in the local branch of the NAACP. Stuart Davison's family urged him to "get in with the better class as we usually do." After Davison entered the army, his status-conscious sister inquired if the "girls realized you were a coming man" and asked, "Did they introduce you as Mr. or Dr.?" The family also cautioned Stuart against casual social alliances, but his mother instructed him, "if you meet a nice girl who will show you around, take her."[7]

The black elite consisted of a small cluster of long-standing black families, several of which had migrated to San Francisco in the nineteenth century. The social rank of individuals from these families was primarily determined by their family's longevity in San Francisco and their association with prominent whites, who often helped them obtain minor political appointments or jobs in city or state government. Among this privileged group were the Fishers, Graves, Sands, Foremans, Brooks, Ruggleses, Butlers, Albergas, Clarks, Stewarts, and Thompsons.[8]

The Ruggleses typified the elite black pioneer family. David W. Ruggles, a native of San Francisco, was a direct descendant of one of the oldest black families in San Francisco. His father, who bore the same name, had been a merchant on the fringes of the city's financial district during the 1860s.[9] The younger Ruggles improved his social standing by marrying Irene P. Bell. Although neither was financially well endowed, the Ruggleses were important members of the social elite, distinguished guests at countless teas, bridge parties, and prestigious formal affairs. Not content to be merely a social figure, Irene Bell Ruggles was active in local politics, social work, and women's clubs. Her association with the California State Federation of Colored Women's Clubs earned Ruggles the office of state president from 1923 to 1924. Under her tutelage, the San Francisco members of the state federation formed a local federation. In an effort to aid young working black females, she cofounded the Madame C. J. Walker Home for Motherless Girls. The home provided shelter, recreation, and companionship for a limited number of black women in San Francisco.[10]

The black elite generally shared the same values, attitudes, and lifestyle as the Davisons and the Ruggleses. They did not permit their children to work in the menial jobs that were available to black San Franciscans, because they believed they were degrading. As a young woman, Katherine Stewart was not allowed to work because "there were no jobs for Negro girls that mama approved [of]." Mary Stewart would not permit her daughter to work in domestic service or engage in any form of menial labor.[11] The Anderson family also reflected these values. Although they were only the daughters of a redcap, the "Anderson girls" were revered by local blacks for their academic excellence and community activism. Three of the four sisters attended Lowell, San Francisco's prestigious senior high school, and all four of them pursued professional careers.[12] Of the four, Tabytha Anderson made the most memorable impression. A rather stout girl with a husky voice, Tabytha excelled in public speaking and drama. Her performance of Macbeth's soliloquy still evokes accolades from her peers. Tabytha decided to pursue a law career, a rare decision for a young black woman in the early 1930s. She graduated from Howard University's Law School and became one of the first black females in the San Francisco Bay Area to pass the California State Bar. Tabytha became an important leader in the black community when she successfully unseated incumbent NAACP president Leland Hawkins in a power struggle. Her untimely death in 1935 from a kidney disease cut short a promising career.[13]

The Anderson family's social life, like that of most black professionals, centered around public lectures, dramatic readings, classical plays, piano recitals, and formal outings. The strict social etiquette of the black professional class restricted even dances and parties to closely supervised affairs, in contrast to the more casual middle- or lower-class functions. Moreover, the Anderson family owned its modest residence, which distinguished them from most blacks. Although they never attained even moderate wealth, their experience characterized a sector of San Francisco's black elite.[14]

Ministers, social workers, editors, and community leaders were also recognized as elite blacks. The Booker T. Washington Community Center's executive director, Robert Flippin, was indisputably a member of the black elite. Flippin's education at Nebraska Central College, the University of Nebraska, Washington State, and Northwest Institute in Minneapolis, was an important factor in his rise up the social ladder. Moreover, his occupation as a social worker, his marriage to Katherine Stewart (who came from one of San Francisco's most prominent black families), and his community activism solidified his social standing and his position in the black elite.[15] Black ministers like J. J. Byers and E. J. Magruder of the First A.M.E. Zion Church and F. D. Haynes of the Third Baptist Church commanded a strong following among middle-class blacks and were revered by white city officials as well. Byers, Magruder, and Haynes were major figures in local civil rights activities, and blacks throughout the Bay Area respected their status and leadership. Black ministers occasionally served on local interracial committees and were designated by white officials as liaisons between the city government and the black community.[16]

Few members of the black elite ever earned a substantial income or accumulated wealth comparable to the white upper class. Thus income was not the overriding factor in achieving elite status; the tenor, style, and quality of one's social commitments proved far more important. However, blacks apparently valued the illusion of affluence. Elite blacks took great pride in their posh dinner parties, lavish teas, and bridge parties. Hosting an elaborate social affair for the "correct" element of black society was more important than earning a sizable income, especially if the money came from "illegitimate" activities.[17] So Lester Mapp and Lew Purcell, who operated successful night spots on the Barbary Coast and were reputedly among the wealthiest blacks in San Francisco, were effectively barred from the black elite. Their association with gambling, alcohol, and prostitution blacklisted them from the social circles of respectable blacks.[18]

Religious affiliation was not an important barometer of class in San Francisco's black community before 1940. Neither the black elite nor the black middle class segregated themselves from lower-class blacks in their selection of churches. In contrast to patterns in Chicago and Cleveland, where elite blacks attended separate denominations from middle- and lower-class blacks, no major class differential existed among the city's three large black churches. Although both of the black Methodist churches, First A.M.E. Zion and Bethel A.M.E., received more attention in the black press than did the Third Baptist Church, blacks from all classes attended each of these churches. Similarly, blacks from every social class attended the city's Catholic churches. Nor did the small influx of black migrants during World War I heighten class distinctions in San Francisco's black churches as it did in Chicago and Cleveland, where large numbers of southern rural blacks relocated. Furthermore, migrant and storefront churches, another sign of class distinction in many northern cities, did not proliferate in San Francisco.[19]

The black elite also heightened their status through association with influential whites. Walter Sanford served as an aide and usher for three San Francisco mayors and was one of the best-known blacks in San Francisco.[20] Similarly, black attorney Edward D. Mabson's stature was enhanced by his association with prominent whites, such as Mayor James Rolph, Jr., and Judge Franklin A. Griffin. But associating with influential whites did not guarantee economic success. Mabson's law practice, for example, was modest, and his unsecured personal property in 1934 was valued at less than $300. These particular blacks were nonetheless revered in the black community because of their associations with influential whites. This association would set them apart from the new black elite that appeared in the 1930s and 1940s. This new elite was more dependent on the expanding black population and developed businesses in predominantly black areas of San Francisco. Members of San Francisco's older black elite, on the other hand, were assisted in their careers, in varying degrees, by whites. The careers of men like Joseph Foreman, David Ruggles, Walter Sanford, and Walter Mabson conformed closely to the pattern that many scholars have documented in other cities.[21]

Social clubs in San Francisco's black community also fostered class distinctions in an attempt to isolate their members from the larger mass of blacks. For example, the Booker T. Washington Country Club, the Kalendar Klub, and the Cosmos Club made conscious efforts to establish social circles that were restricted along class lines.[22] Alice Butler, the wife of San Francisco's black funeral director, organized an exclusive group, the "Committee of Fifty," which included black women from the finest families in the Bay Area. It concluded the year with an annual Christmas buffet and dance. Black social clubs in San Francisco, however, did not limit themselves by skin color; light skin was never a prerequisite for admission to the black elite. Here, San Francisco differed from many older cities, such as Washington, D.C., Charleston, and New Orleans, where elite blacks with light skin were very careful to segregate themselves socially from blacks with dark complexions.[23]

The most dramatic social statement of class standing was an annual formal dance given by the Cosmos Club. This club was organized in 1919 by William Henry Lashley, and represented one of the earliest attempts at an interracial social club in San Francisco. Members met monthly at the International Institute and engaged in numerous social and cultural activities. The society's trademark was its formal ball held in February around George Washington's birthday. Admission to the affair, which was always held at one of the city's fashionable hotels, was by invitation only. The expense of attending was beyond the means of the typical working-class black. Blacks from as far away as Los Angeles often attended, along with prominent white San Franciscans. The strictly formal event gave Bay Area blacks an excuse to don their tuxedos and top hats, flowing silk-and-lace gowns, and white gloves.[24]

The program of the Cosmos Club ball reflected the elite blacks' preference for European culture as opposed to traditional Afro-American folk music, blues, or jazz. A typical program included a lyric soprano, a tenor, a Hawaiian ensemble vocal, a Spanish instrumental trio, piano solos, classical singing, and juvenile readings. Formal dancing generally rounded out the evening. Joseph Foreman, the popular doorman at the exclusive Shreve's jewelry store, served as the master of ceremonies.[25]

Foreman, known affectionately throughout the city as "Joe Shreve," was the most recognizable black social figure in San Francisco. A native of Western Kentucky, Foreman migrated to San Francisco before the earthquake and fire. After working briefly as a doorman at the St. Dunstan's Hotel on Van Ness Avenue, Foreman joined the staff at Shreve's. Foreman's name as well as his imposing form became a part of the city's history. Famed San Francisco columnist Herb Caen remembers Foreman "reigning like a king at Post and Grant streets." Caen described Foreman vividly: "He's tall, dark, and handsome, every inch a gentleman of good taste and culture. On Grant Avenue in the heart of the elite shopping district you often see him nodding to the most elegant ladies, who favor him with their prettiest smiles. I can't remember an important social function in the past decade that has not been graced with his presence. An imposing figure, straight as an arrow in his beautiful tailored uniform, he adds the final touch of class to any event."[26]

With Foreman serving as the Cosmos Club's master of ceremonies, the affair became black high society's biggest social event of the year. Not to receive an invitation was the ultimate social snub. Consequently, the guest list for the annual Cosmos Club ball remained a powerful statement of social hierarchy in San Francisco's black community.[27]

The middle-class blacks' world was similar in many respects to that of the black elite. These two groups often had worked side by side, attended the same schools, lived in the same neighborhoods, and engaged in the same social pastimes. Thus the gulf separating the black elite and the black middle class was psychological rather than economic. Unlike the black elite, however, middle-class blacks were rarely educated beyond high school and seldom owned property or traveled abroad. Among their ranks was a small nucleus of black artisans as well as skilled and semi-skilled workers, postal employees, valets, chauffeurs, Pullman porters, redcaps, cooks, waiters, and doormen at the finer hotels. The black middle class also included businessmen, such as insurance agents, real estate brokers, barbers, beauticians, and merchants.[28]

The lives of the black middle class are more difficult to reconstruct than those of the elite, because they left few written records. Alfred Butler was probably typical of many blacks in this class. A native of Oakland, Butler moved to San Francisco in the late 1920s to accept a position as a chauffeur and valet with the Shumates (a prominent white San Francisco family), a position he held for almost five decades. Even though he never finished high school, Butler's steady income placed him solidly in the black middle class. Although he did not consider himself an activist, Butler joined the NAACP, the Masonic lodge, and a local black church. Butler's monthly wage of $100 to $125 was comfortably above the income of most blacks. However, unlike the black elite, he did not own property before 1940, and he lived in the Western Addition, rather than in the more exclusive Richmond or Sunset districts. The fact that his first wife was employed reflected the lack of economic security among middle-class blacks. Moreover, Butler shared black society's image of himself as a successful Afro-American.[29]

Alfred Butler's status reflected the tenuous economic status of the black middle class. Not highly educated and employed as a chauffeur for most of his career, albeit for a socially prominent white family, Butler's situation was similar to that of lower class blacks in many respects. True, his earnings were sufficient to pay the monthly dues to his lodge and church and to provide a membership in the local branch of the NAACP— fees that some members of the lower class often found prohibitive. But Butler's salary was never large enough to allow him to purchase property until after World War II, so like most members of San Francisco's black working class, he rented a series of apartments in the Western Addition. Butler believed that even if he had attempted to improve his economic status, the restricted employment opportunities for black San Franciscans would prevent him from doing so. He could not even consider white-collar employment or a skilled trade. His monthly salary was not large enough to allow him to move into white middle-class neighborhoods like the Richmond and Sunset districts. Thus the lives of the Alfred Butlers of the black middle class must be viewed in the context of the basic economic and social realities of San Francisco's race relations, particularly the near impossibility of securing professional, white-collar, and skilled jobs.[30]

St. Clair Drake and Horace Cayton wrote in their classic study of black life in Chicago, *Black Metropolis*, that middle-class blacks are "great joiners and belongers."[31] Drama groups and organized clubs, with their dances, whist and bridge parties, were enticing to most blacks. The Booker T. Washington Community Center served as an omnibus organization for many of these clubs, but small gatherings often met in churches, lodges, and even private residences. Each club's trademark was a fancy name that rarely designated the aims and objectives of the organization. The Monarchs, Franciscans, Socialettes, Smart Set, Go-Getters, Kalendar Klub, Alexander Dumas Club, Ecclectrics, and the Carpe Diem Club, to name a few, saturated the black weekly society page with notices of their community activities. These clubs generally had between fifteen and twenty members. The longevity of these organizations varied considerably, from several months to several decades.[32]

Office holding was a crucial aspect of club membership. Generally, every club member held an office, no matter how minor. The Kalendar Klub, which organized at the Booker T. Washington Community Center in the early 1930s, limited its membership to fifty-two, but had an elaborate array of elective offices.[33] Purportedly a combined social and benevolent society, the club restricted its membership to males, twenty-one years of age and over, and females, eighteen years of age and over. The group took special pride in its welfare committee, which dispensed funds for worthy causes. Dances and whist parties, however, were the club's primary activities. Like most black middle-class organizations, the club insisted on proper moral behavior. Hence, the club's bylaws restricted membership to persons of "good character who are properly recommended by a current member."[34]

Not all middle-class functions were a picture of fraternal bliss. Tempers occasionally flared, even among the "better class." In one instance, a jealous wife struck another woman at a society party for flirting with her husband. Likewise, the *Spokesman*'s society editor criticized middle-class blacks for their often unruly behavior. "Day by day, we are forming habits of *others* in the social life. Fighting, divorces, black eyes, and pistol shots seem to be regular bed mates of the Demon Bridge."[35]

Church membership was also an important activity for San Francisco's

black middle class. Most middle class blacks attended one of San Francisco's three largest black churches: Third Baptist, A.M.E. Zion, or Bethel
A.M.E. These churches organized numerous social activities, including
picnics, boat rides, bazaars, and fund raising drives. Church choirs generally attracted broad participation among both youth and adults. Equally important were the literary events, such as dramatic and poetry readings and plays, hosted by black churches.[36] Attending services at these
religious bodies allowed status seekers to display their stylish fashions,
divulge the weekly gossip, and seek the friendship of an admiring ac-
quaintance. Moreover, church activities were an essential outlet for "respectable" black women who otherwise felt circumscribed by rigid societal restrictions. For them, church social life offered an alternative to the
drudgery of everyday life.[37]

The black middle class also organized lodges, as they had since the
mid-nineteenth century. In fact, lodges were some of the oldest secular
organizations in San Francisco's black community. By 1862, three separate branches of black lodges had been organized in San Francisco, and
several years later blacks had established a grand lodge. Lodges never
encompassed the vast majority of black working men and excluded
women altogether. Elected officers were established community figures.
Black San Franciscans associated principally under the banners of the
Masonic Order and the Grand United Order of Odd Fellows. Lodge news,
with its pomp and pageantry, often dominated the social page of black
weeklies. The *Spokesman* called lodges "our strongest black institutions,"
because of their wide influence among Bay Area blacks.[38]

Lodges, though primarily social organizations, offered many important
benefits to their members. Lodges paid death and sickness benefits to
members and aided their brethren during periods of severe financial
crisis. They supported several struggling black institutions financially,
including the NAACP and the black press, and made small financial
contributions to black protest campaigns. Lodges also added an important dimension to the social life of the black middle class. The multitude
of lodge dances, picnics, card parties, and social outings contributed to
the richness and social diversity of the black community.[39] Of crucial
importance, however, were the status and recognition that accompanied
lodge membership. Black secret and fraternal societies engendered in
their members a heightened sense of belonging and importance by virtue
of their flamboyant rituals, hushed proceedings, and stern initiation pro-
cedures. Attaining a leadership position within the lodge heightened a
member's self-esteem and his security in the group.[40] Finally, lodge members' stern adherence to bourgeois values and good character perpetu-

ated an elite group within the black community. Ironically, while black lodges took pride in their commitment to community affairs, they purposely avoided contact with the majority of lower-class blacks, an inclination that Willard Gatewood observed in many members of the black elite throughout the North and South. Nevertheless, the black lodge often trained members for leadership roles, while encouraging self-help and good will among its members.[41]

The lower class blacks' plight did not differ radically from that of the black middle class. Although lower-class blacks occupied the bottom rung of the economic ladder, they were only one step below the black middle sector. Within this lower category fell the majority of unskilled laborers, janitors, porters, female domestic workers, and personal servants. In fact, roughly two-thirds of San Francisco's black labor force fell into this category, so many of these occupations were considered the lower echelon of the middle class.

The life-style of lower-class blacks mirrored the middle classes in form, but their associations were quite different. Less of a "joiner" than the middle-class black, the lower-class black's social activities were loosely structured. They consisted mainly of church activities, informal gatherings, San Francisco's vibrant night life, and athletic contests. Although an accurate profile of lower-class blacks is difficult to reconstruct because of the shifting nature of black occupational patterns and the scarcity of written records, the experience of Willie Solomon lends insight. Born in San Francisco in 1900, Solomon was the product of uneducated parents from the Southwest, and he terminated his own education after grammar school to work. Unskilled and poorly educated, he worked in several positions, including waiter, redcap, and laborer. Finally he obtained steady employment as a porter in one of San Francisco's hotels.[42]

Not long a bachelor, Solomon married a young woman from his own social background. The couple's two children presented some unaccustomed hardships in periods of economic slack, and Solomon was forced onto the local relief rolls during the depression. Even though the family's rent was less than $30 a month for a large, two-bedroom flat, it represented a significant portion of their unpredictable income. To supplement the family's wages, Solomon's wife worked as a domestic, and the family occasionally took in boarders. Both Solomons also worked at odd jobs, such as sewing and cleaning for neighbors.[43] Their social life centered around the church and the neighborhood community center. The family possessed a strong religious orientation, and both Solomon and his wife derived special satisfaction from their leadership roles in the church as a deacon and a Sunday school teacher, respectively. Solomon's wife took part in a small sewing circle, and the couple frequently played cards with other young blacks. Both of them expressed an overriding concern that their children attain a higher station in life than they had managed to attain themselves. Much to the Solomons' satisfaction, both children graduated from high school and obtained employment as bus drivers. In effect, they had risen in status to the black middle class.[44]

In general, the values and life-style of the Solomons are those of hundreds of black San Franciscans who sought to upgrade their position in their unskilled occupations and in the social world. They were diligent, law abiding, and religious. Like countless white immigrants, these blacks wished to share in San Francisco's economic growth and to provide a higher standard of living for their children. Most never rose in status to the black middle class and none ever became a member of San Francisco's black elite. So even though class lines were relatively fluid between the lower and middle class, the exclusion of black workers from many areas hampered class mobility.[45]

Black San Franciscans engaged in numerous social activities that reflected both class divisions and class unity within the black community. Lower- and middle-class blacks used street corners, barber shops, shoe-shine stands, smokeshops, newspaper corners, pool halls, and saloons as informal social clubs. There they exchanged information, debated politics and race relations, gossiped, and complained about their latest physical or psychological afflictions. Street life in particular, as James Borchert concluded in his study of alley life in Washington, D.C., afforded not only a great deal of personal freedom, but it also provided a convenient and legitimate forum.[46] These informal social clubs were male bastions. Women were rarely welcomed or allowed to participate. Moreover, members of the middle as well as the lower class interacted in this informal social life, although members of the black elite did not approve of this type of behavior in public. F. L. Ritchardson, a postal employee and a respected member of the black middle class, noted that whenever he walked down Fillmore Street, he saw scores of blacks congregating on street corners, in pool halls, and in barber shops, almost all of whom he knew by name. The concentration of black businesses in the Fillmore district, coupled with the high percentage of blacks who lived in the Western Addition, encouraged this type of informal social activity. And although neither street corners nor barber shops played the roles they did in Washington, D.C. (according to Elliot Liebow) or in nineteenth-century Boston (according to James Horton), they were important diversions and avenues of recreation. These informal activities illustrate that class divisions were more likely to be bridged in the informal social arena than in more structured and formal organizations like the Cosmos Club or the Masonic lodge. They also gave black San Franciscans an alternative social outlet to the church and community center.[47]

Outdoor street life was an important social dimension for many blacks, as it had been for white San Franciscans since the city's formative years. San Francisco was a walking city, as Roger W. Lotchin observed during the mid-nineteenth century. Black residents like Katherine and Mary Stewart and Josephine Cole took advantage of the city's mild weather and the diversity of recreational areas to explore the city on foot. "My mother was a great walker," recalled Katherine Stewart. "She would walk over the hill to Lombard Street, and I'd walk with her." Similarly, Josephine Cole remembers walking from the Western Addition as a young girl to Cow Hollow, where the Marina district is currently located. There was no legal restriction on black access to parks, beaches, hiking trails, and recreational facilities in San Francisco. Nor did blacks fear they would be attacked by whites if they walked into predominantly white ethnic neighborhoods or swam in certain sections of public beaches. So when the Stewarts or other black San Franciscans attended parades, walked through Golden Gate Park, or swam at public beaches, they encountered no difficulties because of their race.[48]

Blacks were spectators as well as participants in numerous competitive activities. Several factors contributed to the black San Franciscans' enthusiasm for organized sporting contests. The location of several major colleges in close proximity, San Francisco's large metropolitan area, the zest for outdoor events, and the mild weather in the Bay Area produced widespread interest in athletics. Baseball, football, boxing, track and field, and horse racing were especially popular with local blacks.

Black athletes were prohibited from competing in many organized professional sports during this period, but local blacks supported professional and amateur boxing, college sports, and high school athletics. Boxing generated considerable interest among black San Franciscans, who took pride in the exploits of the "Brown Bomber," Joe Louis, the undisputed heavyweight champion of the world for more than a decade. Similarly, boxing enthusiasts followed the colorful careers of local black boxers like Gorilla Jones, Kid Chocolate, and Dynamite Jackson.[49] The boxing craze also extended into the local community, as the black disabled war veterans and the Booker T. Washington Community Center both taught and promoted pugilism. The center's highly structured boxing program succeeded in placing several promising prospects in prestigious amateur contests.[50] Athletic competition was also popular with social clubs and some employers. Black lodges, Pullman porters, and redcaps entered the competitive Bay Area colored baseball league. The *Spokesman* reported that colored baseball "draws large crowds" after an estimated crowd of 7,500 attended the opening game of the Colored Baseball League.[51]

The appeal of black baseball in the San Francisco Bay Area during the 1920s and 1930s reflected the national appeal of this sport, not only in western black communities but also throughout the nation. As Janet Bruce wrote in her history of the Kansas City Monarchs, the dominant team in the Negro national leagues, "blacks, no less than whites, fell victim to the baseball craze of the 1920s."[52] Black baseball games were not only significant as sporting events, but also as social gatherings where blacks from all social classes intermingled, wore their finest clothes, and cheered for their heroes. Sports unified the black community and played a "galvanic role" in the acculturation of black youth just as sports had galvanized immigrant communities in the early twentieth century. When black San Franciscans converged to watch or participate in these athletic events, they learned not only the nuances of the individual sport, but they also learned to channel divisive forces into productive use. As Rob Ruck concluded in his study of the role of sports in Pittsburgh's black community, these varied athletic contests "played a supportive role in the coalescence of a black community both during and after the great migrations of the early twentieth century."[53]

Horse racing was also popular among black residents. The *Spokesman* noted that "members of my tribe are playing Tanforan racetrack daily." In another instance, it reported that nearly 30,000 fans turned out to view racing at Tanforan, including "quite a lot of our group." Jokes concerning betting with bookies occasionally appeared in black weeklies. One black gossip columnist requested, "Please run your horses in pool rooms or barber shops and not in dining rooms." Betting on horses did not carry the same stigma as illegal gambling, and blacks from all social and economic classes, such as the prominent black socialites Alice and Estelle Butler, attended Bay Area race tracks. Black San Franciscans enjoyed the multitude of athletic endeavors and the richness of Bay Area sports.[54]

Dancing was popular among all classes of blacks and a part of many social functions. The Oakland *Sunshine* criticized Bay Area blacks for their preoccupation with this art form, insisting that "our young men and women have no other thought but dancing, and the most indecent dances seem to be the most popular." Lodges, community centers, social clubs, and churches probably spent more time and energy organizing dances than any other activity. The Kalendar Klub, for example, held dances on a frequent basis, and their numerous whist and bridge parties generally culminated in dancing.[55]

Black residents frequented the night clubs on the Barbary Coast and danced to popular Afro-American rhythms. Some clubs, including the Acorn, Apex, Sam King's, Purcell's, and Lester Mapp's were particularly popular, and several were organized as cabarets, a popular form of entertainment. Amid the revelry and gay music, San Franciscans saw interracial couples and dancing by members of all races. The cabarets often featured an "all colored revue," to the delight of black and white San Franciscans alike.[56]

Black entertainers were also an integral part of the city. Black artists performed at the established San Francisco theaters, and some of the most popular early Afro-American art forms were the minstrel shows and vaudeville.[57] Originally a product of the eastern states, the minstrel show predated California's admittance to statehood. The early minstrel companies, made up largely of white men in blackface, exploited stereotyped images of blacks and fulfilled the public's demand for music, dance, and ridicule. Thus the characters Jim Crow, the dumb-witted southern black, and Zip Coon, the slick northern Negro, were the most common minstrel characters.[58]

Following the Civil War, black minstrels and dancers performed more frequently in the leading San Francisco theaters. The prestigious Bush Street Theater, Standard, Baldwin, Orpheum, and Grand Opera House gradually opened their doors to black performers. Black minstrel companies, including the Georgia Minstrels, Haverly's Minstrels, and the Tenth Callendar Minstrels, entertained San Franciscans of all races with black entertainers like Billy Kersands and James Bland.[59]

Black dancers and entertainers continued to be popular in San Francisco into the twentieth century. The renowned black artists Bert Williams and George Walker first attracted serious attention on a downtown San Francisco street corner. The appreciation for black entertainment was widespread. "A colored man with a banjo would draw almost as big a crowd as an elephant in a circus," wrote Ann Charters in her biography of Bert Williams. When the team of Williams and Walker consolidated, the young stars worked several years in the clubs and saloons on the Barbary Coast before going to New York to win national acclaim.[60] Interracial audiences were entertained by still other black dance teams: Al and Mamie Anderson, who brought the Cakewalk to San Francisco; the dancing Mitchells, featuring the "black prince with the electric legs"; and Bill "Bojangles" Robinson, who later gained fame when he appeared in movies with Shirley Temple.[61]

Class distinctions had remained remarkably stable in San Francisco's black community until the mid-1930s, when several significant changes occurred. Because there were fewer black children, few blacks could claim to be descendants of pioneer families. It had also become more difficult by this time to be recognized as a member of the black elite without a college degree or professional training. Hence, recent migrants who had come to San Francisco during the 1930s, such as Robert B. Flippin, director of the Booker T. Washington Community Center, the Reverend Fred D. Haynes, pastor of the Third Baptist Church, and Carlton B. Goodlett, a physician, were accepted immediately as members of this prestigious social group because of their education as well as their influence in the black community. The acceptance of these men and others like them into the black elite helped set the stage for a substantial broadening of the black leadership class during the World War II era, when hundreds of college-educated black men and women migrated to San Francisco.[62]

Class distinctions provided status and prestige to black San Franciscans, who were otherwise ignored by the larger society. They also served as a buffer from racial discrimination and exclusion from white social organizations by instilling a heightened sense of importance and reminding status-conscious blacks that they were not all alike. Blacks set themselves apart in their social clubs, lodges, women's clubs, and recreational pastimes. Although blacks from all social classes intermingled at churches, community centers, and outdoor sporting events, these associations were temporary.

Social class was not a fixed category in San Francisco's black community, and the line between the lower and middle classes was particularly fluid. Social rank in these groups was not only interchangeable, but often depended solely on employment. Blacks could obtain middle-class status by upgrading their occupation, altering their social circle, obtaining a college degree, or marrying into an established family. Thus the social distance between the black lower class and the middle class was not as great as between the middle class and the black elite. Moreover, blacks could raise their status by serving as leaders in black institutions like the community center, church, women's clubs, or Masonic lodge. Blacks themselves determined membership in the middle class and the black elite. Although Josephine Cole stated that "most of us didn't know what class structure was," it was apparent through their values, behavior, and social affiliations that San Francisco's black community was based on a rather elaborate class hierarchy that served their needs and resembled the black class structure in many northern and southern cities.[63]

4

PROTEST ORGANIZATIONS, 1915–1930

During the early decades of the twentieth century, San Francisco's black community conducted a long struggle to gain civil rights as well as respect and dignity. Although blacks had made significant progress in eroding Jim Crow laws and caste distinctions during the nineteenth century, they were still earmarked as an inferior class and restricted to the periphery of the city's social life. Forced to rely on their own resources, blacks sought to develop an effective leadership class, a viable institutional structure, and active protest organizations. Through a succession of agencies, beginning in 1915 with the National Association for the Advancement of Colored People (NAACP) and ending in the early 1920s with the Universal Negro Improvement Association (UNIA), blacks succeeded in obtaining status, fellowship, and a degree of influence in their communities. Black leaders served apprenticeships within these organizations and depended on them for information, support, and services. The experiences of these black leaders illustrate that during the early twentieth century, the reputed egalitarianism of the far West, while more evident there than in the South or in many northern cities, was less pervasive than some scholars indicate. They also show that like their counterparts in Chicago, New York, Cleveland, and Milwaukee, San Francisco's black leaders did not stand idly by during these years of discrimination.

San Francisco blacks grappled with racial caste and patterns of social, political, and economic proscription in numerous ways: they filed petitions, denounced racial prejudice through their press, and held public meetings. Most important, however, was their decision to strengthen existing black organizations and develop more dynamic and responsive protest agencies. Beginning in the nineteenth century, black leaders had established many institutions to fulfill the distinctive needs of blacks and to serve as buffers against racial discrimination. These varied bodies, which included churches, literary societies, and ad hoc civil rights organizations, also served as catalysts in the development and training of black leaders. They continued to be cornerstones of the black community into the twentieth century.

Before 1915, however, local protest organizations often experienced difficulties. With small memberships and no broad support, these bodies were the brainchildren of middle-class black elites. Without strong financial bases, they had difficulty sustaining ongoing activities and were usually ill equipped to handle important community problems.[1] By 1915, though, a new group spirit and a new black leadership class had emerged. The creation, in that year, of the Northern California branch of the NAACP represented a fresh commitment to resolve long-standing problems. The reasons that both local and national leaders decided to support the establishment of a Bay Area NAACP are obscure, but its founding suggests a strong racial consciousness among local black leaders and a desire to identify with the plight of blacks in other sections of the nation. Times were changing, and the ideology of self-help and economic independence stressed by such Booker T. Washington–dominated organizations as the Afro-American League and the Afro-American Council was in decline. Although business enterprise, industrial education, and thrift remained important values in the minds of Bay Area blacks, Washington's influence had given way to more vigorous forms of political protest and a new generation of black leadership.[2]

The 1913 West Coast tour of the black scholar and activist W. E. B. Du Bois had sparked the movement to establish an NAACP branch in the Bay Area. Traveling under the auspices of the NAACP, Du Bois recommended to the national headquarters that two chapters be established in California. Although Du Bois noted that rigid patterns of segregation were absent in San Francisco, he wrote that "the opportunity of the San Francisco Negro is very difficult; but he knows this and he is beginning to ask why." Since only 1,642 blacks lived in San Francisco in 1910, the NAACP's national office concluded that it would be more advantageous to combine the efforts of several Bay Area black communities. As a result, the NAACP authorized a Northern California branch in 1915, with its headquarters in Oakland. It embraced the cities of San Francisco, Oakland, and Berkeley, along with Alameda County. Within two years membership figures exceeded 1,000, an impressive segment of Bay Area blacks.[3]

The leadership of the Northern California branch had barely taken office when it faced a major confrontation. Two southerners, novelist Thomas Dixon and director David W. Griffith, stunned blacks across the country with their movie, *The Birth of a Nation.* Adapted from Dixon's novel, *The Clansmen,* the film depicted a southern view of the Civil War and Reconstruction. It quickly sparked an emotionally charged debate.[4]

The Birth of a Nation was only one of many racist films of that era, but it proved the most significant. Film critics conceded that Griffith, an extraordinarily talented filmmaker, had created a cinema masterpiece. Bold, innovative, and artistic, it played to packed houses throughout the nation. Moreover, the film received favorable acclaim in the highest circles in the nation. Even President Woodrow Wilson, a former professor of Dixon's at Johns Hopkins University, praised the film. But Griffith's film was universally denounced by blacks.[5]

The Birth of a Nation made its San Francisco debut in February 1915, amid an outraged black citizenry. Even though local black leaders were unable to agree on an immediate course of action, they overwhelmingly branded the film as vicious, degrading, and dangerous. The black press initially advised its readers simply to ignore the film, but after vacillating for several months, it finally urged the local NAACP branch to "take up the fight against the Clansmen."[6] With the cooperation of three newly formed black protest organizations, the Negro Equity League, the Negro Welfare League, and the Equal Rights League, the NAACP launched an assault. In instigating a protest against the film, it capitalized on the anger of black leaders over its degrading portrayal of blacks. Tabytha Anderson, an attorney who later became president of the San Francisco NAACP, criticized the movie as a "dastardly outrage upon our people," the "result of T. Dixon's misdirected talent," and "an act of misdirected artistic zeal." She urged local blacks to stand behind the NAACP and Negro Equity League's fight against this "belittling picture" and to "put it where it belongs—in the ash heap."[7]

John Drake, however, was the catalyst who rallied the black community. As president of the NAACP branch, Drake voiced the concerns of black residents to the mayors of both San Francisco and Oakland. He argued that *The Birth of a Nation* "tends to be a breach of public peace and [will] create disorders and race riots."[8] Drake also characterized the film as a "malicious misrepresentation of the colored people, which tends to create enmity and hatred among them." Perhaps there was some truth to these charges. During the film's release, the Klu Klux Klan applied for a charter in California. Anticipating a potentially dangerous situation, the San Francisco Board of Supervisors passed an ordinance prohibiting the wearing of masks "except by those attending carnivals conducted in accordance with city ordinances and under the permission of the proper authority of the city."[9]

Other prominent black leaders sent letters of protest to key city officials in San Francisco. Businessman Walter A. Butler pleaded with Mayor James Rolph in the "interest of decency, morality and fair play, to prohibit the production of the picture in this city." The NAACP even appealed to California Governor Hiram Johnson, asking him to state his position on this controversial matter. He declined.[10]

On the other side of the bay, Oakland Mayor Frank K. Mott refused to censor the film and urged black leaders to ignore it. Mott contended that the film did not produce the "slightest indication of race hatred or mob violence" and that suppression of the movie would result in a "thousand times more publicity than if permitted to run its course."[11]

San Francisco's colorful Mayor Rolph, however, was apparently swayed by the protests. He stated publicly that unless the objectionable features of the movie were removed, he was ready to instruct the chief of police to prohibit its release. Under Rolph's influence, the San Francisco Moving Picture Censor Board reviewed the film and agreed that many scenes were objectionable. The board advised specific alterations "to make the picture less offensive to all sides." The criteria that the censor board used in editing the film were particularly interesting. Although it criticized the derogatory characterization of blacks as tasteless, it demanded the elimination of only those scenes involving explicit physical contact between black men and white women.[12]

Despite repeated protests, *The Birth of a Nation* was shown in both San Francisco and Oakland. Independent of the NAACP, a black faction brought an injunction against the picture, but a court denied the motion. The cause was not completely lost, however, as revisions in the inflammatory script had been made. Black leaders hailed this as a partial victory, but they were not content to let the matter rest there.[13]

Aware of the erosion in race relations that the showing of *The Birth of a Nation* might have triggered and hoping to prevent future inflammatory outbursts, the San Francisco Board of Supervisors sought to regulate all motion pictures. City Attorney Percy Long initially informed the supervisors that they had the authority to enact such legislation, basing his opinion on a 1915 U.S. Supreme Court decision, *Mutual Film Corporation v. Industrial Commission*, which declared that such regulation was a "proper exercise of police power." After further consideration, however, Long hedged. The board's proposed regulation, he felt, was "so far reaching that its possibilities in matter of prohibition are almost unlimited where the portrayal of character, individual or type is sought." He seriously questioned the enforcement of the ordinance, "owing to its failures to define what would be calculated to reflect reproach upon any race or tend to incite race hatred or stir up race prejudice."[14]

Following this ambivalent opinion, the Board of Supervisors backed off. *The Birth of a Nation* was not even the subject of public debate again until 1921, when the supervisors' Vigilance Committee condemned "the Clansmen, in San Francisco or elsewhere at any time." With the strong backing of the district attorney and the chief of police, the board finally amended the Moving Picture Ordinance to include only those pictures "having a tendency toward class hatred or race prejudice."[15] The controversial film was temporarily withdrawn from California in 1921 at a Los Angeles conference. Even the film's owner agreed that the movie was "unfair to the Negro and injurious to the public," and that it should be removed from the market and destroyed. More than six years after the controversy began, the black community had finally achieved a victory.[16]

The struggle to suppress *The Birth of a Nation* revealed much about the strategy of black leadership in the Bay Area and the commitment of white city fathers to harmonious race relations. The infant NAACP branch had emerged quickly to assume a dominant role in the civil rights organizations of the San Francisco Bay Area. The growth of the branch was rapid, and not just by local standards; it also ranked among the fastest growing in the nation. With local interest ignited, the new, aggressive leadership adhered strongly to the NAACP's style of protest. This new leadership reflected the growing militancy of blacks throughout the nation, who had been promised greater equality during the World War I era and were now willing to fight to achieve it. Black leaders like John Drake, Edward Mabson, Walter Butler, Leland Hawkins, Tabytha Anderson, and the Reverend J. J. Byers stepped forward to take commanding roles.[17]

The campaign against *The Birth of a Nation* also revealed a high degree of cooperation among black leaders throughout the Bay Area. Because San Francisco and Oakland blacks shared many problems, their leadership could often agree on a common policy and strategy. The unique structure of the Northern California NAACP branch, with its wide jurisdiction over several Bay Area counties, encouraged this kind of cooperation.[18] Moreover, the controversy forced many key city officials to take a stand for the first time on a major race issue. City officials initially vacillated on the matter but eventually supported the suppression of the film. The impact of this belated support was virtually nil. The same year that the San Francisco supervisors took action against *The Birth of a Nation*, the state of California temporarily banned the film.[19]

This victory proved short-lived. After their six-year struggle to suppress the movie, black leaders were angered and perplexed when the film resurfaced in 1930. "Our [executive] board is somewhat divided as to whether we should fight or not," wrote John Howard Butler, local NAACP branch president.[20] After some discussion, the branch decided to work with a predominantly white coalition in an attempt to bar the film from San Francisco. "Citizens and leaders of all classes" were protesting the film, Butler informed Walter White, including women's clubs, local clergy, and Jewish organizations. This display of interracial unity was significant, because the San Francisco NAACP had attracted only a token white membership by 1930. The branch's secretary had noted just two years earlier that the organization "has fewer white memberships than most branches including the South."[21]

The NAACP, which had successfully lobbied Mayor Rolph to suppress the film in 1921, "decided unamiously [sic] to bring all pressure to bear on the Mayor in [the] form of protest."[22] The branch sent a delegation to meet with Rolph. They planned to gain his support and to remind him of the city ordinance that "prohibits [the] showing of any picture or distributing any literature that has a tendency to create race prejudice and bitter race feelings."[23] Although Rolph did not reveal his reasons, he refused to ban the film or to endorse the efforts of the NAACP branch. Nor did the branch succeed in bringing the film under the city ordinance, due to the latitude for varied interpretations of the statute. "We were powerless to stop this picture from showing on account of the laxity of the city ordinance," stated the NAACP's executive board.[24]

With little recourse, the branch decided to redirect its strategy toward curbing the film's publicity and minimizing its appeal to the large and lucrative San Francisco market. Both the local branch and the NAACP's national office were aware that this tactic might ultimately backfire. "The backers of the film quite obviously would like us to wage a campaign against it, which would give it greater publicity," wrote Walter White to John Howard Butler.[25] Nonetheless, White encouraged the San Francisco branch to proceed with its protest. *The Birth of a Nation*, insisted White, "by its very excellence of photography and staging, to which is now added sound effects, makes it to my mind a most vicious and dangerous thing."[26]

The San Francisco branch did not have the resources to wage an effective counteradvertising campaign against the popular and well-budgeted film—the branch's entire budget for 1930 was $645, of which almost $500 was obligated to other matters.[27] On the other hand, the film had already received enormous publicity, and according to Butler, San Francisco "is flooded with complimentary tickets."[28] The NAACP's protest was ill fated, and the film was shown in San Francisco and throughout the Bay Area. The branch achieved a minor concession, though. They were assured that "all objectionable parts had been taken out." But Butler lamented, "we have found this is not true."[29]

The defeat revealed that the NAACP had lost what little political influence it had previously had with Mayor Rolph. Black leaders could no longer depend on the mayor to halt a film that they believed was vicious and racially degrading. Nor could they depend on either the mayor or the district attorney to enforce the city ordinance that prohibited the showing of films that stirred racial hatred. Moreover, black leaders had not allied themselves with East Bay blacks in their attempt to stop the film in 1930 as they had between 1915 and 1921. As a result, black leaders in the Bay cities had drifted further apart, struggling within their own separate protest organizations to resolve racial conflicts.[30] Finally, the fact that the NAACP had worked with a white coalition marked a departure from past operating methods in the San Francisco branch. The local branch had formed no effective interracial coalitions before 1930 and had attracted few white members since its founding in 1923. Whether whites or blacks had taken the initiative to form the coalition is unclear. The alliance, however tenuous, illustrated that some whites were just as angry by the film's re-release and equally concerned that *The Birth of a Nation* would damage San Francisco's race relations.

The campaigns the NAACP waged between 1915 and 1930 established it as the premier civil rights organization in San Francisco. Its status could also be attributed in part to its role as an omnibus organization that supported a broad spectrum of causes. With no rival Urban League, the NAACP was comparable in power and prestige to the nineteenth-century San Francisco Executive Committee, a coalition of the most prominent leaders in San Francisco's early black community.[31] Indeed, the numerous local and national issues that the NAACP espoused attracted many working-class and middle-class blacks and virtually every black professional in the Bay Area. Although few blacks contributed more than their membership fees, they were proud that a national organization worked to improve their welfare.

The branch investigated many local complaints concerning police brutality, employment discrimination, and discrimination in public accommodations. J. M. Brown, a black minister, presented a lecture before the branch on discrimination at the Presidio, the local military base, and the branch membership discussed how it could rectify this problem, though they failed to reach a solution.[32] Attorney Edward Mabson reported discrimination at some Chinese restaurants in San Francisco. The branch also investigated a delicatessen in the civic center that had refused to serve a black customer unless he was willing to be served in the kitchen.[33] Numerous allegations of racial discrimination occupied the branch's attention, such as a white physician who refused to treat a black patient and charges of discrimination against black patrons at the San Francisco Civic Auditorium. Occasionally, the branch investigated charges of discrimination outside of the Bay Area and in communities where no chapter of the NAACP existed. In at least one instance, the NAACP investigated a theater in Fresno that segregated blacks. The local NAACP not only took the lead in fighting this case, but also raised money when the case was appealed to the district court in San Francisco. This case was one of the few in which the NAACP joined in the struggle for civil rights with other black leaders in California. The district court of appeals in San Francisco ruled against the theater, an important victory for the NAACP.[34]

The NAACP also sought to establish a reputation as a racial watchdog agency. They monitored local businessmen and the press to make certain they did not malign blacks in their advertising or their reporting of racial issues. The executive board of the San Francisco branch urged each branch member to "watch the San Francisco *Call* and *Chronicle* for reading matter relating to our Race" and to report instances where public accommodations were closed to blacks. To be sure, not every allegation of racial discrimination was valid, such as the charge that a public swimming pool refused to admit blacks. However, the local branch investigated every allegation that came before the organization. The majority had merit.[35]

The local branch consistently monitored national issues and supported national campaigns, including the Dyer antilynching bill, the Glass extradition case, and the Louisville segregation cases.[36] The NAACP also supported the Brotherhood of Sleeping Car Porters in their successful fight against the Railway Union to increase wages and improve working conditions. Many of the branch's members were Pullman porters. The NAACP expressed outrage with the East St. Louis race riot and the accompanying racial violence. The branch secretary wrote the national field secretary, James Weldon Johnson, that all blacks imprisoned as a result of the rioting in East St. Louis "are victims of a monstrous miscarriage of justice," and that "this branch is ready and willing to make every sacrifice in order that justice be done in these cases." The branch enclosed a check for $25.[37] The branch took an even stronger interest in the Glass extradition case. It organized a defense fund, held mass meetings, and contributed $258. Additionally, the white San Francisco Women's Club raised $500 on behalf of the Glass case, probably at the urging of the local branch, and wrote apologetically that they were "sorry that we were not able to do more for this needed case." Not only did this represent a significant monetary contribution from a white organization to the NAACP, but it also marked one of the earliest efforts by white women's clubs in San Francisco to participate in the affairs of the branch and the larger question of civil rights in San Francisco.[38]

The branch also took a keen interest in the plight of the Scottsboro Boys, who were imprisoned after allegedly raping two white women in Alabama. The branch sent small monetary contributions to the Scottsboro Defense Committee and held several meetings to inform the public about the status of these young men. Apparently the concern with the Scottsboro case resonated throughout the Bay Area, for the State Federation of Colored Women's Clubs sent $10 to assist in their legal expenses, and Oakland's black community established an East Bay Scottsboro Defense League to raise funds community-wide. The interest of both San Francisco's and Oakland's black community in national affairs illustrates not only a strong racial consciousness, but also an awareness that Bay Area blacks were also affected, though perhaps indirectly, by events on the national level. The mass meetings, letters of support, and financial contributions also demonstrated that black San Franciscans felt an obligation to assist blacks less fortunate than themselves and to ally their own struggle for racial equality with the struggles of other black communities.[39]

Despite its early success, the NAACP branch found its effectiveness limited. After an initial upsurge in membership, which drew praise from the national office, membership in the branch declined by the late 1920s. Funds evaporated and participation steadily declined. Local meetings were so poorly attended that it became difficult to obtain a quorum. The fate of the branch followed the pattern of traditional black civil rights organizations: it became controlled and administered primarily by a small clique of black professionals.[40]

Factionalism and infighting within the branch further divided the association. Disputes over policy and procedure created dissension and degenerated into leadership struggles. During one confrontation, H. L. Richardson, a black attorney, wrote to Mary White Ovington at the national office protesting the policies of the current leadership. Richardson stated that "since the present regime has been in power, their high handed methods have caused a large number of the most ardent supporters to refrain from taking any part in the branches work." Ovington replied that although there had indeed been "irregularities" in a recent election, her office could not find sufficient grounds for a ruling.[41]

Angered by Richardson's charge, the Northern California branch president, John Drake, retaliated. He denounced Richardson as "absolutely no help to the organization" and as one of its "most destructive critics." He noted that Richardson "had not attended an executive board meeting for over six months." Drake urged the national office to support him in this crisis by letting the branch work out its own affairs. Although James Weldon Johnson found Drake's tone "truculent" and resented his "hands off sentiment," he nevertheless left the matter to local leadership.[42]

NAACP members in San Francisco desired complete autonomy, which sparked other divisions in the branch. In the 1920s a schism developed between the Bay Area communities of San Francisco and Oakland. Many black San Franciscans felt that their city's identity was unique and separate from Oakland. Charges of insensitivity were voiced, and several black leaders wrote the national office urging the creation of a separate NAACP branch in San Francisco. "I am a young woman imbued with the spirit of the Association and feel confident that if you empower me I will be able to add members," one black woman wrote. "A number of influential white people," she added, "are urging a drive here, and I think that we will be able to surprise you."[43]

The strongest proponent of a separate San Francisco branch was the Negro Equity League. A small-scale operation with little financial backing, the league first emerged during the controversy over *The Birth of a Nation*. Its objectives were political, social, and economic equality for black San Franciscans. In many respects the league was a forerunner of the San Francisco NAACP. Although its financial base was weak, it had strong, vocal leadership in the person of Edward D. Mabson, its president. A native of Columbus, Ohio, Mabson rose from lowly origins as a bootblack and newsboy to become shipping head for a prominent publishing firm. Mabson purportedly earned the acclaim of his employer by entering a burning building to rescue the company's account books. After attending night school, he was admitted to the California State Bar in 1919. Mabson associated with prominent white city officials as well as traditional black social organizations. Recognizing his abilities, Mabson's white associates proposed his name as a possible justice of the California Supreme Court, although he had no realistic chance of being nominated for this post.[44]

Through the Equity League, Mabson and a small cadre of supporters voiced their concerns and sought political leverage. They were particularly interested in establishing a separate NAACP branch in San

Francisco. Mabson conferred with Robert Bagnall, director of NAACP branches, and reminded him that the Northern California branch had "its hands full in Oakland, and does not function in San Francisco." Thus, he pointed out, officers of the current branch "would not carry the weight in this city." A branch in San Francisco, Mabson believed, could challenge the racial caste system there and curb "its influence before it grows into a monster." He was particularly concerned over residential segregation. "At the present time," Mabson remarked to Bagnall, "it is almost impossible for us to find places to live." The attorney challenged Bagnall to consult other black leaders who "have been out here and can probably give you first hand information." Unlike many northern cities, San Francisco had no "colored section" where blacks could find housing on short notice. "The situation that confronts us," Mabson concluded, "is indeed serious."[45]

Bagnall wavered on Mabson's request for a San Francisco branch, but eventually the national office acknowledged its merits and approved his application for a charter. In 1923, eight years after the Northern California branch was chartered, black San Franciscans formed their own organization. By design, the activities of the NAACP branch in San Francisco did not deviate radically from those of its East Bay counterpart. The new branch occasionally handled cases involving discrimination, but like its predecessor, it devoted most of its energy to fund raising and recruiting new members.[46]

One organization that caused consternation at the NAACP branch in San Francisco was the local unit of the Universal Negro Improvement Association (UNIA). Founded in 1914 by the charismatic West Indian leader Marcus Garvey, the UNIA emerged as one of the most powerful black mass movements in history. Its growth was phenomenal. By the 1920s Garveyism claimed 800 chapters in forty countries and nearly a million members. Bay Area affiliates of the parent organization were established in San Francisco and Oakland in the early 1920s. These local groups attracted small memberships, but they compensated for their size with active programs. Arthur S. Gray, a black businessman and *Negro World* columnist, directed the California section of UNIA, with Jean Joseph Adams heading the San Francisco division. As with most minor UNIA officials, Adams's background is obscure. A native of Haiti who had been educated in Europe and at Tuskegee Institute, Adams served as an official translator for the UNIA mission to the League of Nations and as the UNIA ambassador to France.[47]

The UNIA's presence created a stir among local NAACP officials. As early as 1922, the secretary of the Northern California branch informed

Robert Bagnall that the Garvey movement "is just reaching our section of the state" and "has had much to do with retarding our progress."[48] Just how UNIA retarded the progress of Bay Area blacks remains unclear, and NAACP officials offered no clues. Perhaps the NAACP sensed a serious rival for members and status. The growth of the Garvey local was indeed impressive. It reported a rise in membership from 100 to over 500 adherents between 1922 and 1924. Moreover, the financial status of the UNIA was secure enough to enable it to send delegates to the 1922 international convention and to rent local auditoriums for their meetings. Perhaps the ability of UNIA leaders to organize the lower sector of black society also disturbed NAACP officials. Since the NAACP had made only marginal progress in this area, the Garvey movement's success in recruiting lower-class members was a slap in the face.[49]

Ironically, there were striking similarities in the activities of the UNIA and the NAACP branch in San Francisco, although the ideologies and programs of the two organizations were quite different. UNIA meetings, dances, and public celebrations were generally formal, well organized, and orderly. Like their NAACP counterparts, Garveyites held rallies, sponsored guest speakers, and devoted considerable time to fund raising. A regular UNIA meeting might include a poetry reading, classical piano recitals, drama skits, public speeches, and numerous references to Marcus Garvey's political philosophy. By no means was the range of topics confined to a narrow, didactic repetition of Garveyism. Garveyites were as likely to hear a lecture on the importance of education as a talk on the history of the Chinese and Indian nationalist movements.[50]

Nevertheless, the local black press and black leaders criticized the UNIA as an ill-advised scheme perpetrated on a gullible population. Although an early editorial stated that the "UNIA and other kindred organizations are laboring for one and the same purposes," the press's overriding reaction to Garveyism was hostile. Garveyism, the *Western Appeal* wrote, accomplished "absolutely nothing, outside of collecting a lot of money from a number of unthoughtful dupes, and squandering the same." The editor urged the black populace to "do away with all fly-by-night or day dreams of migrating to Africa" and instead "put our money to working in cooperative businesses." Nor was the anti-Garvey sentiment limited to the Bay Area. The influential *Los Angeles Eagle* also denounced the movement. The black press did not soften its assault on Marcus Garvey until after his imprisonment for mail fraud in 1925.[51]

In spite of Garvey's appeal to race, self-sufficiency, and black nationalism, most blacks rejected the lure and romance of African redemption and continued to affiliate with the more moderate NAACP. With the imprisonment and eventual deportation of Marcus Garvey, the San Francisco chapter faded into obscurity. By 1928, the local UNIA was essentially moribund. Nor did the San Francisco UNIA chapter have the lasting influence of the larger and more active Garvey chapter in Los Angeles, which functioned until the early 1930s.[52]

In addition to their quest to eliminate racial discrimination in local affairs, San Francisco's black protest organizations attempted to provide social services for both the established black community and the newly arrived black migrants. Edward Mabson reminded Robert Bagnall that an "NAACP branch in San Francisco will also give us an organization through which we can help assimilate those of our Race coming in from the South." This service, noted C. Eric Lincoln and Lawrence H. Mamiya in their study of the African American church, had traditionally been performed by black urban churches, not racial protest organizations. Despite its multifaceted character and role, the NAACP could not effectively provide leadership or programs in benevolent institutions and social services. It lacked the personnel, the skill, and the funds.[53]

In many northern and southern cities the Urban League performed a wide range of social services, but several factors worked against the establishment of an Urban League branch in San Francisco. Notably, the city's liberal image convinced civic and political leaders of both races that San Francisco had no "Negro problems" commensurate with those of comparable metropolitan centers. The renowned sociologist Robert Park's monumental survey of race relations on the Pacific Coast in the mid-1920s further reinforced the image of the Bay Area's liberalism in comparison to other cities—at least in the minds of San Francisco's leadership. Although Park's research focused largely on discrimination against Asians, his findings confirmed that the Pacific Coast was not a racially troubled region.[54]

In spite of this optimism, discussions were underway by 1926 for the formation of a Bay Area Urban League. The popular Reverend J. J. Byers, pastor of the A.M.E. Zion Church, one of the largest black congregations in San Francisco, organized the San Francisco drive. Byers attempted to persuade National Urban League Secretary T. Arnold Hill that San Francisco desperately needed a permanent social service agency. Byers was instrumental in gaining the endorsement of the influential black Ministerial Alliance and in establishing an interracial fact-finding committee.[55]

Most black leaders enthusiastically supported the establishment of an Urban League. In stating his case for a San Francisco Urban League, E. B. Gray, a black real estate agent, described black migrants as "a ship at sea without a rudder" and urged the Urban League's national secretary to establish an agency to "direct these people."[56] The executive director of the Booker T. Washington Community Center in San Francisco agreed that the Bay City should have an Urban League, but argued that it would operate most effectively "in connection with Oakland." Oakland's black columnist Delilah L. Beasley stated that she had for "many years made some attempt to secure an Urban League." Ruth Moore, the executive secretary of Oakland's colored YWCA also pledged her support. "The community is already interested in the Urban League movement," she said, "but needs someone to help crystallize this interest." She also pointed out that the board of managers of the colored YWCA could not do the work of the league.[57]

Enthusiastic about the possibility of a new affiliate, T. Arnold Hill visited the Bay Area to ascertain firsthand the economic and social status of blacks. Hill made special note of the number of "well trained men and women" and the "good proportion of successful business enterprises." He also noted the access of blacks to public accommodations and the absence of overt racial tension. Hill and other Urban League officials met with local leaders to discuss the feasibility of establishing a new branch. The white community apparently sensed the importance of these meetings, as representatives from the leading civic organizations participated. The interracial fact-finding committee chaired by Reverend Byers included the directors of the Community Chest and the Public Welfare League, Rotary and Kiwanis Club officials, and the complete board of directors of the Associated Charities.[58]

Hill pronounced the meetings a success. The participants agreed that an Urban League branch would prove beneficial to black San Franciscans. Particularly attractive was the idea of a watchdog agency maintaining "constant vigilance" in social and racial matters. Apparently, there was concern that an increase in the black populace would be accompanied by a corresponding increase in racial prejudice. Some Urban League supporters argued that a Bay Area branch might defuse in San Francisco and Oakland the problems that had triggered post–World War I racial disorders in other sections of the country.[59]

Others felt that an Urban League would accelerate the integration of Afro-Americans into the general populace and provide the leadership essential for a viable interracial organization. With its national status and prestige, the Urban League could go beyond traditional social agencies and influence local, state, and national issues. Most important, an Urban League branch could help black workers find jobs. Hill pointed to the lack of "continuous planning for the occupational advancement

of Negroes" in the Bay Area, adding that he knew "of no effort to advance Negroes in labor, other than limited placement work in domestic
and personal service done by the YWCA's, YMCA's and employment
bureaus." The only successes reported by the two Bay Area NAACP
branches were the hiring of a single colored school teacher, Ida Louise
Jackson, by the Oakland public schools in 1926 and the creation of a "Jim
Crow" Fire Company in Oakland.[60] An Urban League could apply pressure to major corporations and other employers and conceivably obtain
major occupational breakthroughs for blacks, particularly in white-collar
jobs and in the skilled trades, where blacks had made little progress. At
the very least, an Urban League branch could test the facade of liberalism in the employment sector that had characterized San Francisco's
race relations for so long. Whatever strategy the Urban League might
adopt, local leaders knew it would have its hands full in the Bay Area.

Secretary Hill was moved by the enthusiasm of Bay Area Afro-Americans, but concluded that their problems did not warrant an Urban
League branch. Meeting with black businessman Walter Butler, Hill
characterized the problems of local blacks as "not very acute." Hill was
aware that the Booker T. Washington Community Center and the Madame C. J. Walker Home for Motherless Girls were both engaged in
social work for blacks. (A prominent social worker had recommended the
consolidation of these and other existing social agencies into one effective
organization). The final straw was the collapse of the Byers fact-finding
committee that had been organized to consider the feasibility of an Urban League branch. The interracial committee dissolved when influential whites withdrew their support.[61]

In the final analysis, several factors dissuaded Hill and the interracial
committee, but the fact that the region's black population was relatively
small and nonindustrial was pivotal. There were ten thousand blacks in
the Bay Area during the 1920s, in contrast to Los Angeles, where there
were almost thirty-nine thousand by 1930. Because of the dramatic
growth occurring in Los Angeles, the National Urban League office felt
that Southern California's black migrants faced greater difficulty in adjusting and demanded more elaborate social services than did Bay Area
blacks. As a result, the first California branch was established in Los
Angeles in 1930. Sixteen years later an Urban League chapter would be
founded in San Francisco.[62] For the time being, though, Bay Area blacks
had to depend on traditional agencies—churches, lodges, fraternal orders, benevolent societies, and community service centers. These institutions offered the services generally provided by an Urban League and
were the nuclei around which Afro-Americans structured their lives.[63]

Community service centers and political leagues served also as important agencies of social protest for black San Franciscans. Several black
political organizations were established between 1915 and 1930 to es-
pouse a popular cause or protest an injustice. Typically centered around
one dominant individual, these bodies faded into oblivion after supporting a particular issue. Black political leagues also left few records to
describe their philosophy, objectives, or activities, but their names, such
as the Negro Welfare League, Negro Protective League, or Negro Equity
League, reflected their focus on racial issues. In addition to providing a
degree of stability and cohesion to a relatively small population, community centers and political leagues served as forums for black leadership
and encouraged social commitment on the part of black residents.[64]

The most important service organization in San Francisco was the
Booker T. Washington Community Center. An outgrowth of the Victory
Club, a World War I facility for black soldiers, the center evolved into a
multipurpose organization serving an energetic black community. Under
the leadership of Reverend J. J. Byers, Mary McCants Stewart, and John
Fisher, it gradually expanded both its scope and direction. Black women
were particularly active during its early years, drafting the incorporation
papers, serving as the fund raisers, and persevering during troubled
times. In one such difficult period, black social leader Alice Butler organized a "Committee of Fifty" women who successfully raised $2000 to
bail the center out of financial doldrums.[65]

The community center's program blossomed in the late 1920s under
the guidance of Ethel Riley Clark. Clark, a black social worker from New
York, served as executive director of the center for nearly a decade.
Under her leadership, it expanded its educational and social programs
and attracted members from virtually every segment of the black community. Black youth engaged in boxing, basketball, and industrial crafts
and participated in the center's social clubs. Black women devoted their
energies to singing, dancing, homemaking, or sewing. Young adults
staged plays and drama productions, while senior citizens reminisced
over teas, bridge, or whist.[66]

Although it was primarily a social organizer, the center also served as
a forum for the discussion of racial issues. Informal gatherings, debates,
and public lectures were frequently held to explore issues of concern. The
center's Negro Dramatics Club, for example, produced plays relevant to
black life, and singing clubs, through their public concerts, exposed
young blacks to a larger segment of the community. Rob Ruck noted in
his study of the importance of sport in Pittsburgh's black community that
sports were a "bridge" for blacks into the white community. The commu-

nity center was also a bridge, for it served to integrate young blacks into the larger society of San Francisco.[67]

Finally, the community center was an important training ground for black leaders. Here prominent blacks exchanged ideas and came into daily contact with a large portion of the black populace. Virtually every black leader in San Francisco had some contact with the community center. In fact, the list of prominent blacks associated with the organization reads like a social register of the black community. The center also represented a connection with established civil rights organizations. The NAACP held many of its monthly meetings at the center, and some NAACP officials, including Joseph Foreman, Lelia Flippin, and Edward Mabson, were closely affiliated with both organizations. Consequently, the center was able to redirect the focus of its activities from recreation and social reform to protest with a minimum of effort.[68]

Twentieth-century black protest organizations were largely continuations of nineteenth-century institutions, with ideologies and strategies that offered little in the way of change. The most significant developments of the new century were the emergence of a new leadership class and the creation of local branches of national organizations like the NAACP and the UNIA. These institutions generated considerably more stability and status than the short-lived protest organizations of the nineteenth century, but black protest organizations trained leadership and offered a forum for public interaction. Most importantly, they attempted to eliminate the barriers in housing, employment, and public accommodations that had plagued black San Franciscans. But black protest organizations were limited in their goals and objectives and in their ability to eradicate discrimination in either housing or employment. They had considerably more success in halting discrimination in public accommodations, for the stakes were not as high in this area and white San Franciscans were more willing to give ground. However, these organizations never purported to offer panaceas, and even their narrow programs were often hampered by shortage of funds, ineffectual leadership, community apathy, and internal dissension. In spite of these problems, the majority of black San Franciscans relied on these bodies in times of crisis. For however great their liabilities, local community institutions were generally blacks' only defenses in their fight against the racial caste system and their lowly status.[69]

5

POLITICS, PROTEST, AND
RACE RELATIONS, 1920–1940

Interest in political affairs and protest resurfaced in San Francisco's black community between 1920 and 1940, reflecting the renewed desire for political power of blacks throughout the nation. By 1920, San Francisco's black leaders had identified political power as their entrée to the city's decision-making process. To obtain political influence comparable to that of San Francisco's diverse ethnic groups, black leaders decided to take an active role in political affairs and exert their influence as a solid bloc. Blacks demanded from the established political parties a new commitment to racial issues. They also hoped to speed the pace of racial progress.[1]

Scant information has survived regarding the political activities of Bay Area blacks before 1920. However, it is known that several short-lived political organizations were established to improve the status of black San Franciscans. In 1891, the Afro-American League of San Francisco was founded as an auxiliary of the National Afro-American League, which had been established by T. Thomas Fortune in 1890. The inaugural meeting of the San Francisco League, the first chapter established in California, attracted 150 members. Theophilus B. Morton, a Virginia-born black and former slave, served as its first president. Morton had migrated to California in 1875, where he became active in Republican party politics and was described by one writer as "the most forceful speaker and profound thinker of the race on the Pacific Coast." Morton's loyalty to the GOP was rewarded with an appointment as messenger for the United States Circuit Court of Appeals. He was subsequently appointed by the National Republican Committee in 1896 to organize the black vote in California.[2]

With Morton at the helm for seven years, the San Francisco Afro-

American League attempted to mobilize the black vote and to restore black confidence in the Republican party. The organization vowed to "uphold the principles of the Republican party," assist blacks in gaining their full political rights, and help them gain employment. By 1895, the league boasted that it had succeeded in obtaining employment for one mail carrier, a United States gauger, three messengers, three clerks, thirteen porters, eleven laborers, and sixty deputy U.S. Marshals who served as election officers. Although these patronage positions were not impressive in absolute numbers, they were important achievements for a relatively small black community with few eligible voters. The league, in an effort to promote racial unity, also encouraged blacks to "invest their surplus money in manufacturing and other enterprises that gave employment to members of the race."[3]

Black women were also active in the activities of the league. A women's auxiliary of the Afro-American League was organized in San Francisco in 1892, and Ida B. Wells, the renowned journalist and racial activist, visited San Francisco through its efforts. The active presence of black women was noteworthy at local meetings and conventions. At least four women presented speeches at the State Afro-American Congress, an indication that women's views were welcomed and respected. The topics of their speeches, however, reveal the role of women in relation to the larger body. Though one woman spoke on the "Woman's Influence in Politics," the remaining speeches addressed the role of women as homemakers or supporters of men. Sarah B. Cooper's address, "The Home—The True Foundation of the State," illustrated the roles assigned to black women. Black women did not hold leadership positions within the larger body, and their separation from the parent society seems to represent an attempt to curtail their potential leadership and decision making.[4]

The San Francisco Afro-American League proved to be only a preliminary attempt to obtain political power and influence, for it provided little employment for black residents and only token political patronage. Nor did the league stimulate significant economic activity based on racial cooperation, as it had promised. Although T. B. Morton established the Afro-American Cooperative and Investment Association, which he believed would enable blacks to "become, in part at least, a community of businessmen and women, engaged in every pursuit which will reward us with wealth and honor," the league accomplished little in this area. Following the pattern of the National Afro-American League, the San Francisco Afro-American League was ineffectual by 1910.[5]

A number of black San Franciscans, such as J. B. Wilson and Walter Maddox, also worked within the Afro-American Congress, a statewide organization of local Afro-American leagues organized in 1895 in San Francisco. The congress traditionally supported Republican candidates and hoped that its loyalty would reap political appointments for their members. It supported California Republican George C. Pardee, for example, in the 1903 gubernatorial election, and Pardee secured the governorship with little difficulty. However, Pardee ignored his black supporters as well as the congress after the election. James Alexander, secretary of the congress, was especially angry, because Pardee had hedged on his promise to appoint him to a post in the harbor office. Perhaps believing that its integrity was at stake, the Afro-American Congress throughout the state united behind the appointment of Alexander. It denounced Pardee's betrayal and pleaded with the governor to reconsider Alexander's application. "You realize how valuable the solid Negro vote was in electing Gov. Pardee, but we have not received the slightest recognition," wrote the congress. Black voters were not merely deceived by Pardee, they continued, "they were thrown down and their hopes shattered by a false God."[6]

Whether Alexander ever received the desired post is unclear, but J. B. Wilson, president of the congress, continued to plead with Pardee to consider the appointment of an Afro-American "in some position around the State Capitol, either around the Capitol grounds or elsewhere." Despite his dissatisfaction with Pardee's indifference toward blacks, Wilson nonetheless pledged himself "an uncompromising advocate of the present administration."[7]

These early relations between San Francisco's black leaders and the Republican party set the tone until the 1940s. Like their black counterparts throughout the nation, the majority of black San Franciscans were Republicans. In return for their solid GOP support, black leaders expected recognition, sympathetic allies, and limited political patronage.[8] But since the black voting population was less than 1 percent of the city's total between 1920 and 1940, black leaders were in no position to demand major concessions. And because the majority of black San Franciscans were unwilling to embrace the Democratic party until the mid-1930s, Republican party leaders had little motivation to increase black political patronage. By the 1920s, however, several blacks had been appointed to minor political posts: for example, Gregory Hobson was appointed deputy internal revenue collector of San Francisco and served as a member of the Republican Central Committee in Sacramento, and Walter Sanford worked as an aide in the mayor's office for almost two decades. Sanford, who was essentially an usher, had no power in political decision making and never influenced the course of black political appointments. Yet black San Franciscans were proud, recalled Josephine Cole, a retired black school teacher, that one of their own had received this symbolic appointment to city hall. Blacks such as William H. Blake were occasionally granted commissions as notary publics, although this practice became less common after 1900. Political patronage for blacks included little more than positions as clerks, messengers, and pages, but black leaders were proud of these positions and expected regular appointments to these traditional "Negro posts."[9]

Blacks established segregated political organizations that worked closely with white Republican leaders. John Drake, former president of the Northern California branch of the NAACP, chaired the Northern California Colored Hoover-Curtis Committee; East Bay black editor E. A. Daly served as secretary of the Republican Colored Citizens of Northern California; San Francisco's black funeral director, John Howard Butler, organized the Colored Citizens Committee, a black political pressure group; and in 1939, black San Franciscans established the Negro Progressive Unity League. Aside from their names, little is known about these organizations. None left detailed organizational records or descriptions of their goals, objectives, achievements, and failures.[10]

San Francisco's black Republicans also organized formal political organizations that were affiliated directly with the Republican State Central Committee. The most significant of these was the California State Colored Republican League (CSCRL). Organized in January 1932, the CSCRL was headquartered at 1898 Sutter Street, in the heart of San Francisco's black community. Apparently, black Republican leaders did not find the segregated political body awkward. Wesley C. Peoples, the organization's secretary and a respected political leader in San Francisco's black community, informed Herbert Hoover that a separate Republican colored association was "necessary because of the peculiar situation of the Negro group, for while being a part of the body politic, he is necessarily a separate and distinct entity in our complex social structure."[11] The organization drew its leadership primarily from San Francisco's blacks, but power alternated between San Francisco and East Bay black leaders. Several San Franciscans, such as Peoples, Aurelius P. Alberga, and William J. McLemore, were prominent in the hierarchy of the organization. Peoples, one of San Francisco's best-known black politicians, was instrumental in organizing the CSCRL. In his attempt to enlist black voters into the Republican ranks, Peoples conceded the "stiff problems we are up against in the matter of endeavoring to again re-register the Negro group within the ranks of the Republican Party." Peoples wrote Earl Warren, chairman of the California State Republican

Committee, that a "tremendous amount of work remained to be done, especially in view of the splendid recognition . . . Democrats of California have given members of the group in the Los Angeles section." Shoring up the black ranks was particularly crucial, because black voters across the state were growing disillusioned with the Republican party and joining the Democratic party in increasing numbers, particularly in Southern California. The majority of San Francisco's voters shifted from Republican to Democratic in 1934, and the GOP rapidly lost voters of all races.[12]

The shift in black political allegiance troubled Republican leaders. Although Wesley Peoples assured Herbert Hoover that he could count on the solid support of local black Republicans, white GOP leaders agonized over Southern California. One Republican committee official noted that the sixty-second assembly district in Los Angeles had more than 42,000 black voters, more than the combined totals of twelve western states. A Republican position paper on black voters in the state corroborated the fear that they would leave the Republican party. "This Negro vote may easily become the big factor involving California's electoral vote," wrote one official. Republican committee leaders had no solution, but they agreed that attention should be focused on Southern California's black voters, rather than on San Francisco's small black population. Even Frederick Roberts, a longtime Republican politician, was summoned to the party's defense. White Republican leaders did not perceive Roberts, a black, as the "ordinary type of petty, chiseling politician" and regarded his allegiance as a valuable asset.[13] In short, San Francisco blacks were ignored in light of the more urgent political concerns of Los Angeles.

Another black politician, Aurelius P. Alberga, was an important figure in the activities of the CSCRL. A resident of San Francisco since 1884, Alberga participated in early San Francisco politics. He allied himself with Mayor James Rolph, Jr., and worked in numerous Republican campaigns. Alberga's reputation stemmed from his association with prominent white political figures and his long tenure as vice-president and treasurer of the CSCRL. His close friendship with Wesley C. Peoples and his rank as a colonel in the army during World War I also enhanced his status among San Francisco's blacks. Despite his lifelong loyalty to Republican politics, Alberga was never rewarded with a formal political appointment—only the "lucrative" shoeshine stand at San Francisco's Ferry Building.[14]

Many questions regarding the colored Republican organization remain unanswered, such as its size, its funding, and the roles of members. Almost nothing is known concerning recruitment or the makeup of the association's membership. About 100 delegates and visitors gathered at one local meeting, yet A. P. Alberga insisted that between 1,200 and 1,500 blacks claimed membership in the organization. His figures are clearly inflated. Similarly, the relationship between the CSCRL and the Republican State Central Committee is also obscure. The central committee probably contributed to the financial affairs of the CSCRL and absorbed the majority of the organization's expenses, but few records of the organization's activities have survived.[15]

Black women occasionally occupied leadership roles in politics, although none appear to have attained leadership posts within the CSCRL. Vivian Osborne Marsh and Ada Wilson were considered as candidates for the Republican National Committee. Esther Jones, a high-ranking official in Bay Area colored women's clubs, directed the colored women's division for Herbert Hoover under California's State Central Committee. The San Francisco League of Colored Women Voters and the segregated Alameda County League also took an active interest in political affairs. These organizations held debates and public forums on political issues and, in several instances, registered Bay Area black voters. The *Spokesman*'s editor, John Pittman, wrote that "women get things done" and characterized "our menfolk as either jellyfish or asses, and in most cases, both."[16]

The Bay Area black press was perhaps the most important vehicle for disseminating political information, and black editors were key political spokesmen. Black editors stressed the importance of voting, particularly of voting as a bloc. The *Western American* urged blacks to "consolidate the Negro vote that it might obtain the greatest result in all political areas."[17] The *California Voice* affirmed this view and wrote, "Through politics only can we hope to eliminate some of the evils of race prejudice and sinister influences working against us."[18]

The paramount figure in Bay Area black journalism was Oakland editor E. A. Daly. A Tuscaloosa, Alabama, native, Daly had migrated to California in 1922, "looking for greener pastures." After experiencing considerable difficulty earning a livelihood in San Francisco, Daly promptly moved to Oakland. He found the East Bay community more to his liking and invested in several business ventures. By 1927, Daly's success in real estate allowed him to purchase the *Oakland Voice*, an established black weekly. The enterprising editor later purchased the *Western Outlook, New Day Informer*, and the *Western Appeal*. By the early 1930s, Daly consolidated all these weeklies into the *California Voice* and thereby virtually monopolized the Bay Area black press. Because of the small size of San Francisco's black population and the absence of a weekly black newspaper in San Francisco during most of the

1920s, blacks relied principally on Oakland papers during the 1920s and early 1930s for information about black political activity.[19]

Daly was also an influential figure in black political circles. A lifelong Republican, Daly served as the Alameda County Republican League organizer for blacks and occupied a seat on the prestigious Republican County Central Committee. Moreover, Daly enjoyed the support of Bay Area black labor leaders and the Northern California NAACP. He remained the dominant force in Bay Area black journalism before the Second World War.[20]

Because of Daly's political connections and his stranglehold on the circulation of newspapers to blacks, a strong black press did not develop in San Francisco until 1931. Early journalistic efforts in the city floundered or yielded to domination by the East Bay black establishment. The policy of the *Western American* was typical. Although the paper originally served the black communities of Oakland, San Francisco, and Berkeley, it was, after one year, essentially an Oakland paper, devoted to East Bay black affairs. On its first anniversary the paper failed even to acknowledge the support of San Francisco's blacks.[21]

San Francisco's black press continued to develop under a dark cloud until the emergence of two young black journalists in 1931, W. J. Wheaton and John Pittman. Wheaton, a veteran of political journalism, had been educated in Pittsburgh. After spending two years at Western Reserve College, he wrote for the *Pittsburgh Dispatch, Minneapolis Tribune,* and *Helena Independent.* He would later write a political column for the *California Eagle.* A devoted Republican, Wheaton represented the GOP on the Republican National Committee. By the early 1930s, he wrote the political column for the *San Francisco Spokesman.*[22]

John Pittman, the *Spokesman's* editor, was San Francisco's most vocal black political agitator during the 1930s. One of the outstanding intellects in San Francisco's black community, Pittman personified the campus radical. Articulate, energetic, and critical of American society, he was a formidable social critic. Reared in Atlanta, Georgia, Pittman attended Morehouse College as an undergraduate. He developed an early interest in black labor and subsequently enrolled in the University of California, Berkeley, where he earned a master's degree in economics in 1930. His thesis was titled "Railroads and Negro Labor." The following year, Pittman founded the *San Francisco Spokesman.*[23]

Pittman's brand of journalism often transcended racial issues. In scope, his paper compared favorably with Robert L. Vann's *Pittsburgh Courier* and T. Thomas Fortune's *New York Age.* He felt equally comfortable discussing Marxist economic theory and the dilemmas of black fraternities. Pittman's editorials criticized miscegenation laws, advocated birth control measures, supported cooperative health care, and urged protection for the rights of homosexuals. These were progressive stances for any journalist during the 1930s, but particularly for a black journalist since, by and large, black journalists were provincial in their coverage of important social issues. As Gunnar Myrdal would later note in his monumental study of American race relations, "another observable characteristic of the Negroes' thinking about social and political matters is its provincialism."[24]

Pittman and Wheaton were at their best when discussing politics, particularly the problems that black voters faced in their attempts to gain recognition from the Republican party. Both journalists denounced the Republican party's indifference to black voters but agreed that political action was a prerequisite for social change. Wheaton charged the GOP with deviating from its traditional principles: "There is a vast abyss separating the Republican Party of Lincoln, Zack Chandler and Charles Sumner, and their policies from the Republican Party of this day." The present administration, he added, "has become the Party of expediency."[25]

Wheaton also felt Republicans had betrayed Afro-Americans. He attacked the GOP for excluding Afro-Americans as delegates to the 1932 Republican National Convention and criticized the party's choice of the incumbent, Herbert Hoover, as the Republican candidate for president. "We made a careful search of the present administration and have found nothing that would warrant us in going into hysterics over it, unless it was its abject failures," wrote Wheaton. He accused Hoover of showing no concern for blacks. "Never in the history of the Republican Party has the Negro citizen been so openly humiliated as under this administration," he charged. He nonetheless affirmed political loyalty to the Republicans, even in the face of despair. "We belong to the Republican Party," he wrote, "and intend to stay in it and fight for the principles for which the Party was organized." Wheaton later qualified this affirmation: "We are Republican in principle, but Progressive."[26]

Black leaders were dissatisfied with Republican party officials locally and throughout the state. Governor James Rolph, Jr., though an early advocate of equal rights, had become largely indifferent to black political affairs by 1930. As mayor of San Francisco for nearly twenty years, Rolph supported a number of black causes. Blacks had praised his stance against the showing of "The Birth of a Nation" as well as his concern that black World War I veterans did not receive proper celebrations after their return from France. The robust mayor gained the reputation as a fair-minded city official and earned the respect of San Francisco's most prominent black leaders.[27]

When Rolph was elected governor of California in 1930, black leaders were confident that the state's chief executive was a political ally. For many reasons, though, the relationship deteriorated. Rolph probably sensed the lack of black political influence in San Francisco and, unwilling to alienate more important voting blocs, ignored blacks. The black press also accused the governor of overlooking segregation in New Deal labor camps operated by the state, refusing to attend black social functions, and withholding political patronage from blacks.[28]

Rolph further lowered his stature in the black community when he condoned a lynching in San Jose. Black leaders were so infuriated that they called for his resignation. The Reverend Fred Hughes, who had helped manage Rolph's 1930 statewide campaign, deplored the Governor's "recent condonation of lynching." Similarly, the black female activist and attorney Tabytha Anderson criticized Rolph and urged his removal from office.[29]

The San Francisco NAACP also worked for Rolph's removal. Branch president Leland Hawkins requested permission from the national association to write an article on Rolph's record to be published in *Crisis*.[30] Hawkins believed that this article would be "circulated by all his opponents throughout the state," and that "it would have a stronger influence in lining the Negro vote against Rolph than the various little Negro papers would." He insisted that his only intention was to defeat "this advocate of mob rule." Rolph "reminds me of a clown who cracks an obscene joke in a church," wrote Hawkins. However, the governor's death in 1934, wrote Hawkins, "eliminates the necessity of the Association working for his defeat."[31]

Black editors also criticized the GOP's indifference to national civil rights issues during the 1930s. W. J. Wheaton was appalled at the degree of "lawlessness enacted in this country under the present administration," and the heinous crime of lynching provoked the most heated debate. Black leaders denounced lynching as vigorously as their counterparts in other parts of the nation and demanded serious reprisals. The *Western Appeal* wrote that "lynching would cease if law enforcement officers fired on crowds."[32] John Pittman stated that if the federal government had passed the Dyer bill, lynching could have "taken its rightful place beside cannibalism." Black leaders also urged blacks not to vote for public officials who opposed antilynching laws, and the black press kept its readers informed of the voting records of California legislators on this sensitive issue.[33] The *California Voice* endorsed Senator Samuel Short-ridge over Hiram Johnson for governor in 1926, primarily because Shortridge had supported the Dyer antilynching bill.[34]

Bay Area black leadership expressed confidence in the NAACP's ability to lobby and obtain tougher antilynching laws and pointed with pride to the NAACP's persistent fight against lynching. The San Francisco NAACP's crusade against lynching during the 1930s was similar to that of the national office. Petitions supporting a federal antilynching law were submitted to the national body, and local citizens were encouraged to write their congressmen. San Francisco branch president Tabytha Anderson informed Walter White in 1935 that she was "enclosing six completely filled petitions" and "should have more soon."[35] Walter White was pleased with the efforts of black leaders. Attempting to capitalize on their aggressive lobbying, he urged them to "pass the word through San Francisco and other parts of the state to flood [Senator] McAdoo with messages." White added optimistically, "We have enough votes according to present indications to ensure passage—but a great deal depends on California." White predicted correctly that the Wagner antilynching bill "is going to be a bitter fight." It was, indeed, a bitter fight. In the midst of the Great Depression, blacks throughout the nation saw the bill defeated.[36]

Disenchantment with Republican leadership and policies prompted some blacks to leave the GOP during the 1920s and early 1930s and switch to the Democratic party. Attorney Edward Mabson informed the colored voters division of the Republican state committee in 1928 that he had "no intention or desire of having [his] name connected with the Hoover Campaign." Mabson stated that he was "not at all in sympathy or in accord with the national political scheme of the Republican Party," and that under the present circumstances, "it is high time for a person to change his politics, particularly in California."[37] The black businessman Walter A. Butler also joined the Democratic party, after more than three decades as a Republican. Butler had grown "weary and tired of the unkept promises of the Republican Party," promises that were made in the convention platforms but never kept. Black attorney H. Leonard Richardson denounced the Republicans as the party of "banks, big industrialists, big insurance companies and financiers." He believed that the GOP could offer blacks little except the worn slogan, "The Republican Party is the deck and all else is the sea." Reverend H. T. S. Johnson declared himself neither a Democrat nor a Republican. Nonetheless, he urged blacks not to forget that the "Negro's duty is to cast a ballot against

Hoover." Yet the number of black San Franciscans who switched party allegiance during the 1920s and early 1930s was small and apparently confined to a group of vocal black leaders.[38]

The majority of black San Franciscans did not shift immediately to the Democratic party. Most black voters probably agreed with the position of Lelia Flippin, a local NAACP official, who stated after the 1932 presidential election, "I feel that the elected one is the lesser of the two evils; though I am a Republican at heart." The majority of black San Franciscans, along with blacks throughout the nation, remained loyal to the GOP until the mid-1930s, when they shifted to the Democratic party in response to Franklin D. Roosevelt's New Deal.[39]

Black leaders grappled consistently with the question of how to use the bloc of black voters to the best advantage. Some leaders incorrectly saw San Francisco's small bloc of black voters as the balance of power and pointed to the electoral successes of Oscar De Priest in Chicago. Apparently, they were oblivious to the fact that black votes represented less than 1 percent of San Francisco's total voting population. Consequently, the black vote was insignificant, except in extremely close elections. Blacks could not even consider running a black leader for an important political post as larger black communities like Chicago or Los Angeles had done.[40]

W. J. Wheaton and John Pittman argued that the weak political position of black San Franciscans derived from political inexperience, particularly in matters that required political bargaining. Black voters, they believed, were politically naive and unaware of the forces that determined political success among competing ethnic and racial groups. However, the *Spokesman* also charged that much of San Francisco's black leadership was apathetic, self-serving, incompetent, and uninterested in the welfare of the black masses. "The economic condition of the masses concern him not so much as how he will be considered in the political plums," wrote John Pittman. "Nine out of every ten Negroes have been skilled in leadership" since Emancipation, he continued, but Afro-Americans have little "political acumen or astuteness." The brash editor contended that "politics is a great business and business principles regulate it." But black San Franciscans were in no position to demand political favors, a fact that Pittman acknowledged but found difficult to accept.[41]

John Pittman never deviated from the position that the subservient status of blacks resulted from their inability to obtain power in the political and economic arenas. Jobs, wrote Pittman, were "a matter of politics and politicians listen to organized groups." He pointed to California Governor James Rolph, who had thwarted the appointment of a black judge

after opposition was raised among white political groups.[42] The weak
political position of black San Franciscans, Pittman believed, also hurt
race relations. When the San Francisco Police Commission cleared a
white officer on charges of police brutality against a black male, Pittman
stated that the commission's decision had been anticipated, because the
commissioners were "in no way obligated to the Negro population of this
city." Nonetheless, the *Spokesman's* editor had little tolerance for these
actions, and he attacked the police commission and the white politicians
who disregarded black causes. When Pittman asked an incumbent white
supervisor what he had done for the black electorate in his previous
term, the supervisor replied that he had set aside $150 for a Negro navy
ball. "What difference is it that only four sailors were present," chided
Pittman. Black voters, Pittman charged, have become the "playthings of
politicians who despise them even while they are being elected into office
by Negro voters."[43]

The *Spokesman's* editor also felt that blacks were too provincial. Although he argued that race pride was a fundamental prerequisite to
racial organization, Pittman believed that "only a handful of Afro-
Americans are able to look at the world except through Negro colored
glasses."[44] Thus Pittman abhorred any sign of self-segregation and encouraged blacks to broaden their narrow racial perspective. Black institutions fostered divisions, he argued, and called for their dissolution. "In
exact proportion as Negro institutions multiply, segregation and discrimination increase," he maintained. Pittman went so far as to denounce the
celebration of Negro History Week. "We shouldn't study one race's history," he protested, "but universal history." Viewing race as the primary
frame of reference was not only dangerous, he wrote, but represented a
"fallacy of race pride." Rejecting cultural pluralism, Pittman contended
that "no American is more thoroughly American in culture, background,
language and social outlook" than the Negro, and that blacks could not
afford to isolate themselves. The solution, he argued, lay in a "broader
perspective in order to overcome the enervating toxin of our own self-
pity." Despite his criticism of black provincialism, Pittman was optimistic. He believed that an egalitarian, biracial form of society for America
was "inevitable."[45]

Pittman's assessment of the race problem was a bundle of contradictions. While he denounced the provincialism of blacks, his paper was
foremost a voice of the black community. Although he urged blacks to
seek out and welcome white allies, he criticized interracial organizations
as a waste of time. Similarly, Pittman discouraged blacks from forming
political coalitions, but later cautioned blacks against splitting their vote.

"Will misery and humiliation never teach a minority group that its power lies in a consolidated vote?" he asked his readers. By the end of 1932, however, Pittman warned of the "Perils of Band-Wagon Jumping" and stated that the "immediate circumstances, whether it be for good or for ill, is the opportunist's guiding star."[46]

Pittman's candor and personal attacks on both black leaders and black institutions weakened his base within the black community. He attacked his black editorial colleagues, fraternities, educated blacks, and ministers. "Educated Negroes," Pittman wrote, "do little else but keep alive the great pastimes of whist and bridge," and their "chief value" was the "prestige and dignity they lend to the Greek tradition."[47] Nor did Pittman hesitate to criticize civil rights organizations like the NAACP. Although the *Spokesman* generally praised the local branch, Pittman grew increasingly disillusioned with the NAACP's apathy and its inattention to economic and political problems. He described the leadership of the San Francisco branch as a "board of directors whose meetings are so infrequent that they lose touch with community needs, and whose decisions are so unimportant that the directors themselves immediately forget them." In a similar editorial, Pittman ridiculed the association: "To our way of thinking, the people of this community are bored to tears with the lifeless, mediocre activities offered them continuously by unimaginative organization heads." Again mocking the NAACP, he wrote, "Not even the dullest of humans can attend teas, bridge parties and dances, 365 days a year without suffering some feelings of ennui."[48]

Several additional factors hampered the *Spokesman's* effectiveness. The necessity of competing with the more moderate journalism of E. A. Daly hurt the paper's circulation, since the small black population in the Bay Area communities could not support numerous black weeklies. San Francisco's black community also viewed Pittman as an outsider and never accepted him into the leadership circle. Despite his marriage to Gladys Wysinger Crawford, a respected black woman from the East Bay, Pittman never involved himself in established black institutions. Most of his friends were whites, intellectuals, or students. Though he had won respect, he had not won a base of power within the black community.[49]

By supporting the Communist party during the 1930s, Pittman alienated himself from the black community even further. As Wilson Record observed of the relationship between blacks and Communists, blacks were "aware of the stigma that would result from such a commitment, and aware too, that Party discipline and doctrine would involve numerous restrictions on their ideas and actions." Nonetheless, by 1935 Pittman had embraced communism. Although the paper's early columns were in the political mainstream, within four years the *Spokesman*'s editor had become disillusioned with capitalism and democratic institutions. "The process of government as it now exists in this country is incomplete, undemocratic and chaotic," wrote Pittman in one of his final editorials. He embraced communism "in the interests of the common people," because both political parties had failed in this regard. Less than six months later, the *Spokesman* ceased publication, and Pittman moved further into the Communist party's camp. He became one of the founders and the executive editor of the daily *People's World*, a left-wing political paper in San Francisco, and he eventually traveled to the Soviet Union.[50]

Black San Franciscans did not improve their status significantly through politics, because the Republican party was largely indifferent to black political appointments and civil rights issues, and black politicians were relegated to working within a segregated organization. After considerable frustration and years of neglect, the majority of blacks switched to the Democratic party in the mid-1930s, in response to Franklin D. Roosevelt's New Deal reform programs. They were represented by black advisers in important New Deal programs such as the National Youth Administration and the Civilian Conservation Corps. But whether blacks aligned themselves with the Democrats or with the Republicans between 1920 and 1940, they played only a marginal role in political decision making. Major black political appointments in San Francisco were just as rare after 1933 as they had been before the Democrats won national office. Moreover, no black San Franciscan even attempted to obtain political office before 1940, in part due to the small size of the black population and its resulting lack of political influence. Blacks in Los Angeles, on the other hand, were represented by black Republican Frederick M. Roberts between 1919 and 1934 and black Democrat Augustus F. Hawkins, who defeated Roberts for his seat in 1934. Not until 1948 did a black candidate from the Bay Area, William Byron Rumford (representing the Oakland-Berkeley area), win an election to state office.[51] Nor were more than token efforts made by black leaders in San Francisco to work cooperatively with black leadership in larger black communities, such as Oakland or Los Angeles, although there had been considerable cooperation and interaction between San Francisco and other black communities throughout the state before 1915. The question of how to obtain power and influence given the small black population remained the persistent riddle for black San Franciscans.

The frustration that black San Franciscans experienced in the political arena led them to stress internal race organizations and the development of their own community institutions, a characteristic they shared with black communities throughout the nation. Once again, black San Franciscans turned primarily to the NAACP to provide leadership and to break down the remaining impediments to racial equality. Thus the San Francisco branch of the NAACP continued to be the most effective black protest organization throughout the era of the Great Depression. The branch devoted the majority of its time and resources during the 1930s to investigating allegations of racial discrimination, particularly in the areas of housing and public accommodations, working with the national office to block the confirmation of Judge John J. Parker to the U.S. Supreme Court, and protesting discrimination within the American Federation of Labor (AFL). The branch also continued to support the Dyer antilynching bill and the Scottsboro Boys, and NAACP officers worked with civil rights leaders on the state and national level in their attempt to secure a federal antilynching law. These multifaceted campaigns illustrate the strong racial consciousness that black San Franciscans felt during the 1930s. It also revealed that local black leaders were sensitive to the plight of blacks in other parts of the nation, for they provided assistance in attempting to break down racial barriers in the North and South as well as the far West.

San Francisco's black community joined with its counterparts throughout the nation in opposing the confirmation of Judge John J. Parker as a justice of the United States Supreme Court and protesting discrimination within the AFL. The San Francisco NAACP's opposition to the confirmation of Parker was part of a national campaign orchestrated by the NAACP's national office and organized labor.[52] The San Francisco branch, which had supported national issues that included the Scottsboro Boys, the Dyer antilynching bill, and the Glass defense fund, was enthusiastic about this campaign. Branch leaders sent letters and telegrams to California Congressmen Hiram W. Johnson and Samuel M. Shortridge opposing Parker's confirmation. "The Negro citizens of San Francisco strenuously oppose the nomination of Judge John J. Parker to the U.S. Supreme Court," wrote branch president John Howard Butler.[53] Although Butler did not enumerate the branch's specific objections to Parker, he argued that Parker's nomination would "endanger the status of all Negroes."[54]

Parker, a Hoover appointee to the Supreme Court, had angered blacks in 1920 as the Republican gubernatorial candidate in North Carolina by stating in a speech that blacks should not participate in politics. "We recognize the fact that he has not yet reached the stage in his development when he can share the burdens and responsibilities of government," Parker declared. The San Francisco NAACP rejoiced when Parker's nomination to the Supreme Court was rejected by the Senate.[55]

The San Francisco branch also worked directly with the national office to protest discrimination within the AFL. The NAACP's national office had been pressing the AFL to integrate its affiliate unions for several years. "We did tackle the A. F. of L. itself at the outset of the New Deal programs," wrote the NAACP's assistant secretary at the national office in response to an inquiry by Horace Cayton.[56] The NAACP had also asked the AFL to go on record at its annual convention in 1933 in opposition to "wage and geographical differentials" based on race. "I feel sure [the] A. F. of L. will act decisively upon race," Walter White commented optimistically in 1933.[57]

The AFL did not press its affiliate unions to alter their racial policies as a result of the NAACP's pressure. In 1934, black labor leader A. Philip Randolph encouraged Walter White to "sanction a picket of the AFL convention in San Francisco."[58] White agreed with this strategy and directed the San Francisco branch to picket the AFL's fifty-fourth annual convention to protest organized labor's Jim Crow policies. During the demonstration Leland Hawkins, San Francisco branch president, stated that he was acting under direct orders from Walter White.[59] National Field Secretary William Pickens wrote that the signs used by the protesters "were made up in our [national] office mostly by getting different persons to contribute to the list." The national office was pleased with the protest by the San Francisco branch and Pickens congratulated the branch "on your effective protest before the delegates of the American Federation of Labor."[60] The picketing, however, was largely symbolic and did not change the AFL's policies toward integration or racial equality within their unions. The protest did reveal that local black leaders were willing to oppose racial discrimination on the national level, even when they knew that their actions stood little chance of changing the status quo. Most Bay Area affiliates of the AFL did not integrate until after 1945.[61]

The San Francisco branch also continued to attack racial discrimination locally and to serve as a watchdog for violations of the state civil rights law. "This [NAACP] branch is on the alert to see that no deserving case goes without a fight," announced branch president Walter G. Maddox.[62] Between 1930 and 1940, the NAACP demanded the lifting of all racial barriers that prohibited blacks from using public accommodations. Generally, black San Franciscans were already patronizing public facilities without incident, but some establishments, particularly hotels and restaurants, discouraged black patronage. The posh St. Francis Hotel, for example, barred two black couples from their senior ball. When first questioned about the incident, hotel officials stated that management prohibited blacks, but later they admitted that no such policy existed.[63] Similarly, a well-known black singer was directed to a freight elevator when he entered the Sir Francis Drake Hotel. But on another occasion the St. Francis Hotel rented the Cosmos Club a ballroom for their gala annual affair. Perhaps this duplicity in the hotel's policy might be explained by the fact that the Cosmos Club's annual ball was interracial, and the club permitted only members of San Francisco's black and white social and political elites to attend. Yet black San Franciscans always faced the possibility of being turned away from public establishments simply because of the color of their skin.[64]

San Francisco's restaurants also occasionally barred black clientele but, as was the case with hotels, there was no consistent pattern in the policies of these establishments. San Francisco's race relations resembled those described by John Blassingame in nineteenth-century New Orleans: they "swung like a crazy pendulum back and forth between integration and segregation."[65] For instance, the wife of a respected black businessman was refused service at an Italian restaurant and told that the establishment did not serve blacks or solicit black trade. The woman retained San Francisco's two most prominent black attorneys and sued the restaurant for $20,000. The head waiter, an Italian with a dark complexion, defended himself on the grounds that he was a Negro and that his grandmother was a mulatto, originally a native of Liberia. Although he still considered himself an Italian, he could not possibly discriminate against blacks, he stated, because of his unique racial heritage. The court disagreed and awarded the plaintiff a judgment of $250. Black attorney Leland Hawkins noted in a sober tone the increasing incidence of civil rights violations and warned that "this is but one of the many cases of violations of the Civil Rights Act by San Francisco merchants. The situation is becoming acute."[66]

Leland Hawkins was correct when he stated that the California Civil Rights Act was being violated during the 1930s with greater frequency. A black businessman reported that blacks were being charged $1.50 for a glass of beer at a Market Street bar and that their "glasses would be broken as soon as they were used," so not to offend the establishment's white clientele. "It is common knowledge that similar outrages happen frequently," reported the *Spokesman*.[67] The *Spokesman* noted, for example, that public baths and funeral homes also drew a color line. Blacks were allowed to enter the Sutro Baths only if they possessed certificates of good health, but they were barred from the Lurline Baths under any circumstances. Some funeral homes also discriminated, although this policy did not appear to be widespread. One white undertaker "accepted the business and remunerations" of three black veterans buried in the San Francisco Presidio, but "discouraged colored mourners who desired to attend the funeral." Howard Thurman, a black minister, discovered later that discrimination in some San Francisco funeral homes continued into the 1940s.[68]

Racial discrimination also pervaded San Francisco's nightclubs during the 1930s. The city's entertainment sector had generally provided a place for blacks, whites, and Asians to associate, and the races mixed openly during the early twentieth century at cinemas, vaudeville shows, and in smoke-filled cabarets. Interracial dancing was commonplace at clubs like Purcell's, the Show Boat, the Apex Club, and Lester Mapp's. Although some whites objected to these establishments, city officials were tolerant since they catered to interracial couples.[69]

By the early 1930s a more rigid racial pattern had developed, and whites grew apprehensive over the idea of interracial mixing. In 1932, for example, a recreation center in the Western Addition was denied a dance permit by the police commissioners because a police captain had seen "Negro, Filipino, and white women" dancing at the hall ever since it opened. "You wouldn't want your sister to dance with a nigger" he commented at the hearing in an attempt to justify the change in policy. The police commissioners agreed and decided later that blacks and whites could not dance together even on the Barbary Coast. "While tacitly observed," observed the *Spokesman*, the rigid policy against interracial dancing "has never been openly advocated by the [police] department."[70]

The police commissioners' reluctance to grant a dance permit illustrated the uneasiness and anxiety that whites had begun to feel toward interracial relations, particularly between black men and white women. The sight of white women intermingling with black men was unacceptable in most social situations in San Francisco. A black man was reportedly given thirty days in jail and assessed a $250 fine when a white policeman saw him touch the neck of a white woman at a party as they drank a toast. The man and his wife were taken into custody and charged with "keeping a disorderly house."[71] Similarly, Eluard Luchell McDaniels, a black chauffeur, was arrested for escorting two white female passengers. "This is suspicious, two white women and a big nigger," stated one police officer.[72] When they were interrogated, one woman stated that McDaniels was employed by her as a chauffeur. Nonetheless, the officers arrested the three occupants, took them to the San Francisco Hall of Justice, and processed them. The lieutenant on duty allegedly remarked that "any white women who ride around with Niggers and Filipinos should be thrown in jail and kept there."[73] "Down South where I come from," said one of the arresting officers, "such things do not happen. When I see white women with a Negro, I intend to take them in and let them explain. This is my job as a police officer, and the public pays me for it, and I will not make many mistakes when I follow my suspicions in such cases."[74] Rarely have public officials been so candid about interracial relations in San Francisco.

McDaniels and the two women were later released without being charged, but black leaders were outraged nonetheless. NAACP President Leland Hawkins informed Walter White that he would "fight for some disciplinary action in this case," and the branch filed a complaint before the police commission. "The bucket of white-wash which usually sits behind these commission trials is surely going to be embarrassed as I will fill the room with prominent white and black people," Hawkins boasted optimistically.[75]

The officers' counsel based his defense on the argument that interracial relations were so unusual in San Francisco that the two officers were within their rights to stop an automobile that contained a black man and white women. "An automobile with white women and black men attracts attention," he said, "and the sight may be so unusual as to warrant questioning by an officer." The police commission agreed and ruled that the officers had not overstepped their authority. They were cleared of all charges. "It is no more than any police commission in the Old South would issue to newspapers after a lynching," wrote the *Spokesman*.[76] The McDaniels case revealed that during the 1930s some whites had begun to exhibit a great deal of anxiety over the prospect of interracial contact between black men and white women, even though this concern had not been evident between 1900 and 1920. It also illustrated that the NAACP could not expect the San Francisco Police Commission to discipline white officers who harassed blacks. The *Spokesman* spoke for the black community when it wrote, "We cannot conceive of a police department more contemptuous of the rights of Negro citizens than the police of this cosmopolitan city."[77]

The police commission's attitude toward interracial relations was consistent with the mandate state lawmakers perceived. The California State Legislature banned the marriages between whites and members of other races in 1872 and expanded the statute's scope in 1905 and 1933.

California state law required that "no license may be issued authorizing the marriage of a white person with a Negro, Mulatto, Mongolian, or member of the Malay race."[78] Thus public interracial contact in San Francisco was formal because of the strict legal and societal standards.

Although the black community's relations with the mayor and the police department had deteriorated, its relationship with the white press had improved. Though it had been guilty of racist journalism during the early decades of the twentieth century, the white press was much more restrained in its coverage of racial issues by 1930. Even though the *Spokesman* criticized the *San Francisco Chronicle* for "daily insulting Negroes by failing to capitalize the word Negro in its news and editorial columns," the more inflammatory racial reporting had disappeared. In fact, the *Chronicle* published biographical sketches of prominent black leaders, reported on the progress of black organizations, and printed the opinions of black leaders on controversial issues.[79]

Chester Rowell, the *Chronicle*'s editor from 1932 to 1939, advocated a gradual approach to the integration of blacks into American society. He maintained incorrectly that discrimination against blacks was not part of the American law or government policy and that "legally the Negro has exactly the same rights as the white man." Rowell also rejected an immediate solution to the race problem. "If he [the Negro] does not always get these rights, that is a part of the slow adjustment of two racially contrasted peoples to a relatively new and difficult situation. We are at least trying to solve it." Rowell concluded that "there is nothing to do about the problem but wait for time to cure it, as it has long since done with many of the older groups."[80]

Until the 1920s, San Francisco's black community had been relatively free of racial violence, police brutality, and serious racial friction. By the late 1920s, however, blacks reported an increasing number of cases of interracial violence. In one instance, a black man who stole a box of cheese was chased by a mob of white stevedores, who eventually caught him and tied a rope around his neck. The man was released without harm. This incident was unusual in two respects. First, it is one of the few documented cases of interracial violence between blacks and whites in San Francisco. Second, there had never been a lynching of a black in San Francisco and only two in the state of California. Thus this behavior by whites was uncharacteristic, but particularly so given the petty nature of the crime. According to William Pickens at the NAACP's national office, the episode "disclose[s] a very serious situation and a bad state-of-mind."[81]

The NAACP also investigated several cases of police brutality against blacks. The Reverends J. B. Wilson and E. J. Magruder had noted an increase in police brutality in San Francisco and introduced a resolution before the San Francisco NAACP to remove one white officer from the police force for "his brutal and inhuman treatment against members of our group."[82] The NAACP presented the case before the police commission, but the charges against the officer were dropped.[83] The NAACP also reported that a black girl was beaten by white officers, but branch records do not reveal the specific circumstances in this case.[84] It would be incorrect to conclude that San Francisco had a history of police brutality against blacks comparable to those of many northern and southern cities.[85] These intermittent examples were nonetheless troubling to black leaders, because they represented a departure from San Francisco's relatively peaceful race relations and evidence that racial tensions were increasing during the 1930s. It disturbed black leaders even more that their cries for justice were ignored by the city's police commission.

Even though the NAACP did not achieve its goal of full equality for blacks, there were several reasons to be optimistic by the close of the decade. Black leaders and white city officials generally worked together successfully to eliminate the most odious examples of racial friction. The NAACP continued to serve as an effective protest organization locally, and the cooperation between the San Francisco branch and the NAACP's national office revealed that black leaders were deeply concerned with national as well as local issues. On the other hand, racial discrimination, though not as virulent in San Francisco as in Chicago or Cleveland, had been consistent throughout the decade.[86] The intermittent examples of police harassment and brutality, as well as racial discrimination in employment and public accommodations, indicate that not all forms of caste had been eradicated and that many whites still refused to accept blacks as equals. Black San Franciscans would continue to protest these indignities, largely through their internal community institutions, which they saw as the best route to respect and full equality.

6

THE WORST OF TIMES: BLACKS
DURING THE GREAT DEPRESSION
AND THE NEW DEAL, 1930–1940

The Great Depression was a giant step backward for San Francisco blacks, as for blacks across the nation. These were the most difficult years economically. Never before in San Francisco's history had so many blacks from all classes been either unemployed or chronically underemployed. Confined primarily to semiskilled and unskilled labor, domestic, and personal service jobs, most black workers had no protection or security whatsoever in a depressed economy. The majority had difficulty even holding the line, an indication that whatever gains they had made in the previous three decades were tenuous. Consequently, the depression exacted a heavier toll on San Francisco's black population than on any other race or nationality. Blacks had the highest rate of unemployment, the highest percentage of temporary workers in the labor force, and the fewest opportunities to enter the work force as permanent workers. As the decade came to a close, the prospects for black workers were dim.[1]

California was "particularly hard hit" by the Great Depression, wrote David S. Lavender.[2] Virtually every segment of the state's economy, including tourism, real estate, retail commerce, and agriculture, suffered steep declines. Banks foreclosed on thousands of residential mortgages, and workers in all segments of the labor force lost their jobs. By 1933, the number of freight-car loadings had declined to less than half its 1928 level. By 1934, one-fifth of all Californians were "dependent upon public relief."[3]

California's governor, James Rolph, Jr., provided little leadership during this crisis. "In his long tenure as mayor of San Francisco," wrote John W. Caughey, "the major qualifications Rolph had evinced were as official greeter, hand shaker, and parade reviewer."[4] Although Caughey overstates the case, Rolph, who had served as mayor of San Francisco from

1911 until his election as governor in 1930, did not possess the skill or the political acumen to confront the grave situation. "He had no idea how to cope with massive unemployment and poverty," concluded Andrew F. Rolle.[5] Rolph neither devised nor advocated any significant programs to relieve the state's high level of unemployment or to lessen the despair that gripped the state.

The mood in San Francisco typified the gloom in the major urban centers throughout the state. When Lorena Hickok visited San Francisco in 1934 as the chief investigator for the Federal Emergency Relief Administration, she wrote a status report for acting administrator Aubrey W. Williams on the attitude of San Franciscans. "What are people [in San Francisco] thinking about? I asked everyone I saw. Again and again the answer was: their jobs, and whether they are going to keep them or not."[6] The 1930 federal unemployment census reported 21,448 persons out of work in San Francisco, excluding those who were on layoff without pay, workers who were sick, or voluntarily idle. This figure included 4.1 percent of the white workforce and 5 percent of the black; 953 members of other races were unemployed or 3.5 percent of their labor force. Oakland's black community was hit even harder than San Francisco's, for 7.3 percent of East Bay blacks were unemployed, compared to 6.4 percent of white workers. In both Oakland and San Francisco, a smaller percentage of other races (2.6 percent) and whites were unemployed than blacks. Los Angeles, which had the largest black population in the state in 1930, reported a black unemployment rate of 5.5 percent, with 6.3 for other races. Yet Los Angeles also reported an unemployment rate of 4.4 percent for white workers and a rate of 6.3 percent for other races. The high percentage of unemployed workers in the category of other races was the result of the large pool of unemployed Mexican workers, larger in Los Angeles than in any other major urban center in California.

As the depression deepened, particularly in the industrial and manufacturing sectors, San Francisco's black unemployment rate increased significantly. By 1937, the federal relief census reported that 459 blacks in San Francisco were unemployed, 1.5 percent of all unemployed workers, but almost three times the number unemployed in 1930. And although it is impossible to calculate precisely the unemployment rate of any racial group between censuses, the number of black workers who were unemployed in 1937 represented 13.7 percent of all black laborers reported in the 1930 census.[7] Both white workers and members of other races fared considerably better than blacks, for their unemployment rates were 5.7 percent and 3.4 percent respectively. Oakland's black unemployed workers, however, constituted 15.3 percent of its black labor

Table 6.1. Unemployment in Selected California Cities
by Race, 1930

	Unemployed and looking for a job	Unemployed through layoff without pay
San Francisco	21,448	3,019
White	20,327	2,658
Black	168	28
Mexican	262	54
Other races	691	279
Oakland	8,257	1,093
White	7,663	1,054
Black	435	27
Mexican	110	10
Other races	49	2
Los Angeles	44,480	6,438
White	37,788	5,241
Black	1,696	197
Mexican	4,473	925
Other races	523	75
San Diego	4,835	896
White	4,219	749
Black	157	19
Mexican	412	107
Other races	47	21

Source: United States Bureau of the Census, *Fifteenth Census of the United States: 1930, Unemployment,* vol. 1 (Washington, D.C.: Government Printing Office, 1931), pp. 151–52, 155–56.

force, still another sign that black workers in this industrial city were losing their jobs at a faster pace than blacks in San Francisco. Los Angeles had almost fifteen times as many unemployed blacks as San Francisco in 1937—22 percent. The higher black unemployment levels in Oakland and Los Angeles can be attributed to the larger black populations in both cities and the concentration of black workers in unskilled labor, manufacturing, and domestic and personal service jobs—occupations that were hit especially hard by the depression.[8]

The majority of unemployed black San Franciscans, as well as blacks throughout the state, were seeking work as semiskilled workers, unskilled laborers, domestics, and personal servants. Fifty-five percent of all unemployed blacks in San Francisco were seeking work as servants. Sixteen percent were looking for work in semiskilled jobs, and 11 percent reported their former jobs as laborers. Black females were much more likely to report domestic and personal service jobs in the 1937 unemployment census than were black males: 69 percent of black females reported these categories as their former occupations, compared to 44 percent of black males.[9] The high percentage of black women seeking domestic work is not surprising, given their widespread exclusion from professional, white-collar, clerical, and skilled jobs. Black women in San Francisco understood employment discrimination all too well, and during the depression, they struggled to maintain even their menial jobs.[10]

Since San Francisco was not as dependent on industrial employment as many northern and eastern cities, neither black nor white workers lost their jobs immediately. "Due to the comparatively slight industrialization of California, the disastrous results of the crisis were felt in the industries and trade of the state somewhat later, and to a lesser degree, than in the highly industrial states of the East," reported the California State Relief Administration.[11] California's manufacturing employment reached its peak in April 1929, but "from that point a rapid decline set in, and by March 1933, the proverbial rock-bottom had been reached." However, the relief administration concluded that between 1929 and 1935, California's economy "enjoyed a relatively more favorable position than the country as a whole."[12]

The diversity of San Francisco's economy served as a temporary buffer for blacks, who lost their jobs at a slower rate and in smaller percentages than their counterparts in heavily industrialized cities. Since black work-

Table 6.2. San Francisco's Labor Force: Unemployment and Emergency Workers by Race and Sex, 1937

	Totally Unemployed*		Emergency Workers		Partly Unemployed	
	Number	Percent	Number	Percent	Number	Percent
City total	29,506	100.0	14,487	100.0	11,946	100.0
Male	19,952	67.6	10,272	70.9	9,258	77.5
Female	9,554	32.3	4,215	29.0	2,688	22.5
White	28,118	95.3	13,637	94.1	11,581	96.9
Male	18,841	63.9	9,640	66.5	8,978	77.5
Female	9,277	31.4	3,997	27.6	2,603	22.5
Black	459	1.5	436	3.0	159	1.3
Male	266	0.9	277	1.9	103	.8
Female	193	0.6	159	1.0	56	.5
Other races	929	3.1	414	2.8	206	1.7
Male	845	2.8	355	2.4	177	1.5
Female	84	0.3	59	0.4	29	.2

*Persons ages 15–74 who registered in the unemployment census. Totally unemployed does not include emergency workers.

Source: United States Bureau of the Census, *Partial Employment, Unemployment, and Occupations,* vol. 1 (Washington, D.C.: Government Printing Office, 1938), pp. 319, 330.

ers in San Francisco had never had the relatively secure industrial foothold of blacks in Milwaukee, Cleveland, or Pittsburgh during the 1920s and 1930s, they were not immediately devastated by the depression. The number of black households on relief in San Francisco never approached that of a city like Norfolk, Virginia, for example, where 79.6 percent of all black households were on relief in 1934. However, the paucity of industrial jobs in San Francisco also made it more difficult for unemployed blacks to regain employment, because their prospects were even more limited during the depression.[13]

Competition with nonwhite workers also made it more difficult for unemployed blacks to reenter San Francisco's labor market. By 1930, over 35,000 members of other nonwhite races, primarily Asians, competed with approximately 3,000 blacks for employment. Whereas the number of Asian and Mexican workers was relatively small in a northern city like Milwaukee or a border city like Louisville, Kentucky, nonwhite groups outnumbered San Francisco's black labor force significantly. Thus black workers were forced to compete with them for many unskilled and semiskilled jobs. It stands to reason, then, that Asian and Mexican workers also had a high percentage of unemployment relative to white workers. Yet the percentage of unemployed Asians and Mexicans in San Francisco's labor force was lower than the percentage of unemployed blacks in 1930 and 1937.[14]

Although black families struggled during the depression and were forced to use their ingenuity in allocating scarce resources, most managed to persevere economically and to maintain their dignity. Few individuals or families left records describing how they coped during these difficult times, so we are left with little besides the federal relief censuses in evaluating the impact of the Great Depression on black San Franciscans. Several preliminary conclusions, however, can be drawn from the extant records. Blacks were aggressive in attempting to cope with economic hardships, rather than passively accepting the dire consequences of a rapid economic downturn. Many worked two jobs, while others, such as Robert B. Flippin, waited tables at a San Francisco restaurant, despite his college degree and marriage into an elite black family. The alternative to underemployment for Flippin and many other black workers was unemployment, so most gladly chose the former. Similarly, black San Franciscans were creative in juggling limited resources and in earning additional income. Many took in boarders, and others took on odd jobs, such as sewing and domestic work, in addition to their normal employment. Out of necessity, the majority made monetary sacrifices or delayed purchasing goods and services altogether, for the depression caused San Franciscans of all races to recast their priorities. Some blacks were forced to pool their resources and to share the same dwelling with family members, relatives or friends. These short-term remedies only buffered the impact of the depression; they did not restore full employment to black workers who were unemployed or working in relief jobs.[15]

The stories of Tarea Hall Pittman and Walter A. Butler illustrate the difficulties that middle-class blacks experienced during the 1930s and how unemployment transcended class lines within the black community. Tarea Hall Pittman was a member of the Bay Area's social and economic elite by 1930. She had attended the University of California, Berkeley and earned a degree in 1925. She soon began to make inroads into the East Bay black communities through her work in the California State Association of Colored Women's Clubs. In 1927, she married Dr. William Pittman, a black dentist and a member of the Bay Area's small black professional class. Together they settled in Berkeley.[16]

Despite their status and relatively comfortable position in the black community, the Pittmans encountered numerous financial hardships during the depression. William Pittman's dental practice could not support his family, so he worked as a chauffeur "temporarily," even though he earned only $80 a month. Tarea Pittman, though trained in social work, worked in a cannery until her position was terminated. "Since that time," she lamented in 1932, "I have been unable to find work." Tarea attributed her difficulty, in part, to racial discrimination. "Positions which I am best capable of filling are closed to me on account of my race," she wrote. But she also added that any job was difficult to obtain in the Bay Area and that even "in domestic service people are staying on their jobs."[17]

These economic hardships forced the Pittmans to reduce their standard of living. Social engagements and entertainment, for example, were either curtailed or eliminated. "We haven't been to the theater for months and were unable to go to the opera to hear Paul Robeson or Roland Hayes," wrote Tarea. The Pittmans were also forced to borrow money to pay back taxes on their home. "The urgency of my request, and the nearness of ruin have prompted me to write you," noted Tarea in her plea to borrow $500 from Noel Sullivan, the respected white literary patron.[18] This experience must have been humbling to the Pittmans, who had been in a much stronger economic position to withstand the exigencies of the depression than most Bay Area blacks. Nor were most blacks in a position to request a substantial loan from a wealthy white patron like Noel Sullivan.

The Pittmans were not alone in experiencing economic hardships. Walter A. Butler, a black businessman who worked in San Francisco but lived in Oakland, also had considerable difficulty during the depression. Butler, who had been active in the affairs of the Northern California Branch of the NAACP since its founding in 1915, was one of the Bay Area's most popular and respected black leaders. Although Butler had never owned a lucrative business, he had built a steady clientele with a small moneylending business that made loans to Bay Area blacks. The depression, however, crippled his business. Unemployed blacks, who comprised the majority of his clients, were in no position to repay their debts. "When the Depression came," recalled his nephew, Alfred Butler, "a lot of people didn't pay him back and that's how he went down. Nothing you could do about it."[19] Walter Butler also lost his modest home in Oakland, but he did succeed in obtaining a job as a messenger with London, Liverpool, and Globe, a San Francisco insurance firm. However, neither Butler's income nor standard of living reached their predepression levels until the 1940s.[20]

Tarea Pittman and Walter Butler's plight was shared by other members of San Francisco's black professional and middle class, who struggled to maintain their jobs and homes during this trying era. Most, like Butler and Pittman, cut their spending significantly, worked at any available job, scraped to supplement their incomes, and struggled to keep their homes. Some, like Walter Butler, did not succeed. Blacks at the lower end of the economic spectrum, with fewer resources or allies, relied on public relief employment, ingenuity, and faith to survive during this economic ordeal.[21]

As a consequence of their economic hardships, black San Franciscans took in lodgers, as did their counterparts in many northern and southern cities, at a higher rate than native white or foreign-born white families. While only 12 percent of San Francisco's native white and 13.3 percent of foreign-born white families took in lodgers in 1930, 28 percent of black families did so. Both black homeowners and renters took in lodgers at a higher rate than white families, an indication of the hardship that both groups experienced. One in five black homeowners and nearly one in three black renters had lodgers residing with them. This income supplemented the nominal wages that black families earned during the 1930s.[22]

Blacks also had the highest number of females in the work force. By 1930, 55.1 percent of black females were gainfully employed in San Francisco, compared to 37.2 percent of native white females, 27.7 percent of foreign-born white females, and 28.3 percent of women of other races. The high percentage of married black working women is particularly striking. Forty-two percent were employed compared to 18.7 percent of married native white women, 14.5 percent of married foreign-born white women, and 18.5 percent of married women of other races.[23]

By 1940, black women were still in the labor force in higher percentages than other women. Almost 49 percent of black females fourteen years of age or over were employed in 1940, compared to 34.7 percent of white females and 32.8 percent of females of other races. An additional 16.9 percent of black females were seeking work, virtually all of whom were experienced workers. Black women had always worked in higher percentages than white women, in San Francisco as well as in other American cities, and most had worked out of necessity. During the depression, their employment was even more vital to the security and stability of their families, because of the high unemployment rate among black men.[24]

Despite the numerous difficulties they faced, black families had one factor in their favor: they had, by 1930, the smallest median family size and the fewest number of children of any race. Of the 988 black families reported in the 1930 federal census, 817 (82.6 percent) had no children under the age of ten. Only 10 percent had two children under ten years of age and a mere thirty families (3 percent) had three or more children in 1930.[25] Little had changed by the close of the decade, for over 80 percent of all black San Franciscans were twenty-one years of age or older, and only 8 percent were under the age of ten in 1940.[26] These small family units were, for the most part, spared the burden of feeding and clothing young children, which probably decreased the anxieties associated with poverty and deprivation.

In light of the high rate of black unemployment, relief programs were welcomed in San Francisco's black community. Blacks and other workers received assistance through both the California State Relief Administration (SRA) and the New Deal relief programs. The SRA was established in March 1933 to distribute federal and state bond monies and to assist Californians who were unable to secure employment through the New Deal programs. The establishment of this agency represented a new commitment for California, which had budgeted no funds for relief in 1931. Between 1937 and 1939, the state's relief budget soared to $80 million, and an estimated $110 million was projected for relief between 1939 and 1941.[27] By 1938, SRA clients "comprised 38 percent of all relief cases handled by state and federal governments in California at the time."[28]

White workers comprised two-thirds of all SRA relief cases by 1939. Mexicans, who represented only 6.5 percent of California's population in 1930, received 25 percent of SRA relief. Blacks also received a disproportionate share of SRA relief, 4.3 percent, approximately three times the percentage of blacks in the San Francisco population according to the 1930 census. Asians had the lowest SRA relief caseload of any group in the state, accounting for only .9 percent of all SRA relief cases.[29]

A disproportionately high number of black San Franciscans were employed in most New Deal programs, such as the National Youth Administration (NYA) and the Works Progress Administration (WPA), an indication of their greater need and evidence that the New Deal in San Francisco was responsive to the economic needs of blacks. By 1937, 436 blacks worked on relief projects in San Francisco, a figure surpassed in California only by Oakland and Los Angeles. Both cities had substantially larger black populations and a larger number of unemployed black workers. Oakland, for example, reported 860 black relief workers in 1937, almost twice as many as San Francisco. Los Angeles reported 3,752 black workers on relief projects, more than eight times as many as San Francisco.[30]

By 1940, 17.3 percent of San Francisco's black laborers were classified as emergency workers, compared to 3.9 percent of white workers, and 3 percent of other races. One in five black males and 13.5 percent of black females worked on relief projects, compared to only 4.1 percent of white males and 3.5 percent of white females. Males and females in the category of other races had the lowest percentage of relief workers in 1940, at 3.3 percent and 1.7 percent respectively. White workers and members of other nonwhite races also recovered from the depression much earlier than blacks and reentered the permanent labor force. Thus by 1940, only two-thirds of all blacks were employed in nonemergency work, compared to 85.9 percent of whites and 84 percent of other races. Blacks continued to work in public relief jobs in higher percentages and longer than any other race in San Francisco, an illustration that the New Deal relief agencies continued to serve their needs, but also an indication that black workers had a more difficult time obtaining nonrelief work than any other group.[31]

The majority of San Francisco's black relief workers were employed as unskilled workers, domestics, and personal servants. Approximately a third of black male relief workers and almost half of black female relief workers were servants. Twenty-eight percent of black males were classified as laborers, but 15.3 percent were listed as semiskilled workers. Only 6 percent were employed in professional, proprietary, managerial, or white-collar jobs.[32]

Black female relief workers actually upgraded their occupational status, in some instances, when they worked in relief programs. Although

Table 6.3. Unemployed and Emergency Workers by Race
and Sex, San Francisco, 1940

	Population*	Total in labor force*		Employed on emergency work		Seeking work	
		Number	Percent	Number	Percent	Number	Percent
Male	279,591	222,803	79.7	9,305	4.2	23,531	20.6
Black	2,189	1,726	78.8	338	19.6	255	14.8
White	261,868	209,275	79.9	8,579	4.1	21,602	10.5
Other races	15,534	11,802	76.0	386	3.3	1,674	14.0
Female	270,420	93,856	34.7	3,378	3.6	9,139	9.7
Black	2,097	1,020	48.6	138	13.5	172	16.9
White	262,106	90,795	34.6	3,206	3.5	8,842	9.7
Other races	6,217	2,041	32.8	34	1.7	125	6.1

*Includes all those fourteen year of age and older.

Source: United States Bureau of the Census, Sixteenth Census of the United States, 1940: The Labor Force (Washington, D.C.: Government Printing Office, 1943), vol. 3, pt. 2, pp. 205, 663.

half were employed as servants in 1937, 43 percent worked in semi-skilled jobs, a percentage almost three times higher than their male counterparts and significantly higher than the percentage of black women employed in this category in 1930. Few black female relief workers were classified as professionals in 1937, and none were skilled workers or foremen. However, black female relief workers in San Francisco were still less likely to be employed as domestics and personal servants during the 1930s than were members of the city's black working female population in general. This evidence refutes the conclusion of historian William H. Harris that some federal relief agencies, such as the Works Progress Administration and the Public Works Administration, "actually lowered the occupational level of black workers because blacks rarely found relief work commensurate with the work that they had performed in the private market." In San Francisco, and perhaps in other western cities, black workers gained access to semiskilled jobs that had been closed to them before the depression. And although relief jobs did not pay lucrative wages, semiskilled employment did represent an upgrading in the status of many black workers. The progress that black women experienced may well have been predicated on the fact that relief inadvertently upgraded black female occupations because there was little relief work in domestic service, where the vast majority of black women had been employed. The number of domestic jobs available to all female emergency workers in San Francisco confirms this suspicion, for only 324 domestic jobs were listed for female relief workers in San Francisco from a total of 4,215 positions. In contrast, 1,544 jobs were listed as semiskilled and 1,228 positions were classified as "clerks and kindred workers."[33]

Black workers received jobs from every New Deal agency, but the Works Progress Administration and the National Youth Administration were most responsive to their needs. Both agencies employed blacks in higher percentages than their proportion in San Francisco's population. The NYA's state director, Robert Wayne Burns, informed Mary McLeod Bethune, head of the NYA's Division of Negro Affairs, that "while Negroes constitute only 1.4 percent of California's population, the NYA caseload has 5.4 percent Negroes." Three years later, the black caseload in California had increased to 6.5 percent, although blacks between the ages of fifteen and twenty-four still made up only 1.4 percent of the state's population. The disproportionate percentage of blacks on the NYA rolls was true in almost every western state, except Wyoming.[34]

A number of people contributed to the success of blacks in gaining employment on NYA projects, but most important was Mary McLeod Bethune, the NYA national director of Negro affairs. Bethune was one of the nation's most influential black leaders during the 1930s, and she used her influence with both Eleanor and Franklin D. Roosevelt to ensure that blacks were fairly represented in NYA programs throughout the nation. Although the total number of blacks who worked on NYA projects in San Francisco never exceeded forty, the National Youth Administration was still an important source of employment for the city's school-aged black population. In the Los Angeles metropolitan area, almost ten times as many blacks were employed on NYA projects as in San Francisco; Oakland and San Diego both utilized more blacks on NYA work projects than did San Francisco.[35] Few New Deal programs were as successful as Bethune and her state directors in putting black youth back to work: blacks filled almost 21 percent of all NYA jobs in 1941.[36]

Local black leaders also deserve considerable credit for the NYA's success in the Bay Area black communities. Black leaders attempted to exert their influence through advisory committees and in the California office of the Division of Negro Affairs. As B. Joyce Ross wrote in her study of Mary McLeod Bethune and the National Youth Administration, the heavy geographical concentration of blacks in specific cities and strong black leadership "led Blacks to seek voluntarily control of Negro NYA activities as a reflex action to actual and potential white discrimination."[37]

Table 6.4. Negro Youth Representation in the Out-of-School
Work Program and in the General Population in Selected
Western States NYA Youth Employment—February 19, 1941

State	NYA youth employment		% Negroes in total population	
	Total	Negro (%)	15–24 years	All ages
Arizona	1,557	103 (6.6)	2.38	2.47
California	20,904	1,362 (6.5)	1.36	1.43
Colorado	3,701	114 (3.1)	.92	1.14
Idaho	1,597	5 (.3)	.10	.15
Iowa	11,897	301 (2.5)	.65	.70
Kansas	7,552	553 (7.3)	3.24	3.53
Montana	2,431	4 (.2)	.14	.23
Nebraska	5,282	129 (2.4)	.82	1.00
Nevada	319	1 (.3)	.31	.57
New Mexico	1,772	14 (.8)	.61	.67
Oregon	2,762	5 (.2)	.18	.23
Utah	2,735	4 (.1)	.11	.22
Washington	5,569	29 (.5)	.33	.44
United States & territories	487,332	64,686 (13.2)	NA	NA

Source: National Youth Administration, Division of Negro Affairs, *Final Report*, 1943,
National Youth Administration Papers, National Archives.

Although California's black population was sizable only in Los Angeles
during the 1930s, black leaders in San Francisco, Oakland, and Los
Angeles all attempted to shape NYA policy in their respective cities,
independent of white control. Vivian Osborne Marsh, who headed the
segregated office of the Division of Negro Affairs for the state, C. L.
Dellums, a respected black labor leader, and Augustus Hawkins, an assemblyman from the sixty-second assembly district in Los Angeles, were
especially influential. Dellums and Hawkins served on the black statewide advisory committee, which functioned as a subcommittee of the
California State Advisory Committee. Established in 1941, the black
advisory committee had eight members, and its objectives were to represent the interests of blacks throughout the state and to publicize the
NYA's activities in black communities. The committee also encouraged
the training and placement of blacks in permanent jobs in the civilian
labor force. In addition to addressing the needs of blacks, the advisory
committee later broadened its focus and agreed to consider "problems
common to all racial minorities."[38]

Black women constituted half the membership of the state advisory
committee. The division of power on this committee between black males

and females illustrates some of the multifaceted roles that black women played in state politics and in some New Deal agencies. Black leaders chose their own representatives for the advisory committee, which suggests that black males were willing to accord black women more than token representation. Apparently, black females were also demanding representation on this committee, and black men were more than willing to grant them their wishes.[39]

Even though the establishment of a black state advisory committee drew an inquiry from the NYA's national office regarding its purpose, structure, and objectives, the committee's activities were encouraged by Robert Wayne Burns, state administrator for the California NYA.[40] "We are fortunate in having the services of a prominent, sympathetic, and active State Negro Advisory Board," wrote Burns.[41] He also praised the committee's "contribution to promoting better race relations with Negroes generally because among the members we have the most prominent Negroes in California."[42] Thus Burns believed that the black advisory committee could sensitize whites to racial issues, and he favored black representation on the California State Advisory Committee. As a result, three blacks, C. L. Dellums, Floyd Covington, executive director of the Los Angeles Urban League, and W. R. Carter, the general missionary for blacks in the Southern California Baptist Conference, served on the more prestigious integrated committee, in addition to serving on the black advisory committee.[43]

Black advisers served many functions, but their role as advocates was particularly important. Dellums, for example, praised the California NYA because "Negro boys in the Bay Area have been able to gain work experience which qualifies them for employment under union control where they would have to pass tests in order to qualify."[44] Like Burns, Dellums also believed that the presence of black advisers within the NYA helped contribute to better race relations in California. "The actual working together in projects of all races is invaluable," he concluded.[45]

Black advisers such as Dellums and Augustus Hawkins also played an important role in several areas of NYA policy other than race. Dellums protested cuts in the agency's entire California appropriation in 1941, and he urged the NYA's national director, Aubrey Williams, to "do everything within your power to maintain a quota of about ten thousand [workers] in California."[46] Dellums and Hawkins also believed that NYA job training could serve as a potential bridge to more lucrative and permanent defense industry employment for black workers, and accordingly, they pushed in this area. "Your efforts to interest more Negro youths in sheet metal, machine, radio, and aircraft projects of NYA will be appreciated," wrote Robert E. Brown, a black assistant to Burns. Brown agreed with Dellums that job training in some NYA projects "will prepare them [blacks] for employment in defense industries."[47]

Although Dellums may have been the linchpin in the black state advisory committee, Vivian Osborne Marsh, the state supervisor of the Division of Negro Affairs, ran the day-to-day operations of the segregated California division. A native of Houston, Texas, Marsh had migrated to the Bay Area in 1913 to take advantage of California's excellent schools. She enrolled at the University of California and earned a bachelor's degree in 1920 and a master's degree in anthropology in 1922. Marsh developed an early friendship with Mary McLeod Bethune as a sorority affiliate, and the two women remained lifelong friends. When Bethune became head of the NYA's Division of Negro Affairs in 1936, she appointed Marsh the state supervisor of California's segregated program.[48]

Marsh initially received widespread support from the Bay Area black communities and throughout California. "Much favorable publicity in the Negro press has been given to the creation of the Division of Negro Affairs," she informed Mary McLeod Bethune.[49] Marsh appealed to many black organizations to provide employment opportunities for black youth and adults, and in at least one instance, this strategy succeeded. "As a result of my plea," she wrote, "the California Federation of Colored Women's Clubs, Inc. has organized an employment division on their program." Playing the role of advocate, Marsh also encouraged the San Francisco Civic Advisory Committee for the NYA to conduct a survey of the city's black population to determine their employment needs and to gauge the job opportunities available to them.[50]

Some black leaders criticized the segregated policies of New Deal agencies, and others demanded that blacks receive a larger share of jobs. San Francisco's black press, for example, criticized the California Civilian Conservation Corps (CCC) because it segregated blacks in the dining facilities at some of its camps. "It never was the policy of CCC officials to create a nationwide system of integrated camps," wrote John A. Salmond. However, in western states, where the black population was small, blacks and whites were generally assigned to the same camps. But discrimination existed.[51]

Most Bay Area black leaders accepted segregation within New Deal agencies, because they believed that they would gain greater control over their affairs in a segregated program. Others, such as Dellums and Hawkins, protested the NYA's segregated Division of Negro Affairs because they believed that segregated New Deal agencies established a dangerous precedent in California. Dellums, in particular, believed that Vivian Osborne Marsh had persuaded Mary McLeod Bethune to establish a segregated California unit in order to give her the top post. "I just couldn't see Mrs. Bethune setting it up without being convinced that a Negro division was needed," he stated.[52]

Dellums was also troubled by Marsh's political affiliation, her alleged opposition to some New Deal programs, and her gender. Marsh, he wrote, "has always opposed the New Deal and everything it stands for." He described her as a "renowned reactionary Republican" who was "in some way appointed to the [NYA] job." Instead of Marsh, Dellums felt that a "qualified and suitable young Negro man may be [of] better service than a woman." Not content to let this matter rest, Dellums wrote Hawkins to gain his support: "We must press this NYA matter because this Republican dame is still criticizing [us]." Dellums also wrote Mary McLeod Bethune to express his disapproval of Marsh. Bethune, obviously annoyed that a friend and colleague was being maligned for political reasons and because she was a woman, informed Dellums that "I have been most disturbed over conditions in California."[53]

Marsh related a different story than either Dellums or Hawkins. According to Marsh, it was not she but Bethune who had seen the need for a segregated Division of Negro Affairs in the state. But Marsh also believed that the opposition spearheaded by Dellums was merely an attempt to replace her with a black male at the helm and was not in fact opposition to a segregated relief agency. The correspondence between Dellums and Hawkins appears to confirm Marsh's version.[54] Dellums and Hawkins eventually succeeded in persuading Burns to abolish the Division of Negro Affairs in California. By 1941, the segregated unit had been disbanded.[55]

San Francisco's black leaders also demanded a larger share of jobs in New Deal programs, where federal funds were used to complete construction projects or to improve San Francisco's civic facilities. When the Reconstruction Finance Corporation began negotiating loans to finance construction of the Golden Gate and the San Francisco-Oakland Bay bridges, the Spokesman encouraged blacks to demand some of the jobs. The paper also criticized white workers who had migrated to the Bay Area to fill these positions. "There are worthy [black] families who are in dire distress—families who by their length of residence, have a prior claim on our assistance," wrote the editors.[56] Local NAACP president Leland Hawkins also pushed for jobs on the Bay Area bridges, but was not optimistic. "As usual," wrote Hawkins to Walter White, "we must expect a fight."[57]

Black leaders also investigated complaints of employment discrimination outside of the Bay Area, such as alleged discrimination in the construction of the Boulder Dam project at Lake Mead. The *Spokesman* reported at the onset of the project that absolutely no black workers had been hired to construct the dam and that a private company in San Francisco had refused to hire blacks in "any capacity." The *Spokesman* and the NAACP pushed for a formal investigation.[58]

The San Francisco NAACP directed its president, Leland Hawkins, to investigate the matter. However, the San Francisco branch was under the close supervision of the NAACP's national office, for Hawkins had assured Walter White that he would "carry on in San Francisco as you instruct me, in an attempt to secure some work for Negroes on these projects which are supported by finances of government." With the weight of the NAACP behind the investigation, the secretary of the interior agreed that some blacks would be hired. Then later he stated that "no new blacks would be hired at Hoover [Boulder] Dam."[59]

The Boulder Dam investigation uncovered a pattern of discriminatory and segregated employment practices and illustrated the chronic underemployment of black workers. Leland Hawkins found, for example, that black workers were hired in modest numbers to build the dam, but by late 1933, only fourteen blacks were employed in a work force that exceeded four thousand men. At no time, noted Hawkins, did the number of black workers exceed thirty. Hawkins also reported that black workers had been fired without explanation on several occasions.[60] Despite their small numbers, black workers were segregated in the workplace. A separate truck transported black laborers to and from the job, twenty-eight miles away, while white workers were permitted to reside conveniently at the project site. Blacks were also segregated in dormitories, dining accommodations, and recreation facilities. The investigation did not reveal whether blacks were forced to work in separate gangs or if a dual wage system prevailed. It is doubtful that black workers were employed in supervisory or management positions. Although black leaders were powerless to change the racial policies at Boulder Dam, they continued to protest the discriminatory employment practices of New Deal programs.[61]

In light of the Great Depression's pernicious effects on San Francisco's economy, neither black nor white workers experienced many significant employment breakthroughs during the 1930s. Only the status of black longshoremen improved significantly between 1934 and 1940. Two interrelated factors, the passage of the National Industrial Recovery Act in 1933 and the 1934 maritime strike, provided the opportunity for black workers to integrate into the emerging International Longshoremen's

Association (ILA).[62] Radical labor leader Harry Bridges, concerned because blacks had been used effectively as strikebreakers in the 1916 and 1919 waterfront strikes, urged the segregated black work gangs to join the parent union if they supported the 1934 strike. The *Waterfront Worker*, the ILA's official newspaper, cautioned white workers to "well remember the 1916 and 1919 strikes on the front where Negroes were used as strikebreakers." Bridges and other ILA officials agreed and advocated "mixed gangs based on racial equality."[63]

Black longshoremen had considerable experience as pawns in these volatile situations. The *Spokesman* reminded black longshoremen that "union labor never seems to need the loyalty of Aframerican workers until it calls a strike."[64] Nonetheless, the *Spokesman* agreed with Bridges's position that once a truce had been declared, the ILA should enroll more blacks as members and integrate them into white work gangs. Bridges kept his promise after one black work gang agreed to support the

Table 6.5. Occupations by Race and Sex, San Francisco, 1940 (in percentage)

	White	Negro	Other nonwhite
Males			
Professional and semiprofessional	7.5	2.8	3.7
Proprietor	13.3	2.9	10.5
Clerical, sales	23.4	7.0	13.6
Craftsman	15.9	4.7	3.4
Operative	15.6	9.9	14.1
Domestic	.2	3.3	15.9
Protective	5.3	2.0	.5
Service worker	9.7	51.0	34.3
Laborer	8.0	15.4	2.9
Nonmanufacturing	2.4	1.9	1.2
Females			
Professional and semiprofessional	14.4	2.8	6.6
Proprietor	6.3	1.5	4.8
Clerical, sales	45.4	1.7	16.2
Craftsman	1.1	.4	1.2
Operative	12.2	2.5	26.0
Domestic	7.4	63.8	31.2
Service worker	11.9	25.1	12.6
Laborer	.4	.7	.4

Source: United States Bureau of the Census, *Sixteenth Census of the United States, 1940: The Labor Force* (Washington, D.C.: Government Printing Office, 1943), vol. 3, pt. 2, pp. 268–73.

strike. Shortly after a settlement had been reached between the union and management, the *Spokesman* reported that more than "a hundred Negro union men" were put to work, that their salaries were on a parity with white workers, and that Bridges had disciplined white workers who failed to conform to the union's egalitarian code.[65] Bridges reflected later that the union "would never have grown and prospered without the help of its Negro workers and friends."[66]

Even with the integration of black workers into the ILA the Great Depression affected black workers in San Francisco more severely than any other race or nationality. Although the New Deal relief programs and the relief programs of the California State Relief Administration assisted a disproportionately high number of black workers, these programs also underscored the depths to which black workers in San Francisco had sunk. To many black workers, it appeared that the bottom had dropped out altogether. Although the New Deal did provide black San Franciscans with jobs, encouragement, and a ray of hope, it never devised specific programs in San Francisco or throughout California that effectively addressed their more acute employment needs. Finally, black San Franciscans, like their counterparts in Los Angeles and Milwaukee, had a more difficult time than white workers in making the transition from public emergency work to permanent employment when the economy began to rebound in the early 1940s.[67] Many white employers in San Francisco refused to hire blacks in any capacity, since they were competing with white workers for scarce jobs. The economic status of black San Franciscans only began to improve when World War II mobilization required the full utilization of San Francisco's labor force.

PART TWO

THE GREAT DIVIDE: WORLD WAR II AND ITS AFTERMATH, 1940–1954

7

THE GROWTH OF BLACK
SAN FRANCISCO, 1940–1945

The Second World War was a demographic watershed in the history of black San Francisco. Although the city's black population had grown slowly throughout the twentieth century in relation to other black urban communities, it swelled by more than 600 percent between 1940 and 1945. And in the five-year interim between 1945 and 1950, black migrants continued to stream into San Francisco. By 1950, 43,460 blacks lived in a city where fewer than 5,000 had lived a decade earlier. Few northern or western urban communities had ever experienced such rapid growth in a comparable period. With the phenomenal increase in the city's black population, San Francisco suddenly faced demographic change on a scale it had not experienced since the 1849 Gold Rush.[1]

When the United States entered World War II, the nation's economy was transformed. Suddenly the entire San Francisco Bay Area became a focal point of massive black migration. High-paying jobs had become available, and despite the distance, blacks from across the nation, particularly from the South, were eager to move to San Francisco. It was the immediate availability of jobs, particularly in defense industries and in the Bay Area's shipyards, that provided the major impetus for this demographic shift. By 1943, according to the San Francisco Chamber of Commerce, the Bay Area was the "largest shipbuilding center in the world." Black migrants during the 1940s were as pragmatic as their World War I counterparts; they moved west in search of racial equality and the opportunity to improve their economic status and play a decisive role in shaping their own destinies.[2]

The World War II black migration to San Francisco was part of a general demographic shift to the city. The local chamber of commerce reported that between 1940 and 1943, 94,000 people migrated to San

Francisco, "the majority in less than one [year]." Although it is difficult to estimate population changes between census years, the San Francisco Air Raid Warden Service conducted its own 1942 census to "determine the quantities of rationed foods and other commodities which will be made available to the people of San Francisco." Eugene Broderick, chief of the Air Raid Warden Service, revealed that 728,236 people lived in San Francisco as of December 1, 1942, a 15 percent increase from San Francisco's 1940 population.[3]

Several indicators suggest, however, that blacks were migrating to the San Francisco Bay Area in proportionately greater numbers than whites. "Negroes are rapidly becoming the most significant minority group in California and if the six Bay counties are taken together, it is seen that the largest growth of population, both absolutely and proportionately, occurred in this section of the state," wrote Davis McEntire, a professor at the University of California's School of Social Work. McEntire estimated that the six Bay Area counties reported an increase of 324,000 blacks in 1943 from their 1940 figures. McEntire added that "the end of wartime migration to California is by no means in sight."[4]

McEntire based his population projections on two factors. First, major employers throughout the Bay Area had not met their hiring schedules as stipulated in wartime defense contracts. Second, both federal agencies and major employers were recruiting workers to California. The United States War Manpower Commission, for example, attempted to recruit 100,000 additional workers for major Bay Area industries during 1943 alone. Similarly, the United States Civil Service Commission worked with large Bay Area employers, such as the Kaiser shipyards, to recruit workers to the Bay Area. These factors, coupled with the eagerness of blacks to pursue the unprecedented economic opportunities of the West Coast, almost assured a consistent westward flow of black and white migrants alike.[5]

But black migrants did not need encouragement from federal agencies, even though the decision to move west could not have been an easy one, even in the best of times. Many black migrants, however, had suffered through more than a decade of economic deprivation, so their decision to migrate to San Francisco, a community where the vast majority had neither friends nor family members, was a rational one under the circumstances. Particularly southern tenant farmers, sharecroppers, and farm laborers, who depended on the land for subsistence, had little to lose, though potentially a great deal to gain by making the uncertain westward trek.[6]

And so they came by the thousands, each month, crowding into established black settlements and creating new ones. Sue Bailey Thurman, who would later organize the San Francisco chapter of the National Council of Negro Women, recalled that blacks were "scattered all over the city" in 1942, when she visited San Francisco for the first time. When she returned to San Francisco two years later she stated that "upwards to 40,000 blacks" were living in the city. "It had changed in just that time," she exclaimed.[7]

Although Sue Bailey Thurman was not a demographer, her impressions were largely confirmed by the U.S. Census Bureau. The census bureau had conducted a special census of San Francisco's population by age, color, and sex in 1945, and the findings illustrated the rapid wartime growth of San Francisco's population in general and the city's black population in particular. By 1945, San Francisco's total population had increased to 827,400, an increase of 30.4 percent in five years. But while the city's white population grew at a rate of 28.1 percent during this period, the black population had increased by 665.8 percent. Approximately 32,000 Afro-Americans resided in San Francisco by 1945. The total number of blacks who migrated to San Francisco between 1940 and 1945 is larger than the combined totals of every decennial census of San Francisco's black population in the previous nine decades.[8]

This dramatic increase within the space of five years altered the percentage of blacks relative to other minority groups within the city. Blacks had composed only 15.2 percent of the city's total nonwhite population in 1940. By 1945, however, the black populace was 53.1 percent of San Francisco's nonwhite population. True, the wartime relocation of the Japanese accounted, in part, for this startling turnabout, as the number of nonwhites other than blacks declined by almost 4,000 (14.6 percent) during this period. However, 27,155 black migrants moved to San Francisco during the same five-year interval. Thus the wartime black migration pushed the city's black population far ahead of the Chinese, Japanese, and other nonwhite races in absolute numbers.[9]

San Francisco was not the only black community in California to register impressive increases in its black population. Davis McEntire noted that six Bay Area counties made relatively large gains. Oakland, for instance, recorded an increase of 37,327 blacks between 1940 and 1945, a 341.1 percent gain. The East Bay community of Richmond, profiting from defense contracts and shipyard employment, registered an increase of 5,003 percent in its black population between 1940 and 1947. Fewer than 300 blacks had lived in Richmond in 1940, but the lure of shipyard employment had swelled that number to nearly 14,000 by 1947. Similarly, blacks flocked to Southern California, particularly to Los Angeles, in large numbers. The black population of Los Angeles was 63,774 in 1940, already the largest black community in California. Between 1940 and 1946 it increased 108.7 percent. Clearly, blacks were migrating to cities throughout the state in search of employment, but the San Francisco Bay Area registered the largest increases in the percentage of its black population.[10]

No one attempted a demographic study of these new migrants until 1944. In fact, Davis McEntire wrote in 1943 that "no systematic data are available concerning the social characteristics of the migrant group." Yet, several preliminary conclusions could be drawn, he argued. First, a significant proportion of the newcomers of all races came from the southwestern states of Texas, Oklahoma, Missouri, and Arkansas. McEntire believed that most of the migrants came as family units. If they came as single individuals, they generally planned to send for their families as soon as they found employment and shelter. McEntire also observed that many migrants were employed in the manufacturing sector. "Thus the war," he concluded, "has brought to California not only many people, but a large industrial population." McEntire made these observations in reference to California's total migrant population, of which blacks were not the majority, and he conceded that "there is an almost complete lack of reliable information on the size, growth, and characteristics of the new Negro population."[11]

While McEntire speculated about these questions, Charles S. Johnson, black sociologist and president of the race relations department of the American Missionary Association, was conducting an intensive study of San Francisco's black migrant war workers and their families. His study, *The Negro War Worker in San Francisco*, published in 1944, was funded by a local foundation and conducted with the assistance of leading civic and civil rights organizations in the Bay Area.[12] It proved to be one of the most ambitious of its kind. Never before in the city's history had so many diverse groups combined to study an aspect of race relations. With the help of more than 150 agencies, numerous "unaffiliated laymen," scores of female volunteers, and the local sponsorship of a citizen's committee organized by the YWCA, Johnson began systematically collecting information in October 1943. Local agencies and institutions, such as the San Francisco Board of Education and the Juvenile Courts, opened their doors to him. Major employers in both the private and the public sector cooperated in sharing employment data, and labor leaders, housing experts, and public policy analysts granted interviews.[13]

Virtually all of Johnson's volunteer field workers and interviewers were white middle-class women. Only one black female and two black

males were among the more than fifty volunteers, who assisted in virtually every phase of the project. They collected material, organized and
planned the direction that some phases of the study would take, interviewed migrants, and distributed questionnaires. Josephine Whitney
Duveneck, a field worker in the study, was among the earliest organizers
of the project. She recalled that a meeting was held at the Young Wom-
en's Christian Association (YWCA) in San Francisco of "all the prominent
people in San Francisco" to explain the need for the survey and to request their participation. Several prominent white women organized a
group of volunteers, who went into black neighborhoods to survey housing conditions. "You had these really prominent women, who'd always
lived in luxury, going into those places and seeing with their own eyes
what went on," Duveneck mused. She concluded that women's participation "was just great" and "one of the best things I've ever known to
arouse public opinion."[14]

Apparently the committee that sponsored Charles S. Johnson's survey
had a specific purpose in mind. They intended Johnson's findings to
serve as a catalyst for organizing an effective program to circumvent
racial problems that had emerged as a consequence of the wartime migration and prevent potential problems. Hence, the contributors to the
survey met in a series of community-wide forums to formulate recommendations for community action. An interim steering committee report
recommended the creation of a "broad community organization mobilizing all of the elements of the community to meet effectively the problems
of group interracial and intercultural relations." The committee report
was adamant in its charge that "existing [local] agencies are not adequate to meet the [racial] problem, and that a separate community-wide
committee is needed to carry through the basic purpose of the [Johnson]
survey."[15]

Johnson's research also produced the first extensive social profile of
the city's black migrant population. Johnson studied both migrant and
nonmigrant black families in the systematic, analytical fashion that
characterized his scholarship as one of America's premier sociologists.
Undoubtedly, Johnson's research experience in other urban communities, including Pittsburgh, Detroit, St. Louis, and Minneapolis, gave both
his staff and his local sponsors confidence that the San Francisco survey
would be noteworthy.[16]

The survey's findings, which compared 149 black migrant households
with 123 nonmigrant black households, clarified and confirmed many of
the preliminary conclusions that Davis McEntire had drawn the previous year. Johnson concluded, for example, that the majority of black

migrants had relocated from southern states, as McEntire had suspected. Approximately two-thirds of the city's total black population came from the South. Yet the entire South did not contribute uniformly to San Francisco's large black influx. Instead, 51 percent of blacks had migrated from Texas, Louisiana, and Oklahoma. Arkansas and Mississippi also contributed large numbers of black migrant families. Northern and western states, in contrast, contributed significantly fewer black migrants. Johnson noted that only 14.3 percent of black family heads residing in San Francisco one year or less came from western states and only 8.5 percent came from the North. Hence, by 1944, San Francisco's black community was overwhelmingly dominated by southern migrants.[17]

Although most blacks who migrated to the San Francisco Bay Area came from the southern states, we do not know how that percentage was divided between rural and urban migrants. Although Johnson wrote that the "migrant families are to a large extent of rural southern origin," his study offered no reliable statistics on that question, and his evidence on the median number of school years completed by San Francisco's black migrant population appears to refute this assumption. Johnson may well have relied too heavily on the patterns of southern rural migration to northern and midwestern cities that had been typical during the Great Migration between 1916 and 1919. The 1950 census reported that between 1940 and 1950, "more persons moved from rural to urban areas than in any previous decade" and that the majority came from rural-farm areas, which registered a net out-migration of 8.6 million. Black out-migration from southern rural farm areas was approximately 1.7 million, almost 50 percent of all blacks who had resided in these regions in 1940. Given the large influx of blacks into western states between 1940 and 1945, it is reasonable to speculate, as Johnson did, that a large percentage were indeed drawn from the rural South.[18]

Johnson's survey also confirmed Davis McEntire's conclusion that most blacks migrated as family units. Slightly more than half of black migrant families came to San Francisco as family units, according to Johnson. In most other cases, the family reunited within one or two months. Three-fourths of migrant blacks were married compared to 67 percent of nonmigrant blacks. "The large proportion of married persons in the migrant population suggests a relatively high degree of stability among the new people," wrote Johnson.[19]

The majority of black migrants were ambitious, enterprising, and industrious young men and women in the prime of life. These young adults, who were, on the average, twenty-three years old (compared to twenty-six years for the total black population), worked in one of the principal Bay Area industries. Migrant females were slightly younger, 22.9 years on the average, than migrant black males, who averaged 23.4 years. Moreover, one-third of the migrant family heads were less than thirty years old, compared with one-seventh of the nonmigrant family heads. Almost half of black nonmigrant family heads were forty-five years old or older, compared with only 19 percent of migrant family heads. Clearly, the black migrants were a more youthful population, and this was especially true among heads of families.[20]

The influx of black migrants apparently had no immediate impact on the disproportionate black male-to-female ratio in San Francisco, but Johnson argued that the new black migrant population was characterized by a "slight predominance" of females over males. In a sample of 618 blacks who had lived in San Francisco less than four years, 53 percent were females. The greatest disparity was found among young adults, ages fifteen through twenty-four, where twice as many females as males were recorded. While Johnson noted that these findings were "contrary to the sex composition of most migrant populations among which males usually predominate heavily," he speculated that the large demand for black female labor in defense industries was "an important underlying factor." Yet Johnson offered another plausible explanation. He speculated that a number of black females followed their husbands to San Francisco's port of departure and remained in the city to work in defense industries after their husbands were shipped abroad. Johnson also believed that some young black males might have migrated to San Francisco as civilians, but were promptly drafted into military service, leaving their wives behind.[21]

Johnson's figures on the black male-to-female ratio, however, conflict with the Special Census of San Francisco's black population conducted in 1945. The Special Census counted 32,001 total black residents, of which 17,160 (54 percent) were male, and 14,841 (46 percent) were female, exactly the inverse of Johnson's findings. Johnson's sample of black families in San Francisco is too small to compete with the Special Census, which is a far better gauge of this question. Johnson never conceded that a sampling error might have resulted in his reporting a disproportionate ratio of black females to males. Instead, he predicted that manpower needs in the military and defense industry would stimulate a still larger female population within the black migrant population.[22]

In addition to being young and ambitious, black migrants were almost as well educated as San Francisco's established black residents. The average level of education for black migrants, 8.6 years, compared favorably with the educational level of nonmigrant blacks. Although fewer migrants had completed only the lower grades, the proportion of high school, college, and professional students in both groups was roughly equal. These findings, among others, led Charles S. Johnson to conclude that the "grade achievement of the San Francisco Negro migrant population, as revealed in our sample, reflects a relatively high degree of formal education."[23] This finding also cast serious doubt on Johnson's assumption that the majority of these migrants had come from rural areas, where the school term was shorter and the level of instruction significantly inferior to urban schools.

Black migrant women outstripped their male counterparts in educational achievement beyond the elementary school level. Whereas black male migrants predominated in grades one through eight, females recorded higher percentages than males at the high school, college, and professional school levels. The disparity was most pronounced in high school education: almost 30 percent of female migrants had completed three years of high school, compared with only 19 percent of black male migrants. Similarly, 27 percent of black female migrants were high school graduates, compared to 18 percent of males. Only at the college and professional-school level did this gap narrow appreciably, but even then, black women still held a slight advantage, as 8.7 percent of black female migrants had attended either college or professional school, compared to 6.9 percent of black male migrants.[24]

The families of black migrants were larger (3.2 persons) than those of nonmigrants (2.8 persons). Although this difference was not extraordinary, the migrants were much more likely to settle as a family unit. Hence, black nonmigrant families had proportionally more than twice as many one-person families as migrants. Moreover, nonmigrant black families were far less likely to have five or more members; proportionally the nonmigrant population included half as many of these large families as the migrant population. Only when two and three person families were compared did migrant and nonmigrant black families conform, though in both categories, migrant families held a slight edge.[25]

Another important distinction between migrant and nonmigrant black families was the large number of relatives that were reportedly living in migrant homes. Whereas 548 relatives per 1,000 migrant heads were reported in 1943, only 413 per 1,000 nonmigrant heads were noted. The significance of these extended kinship ties had also been noted by James Grossman during the first Great Migration in Chicago. He wrote that they "not only facilitated migration, but helped to check whatever centrifugal pressures family division during migration might have produced."[26] The percentage of nonfamily lodgers residing with both migrant and nonmigrant black families was also high, but higher with nonmigrants. In fact, nonmigrant black family heads were actually outnumbered by lodgers, perhaps an indication of their economic foothold in a restricted housing market.[27]

Although the Johnson and the McEntire studies provided a wealth of information concerning black migrants, numerous questions remain unanswered. Neither scholar explained the role that Bay Area black leadership, government agencies, and industrialists played in the recruitment of black migrants to San Francisco. There is evidence that recruitment of laborers on a nonracial basis took place throughout the state. The commander of the ship repair base at the Hunter's Point Naval Shipyard in San Francisco reported that 24,000 workers had been hired within two years after a recruitment program went into effect.[28] Yet there is little evidence to support Douglas H. Daniels's conclusion that industrialists like Henry Kaiser "brought Blacks here from all over the South—every state—and he brought them in train loads." Rather than being brought to the West Coast like cattle by the train load, black migrants were most likely influenced by the letters and stories of immediate family members, relatives and friends. The "grapevine," an informal information network that had endured from the antebellum era, was also of paramount importance. The 1941 Tolan Congressional Committee, investigating "National Defense Migration," noted that "almost every defense migrant who testified before the committee explained that he had heard from relatives, or from neighbors or friends, about the job openings." The committee concluded that the "grapevine" or "this information put these workers on the road."[29]

The surviving evidence regarding the method of transportation that black migrants used to come to Bay Area urban centers is even more scant. Apparently, few social scientists or public policy experts were concerned with this question. Most blacks probably came by train or bus. Train was the mode of transportation that Sarah Hastings, a black domestic worker, chose when she migrated from Kansas City, Missouri, to San Francisco with her two children during the war. Rail transportation had also been the preferred mode of travel for southern blacks during the First World War, and given twelve years of economic depression, it was unlikely that the majority could have purchased automobiles.[30] But not all black migrants were poor or destitute. Some owned automobiles as well as land and homesteads, and blacks driving along Route 66 were more than just a passing curiosity. Otis Porter, a migrant of undetermined race, testified before the Tolan Committee that he drove a woman from Oklahoma to Long Beach, California, in return for passage to the

Pacific Coast. Porter stated that he made the journey on the "strength of a telegram" that he received from a friend who worked for the aircraft industry in San Diego. Thus perhaps black and white migrants alike, motivated by the promise of economic opportunity and a better life, migrated to the West Coast along similar routes and by common modes of transportation.[31]

Although San Franciscans demanded certain adjustments on the part of black migrants, the migrants also left their imprint on the city, and their very presence prompted a reappraisal of San Francisco's race relations. The black migrant population, because of its size, also faced friction with the black residents, who sometimes resented the burden of assimilating them into the black community. The new black migrants were not content to settle for the menial jobs and racial caste that the black residents had been fighting for decades. Instead, black migrants expected a greater degree of personal freedom and economic equality than white San Franciscans were willing to concede immediately, and in their pursuit of these objectives, they would ally themselves with both the established black leadership and white liberals. Through racial protest and interracial alliances they hoped to eliminate the remaining caste barriers and impediments to racial equality. Although some discrimination continued in employment, housing, and public accommodations, the black migrants' wartime status in San Francisco was a marked improvement over that of blacks who had remained in the South. Small wonder that the majority of black migrants remained in the San Francisco Bay Area after the war. For the first time in the city's history, white San Franciscans would have to adjust to a large black community.

8

WORLD WAR II, FAIR EMPLOYMENT, DISCRIMINATION, AND BLACK OPPORTUNITY

The era of the Second World War was a period of rapid economic progress for black San Franciscans. The wartime emergency created an unprecedented demand along the entire Pacific Coast for laborers, and the San Francisco Bay Area was the focal point for large-scale black migration. Hearing the cries of the federal government, business, and industry to support the war effort, both at home and abroad, blacks aspired to participate fully in the mainstream economic opportunities of the era. Black workers sought and demanded employment in the traditional areas open to nonwhite workers, but they pursued, with equal fervor, nontraditional employment avenues in both the skilled and semiskilled sectors. Blacks' entrance into new sections of the labor market was supported by a presidential executive order, a federal Wartime Commission, the prodding of black leadership, and the efforts of the California CIO, whose racial policies toward the admittance of blacks to organized labor were far more egalitarian that the AFL's. It would restructure black employment patterns throughout the Bay Area. Like their mid-nineteenth century black counterparts, who had migrated to the western Promised Land in search of gold and economic opportunity, these newest black migrants from the south were also optimistic that San Francisco offered a fresh start, economic opportunity, and a better life for their children.[1]

San Francisco's economy, together with the economies of many West Coast and Sunbelt cities, grew rapidly during World War II. As Carl Abbott wrote in his history of urban growth and politics in the Sunbelt, "More than any other single factor, it was the American mobilization for World War II that marked the emergence of the Sunbelt." The rapid, large-scale expansion of defense production and the corresponding growth of the military were pivotal factors in shifting both economic and demographic growth toward the Pacific Coast, South Atlantic, and Gulf states. Thus not only California, Oregon, and Washington expanded and prospered during World War II, but also Arizona, Nevada, Utah, Florida, Virginia, and Maryland. Moreover, Abbott continued, World War II "laid the basis for continued prosperity" in many western and southern cities. The growth of San Francisco's population and economy during the war presaged the post–World War II growth that was a part of a larger pattern throughout the Sunbelt and along the Pacific Coast.[2]

Black migrants had many reasons to be optimistic about their immediate prospects as well as their longterm opportunities. Jobs were plentiful, wages were relatively high, and compared to most major cities, San Francisco had made tremendous strides in combating segregation. But black migrants were not naive. As Davis McEntire concluded in a study of California's wartime population problems, blacks "are acutely conscious of the disparity between democratic professions and the fact of Negro life." But, he added, "their own hopes and aspirations are identified with democratic war aims."[3] This guarded optimism would characterize many black migrants. On the one hand, they believed that the nation had an obligation to honor its democratic credo during the wartime emergency. But they also knew that the reality of race relations in the far West meant that blacks could not enjoy the full range of amenities that their white counterparts claimed as their birthright.

The first year of World War II produced few alterations in employment opportunities for Bay Area blacks. McEntire noted the precarious nature of black employment throughout much of California industry when he wrote, "Industrial opportunities for Negroes [in 1941] are extremely limited, being confined almost exclusively to custodial and heavy labor jobs with little prospect of advancement."[4] The California CIO was especially vigilant during World War II in monitoring the conditions of black workers in the defense industry and suggesting more effective ways to integrate black workers into the burgeoning labor force. The CIO organized a minorities committee in the early 1940s specifically for this purpose, headed by the black labor leader Matt Crawford. The minorities committee concluded what many black leaders had suspected: "Minority groups were being effectively kept out of industry and that America's vast labor force was far from being integrated."[5] In his detailed study of California's wartime labor, McEntire confirmed that black workers were indeed "slow to gain a foothold in the war industries, but as the manpower shortage has intensified, the area of acceptance has steadily enlarged."[6]

Within two years of the United States' entrance into the war, that proverbial foothold had been attained in many critical wartime industries. Blacks could find employment in the aircraft, construction, iron and steel, and shipbuilding industries. Several agencies, including the War Manpower Commission and the Civil Service Commission, cooperated with Bay Area employers to recruit workers to the area. The War Manpower Commission, for example, had hoped to recruit 100,000 "additional workers for Bay Area essential industries during the last half of 1943." By spring 1943, the manufacturing sector employed an estimated one-third of California's labor force, twice the percentage reported in the 1940 census. Clearly, workers of all races and nationalities would find these economic opportunities attractive, but black workers found unprecedented employment opportunities available to them in the Bay Area as a direct consequence of the World War II mobilization and the rapid growth of defense industries.[7]

The Bay Area's shipyards, in particular, hired black workers in large numbers. As shipyards like the Kaiser companies frantically attempted to meet their hiring schedules and honor their defense contracts, workers of all races were in demand. The number of black shipbuilders varied from locality to locality and precise figures are impossible to ascertain. However, several reliable organizations, such as the California CIO and the Bay Area Council against Discrimination (BACAD), a local civil rights organization, estimated that 15 to 16 thousand blacks worked in Bay Area shipyards in 1943, a figure that exceeded the 1940 black populations of San Francisco and Oakland combined. The United States Fair Employment Practices Committee (FEPC) corroborated the progressive employment practices in Bay Area shipyards. The FEPC stated unequivocally in its *Final Report* that by September 1945, "more than twenty-six percent of the Negro working force were engaged in shipbuilding or ship repair. Another twenty-five percent were employed in servicing water transportation, which was largely government work." These two industries alone, concluded the report, accounted for approximately 12,000 black workers.[8]

By 1943, the CIO's minorities committee could correctly boast that the San Francisco Bay Area was the premier shipbuilding area in the state. This burgeoning industry, as well as most major industries in San Francisco, had employed few black workers in 1940. The CIO surveyed fifty-six San Francisco plants that year and found that only fifty-six blacks were employed, out of a total work force of 38,454. In the span of three years, these same plants expanded their total labor force to 192,000, but employed over 15,000 black workers. These industries were increasing their labor forces dramatically as a direct result of the wartime emergency, but they were also employing large numbers of blacks for the first time.[9] This finding led the CIO's minorities committee to conclude that the increase in the number of black workers could be attributed in large measure to "Kaiser shipyards, Marinship and other newly developed ship repair and construction industries of the Area." The CIO singled out the shipbuilding industry in the San Francisco Bay Area as a place where "the Negro worker has been able to make a successful adjustment."[10]

Despite their rapid integration into Bay Area shipyards, black workers did not make comparable gains in other sectors of the work force. Even the laudatory CIO minorities committee report conceded that "fortunate conditions in the shipyards dominate the picture and camouflage less favorable attitudes and policies toward racial minorities characteristic of other industries."[11] Yet it would be inaccurate to minimize the changes that did occur. Most industries had employed few blacks on the eve of the war, but were committed to hire a nominal percentage as a result of the wartime mobilization. Whether these industries were motivated by pragmatism or by a commitment to a new racial order, black workers were the beneficiaries nonetheless.

The records of the Fair Employment Practices Committee (FEPC) were one of the best indicators of blacks' employment status during the war. An outgrowth of Franklin D. Roosevelt's Executive Order 8802, the FEPC was one of the most ambitious federal agencies ever created to eliminate employment discrimination. Louis Ruchames concluded in his history of the agency that Executive Order 8802 "constituted the most important effort in the history of this country to eliminate discrimination in employment by use of governmental authority."[12]

The FEPC's jurisdiction was later expanded by Executive Order 9346, which provided the committee with a number of sweeping powers. They included the adjudication of complaints against "all departments, agencies, and independent establishments of the Federal Government"; complaints against "all employers, and the unions of their employers, having contractual relations with the Federal Government which contain a nondiscriminatory clause"; and finally, complaints against "all employers and unions of their employees, engaged in the production of war materials," whether or not the employers had government contracts.[13] However, the FEPC did not have the full authority to enforce the presidential mandate; nor could it interfere with "privately owned and operated plants which do not hold government contracts or subcontracts and which are not engaged in activities essential to the war effort." Moreover, the FEPC had no jurisdiction over the armed forces. It took another executive order before Jim Crow was eradicated formally from the military in 1948.[14]

Although issuing an executive order to cease discrimination in defense-related industries was a bold gesture, enforcing it was quite another matter. The FEPC established fifteen regional and subregional field offices throughout the nation to enforce the salient features of the executive order and to investigate alleged complaints of discrimination. Noncompliance was financially risky, because the law stipulated either cancellation of wartime contracts or failure to renew expired contracts for offenders.[15]

Region twelve, one of the most active regions, judging by the number of cases docketed, included San Francisco within its jurisdiction. Harry Lees Kingman, a prominent Bay Area white liberal, served as the region's director from 1943 to 1945. Born in Tientsin, China, where his parents were stationed as missionaries of the American Board of Foreign Missions, Kingman moved to the West Coast, where he completed his undergraduate degree at Pomona College and his master's degree at the University of California, Berkeley. At that point Kingman was already associated with several liberal organizations, an association that would set the tone for his activities throughout his life. In 1916 Kingman accepted a post as secretary of the University of California YMCA, better known as Stiles Hall, and in 1932, he was elevated to executive director.[16]

As executive director of Stiles Hall, Kingman gained the admiration and respect of the black and white communities alike. A highly respected community activist, Kingman joined several organizations, from the American Civil Liberties Union to the Massachusetts Society of Mayflower Descendants. With the outbreak of World War II, Kingman directed his energies almost exclusively to working on behalf of Japanese-Americans and blacks. In 1942 he cofounded the Student Relocation Council for Students of Japanese Ancestry Evacuated from the Pacific Coast, which attempted to prevent anti-Asian racial incidents on the campus in the wake of Japan's invasion of Pearl Harbor. Yet Kingman's interest in Asians and race relations predated the Japanese attack on Pearl Harbor, for as early as 1940 he had urged Robert Gordon Sproul, the University of California's president, to sponsor a series of programs on race relations, arguing that addressing the problems of racial minorities was in the best interest of the community.[17]

The plight of black migrants in the San Francisco Bay Area also troubled Kingman, for he feared that the large influx of southern blacks could potentially heighten racial tensions. He joined every major civil rights organization in the Bay Area, including the San Francisco Council for Civic Unity, National Association for the Advancement of Colored People, and later, the National Urban League. Kingman's most significant contribution, however, resulted from his appointment as West Coast regional director of the FEPC. As director of region twelve from its creation in September 1943 to its demise in August 1945, Kingman influenced many large industrialists to adopt egalitarian hiring practices, to cease discriminating on the basis of race, and to enlarge their minority work force.[18]

With the support of the white liberal community already behind him, Kingman successfully courted California's black leaders. In some cases, Kingman called upon black San Francisco leaders, such as Joseph James, NAACP president, and Jefferson Beaver, a prominent businessman, as FEPC consultants. Yet Kingman's black contacts were not limited to the Bay Area or even to the state of California. He also sought advice and counsel from national black leaders, such as George M. Johnson, deputy chairman of the FEPC, and Clarence Mitchell, who served as the NAACP's labor secretary between 1945 and 1950. In a relatively short time, Kingman succeeded in mobilizing an impressive group of interracial leaders to work in tandem with the FEPC.[19]

With Kingman at the helm and a shoestring staff (consisting initially of Edward Rutledge, the chief examiner, and secretary Virginia Seymour), the FEPC's West Coast Regional Office was one of the most successful in the nation. Kingman and his staff spent most of their time investigating complaints of discrimination by blacks and other racial minorities. When a formal complaint of discrimination was made and the case docketed, the regional office would investigate. The investigation generally involved a meeting between the company in question and a member of the FEPC Regional Office staff. The FEPC officer would summarize the charges as they had been presented, and the company would be informed that Executive Order 8802 prohibited discrimination in defense industries. If an employer agreed to stop the alleged discriminatory practices, the FEPC staff would test "actual compliance by subsequent checks" and "provide expert advice and counsel on techniques for integrating minority workers." If an employer refused to comply, the FEPC officer might arrange subsequent meetings. If an employer adamantly refused to cease discriminating, the FEPC officer would recommend the cancellation of his defense contract. This drastic step was never taken.[20]

For two years, Kingman and his staff methodically investigated numerous discrimination complaints. In December 1944, for example, the regional office docketed eighty-five cases. By the following spring, there were still 130 cases pending. Kingman and his minuscule staff did not believe in dragging their feet. Between January and March 1945, the regional office docketed 105 cases, and an equal number were closed during the same period. Of those that were closed, fifty-four were "satisfactorily adjusted." Nor was the heavy case load during the formative months atypical, for the regional office reported that in its first full year of operation, 823 cases were docketed, an average of almost seventy per month. By September 1944, the regional office reported that 62 percent of these cases were closed, and 32 percent were pending[21]. The case load did not taper off during the final year that the regional office was in operation. In January 1945, the region's case load totaled one thousand docketed cases, of which 754 were closed. In early February Kingman wrote to George M. Johnson, FEPC deputy chairman, that "you have heard that Region XII led the league in cases during 1944."[22]

To no one's surprise, the majority of employment discrimination complaints were filed by blacks. During the regional office's first year of operation, blacks filed approximately 80 percent of the total cases. Mexicans comprised the next largest group, accounting for a distant 8 percent of all complaints, followed by Jews, with 7 percent. Moreover, blacks unanimously cited racial discrimination as the reason for an employer's refusal to hire, promote, or upgrade them.[23]

The volume of these complaints, as well as their consistency, revealed the degree to which blacks believed in the wartime credo of equal opportunity. Some black victims, so imbued with the wartime spirit, wrote the president of the United States directly. "I am a Negro and I am coming to you for help, because we know that you have proven to be more than a president to our country. And we don't think that we as a whole, see any different," wrote one black worker. Still others wrote the president protesting discrimination in the military, merchant marine, and trade unions. These letters, certainly acts of faith, also illustrated that some black workers believed they had an ally in the White House, a man who had pledged to the nation in 1941 that he would not tolerate discrimination in defense industries. Apparently some blacks took him at his word.[24]

The FEPC's West Coast Regional Office investigated a wide range of cases, for hardly a major San Francisco employer was spared at least one discrimination complaint. Two-thirds of all complaints were filed against private businesses. Discriminatory complaints against government establishments, in contrast, represented 25 percent of the total cases docketed, and complaints against labor unions made up only 10 percent of the region's total case load.[25] The relatively small number of complaints filed against labor unions, however, was not an accurate indicator of discrimination by unions relative to that of businesses in the private sector. The high wages that blacks earned as union members in the Bay Area shipyards might have been an incentive to "grin and bear it," rather than risk job security. Nonetheless, Kingman and the FEPC regional staff devoted a disproportionate amount of time, relative to the number of cases, handling discrimination complaints against Bay Area labor unions.[26]

The specific allegations black workers levied at private businesses and trade unions were revealing in two respects. First, they suggested the depth and pervasiveness of employment discrimination against black workers. (Nearly half of the 100 leading San Francisco industries did not employ a single black worker in 1944. Ninety percent of black workers were employed by 10 percent of all industries). Second, they revealed that many employers were not willing to integrate their labor force simply because of a wartime executive order, but had to be convinced that blacks were capable workers and that integration would not hurt the morale of their employees.[27]

Some of the barriers the FEPC's Regional Office attempted to penetrate were sources of long-standing anxiety and frustration for black workers, such as the policy of San Francisco's hospitals that prevented black physicians from using their facilities. To Kingman's chagrin, the FEPC failed to persuade a single hospital to change this policy. After some initial resistance, most hospitals did agree to employ blacks as menial workers. By 1944, a private San Francisco hospital asked a black minister to recruit black workers for them, presumably to insure that the workers were reliable and of good character. The Ford Motor Company used the same procedure in Detroit during the Second World War. Not to be outdone, the University of California Hospital in San Francisco and Stanford Hospital both increased the number of black service employees on their staffs. This turn of events led Kingman to inform Sam Kagel, state manpower director of the War Manpower Commission: "We have commended the Stanford Hospital for its relatively fine record in the employment of minority workers."[28]

Kingman and his staff achieved mixed results in their quest to integrate other areas of the private sector. Black women, in particular, faced stiff resistance in their pursuit of jobs; in many respects, they fared worse than black males in both San Francisco and throughout the nation during the World War II era. As a former executive director of a YMCA, Kingman must have been shocked to learn that a black female accused the navy branch of the YMCA of discrimination for refusal to employ her as an elevator operator. Another black woman filed a complaint when she was denied a position as a domestic in a laundry company. A black male pleaded to President Franklin D. Roosevelt to halt employment discrimination against his wife: "My wife was sent out today as a cable worker but was refused and given janitor's work. The only jobs we can get is unskilled labor." Harry Kingman agreed that black women faced special problems in finding employment and that they represented a large number of the unemployed minority workers in Region XII."[29]

At the start of World War II, the range of employment opportunities for black females in San Francisco was no different than in most northern or southern cities. However, with the coming of the war, the expansion of defense industries, and the president's executive order to prod them to greater achievement, black women gradually began to break the familiar mold of menial work. To be sure, the war produced rising expectations in black females because they took the initiative to apply for white-collar and skilled employment as well as unskilled jobs. Given the low percentages of black women in white-collar, skilled, and professional positions before the war, employers were uneasy about the prospect of integrating their female work force. Thus, an official of the Boy Scouts of San Francisco refused to hire a black female office worker because he "didn't know how a colored girl will work out." But even though this woman was turned away, others refused to let their hopes and ambitions be thwarted so easily.[30]

The FEPC Regional Office occasionally ventured into the terra incognita of major San Francisco employers like the Pacific Telephone and Telegraph Company (PT&T), testing the limits of the wartime patriotic fervor and hoping to advance the employment opportunities of black women. Disturbed that PT&T was shirking its responsibility to minority workers in general, the FEPC reported that the company employed only thirty-five blacks out of more than 17,000 employees. One Bay Area newspaper, the *People's World*, reported that PT&T "has not a single Negro operator at work on its Pacific Coast switchboards."[31]

Determined, many black females pushed their claims for employment. Most were rebuffed in their quest for white-collar respectability and career advancement, as was a black woman who responded to an advertisement for an operator, but was turned away with the familiar claim that no positions were available. Another black female attempted to circumvent the racial classification section on her application by writing in "American." The interviewer, apparently in no mood for deception or for black females, told her candidly, "That won't do," and refused to hire her. A distressed Harry Kingman voiced his dismay at the PT&T's hiring policies. "The company's policy has resulted in the employment of Ne-

groes as janitors only or menial jobs," Kingman informed his director of
field operations, Will Maslow. "During the whole course of our dealings
with the PT&T Company representative it was clearly obvious that the
company will not state whether it is willing or unwilling to abide by the
President's Executive Order. Our conferences were absolutely unsuccessful."[32]

Black women not only complained that they were denied employment
opportunities, but that they were forced to bear the added indignity of
employers inviting white women to apply for positions that they had
been denied. One black female college graduate with fifteen years teaching experience was denied employment as a secretary, a position that
was frequently difficult for a black woman to obtain. Another black woman lamented, "They were hiring girls, but not my color of skin." As late
as October 1945, the FEPC Regional Office was still receiving inquiries
and complaints concerning the tenuous status of black female employment at PT&T.[33]

The opposition to hiring black women can be explained on several
levels. Many employers had not hired blacks of any gender, so black
women were at the same competitive disadvantage as their black male
counterparts. But black females generally faced an even bigger obstacle.
They had made less progress in breaking the cycle of domestic service
and menial labor than white females or black males. Consequently, black
women were typecast by the general working population and major
employers—they were seen as suitable only for menial labor. It was
one thing to hire a black woman to scrub a toilet, yet quite another, as
several employers indicated in their refusal to hire black women, for
black women to share toilet facilities with white women.[34]

A more common argument against hiring black women was the charge
that the morale of white women would suffer if black women were hired.
No doubt, many white women felt a bit apprehensive at the prospect of
black women sharing the same offices and becoming, in effect, economic
equals. Some white women took refuge in the monopoly they held on
secretarial and white-collar privileges at the expense of black women—
that was evident from the stern opposition of their employers and personnel directors to hiring black females. But many employers probably
hid behind the excuse that hiring blacks would cause poor morale or
mass walkouts. If these predicted walkouts ever occurred in any industry
in the Bay Area, they were never reported.[35]

Finally, companies balked at hiring black women because they did not
wish to establish a precedent within their industry. This was the fear of
one employer, who stated that "no [San Francisco] envelope manufactur-

ing companies had as yet employed colored girls and that he would not be the first to do so." Other black women must have felt bitterly disgusted after they were referred to jobs by either the Civil Service Commission or the United States Employment Service and politely rejected or told that there was no opening. Why else would the Civil Service Commission have "sent me to the job?" a black female asked in her complaint to the FEPC's Regional Office. "I feel that there was an opening," she wrote, "and that refusing to employ me was based on racial prejudice." Even though labor shortages continued to plague Bay Area businesses and industries throughout the war, black females, like their male counterparts, encountered resistance in their attempts to find jobs in the private sector. Black women gradually penetrated some of the barriers prohibiting their progress, but the walls of employment segregation eroded even more slowly for them. Their dreams of occupational advancement continued to be frustrated by employers who resented their race as well as their gender.[36]

Employment breakthroughs of a different sort transpired on the city's buses, streetcars, and cable cars. Without exception, blacks had been frozen out of employment opportunities in these areas. Employers gave few clues to their reasons for excluding blacks, but the extensive public contact of their employees and discriminatory union policies must have loomed uppermost in their minds. Nonetheless, blacks pushed for admittance into these exclusively white employment domains.

Audley Cole, a twenty-three year old male and formerly a member of the AFL's Janitors Union, was the first black to test the limits of this brand of de facto segregation and the conscience of white civic leaders. Perhaps Cole's dogged determinism can be explained by the fact that he was a native of Pittsburgh, Pennsylvania, and did not comprehend the unwritten limits imposed on black employment in the Bay Area. Then again, perhaps Cole understood the civilities of San Francisco's racial etiquette all too well. At any rate, Cole passed the Civil Service examination and the physical without difficulty and qualified as a motorman on the municipal streetcars. But his problems were just beginning. The local Carmen's Union ordered its members to deny Cole any instruction and threatened a $100 penalty in the event those orders were disobeyed. In the course of the dispute, "fourteen motormen were suspended from their jobs."[37]

One white worker placed his job on the line and agreed to train Cole, a show of good will for which he was physically assaulted. Hard won as it was, the progress made by Cole in 1942 opened the door for hundreds of black workers by 1945. Approximately one year after Cole was finally admitted to the Carmen's Union and allowed to work, a black labor leader reported that the problem was solved. Similarly, Harry Kingman wrote that "the San Francisco Municipal line is now doing very well [and] they now employ a hundred Negroes." Nor were these jobs occupied solely by black males. Kingman explained, "the breakdown is sixty conductors, four conductresses, thirteen female motormen, and nineteen male motormen." Kingman and black leaders must have been gratified to learn that within the space of two years, the San Francisco Municipal Railway System employed approximately "700 Negro platform operators." This was an impressive improvement by any standard, but especially noteworthy in an industry that had not employed a single black worker at the start of World War II.[38]

Audley Cole did not fight his battle alone. Several organizations, including the FEPC Regional Office, pushed for his admittance into the all-white union. The Bay Area Council against Discrimination (BACAD), a newly formed interracial society promoting civil rights, also supported Cole. Working through its trade union subcommittee, BACAD issued a resolution condemning the Carmen's Union before the San Francisco Labor Council.[39]

The *Daily People's World*, a communist party newspaper, also supported Cole's integration into the Carmen's Union. Founded in 1938 by several left-wing leaders, including John Pittman, former editor of the San Francisco *Spokesman, People's World* consistently fought to improve the status of black workers during the Second World War. The paper's position concerning Cole's admittance into the Carmen's Union was also consistent with the ideological underpinnings of Franklin D. Roosevelt's executive order. *People's World* called Cole's exclusion a "scandal for the whole labor movement" and "Hitlerism without the Swastika, but Hitlerism nonetheless, with all its racism ready to run riots against not only Negroes, but other groups." The editors of *People's World* believed that they were partly responsible when the San Francisco Labor Council unanimously adopted a resolution informing affiliated locals that discrimination was contrary to AFL principles. This resolution subsequently led to Cole's acceptance as a member of the Carmen's Union.[40]

The Cole case was revealing in several respects. First, it illustrated that new interracial organizations like the BACAD, as well as established black organizations like the NAACP, were willing to unite and fight employment discrimination. Although the support that these two organizations contributed was expected, the *People's World* editorials in support of Cole seemed to take much of the Bay Area by surprise. John Pittman, whom sociologist Herman H. Long described as one of the most knowledgeable men concerning labor conditions in the Bay Area, was the paper's managing editor. Under his leadership, the *People's World* supported Cole more vigorously than any other newspaper, black or white, in the San Francisco Bay Area. And although neither black nor white leaders openly embraced this Communist party ally, they agreed with the bold stance *People's World* took in its editorials about black workers.[41]

The Cole incident illustrated that San Francisco's labor unions were not willing to open their doors to black workers simply because of an executive order. Unions resisted attempts to integrate their ranks until concerted pressure was applied by both black and white leaders as well as organized labor. Apparently the Carmen's Union did not wish to risk continued ostracism by the powerful San Francisco Labor Council. After weighing the consequences, the union admitted Cole as well as other blacks.

The FEPC Regional Office as well as black leaders also pressed for expansion of black employment opportunities within companies that had traditionally employed black laborers. Whether these companies needed additional prodding is unclear. Nevertheless, Kingman and representatives from the BACAD met with company officials intermittently to make their presence felt and to promote continued compliance with nondiscriminatory policies. This apparently was Kingman's motivation when he met with the International Longshoremen's and Warehousemen's Union (ILWU), because the ILWU had employed blacks on an integrated basis for nearly a decade before the creation of the FEPC.[42]

Most black leaders believed that the ILWU was the most progressive union in the Bay Area. Matt Crawford estimated that the ILWU's San Francisco local alone contained 800 black members. The local's president, Richard Lynden, claimed that the ILWU "is perhaps the most significant labor union in the Bay Area, insofar as progressive and democratic practices regarding the Negro worker is concerned." Given this relatively large black membership, his claim appears valid. Lynden stated in an interview that the ILWU "enjoys the reputation of being forthright and honest in all matters involving the Negro worker" and that the ILWU's constitution contained a provision in the master clause of the contract for the Bay Area that prohibited racial discrimination. Lynden agreed, however, that "the clause is not as strong as it might be."[43]

The ILWU's status as the largest CIO-affiliated union in the San Francisco Bay Area offered advantages for black workers. The union did not enact quotas limiting the number of black workers. In fact, the ILWU's black membership was a respectable one-third of the union's total. The FEPC's Regional Office was so impressed that it boasted: "The longshoremen's local in San Francisco has a reputation of adhering closely to the President's nondiscriminatory order more than any other union, C.I.O. or A.F. of L., in the Bay Area."[44]

But the ILWU was not completely above reproach. The BACAD charged that the ILWU requirement of three months experience applied exclusively to black workers, a charge that the ILWU called "erroneous." The FEPC apparently agreed and dismissed the allegation, after conferring with ILWU officials. No other charges against the ILWU surfaced during the World War II era.[45]

As a result of the ILWU's egalitarian policies, a small but influential cadre of black leadership gradually developed within their respective Bay Area locals. Oakland, not San Francisco, boasted the largest number of black union members and, accordingly, elected several blacks to supervisory positions. Matt Crawford and William Chester rose within the ILWU's ranks to become two of the Bay Area's highest ranking black union officials.[46] Despite the ILWU's attempts to promote black leadership within its ranks, black union leaders were a minuscule group within the ILWU hierarchy. Richard Lynden readily agreed that the black supervisory positions in Oakland were among the "few instances where we have minority group people leading the affairs of the union." Lynden was quick to add, "we have never had a Negro in a big office in our union." He did not feel that the ILWU was totally at fault, though. Instead, he explained that the "main reason seems to be that there have been few Negroes in our job classification until recently. Employers just did not hire Negroes in these classifications."[47]

Even though the ILWU could claim the largest black membership of any union in the Bay Area, its record in upgrading black workers was dismal. Almost nothing had been accomplished in this area since the integration of blacks into the union during the mid-1930s. "We have not done anything in upgrading in the plants where we hold jurisdiction for any of the minorities," Lynden said. Since blacks were the newest members of the union and held the least seniority, they were least likely to be promoted. The ILWU's policy was that "seniority shall be the basis of upgrading." Although Lynden and union officials were concerned about upgrading blacks and promised action, little progress was achieved. But as far as blacks were concerned, the ILWU stood head and shoulders above other Bay Area locals in virtually every respect, even though the union acknowledged that there was still room for improvement. The ILWU was as close to a "model" union as black San Franciscans were likely to find during the years of the Second World War.[48]

The ILWU was not the only union to underutilize black workers.

Blacks frequently complained of the lack of opportunities for promotion and additional training. The FEPC Regional Office reported that 58 percent of its active cases, as of September 1943, involved denial of hiring or upgrading. Both union and nonunion employers were guilty of these offenses, and the problem plagued companies of all sizes. The San Francisco-based Pacific Gas and Electric Company employed only four blacks in its work force of 1400 employees, according to a survey conducted by the CIO minorities committee. The survey also revealed that black workers were assigned to the service garage, janitorial work, and washing cars. Hence, the committee concluded that "Negroes are not promoted or upgraded" within the Pacific Gas and Electric Company.[49]

The barriers to upward mobility for blacks within most Bay Area companies were formidable. The typical black worker could expect only a minimum of advancement beyond the entry level, and supervisory positions were virtually impossible for blacks to obtain. After an intensive investigation, David Selvin, secretary of BACAD, reported that "supervisory positions are particularly difficult for Negroes to achieve, because of the common conviction that white workers will not serve under Negroes and the obvious difficulty of establishing all-Negro crews throughout the plants." One personnel director in a Bay Area shipyard reported that blacks could, in fact, be promoted from laborer to journeyman. But he was quick to clarify his position: "Of course we can't make a Negro supervisor over white people. We wouldn't ask the white people to work under a Negro and we shouldn't expect them to." These attitudes of both management and white workers made the black worker's chance of advancing up the ladder exceedingly difficult.[50]

The majority of black workers were affiliated not with the CIO unions, but with the unions of the AFL. The attempt to gain equal union membership for black workers presented perhaps the greatest challenge to the FEPC, black leadership, and interracial organizations. Black leaders as well as white liberals discovered that gaining access to jobs was one thing. Obtaining union membership and its benefits were quite another. Bay Area unions differed considerably in their treatment of black workers, though most were not inclined to admit openly that they discriminated. Both the CIO and the AFL, for example, had clauses in their constitutions "prohibiting discrimination on the grounds of race or color." While the CIO proudly but cautiously "carried its non-discrimination principle into a positive program for the acceptance of all racial groups," the dominant AFL had "not enforced its anti-discrimination policy upon its affiliated unions." In effect, the AFL left the enforcement of its nondiscrimination clause to the respective locals.[51]

This discretionary power on the part of AFL locals was repeatedly abused. Some locals did not admit blacks under any circumstances, either before or during the war. The Steamfitters' Union, for instance, granted work permits to blacks, but not union membership. The International Association of Machinists attempted to disguise its Jim Crow policies in deference to the AFL constitution. Although the union removed its constitutional ban on black membership, it continued to exclude blacks "by a ritual pledge, binding every member to propose only white men for membership." Still other AFL unions excluded black women as a matter of policy. One labor union official went so far as to say that black women make "poor union men" because they "are inclined to be troublemakers." Most union leaders, however, did not share this sentiment.[52]

The most flagrant abuses of the locals' discretionary power did not involve excluding blacks outright, but denying them membership in the parent union. To perpetuate their inferior social and economic position, black laborers were shuttled into separate Jim Crow auxiliaries. The largest industrial craft union in the San Francisco Bay Area, the International Brotherhood of Boilermakers, adopted this policy, which was uniform throughout the union's locals. This strict policy of segregation along racial lines led a distressed Harry Kingman to state that "we would put union cases in the highest priority list and the need for Congress to give the FEPC more authority in dealing with some of the big craft unions which discriminate is constantly being reemphasized out here."[53]

Since the shipyards employed the majority of black defense-industry workers in the Bay Area, bypassing the separate black auxiliary union was difficult. The leading shipyards, Kaiser and Moore Drydock, had contracts with these unions obligating them to hire only union laborers or workers with union clearance. Some companies occasionally hired blacks without union clearance, though when they did, they risked the ire of union officials. Still other companies hired blacks, but demanded that they obtain union clearance before commencing their work. Thus, being hired was no guarantee of a job—the union would first have to grant clearance, as some Afro-Americans learned to their dismay.[54]

Black workers and local protest organizations were outraged by the Boilermakers' insistence on separate unions for blacks. Every feature of the segregated unions was under constant attack and scrutiny. A research team under the direction of the sociologist Charles S. Johnson concluded that "the major problem of labor unions and Negro workers in the Bay Area is the burning issue of segregated union auxiliaries for Negroes within the Boilermakers' setup."[55]

The evolution of separate black auxiliaries in the San Francisco Bay Area was related, in part, to the wartime influx of Afro-Americans as well as a consequence of pre-existing racial attitudes. Before July 1942, black shipyard employees were given clearance for work by the Boiler-makers' Union without specific designation of union or nonunion affiliation. However, for reasons that remain obscure, blacks were required to join a "segregated, subordinated auxiliary" after July 1942. Prior to this change in policy, blacks were apparently led to believe that they could ultimately become "bona fide" members of the union local. No doubt the wartime influx of blacks exacerbated white fears that blacks were serious economic competitors. Consequently, an informal union arrangement would quickly succumb to the formal de jure segregation.[56]

Membership in segregated locals presented black laborers with several disadvantages. The segregated auxiliaries were under the control of the supervising white locals, and auxiliary members were "not parties to the master contract." They were denied voting privileges in the business of the local and "in matters of policy even pertaining to the auxiliary." Auxiliary union membership "carries none of the benefits ordinarily associated with union membership except the opportunity to work, upon payment of union dues," noted an astute observer. Moreover, since the auxiliaries had no contractual arrangement with employers, its members were prohibited from attending meetings of the regular locals. Nor were blacks permitted to take part in the general business affairs of the union or in the collective bargaining process. Finally, the segregated auxiliary could be dissolved by the parent local and the international union at any time. Denied the benefits of regular union membership even during the war, when employment was plentiful, black workers feared that their tenuous status as members of auxiliary unions would make them the most expendable workers during the postwar era. David McEntire confirmed this suspicion: "A significant implication is that the Negro members who have had to be admitted [to auxiliary unions] during the present emergency can be quietly dropped from the union when the war is over."[57]

The auxiliary unions came under sharp attack from both black and white leaders, but none was more scathing than the attack of Joseph James, the San Francisco NAACP's branch president. James, a "young baritone of great promise," and his wife Alberta arrived in San Francisco in 1939 and settled in San Francisco's black community, near Pine and Fillmore streets. The Jameses were embraced immediately by San Francisco's small black community and they responded by playing an active role in community organizations, such as the Booker T. Washington

Community Center and the NAACP. James also found time to continue his singing career by performing periodically at fund raisers, protest meetings, and shipyard launchings and ceremonies.[58] Like many black workers, James obtained employment in 1942 at Marinship, one of the largest Bay Area shipyards. In a matter of months, he had advanced from a welder's helper to journeyman. Despite his own advancement, James protested the segregated auxiliary arrangement and worked toward its abolition.

James organized a broad coalition of interracial opposition against the auxiliary, which included the BACAD and the San Francisco branch of the NAACP. He also spearheaded an interracial committee composed of black shipyard workers and civic leaders to protest the segregated auxiliary union directly. This organization, called the Committee against Segregation and Discrimination, adopted an aggressive approach to solving the union inequities. The committee met periodically at local black churches in November 1943 and appointed an executive committee to devise strategy. The executive committee adopted a number of recommendations, including a walkout; a campaign to send telegrams to responsive agencies like the War Manpower Commission, the FEPC Regional Office, and the BACAD to protest the firing of black workers who resisted the segregated auxiliary; a publicity campaign to elicit the support of sympathetic allies; and a plan for boycotting workers to "return to work immediately but not join the auxiliary." Eugene Small, a black shipyard worker who had addressed the group in James's absence, called the meeting "a somewhat stormy session." Some workers favored an even more militant posture and fought returning to work.[59]

James objected to every aspect of the segregated auxiliary union, and he urged black shipyard workers not to compromise. He called the auxiliary a "Jim Crow fake union." In denouncing it, he drew a familiar parallel between Hitler's racism in Europe and American racism at home. Moreover, he argued that the auxiliary union policy was divisive to the labor movement in general. Both black and white workers, he insisted, stood a much better chance of persevering during the postwar era if they were closely associated with the parent union. Not content to let this matter rest, James informed Harry Kingman that he favored public hearings in San Francisco before the FEPC on this issue. His reasoning was direct and straightforward. This area was "a key," he argued, and the "local labor bigwigs who are behind this segregation policy should be subjected to the discomfort that a public hearing would bring." Thus far, James continued, "no heat has been applied here and it can be best applied by means of a public hearing."[60]

Despite his leadership and a wide spectrum of interracial support, James's committee suffered setbacks. As some had feared, approximately 100 black workers were discharged for failure to pay dues to the Boilermakers' auxiliary, and additional firings in other shipyards appeared imminent. One source reported the "threatened discharge of 1200 black employees at Marinship, Bethlehem, and Western Pipe and Steel for failure to join or pay dues to auxiliary lodge or Boilermakers' Union established solely for Negroes." Although James objected strongly to paying dues to an auxiliary in which he had no voice, there is no reason to believe that he encouraged his fellow shipyard workers to pursue this course. On the contrary, James seemed somewhat restrained. His correspondence suggests that he wished to fight the segregated auxiliary through normal institutional channels rather than civil disobedience.[61]

If James was cautious, he demonstrated the kind of restraint typical of an NAACP branch president. After his election to the presidency of the strife-ridden San Francisco branch in 1944, he worked closely with both black and white allies. He must have been encouraged when an interracial mass meeting was held at the First A.M.E. Zion church to protest the firing of black shipyard workers. Likewise, a week later, Harry Kingman informed FEPC Deputy Chairman George M. Johnson that "Marinship company is reported as not firing any more workers, but not rehiring discharged men without union clearance." True, James could take only partial satisfaction in knowing that the situation had merely stabilized. Yet he was gaining additional allies in both the shipyards and throughout the Bay Area communities.[62]

Although troubled by a stubborn Boilermakers' Union hierarchy, James remained unwavering in his stance. As chairman of the Committee against Segregation and Discrimination, he restated the committee's position to California State Senator Sheridan Downey: "Negro workers are solidly opposed to any auxiliary, and this opposition continually grows stronger. We refuse to join a segregated, disenfranchised auxiliary. We do not consider the auxiliary a rightful bargaining agent, as we have no voice nor vote in union affairs."[63]

James's threat to hold public hearings gave the movement against the segregated auxiliaries new momentum. The BACAD encouraged all blacks involved with auxiliary unions to file complaints at the FEPC Regional Office as evidence in the forthcoming hearings. Nor could the Boilermakers have been pleased to learn that black workers were also protesting the segregated auxiliaries in Los Angeles, Portland, and Seattle. One FEPC official inferred that San Francisco had not been the catalyst for public hearings. Rather, he stated, it "looks as though the protests are spreading into San Francisco." Regardless of who started the trend, black communities throughout the Pacific Coast were advocating the eradication of Jim Crow auxiliary unions.[64]

The Boilermakers' leadership did not appear the least perturbed by the prospect of public hearings. Edward Rainbow, president of the Boilermakers' Union Local No. 6, stated that although he disliked the practice of segregated auxiliaries, his hands were tied. Rainbow argued that "we are governed by the laws of the International [and] it's the law of the International that excludes Negroes and not the locals—certainly not this local." Rainbow also maintained that the local under his jurisdiction was "doing everything we can to get rid of its segregated auxiliaries," but he was adamant that his local would lose its charter if blacks were allowed to join the parent union on an equal basis. The Boilermakers' Union president promised that he and the "delegates from local No. 6 are going to fight like hell at the National Convention to do away with segregated auxiliaries." But in the interim, blacks must continue to join the segregated auxiliaries until the problem could be rectified at the national convention.[65]

Rainbow exaggerated his commitment to establish an integrated union in several respects. To be sure, his hands were tied by the "Master Agreement between the Pacific Coast Shipbuilders and the Metal Trades Department of the A.F. of L." Yet neither Rainbow nor any other Boilermakers' official ever "fought like hell" to correct this problem. Quite the contrary, Rainbow and union officials appeared comfortable with this arrangement. Segregated auxiliaries would not disrupt the precarious race relations within the union. The status of blacks would continue to be marginal at best within the union hierarchy, and consequently, blacks would never be in a position to challenge whites for skilled jobs or union leadership. By November 1943, the Boilermakers' Union did not have a single black foreman, though it had several thousand black members.[66]

The segregated auxiliary increased racial tensions among black and white shipyard workers. The arrangement fostered a false sense of superiority in many white workers, who felt that blacks were inferior and not worthy of exalted positions or equal treatment within the union. A white female shipyard worker, for example, felt that her coworkers harbored a "race hatred that was basic." Although the typical white worker was not likely to boast of his alleged superiority for fear of black reprisals, the attitude of superiority was prevalent among whites. That these beliefs often caused strained race relations within the union is not surprising.[67]

Black workers found several ways to resist the segregated auxiliaries. Some delayed paying their dues, and others refused to pay dues altogether. Passive resistance, however, was not an effective technique in eroding the union's discriminatory barriers. Black workers who refused to pay their dues might find themselves unemployed in short order. Furthermore, union officials did not think that this act of "union disobedience" was either appropriate or legal. The Boilermakers' Master Agreement specified that "all workers . . . shall be required to present a clearance card from the appropriate union before being hired." In the event that union members were unavailable to fill job openings, new workers could be hired but were required to secure a clearance card before starting work. The Boilermakers Union controlled an impressive number of workers: it represented approximately 70 percent of Bay Area shipyard workers. As Joseph James aptly informed Stanley White, a War Manpower Commission official, "You are well aware that the Boilermakers are the key crafts in these yards in the Bay Area."[68] So if black workers continued to work in Bay Area shipyards, they would either have to accept the Boilermakers' segregated auxiliary arrangement or attempt to alter this policy through legal channels. Black workers and black leadership unequivocally chose the latter course.[69]

James initiated a series of lawsuits against the Boilermakers in an attempt to eradicate the segregated auxiliary structure. He was fortunate in attracting the law firm of Andersen and Resner to defend the newly organized Shipyard Workers Committee, which was "allegedly organized because of the inactivity of the San Francisco NAACP Branch." National NAACP leaders like Walter White were concerned that the committee might be a "black front" for the Communist party, and Thurgood Marshall confirmed this suspicion in part. "There is no doubt in my mind that many of the members are Communists," Marshall wrote. "However, all of them cannot possibly be Communists because there are too many of them." Marshall explained that the committee's attorneys, Andersen and Resner, "are not Communists. However, they represent the Communists and have a reputation for taking all types of cases of persons who are persecuted for one reason or another."[70]

James's legal action was successful. Under the aegis of the San Francisco Committee against Segregation and Discrimination, James and his black shipyard colleagues pressed to halt the dismissal of black shipyard workers who refused to pay dues to the segregated auxiliary. Edward Rainbow, president of Local No. 6, considered this act of defiance contrary to union principles and in violation of the Boilermakers' closed shop agreement. Rainbow directed union officials to deny work clearances to 160 black workers, including James. Lawyers representing the black workers promptly sued in federal district court for reinstatement and monetary damages. James was supported by several civil rights organizations and succeeded in allying the national office of the NAACP as well as the San Francisco branch with his cause. Harry Kingman also asked his deputy chairman, George M. Johnson, to wire the management of Marinship, Bethlehem, and Moore Drydock shipyards "insisting that colored workers not be discharged or refused hire because of unwillingness to join or pay dues to auxiliaries." A month later, an elated Kingman wrote Johnson that the "Superior Court just ruled in favor of Negro workers and has granted [a] preliminary injunction." But the FEPC regional director was quick to caution his deputy chairman, "Attorney [George R.] Andersen expects [the] Boilermakers to appeal to [the] State Supreme Court."[71]

The Marin Superior Court also ruled that the Boilermakers' arrangement of "discriminating against and segregating Negroes into auxiliaries is contrary to public policy of the State of California." Accordingly, the Superior Court prohibited the union from laying off workers who refused to pay dues and barred the union from requiring blacks to join segregated auxiliaries as a condition of employment. In short, the court ruled that the Boilermakers must "admit Negroes as members on the same terms and conditions as white persons" if they wished to "retain closed shop privileges."[72]

Union leaders felt that the Marin Superior Court had overstepped its authority and promptly appealed the decision to the California Supreme Court. In a decision, *James v. Marinship*, that both surprised and jolted Boilermakers' officials, the California Supreme Court upheld the Marin Superior Court's decision. In the court's view, "the fundamental question in this case is whether a closed union coupled with a closed shop is a legitimate objective of organized labor. . . . In our opinion an arbitrarily closed or partially closed union is incompatible with a closed shop."[73] The court also found the "discriminatory practices involved in this case contrary to the public policy of the United States and the State." It cited Executive Order 9346, which declared that "it is the policy of the United States to encourage full participation in the war effort of all persons regardless of race, creed, color or national origin, that there should be no discrimination in the employment of any person in war industries because of such." Hence, the court ruled that blacks "must be admitted to membership under the same terms and conditions applicable to non-Negroes unless the union and the employer refrain from enforcing the closed shop agreement against them." The decision was unanimous.[74]

The California Supreme Court's opinion in *James v. Marinship* was a momentous legal decision that could potentially end segregated auxiliary unions, not only in San Francisco, but in other West Coast cities as well. The decision ended the separate auxiliary arrangement in California. Black shipyard workers were theoretically free to join the parent local on an equal basis with white workers. Or were they? Although the Boilermakers Union agreed to abolish its segregated California auxiliaries, the union announced that it would form "separate but equal" local lodges in their place. Hence, blacks would be required to join an all-black local, but they would be given full membership rights within the parent union. If this new arrangement was the Boilermakers' brand of liberalism, it was a most curious liberalism indeed.[75]

The Boilermakers never carried out their plan for "separate-but-equal" lodges. Instead, within three years of the war's termination, the Boilermakers had integrated their union. As fate would have it, black shipyard workers never realized the full potential of the California Supreme Court's decision, because the war ended in a matter of months. With the termination of the second great global conflict, black shipyard workers were laid off in massive numbers, along with their white counterparts. As Harry Kingman and many black leaders had predicted, however, postwar layoffs affected a disproportionate number of black workers. By 1948, the black unemployment rate throughout the San Francisco Bay Area was approximately 15 percent, almost triple the state unemployment rate for all races.[76]

The presence of black wartime workers in the labor force had made profound changes in San Francisco's black community. Blacks had made inroads into occupations beyond the menial positions customarily set aside for them. For the first time in San Francisco's history, blacks competed with white workers for semiskilled and skilled jobs, and even black women had made gains during the war, though they had had much more trouble cracking the color barrier. Although equal employment opportunities were seldom won without a struggle, the Second World War became an important benchmark for black progress. "Although little was accomplished in the way of permanent progress toward equality," says the historian William H. Chafe in summarizing the war's impact on blacks, "the changes which did occur laid the foundations for the development of mass protest activity in subsequent years." World War II was one of the most important developments in the history of San Francisco's black community.[77]

9

WARTIME TENSIONS AND
THE STRUGGLE FOR HOUSING

The assimilation of 27,000 black migrants into San Francisco within a span of four years, 1941–1945, was not easy. An even larger influx of white migrants during the same period exacerbated the problems of housing, race relations, and the black migrants' adjustment. Perhaps under the best of circumstances, race relations would be strained in the wake of a sizable black migration. Yet even though San Francisco suffered from racial tensions in a number of areas, conditions never resembled the volatile situations in Los Angeles or Detroit, where race riots erupted. Black and white San Franciscans coexisted in a state of relative peace and mutual toleration. Indeed, the two races came into contact more frequently than ever before in housing, employment, recreation, and public accommodations. But some whites were visibly disturbed over the growing black presence and showed disdain for blacks. After all, longtime residents, both white and black, had to adjust to the presence of tens of thousands of blacks in a city where less than 5,000 had lived in 1940. The process of was often fraught with racial antipathy and bitterness, but the black migration was also welcomed in some circles as the dawning of a new era in San Francisco's race relations. This duality—toleration and ambivalence—made the adjustment of wartime black migrants unpredictable and uncertain in a city that had been renowned for its racial toleration.[1]

Most San Franciscans were optimistic that their city could assimilate black migrants without difficulty. The black social worker Robert Flippin, for instance, expressed confidence in San Francisco's race relations and optimism about the future. "Today our city holds within its environs some 15,000 to 18,000 Negroes," remarked Flippin. "The city that knows how, along with other great war industrial centers that have swollen and festered with the influx of thousands of black and white workers from other sections of the country, is in the embryonic stage of developing a new and truly democratic mutually agreeable and successful pattern of bi-racial living." Josephine Cole, a native of San Francisco who later became the city's first black public school teacher, welcomed the "infusion" of new blacks. Cole stated that the migration was the "best thing that had ever happened to us as an ethnic group." Similarly, Maurice Harrison, former dean of the Hastings College of Law and a member of the University of California Board of Regents, also believed that San Francisco could assimilate these newcomers peacefully. "San Francisco always had a tradition of toleration," exhorted Harrison. "It has been cosmopolitan always. We want to preserve that atmosphere of good will."[2] Indeed, most San Franciscans probably felt that potential problems could be resolved with the same maturity and sophistication that the city had shown in the past and that the worst features of Jim Crow, such as race riots and racial violence, would never appear in San Francisco.

Black migrants discovered, despite the best efforts of white San Franciscans, that their adjustment to this urban milieu was marred by racial discrimination, ostracism, and even hostility from other blacks. The *Christian Science Monitor* devoted a front-page story to San Francisco's wartime race relations and observed that the San Francisco Board of Supervisors and the public, through a series of open hearings, were "learning that there are many flaws in San Francisco's once-vaunted cosmopolitanism. . . . Segregation is practiced almost rigidly with the use [of] occupancy clauses in deeds and leases restricting colored races to certain rather well defined areas of the city."[3] The *Monitor*'s reference to restrictive covenants is especially noteworthy, for these racially restrictive deeds had not been widely used before World War II. The World War II migration clearly heightened residential segregation, as white developers, realtors, and property owners increasingly felt the need to legally bar blacks from their neighborhoods.

As a direct result of the wartime migration, some local businesses also began to shun black patronage. The Hastings Clothing Store, for example, revised its policy, "because of the influx of southern white and colored," and would not allow black patrons to try on suits or hats before purchases. Only after the city's interracial leadership pressured the establishment did this policy cease. But racial slights were hardly confined to clothing stores. A black woman filed a $25,000 damage suit against Di Maggio's restaurant and retained the services of Edward D. Mabson, San Francisco's leading black attorney, after she was refused service. The number of blacks who were refused service in either public or business establishments may never be known, but Katherine Stewart Flippin expressed what well may have been the prevailing attitude. "We know where we couldn't go; the places we couldn't go, we just kept out of." Thus some blacks consciously minimized the potential of day-to-day racial insults by avoiding establishments that insulted or refused to serve black patrons. Others, however, were eager to test their limits and challenge de facto segregation in public accommodations.[4]

Some whites felt so frustrated and fearful about the growing black presence in their state that they wrote Governor Earl Warren to express their disapproval. Such was the sentiment of Leonard A. Brinson, who deplored the migration of illiterate southerners of both races to the state. He informed the governor that we need "to teach" migrants to be model citizens.[5] Similarly, Edwina Robbins asked the governor to create a fact-finding committee to study the black migration's impact on California and also expressed concern over the political significance of the large number of blacks in the state.[6]

But most Californians who wrote the governor were not this restrained. "I am glad to see you [have] switched over to the Negro side of the house," wrote another resident, "and I hope if you become president you will appoint an entire supreme court of sole black negroes. This will save applying for annexation to liberia."[7] Still another Californian, dismayed over an assault on a white woman by a black sailor, wrote, "This one attack (though unsuccessful) will create a wave of racial hatred which all your talk about racial tolerance will [be] wasted. "He urged "retribution," because the "minds of Negro boys and men" were "for the most part infantile." Similarly, J. F. Anderson criticized the "pugnacious attitude of the colored people who have come here in droves [and] a lot of them seem to have run away with the idea that they are the chosen people." Anderson continued: "I don't believe in intermarriage, residential mixing, or [black] mixing with whites. If the colored folks are not set right on these questions, there will be trouble in this state."[8] And while George Backester would not admit that he was a racist, he feared the devaluation of property when blacks moved into white neighborhoods. Backester described blacks as "permanent charity cases" and he implored the governor, "Let's send the Negro and all others who will go back to their own states, and not try to make an utopian for them here." Finally, a white supremacist not only found the presence of blacks undesirable, but he wrote that the "Negro was a naked savage a very short time ago."[9]

These letters reflect much more than disdain for Afro-Americans.

They also illustrate an irrational, though mounting, racial fear among some whites, that blacks and whites could not live together in California. Admittedly, there is no substantial evidence that a majority of whites shared these abhorrent views of blacks, yet these attitudes did indeed suggest that the rapid influx of black migrants was not welcomed by all segments of the white population, either in the San Francisco Bay Area or in other parts of the state. Quite the contrary, blacks were often perceived as undesirable and unassimilable elements of the state's population. Hence, the sentiment of a woman who asked Earl Warren to "please Governor, segregate us from them" probably struck a responsive chord in a much wider segment of the population than most white Californians were willing to admit.[10] Maintaining the illusion of civility was one thing. Living with blacks in an integrated, egalitarian environment was quite another.

Wartime tensions were also manifested in the increased incidence of sporadic racial violence and police brutality. Racial violence had been uncommon in San Francisco before World War II. The new black migrant population, however, was more likely to feel the wrath of whites than their pre–World War II counterparts. Politically, the black community was too weak to have any recourse. Hence, there were no public outcries when a black longshoreman was beaten by San Francisco police or when two white servicemen deliberately ran over a black male with their automobile after an alleged robbery. White San Franciscans occasionally reported that policemen were more hostile to blacks in public than to whites. A white woman testified before the San Francisco Board of Supervisors that a white policeman in San Francisco threatened to arrest her as a prostitute because she was "talking to a Negro friend." The policeman ordered her off the street with the stern warning that "ninety percent of the Negro men in the [Fillmore] district are sex maniacs."[11]

These examples of racial intolerance and friction alarmed black leaders and white city fathers alike. Some San Franciscans, for instance, were quite disturbed when a black editor received an anonymous letter regarding the reorganization of the Klu Klux Klan in San Francisco and when a black family's residence and a Jewish synagogue were defaced with the Klan's insignia. Bay Area black communities also mobilized after three white men killed an unemployed black man who was collecting garbage in Richmond. After the district attorney, Edmund G. Brown, refused to prosecute the case, the state's attorney general, Robert Kenny, intervened. Kenny, who had a "statewide reputation as a believer in civil liberties and particularly in fair play for racial and political minorities," pushed for a charge of manslaughter, rather than murder. A California

Superior Court jury, however, exonerated the defendants. Racism may well have been the major issue confronting the nation in 1944, as American Civil Liberties Union president Roger Baldwin argued, but at least one white jury in California would not convict whites for murdering blacks.[12]

Racial slurs and insults appeared periodically in the city's leading white daily papers more frequently during World War II than they had in the previous decade. C. L. Dellums, a black labor leader, criticized the *San Francisco Chronicle*'s sports writer after he referred to a black child at the Shrine Hospital as a "pickaninny." Dellums informed the writer that "during the last ten or twelve years, the *Chronicle* has improved greatly and stopped using a number of insulting terms to the race that they formerly used."[13] Davis McEntire noted that the *San Francisco Examiner* also "made a specialty of derogatory news and editorials on the American-Japanese and Mexicans." Robert Kenny agreed and charged that "several newspapers were contributing to the danger of race riots by blowing up small incidents far beyond their actual significance." Similarly, the *Los Angeles Times* "credited the *San Francisco Examiner* with a large share of the responsibility for stirring up anti-Mexican feeling among the servicemen and the civilian population."[14] The BACAD demanded that local newspapers cease "using racial descriptions of criminals or alleged criminals." Through this one policy change, it argued, the white press "could make a substantial contribution to the war effort and to maintaining harmonious relations between all races and nationalities."[15]

White racism was not the only problem that black migrants confronted. Established black residents were often condescending toward black migrants or criticized their behavior as uncivil or countrified. "No one is more anxious than I to see every Negro in the South get out," wrote C. L. Dellums to his cousin. "Unfortunately thousands of the worst type and most ignorant are leaving the South, but those who are a credit to the race and can make a contribution still toward its progress aren't coming out fast enough."[16] Still other blacks complained that the migrants were loud and vulgar, and that they lingered on street corners and lacked the grace and sophistication of nonmigrants. For example, a black family that had recently relocated to San Francisco from Pacific Grove, California, complained to the national office of the NAACP that "our grown ups are loud and noisy. They are sloppy in their dress on the streets." This type of tension between old and new black residents following a large-scale black migration was not uncommon. It reflected, as

James Grossman noted in his study of Chicago's black community during the World War I migration, a difference between urban and rural values and the failure of the black middle class to see any "redeeming value in southern black folk culture."[17]

Negative attitudes toward black migrants were manifested in many ways. Robert Flippin felt a sense of paternalism and noblesse oblige toward black migrants. He argued that even though "the old problems of discrimination, housing, and lack of representation, as well as political and economic problems are being aggravated and multiplied by the influx of Negroes, San Francisco must strive to assist these people and to integrate them into our society. We must reach them and assist in maintaining a high standard of living and of conduct."[18] Flippin displayed patience and understanding, but many black nonmigrants believed that the migrants had actually damaged the position of blacks in San Francisco. Charles S. Johnson discovered, much to his chagrin, that "82 percent of those giving information on the subject and 69 percent of the total old resident families were either definitely sure that all, or some new Negroes, were a handicap to them." Black nonmigrants, however, showed a bit more compassion when asked if black migrants should return home. Only 14 percent replied affirmatively, though an additional 7 percent felt that "some should return home." Nor did the majority of nonmigrants believe that the further in-migration of blacks to San Francisco should be stopped. Instead, most expressed a willingness to live in the same building with migrants and to send their children to schools with the children of black migrant families.[19]

While it is risky to attempt to identify the factors that prompted these attitudes, Charles S. Johnson's study, *The Negro War Worker in San Francisco*, offers several clues. Most blacks who criticized the black migrants were born in the South, but 49 percent had lived in San Francisco at least fifteen years. The overwhelming majority were females who rented apartments in the Western Addition in proximity to black migrants. These women, concluded Johnson, "were either housewives or engaged in domestic work." Perhaps they believed that the security and success they had attained would be threatened by a large influx of blacks, many of whom worked in high-paying defense industry jobs. These nonmigrant blacks had probably grown accustomed to both the relative isolation and the predictability of their status in San Francisco. With the onset of war, the rapid demographic shifts among the black population, and the ensuing dislocation, these residents faced an uncertain future. Moreover, they would compete with the black newcomer for jobs, homes, social services, recreation, and status. Hence, as black migrants sought to adjust to their new urban milieu, acceptance even by their black brethren came grudgingly if at all.[20]

Adjustment to an urban metropolis was one thing, but the black migrant's most immediate and pressing problem was housing. San Francisco had historically been plagued with a shortage of housing, and with the wartime migration housing of any variety was at a premium. By 1943, housing was already in critically short supply throughout the city. The commander of the Hunter's Point Ship Repair Base stated that "we had to stop recruiting workers from February to July, 1943, because we ran out of housing."[21] Caroline MacChesney, executive secretary of the National Conference of Christians and Jews, wrote the *San Francisco Chronicle's* editor that "some city officials have suggested that the program of recruitment of labor be stopped," due to housing shortages. Similarly, Revels Cayton, the black labor leader, found it difficult for the Ship Scalers Union to recruit 4,500 "urgently needed longshoremen and shipscalers" because of the poor housing market. "Housing has been chronically in arrears," wrote Davis McEntire, and "it is a matter of common knowledge that rental units have virtually disappeared from the market."[22]

Black San Franciscans discovered that racial discrimination and restrictive covenants made it more difficult for them to obtain housing in a tight housing market than for their white counterparts. Charges of housing discrimination had surfaced infrequently before World War II, and most San Franciscans were probably smug in their belief that blacks could reside anywhere in the city. Yet it was hardly a coincidence that the vast majority of blacks resided in three census tracts in 1940 and that these areas, though integrated and predominantly white, would continue to define where most blacks would be permitted to live during the war. Charles S. Johnson noted this peculiarity regarding San Francisco when he wrote, "Underlying the entire question of Negro housing in San Francisco—both public and private—is the issue of residential segregation."[23]

Housing discrimination in San Francisco was widespread by World War II. One researcher estimated that "not less than 80 to 90 percent of the residence areas in the San Francisco Bay Area communities are closed to non-Caucasian entry."[24] Perhaps this factor prompted a port agent for the National Maritime Union to write, "We are having a difficult time in securing housing for Negro members of our organization."[25] Blacks were not merely struggling to find shelter during a period of acute housing shortages; they were also forced by custom and legal covenants to confine their searches to a handful of predetermined and highly congested neighborhoods. By 1945, Joseph James, the NAACP branch president, called housing "the number one priority."[26]

Many white property owners, real estate agents, and neighborhood improvement associations were vocal in voicing their horror at the prospect of black neighbors. One white San Franciscan, echoing the sentiment of the Daughters of the American Revolution, admitted, "I wouldn't even want Marion Anderson as a neighbor." Others resorted to age-old stereotypes and complained that blacks were dirty, lazy, thievish, drunken, and quarrelsome. Some white parents objected to their children associating with black children in schools and recreation facilities, while a few feared intimate contact between black men and white women if blacks integrated white neighborhoods.[27]

Real estate interests generally based their opposition to black tenants or property owners on the charge that even a modest black influx into white neighborhoods would cause a sharp depreciation in property values. Few were willing to admit that blacks, in many instances, actually paid higher rents than whites as well as increased the volume of business in their communities. Nonetheless, restrictive covenants, which in some cases barred blacks from renting or purchasing property for as long as twenty years, were present in more than a half-dozen neighborhoods and endorsed by some of the "best established groups in the city." These pillars of San Francisco's business and civic community, wrote Charles S. Johnson, "openly proposed segregation as a solution to housing problems of the Negro population, and no group proposed residential integration of either a complete or modified form as a way out of the present housing dilemma."[28]

The quality of San Francisco's housing also left a great deal to be desired, for little had been accomplished since 1940 to improve the number of substandard dwellings throughout the city. The city's public health director, J. C. Geiger, conducted a house-to-house sanitary inspection in 1943 of one square mile of the Western Addition, consisting of 114 city blocks. The area, bordered by Presidio and St. Joseph's avenues on the west, Gough Street on the east, California Street on the north, and Golden Gate Avenue on the south, housed 37,030 persons, of whom approximately one-fourth were black. Conditions were so squalid that the health department ordered that 288 structures must be "vacated and remodeled or torn down because of fire and health hazards." The health department's ruling had the support of the mayor, despite a chronic shortage of housing.[29]

Blacks occupied a disproportionate share of the Western Addition's substandard housing relative to their percentage of the city's population.

Overcrowding, unsanitary living quarters, and infestations of rodents were typical sights, particularly in the city's Fillmore district. The black press conducted its own survey of black housing conditions in the Fillmore district in 1944 and found that in some instances residents were "crowded 9, 10, 15 to a single room with only one window. They work all day for the maintenance of democracy and the defeat of fascism abroad and come home in the evening to face the realities of domestic fascist practices. . . . No single factor has contributed as much to unity and solidarity of San Francisco's Negro population as had the intolerable housing condition that has been allowed to develop and continues to exist."[30]

Besides being overcrowded, many of these dwellings had no hot water, bathroom facilities, or access to natural light. More than one black migrant must have wondered if he had really left the rural South behind when he saw the Fillmore district. Rodents abounded to such a degree that the United States Public Health Service assigned two ratcatchers to the Fillmore district. After surveying conditions in the area, one public health inspector exclaimed, "This district is worse than ever. It's the worst in the city." The Reverend Thomas Grigsby worked for the public health department and visited "50 to 100 places a day." Grigsby stated that on a "pretty good day," he caught as many as twenty-one rats with the help of a 22-caliber hand gun. Likening his job to going fishing, Reverend Grigsby stated philosophically, "Some days you catch a lot; other days you don't catch any." The *Daily People's World* was probably accurate when it reported, "The rat-catchers don't eliminate the sources of rats—squalid slum conditions. Their job is just to catch them."[31]

Blacks also paid relatively high rents for substandard housing. Herman H. Long, who assisted Charles S. Johnson in his study of black war workers in San Francisco, noted that blacks "pay a greater proportion of their incomes for rent than even the Chinese."[32] Black migrants paid the most of all, averaging $13 a month more than black nonmigrants. Yet the migrants had less living space, an average of 3.3 rooms compared with 5.1 rooms for nonmigrants. Black migrants also housed an average of five persons in their cramped surroundings, compared with 4.7 persons for nonmigrant blacks. The prevalence of relatives and lodgers contributed to the congestion and the lack of privacy in migrant households. One third of all black families that the Johnson research team interviewed "maintained some type of undesirable sleeping arrangement, either by having children of various ages in the same room or same bed with parents or by having children of different sexes sleeping together."[33] As a result of the influx of migrants and the restricted housing market, major adjustments in living space were essential to accommodate an expanding black population that seemed to have no end in sight.

Several measures were undertaken to relieve the acute housing problem. In 1942, the federal government constructed 5,500 temporary units of emergency housing at the Hunter's Point Naval Yard in San Francisco; occupancy was confined to naval yard workers and their families. Black workers in defense industries viewed the community as a vast improvement over the conditions that many San Franciscans had to tolerate. Moreover, Hunter's Point became one of the most thoroughly integrated communities in San Francisco. By 1945, the community's population had swelled to 20,000, of whom one-third were black. The development also contained a community center, an interdenominational church, a community relations program, a newspaper, and a special police force.[34]

Despite its promise, Hunter's Point had numerous problems. Two black tenants complained that the development's physical makeup left much to be desired. "It hasn't been dry around these apartments since the first rains of Autumn," wrote William and Adde Critz. "The children have no place to play save in the mud around the buildings." Other black residents complained that the armed special police force was all-white and not initially under the jurisdiction of the San Francisco police department. The mayor's Committee on Civic Unity, attempting to quell rumors of forthcoming race riots at Hunter's Point, met with the San Francisco Housing Authority on at least four occasions. The interracial committee recommended that blacks be added immediately to the special police force and that all officers assigned to Hunter's Point should be trained in "interracial and intergroup problems." Additionally, the committee suggested that a multiracial tenant's organization be created.[35]

Within a year of the initial meetings, most of the problems had been solved. A Housing Authority official, John Beard, dismissed the story of the impending race riot as an ill-advised rumor.[36] Moreover, Beard was not convinced that white racism alone contributed to racial conflict. "Ninety-five percent of Negroes are law-abiding citizens," argued Beard. Yet he was still concerned because "the Negro [migrant] brings with him certain convictions regarding the law which are deeply seated and come about as a result of his experience in the section of the country when[ce] he comes." Perhaps Beard was purposely vague to avoid offending his liberal audience, but he was straightforward when he stated that the "main source of difficulty on the [housing] project springs from prostitution, illegal liquor sales and gambling."[37]

In 1945, life went on at Hunter's Point much as it did in any San Francisco neighborhood. To be sure, problems of both a racial and nonracial nature emerged from time to time. After all, a war was going on. Thus, instead of becoming a racial powder keg, Hunter's Point developed into one of the most progressive examples of San Francisco's wartime housing. It is curious that the acute housing shortage had prompted an atypical pattern of residential integration.[38]

If most black San Franciscans felt that solving the twin problems of housing discrimination and housing shortages was difficult, they were correct. City officials did almost nothing about the former, but they were embarrassed by the abundance of substandard housing and sought to remedy that situation, at least in part, by constructing thousands of low-income housing units throughout the city. Thus, in the wake of the 1937 United States Housing Act and a California State Enabling Act the following year, a local Housing Authority was created in San Francisco. Eleven permanent housing developments were initially scheduled for construction, but wartime exigencies allowed for the completion of only five by 1943. Preliminary construction planning was begun for the remaining six sites, and their completion would be an urgent postwar priority.[39]

In 1943, the Westside Courts project, an integrated housing development, was completed in the Western Addition. The 136-unit development, which was built at a cost of $700,000, was an attempt to provide adequate housing for families. Westside Courts, noted the San Francisco Housing Authority's *Sixth Annual Report*, "replaced an entire city block of some of the city's worst housing." Robert Flippin managed the integrated development during its first year of operation, a prestigious appointment for a local black leader. Flippin, who had no previous experience in this area, had called upon San Francisco's white leadership as well as his close friend Horace Cayton to help him secure this job. Cayton assured Frank S. Horne, a national housing authority official, that Flippin was a man of "unusual ability" and more than competent to perform the job.[40]

Although low-rent housing projects were never perceived as a panacea for the blacks' housing dilemma, some leaders believed that they were an important step in the right direction. Housing Authority Commissioner John Beard went so far as to state, "Until about two years ago, the Negroes of the city had the best housing situation of all other racial groups; and when the Westside Courts project was built to relieve the housing shortage in that area, they were far better off than other groups." After the wartime migration, Beard tempered his enthusiasm. "Now, of course, it is a different matter. The large in-migration of Negroes has perhaps put them in the worst position for housing."[41]

Beard failed to mention that the housing authority's policy of admitting black tenants only to the Westside Courts project in the Western Addition contributed to their housing difficulties, a policy that he strongly supported. "As a matter of policy, we have never restricted certain projects to either Negro or white occupancy," stated Beard. "We deliberately allowed a few white families to go in [to Westside Courts] so as not to establish a purely Negro project," he continued.[42] However, when the five permanent housing projects were completed, blacks were conspicuously absent from all but the Westside Courts development. The other four housing projects, Holly Courts, Potrero Terrace, Sunnydale, and Valencia Gardens—1,605 housing units—had no black tenants.[43]

The decision to confine black tenants to one housing project in the Western Addition also caused some dissension among Housing Authority commissioners. Alice Griffith resigned her post in protest over the discriminatory policies.[44] The San Francisco Housing Authority's racial policy was consistent with the United States Housing Authority's national policy that tenant selection as well as "development and management of United States Housing Authority aided projects are primarily responsibilities of the local housing authorities." Moreover, according to Clarence R. Johnson, "in the distribution of families of different racial groups, local authorities use state and local law and customs," and "public housing projects [may] not be used to displace minority groups nor to change the prevailing racial pattern of a community."[45]

San Francisco Housing Authority commissioners, though denying that this policy existed during the agency's formative years, would later admit to its use in tenant selection, calling it the "neighborhood pattern." In essence, the Housing Authority maintained that the tenants selected for any housing development must reflect the racial and ethnic composition of the existing neighborhood. Thus, if black families wanted to integrate white neighborhoods, they would not use the San Francisco Housing Authority as a springboard.[46]

Several organizations in the black community protested the Housing Authority's segregated policy. "There has been considerable agitation about the apparent discriminatory policies followed by the San Francisco Housing Authority in the acceptance of Negro tenants," Clarence R. Johnson confided to C. L. Dellums.[47] Herman H. Long concurred that "sentiment from the Negro constituency strongly resented a special segregated Negro housing project and favored a policy of integration of Negro families into all available low rent developments."[48] Exactly who was agitated is unclear. San Francisco's "Negro constituency" may have well resented the segregated policy, but the most heated criticism of the

policy came after, not during the war.[49] Thus black San Franciscans occupied the Westside Courts housing project without a major public out-
cry in 1943, in contrast to their counterparts in wartime Detroit, who
faced considerable opposition and violence.[50]

In Detroit, violence broke out when black families attempted to occupy
a housing project in a predominantly Polish community. As Dominic J.
Capeci, Jr., illustrated in his study of this controversy, Detroit's Polish
community mobilized, enlisting white developers, civic groups, and cler-
ics in their effort to keep blacks out of their neighborhoods. They feared
that blacks would "ruin the neighborhood" and "destroy their way of
life." In San Francisco, interracial coalitions had worked actively to improve the housing status of blacks during the war; in Detroit, many
important business interests as well as Detroit's large Polish community
were openly defiant of the attempt by housing authority officials to build
integrated public housing in their communities. Consequently, more
than three thousand local and state police officers were required to move
black families into the Sojourner Truth Homes in 1942. In contrast, not
a single police officer was needed in San Francisco to integrate public
housing. Nor did San Francisco experience the citywide race riot that
occurred in Detroit in 1943. True, the Westside Courts were located in
the Western Addition, an area of San Francisco where an established
black neighborhood had existed for decades, whereas Detroit blacks were
attempting to integrate a white ethnic community that was not only
hostile to black settlement, but also a community where almost no blacks
had lived before 1941.[51]

On the whole, blacks as well as many white leaders were critical of San
Francisco's housing policies. One black woman complained that she preferred Buffalo to San Francisco, because in Buffalo "people lived in mixed
neighborhoods and little if any discrimination existed."[52] However, few
blacks carried their protests beyond the level of informed complaint.
Furthermore, black migrants rated the Housing Authority as the "least
helpful" of all agencies in San Francisco.[53] Davis McEntire, a white critic
of Housing Authority policies, charged that "a variety of practice and
varying degrees of segregation are found in the public housing projects."
He concluded that "public housing has not afforded opportunity for more
than a very small fraction of in-migration Negroes."[54] Marion Beers Howden, regional management advisor for the Federal Public Housing Authority, also criticized San Francisco's housing policy. "The attitude of the
management of these housing developments is reflected all the way
down the housing personnel from tenant selection to recreation," exclaimed Howden. In addition, "the War Relocation Authority in San

Francisco is not to be trusted," and "there is consistent undercutting of FPHA policy on the housing of Negroes and other minorities by people who are in positions slightly better than clerks. . . . These people are supported by the local housing officials—if not the local authority itself, then certainly the executive director or secretary."[55]

Finally, interracial organizations like the NAACP, the San Francisco Council for Civic Unity, and the BACAD supported blacks in an attempt to curtail housing discrimination in the public and private sector. The BACAD, in particular, adopted some ambitious goals, working with the San Francisco Housing and Planning Association and its statewide counterpart to "investigate and eliminate discrimination in public housing in the Bay Area."[56] In addition, BACAD pushed for a policy of nondiscrimination for the San Francisco Housing Authority and urged the San Francisco Board of Supervisors to adopt a general public policy of nonsegregation in all housing. Finally, it sought to prohibit restrictive covenants through a legislative enactment, arguing that covenants were "probably the primary cause for residential segregation against minority groups."[57]

Despite the best efforts of black and white leaders, housing shortages, substandard housing, and residential discrimination persisted throughout the World War II era. The San Francisco Housing Authority had taken an important first step toward the eradication of substandard housing by the construction of permanent housing projects, but at the same time it established a controversial and volatile policy under the pretext of preserving the racial and ethnic integrity of neighborhoods. It also limited black families to a single development in San Francisco's Western Addition. Herman H. Long was correct in his observation that John Beard and the Housing Authority commissioners represented "a victory of the private real estate faction over public housing interests."[58] Both blacks and white liberals discovered that committing city fathers and Housing Authority commissioners to redress the problem of segregated housing would be a formidable task. Although San Francisco had few segregation laws, its public and private housing patterns conformed closely to the national pattern. The World War II migration of black southerners to San Francisco not only accelerated residential segregation and heightened racial tensions, but also laid the groundwork for the creation of a black ghetto in the postwar era. The large number of blacks who were denied access to housing and public accommodations also raised some serious questions about San Francisco's liberal race relations image.[59]

10

WORLD WAR II AND
THE NEW BLACK LEADERSHIP

The Second World War had a profound impact on San Francisco's black leadership class. For the first time in the city's history, hundreds of skilled, professional, and white-collar blacks worked and lived in San Francisco. These upwardly mobile Afro-Americans became the nucleus for the expanding black leadership class. Though they migrated to San Francisco primarily to improve their economic status, they would also have an appreciable impact upon both the quantity and quality of San Francisco's black leadership. Armed with a presidential mandate to eliminate discrimination in the defense industries and the support of the Bay Area's white liberal community, they would work zealously to end all vestiges of racial discrimination in San Francisco, including discrimination by existing black leadership. Almost all of these individuals would occupy leadership positions in the black community. Through their efforts, committees, churches, and protest organizations would be formed, including the Church for the Fellowship of All Peoples, the National Urban League, and the National Council of Negro Women. Moreover, the new leadership would work with established community organizations like the Booker T. Washington Community Center, the black churches, the YWCA, and the NAACP to advance the cause of racial equality.[1]

The new elite did not represent a revolution in San Francisco's black leadership. Instead of the sudden metamorphosis that occurred in Chicago between 1900 and 1915, and in Cleveland between 1915 and 1930, where a new black elite augmented its power at the expense of the old elite, continuity rather than change characterized the ideologies, programs, and racial strategies of San Francisco's new black elite. The new black leadership differed not in the nature of their demands for racial equality but instead, in the urgency of their message. These leaders,

principally activists rather than ideologues, appeared to believe Gunnar
Myrdal's prophecy that "there is bound to be a redefinition of the Negro's
status in America as a result of this war."[2] Hence, the new black elite was
in the vanguard of every major campaign for racial equality during the
World War II era and the postwar years as well.

Most members of the new elite were born, educated, and came to intellectual maturity in the caste-ridden South. Some of these individuals
migrated to San Francisco directly from southern and border states, the
migration path of the majority of San Francisco's black World War II
migrants. However, the migration to San Francisco was a two- or three-
step process for the majority of the new elite. Most did not come directly
from the South, but had resided in the North or West before migrating to
San Francisco. Thus, their backgrounds were different from those of
most black migrants, who came directly from southwestern, south central, and southeastern states.[3]

Members of the new elite were also younger than the representatives
of San Francisco's old elite, and they reflected the lower median age of
the city's black migrant population as a whole. Most were born after the
turn of the century and were in their thirties or forties when they arrived
in the Bay Area. Almost none were over fifty. Reflecting the youthful
optimism typical of new leadership, these men and women were bold and
energetic. They were also confident that racial conditions would improve
and that they would play a decisive role in the ultimate destruction of
racial discrimination in San Francisco.[4]

Almost without exception, members of the new elite were college educated, many of them trained in the nation's black colleges. Some, such as
Carlton B. Goodlett, had attended predominantly white universities for
their graduate and professional training, after receiving undergraduate
degrees from black colleges. Only a small percentage of the new elite,
including Cecil Poole, a prominent black attorney, and Seaton W. Manning, the Urban League's executive director, had attended predominantly
white institutions for both their undergraduate education and professional training. By the end of World War II, a college education virtually
was a prerequisite for entry into the new black leadership class.[5]

The new black elite inherited the social trappings of the older generation of black leaders. They achieved status in similar ways, through
membership in lodges, fraternal organizations, and exclusive men's and
women's clubs. The majority attended one of San Francisco's established
black churches, where they occasionally served as board members, dea-
cons, and trustees. Many educated their children at Lowell High, the
city's most prestigious high school. These leaders also married within

their social and economic class, much like their prewar counterparts. The new elite also attended the Cosmos Club's annual ball, which remained the most prestigious social event of the year for black San Franciscans.[6]

The new leadership expanded San Francisco's black professional and white-collar class, as more doctors, nurses, dentists, ministers, and social workers migrated to San Francisco. For example, William McKinley Thomas, a native of Bryan, Texas, had been a physician in the army before relocating to San Francisco, where he became one of the city's most respected black leaders. Daniel Collins, a South Carolina native and one of the principal organizers of the San Francisco Urban League, was a prominent dentist before migrating to San Francisco. After completing his training on a scholarship at the Guggenheim Clinic in New York, Collins secured an academic appointment at the University of California's prestigious college of dentistry in San Francisco. A prolific scholar, Collins authored fifteen scientific papers. By 1944, through his teaching post, local practice, and involvement in black institutions and interracial committees, Collins had emerged as one of the prominent black leaders in San Francisco.[7]

Physician Carlton B. Goodlett became the most influential member of the new elite. Although he was born in Chipley, Florida, in 1914, Goodlett grew up in Omaha, Nebraska, where he attended the public schools. He followed the traditional path of the black "talented tenth" and enrolled in Howard University, where he received a degree in 1935. Three years later, Goodlett had earned a Ph.D. in psychology from the University of California, Berkeley, and in 1944 he obtained a medical degree from Meharry Medical College. The following year he moved to San Francisco, where he established a medical practice and became a community activist and trustee of the Third Baptist Church, the city's largest black congregation. He also served several stormy terms as president of the San Francisco NAACP. Shortly after Goodlett's arrival, he and Daniel Collins invested in the *San Francisco Reporter*, a weekly black newspaper that was established in 1942 by a black gambler from the Fillmore district. Goodlett and Collins eventually gained controling interest in the paper. In 1948, Goodlett also became editor and publisher of the *San Francisco Sun*, another black weekly newspaper, after allegedly winning the paper in a poker game from the white San Franciscan who owned it. Goodlett and Collins combined the two papers in 1948 and formed the *Sun-Reporter*, which became an important voice in San Francisco's burgeoning black community. When Collins withdrew his financial support in 1949, after the paper suffered heavy financial losses, Goodlett alone became the leading black journalist in San Francisco. Goodlett would later be acknowledged by his peers as one of the preeminent black journalists in the nation.[8]

Black ministers, though less numerous in the leadership class, were among the most respected leaders. None was more distinguished than Howard Thurman. Thurman had occupied academic posts at Morehouse College and Howard University before moving to San Francisco in 1944. Shunning the provincialism of his black ministerial colleagues, Thurman had achieved international acclaim as a minister and scholar. His reputation was instrumental in arranging a personal meeting with Mahatma Gandhi when he visited India in 1936. He would author nearly two dozen books during his lifetime, and the editors of *Life Magazine* would later name Thurman one of the ten most influential ministers in America.[9]

Although they were less distinguished than Howard Thurman, several other black ministers were no less significant to their respective congregations. The Reverend E. E. Hamilton, who pastored the Church of God, reportedly had one of the largest black congregations in San Francisco by 1943, though he had arrived in the city just two years earlier. The Reverend H. B. Gantt also came to San Francisco in 1941 and pastored the influential First A.M.E. Church, one of the oldest black congregations in San Francisco.[10] These men, along with the Reverend Hamilton T. Boswell, pastor of the Jones Methodist Church, and F. D. Haynes, pastor of the Third Baptist Church, were the leading figures in the Black Ministerial Alliance, which advocated equality in employment, housing, and public accommodations for blacks and also pushed for the election of a black to the Board of Supervisors. The activities of Haynes and Boswell, in particular, illustrated the increasing tendency of black ministers to play a more active role in civil rights organizations than their pre–World War II counterparts and to assume commanding leadership roles in pushing for full equality and greater opportunity for black San Franciscans.[11]

The new elite also included professional social workers, who competed for leadership roles in the expanding black professional community. They included men like Seaton W. Manning, D. Donald Glover, and James Stratten. These men were young, college-educated, and experienced in social work and community services. Manning, for example, had worked as an Urban League official in Boston and New York before coming to San Francisco. After receiving an undergraduate degree in history from Harvard University in 1934 and a master's degree from Boston University four years later, Manning worked as industrial secretary for the Boston Urban League. The Kingston, Jamaica, native showed such promise that he was elevated to executive secretary of the Urban League of Greater Boston within three years. By 1945, the National Urban League office moved Manning to its New York City headquarters as the industrial relations specialist. The following year, Manning agreed to serve as executive director of the San Francisco Urban League, a position he held until 1960.[12]

Manning's industrial secretary, D. Donald Glover, was also a member of the new elite. The Huntington, West Virginia, native and recent Bay Area migrant was educated at West Virginia State College, Ohio State, and Dayton College. Like Manning, Glover brought both a well-rounded education and valuable experience to his post. During the Second World War, for example, Glover had conducted utilization surveys for the War Manpower Commission and developed programs to integrate black workers into the work forces of the Dayton Rubber Company, Frigidaire Corporation, and Inland Steel. By the time Glover relocated to San Francisco in 1946, he had already won a regional reputation for his "outstanding ability in labor-management negotiations." Glover's subsequent election as vice-chairman of the California Federation for Civic Unity, a statewide omnibus civil rights organization, also illustrated his prestige at the state level.[13]

James Stratten, who migrated to San Francisco in 1941, was one of the most popular members of the new elite. During the war, Stratten worked as the associate regional supervisor of the YMCA-USO and the West Coast area director, coordinating the services for black soldiers. After the war, the ex-professional football player became the executive director of the Booker T. Washington Community Center, a member of the San Francisco Grand Jury, a commissioner in the redevelopment agency, and the first black appointed to the San Francisco Board of Education. Stratten's tenure at the Booker T. Washington Community Center, in particular, provided him with a strong base of support in the black community, as it had for his predecessor, Robert B. Flippin.[14]

Occasionally, a black nonprofessional, such as Joseph James, earned the esteem of the black community and occupied a firm position in the new elite. James migrated to San Francisco in 1939 from New York to advance his career as a professional singer. Apparently, James's blue-collar occupation as a welder in a Bay Area shipyard did not hurt his standing in the black community, for by 1944, James was president of the local NAACP. Shipyard employment was among the most lucrative work that blacks of any social class performed during World War II. Moreover, James had been trained at Boston University in music, which made him one of the most culturally refined men in the black community.

By 1944, James had earned the respect of local leadership and the NAACP's national office.[15]

Black women were in the minority among the new elite, and they worked principally as "clubwomen" and community volunteers. Only occasionally were they employed in professional jobs. Sue Bailey Thurman, Frances B. Glover, and Anna Magruder were typical. Thurman was one of the most admired women in San Francisco's black community. The daughter of a black minister who had served in the Arkansas State Legislature, Thurman was reared in comfortable middle-class surroundings, but she did not allow her family background or her marriage to Howard Thurman to compromise her potential or her ambition. After receiving undergraduate degrees from both Spelman and Oberlin colleges, Thurman taught briefly at Hampton Institute before joining the national staff of the YWCA to work with southern and eastern colleges. She also found time, in the course of raising a family, to chair the archival and museum departments of the National Council of Negro Women. Additionally, Thurman founded and edited the *Aframerican Woman's Journal*, the official publication of the National Council of Negro Women. Although Thurman stated later that she "hated leaving her work in Washington, D.C. to come to San Francisco," she organized a local chapter of the National Council of Negro Women in 1945 at the urging of Mary McLeod Bethune. Supporting her husband in the day-to-day affairs of the Fellowship Church, Thurman directed the church's Intercultural Workshop and traveled extensively. She served as a delegate to the first Inter-American Congress of Women in Guatemala in 1947 and also visited India, Burma, Ceylon, and Cuba. In 1949, Thurman led a delegation to the UNESCO conference in Paris. Two years later, she received recognition in a nationwide poll as an "outstanding woman of the year."[16]

Frances B. Glover's career paralleled Sue Bailey Thurman's in several respects, although the two women followed different career paths. Glover had also followed her husband to San Francisco, when he was selected as the San Francisco Urban League's Industrial Secretary. She also worked with Mary McLeod Bethune as an assistant in the National Youth Administration's Division of Negro Affairs in northern Ohio. Educated at West Virginia State College and Ohio State University, Glover served in San Francisco as secretary to the board of directors at the central YWCA, a member of the board of trustees of Fellowship Church, and became managing editor of the *Sun-Reporter* in 1950. Her position at the *Sun-Reporter* was noteworthy, for it was one of the few instances where a female member of the new black elite was employed in a professional capacity, rather than working as a volunteer.[17]

Anna Magruder, the wife of the influential black minister, E. J. Magruder, became a respected voice in the black community. A native of New Orleans, where she attended New Orleans University and worked as a teacher for ten years, Anna Magruder moved to California in 1909, after her marriage to the Reverend E. J. Magruder. While Reverend Magruder served as pastor of the First A.M.E. Zion Church in San Francisco from 1926 until his death in 1941, Anna Magruder began her own crusade. In 1939, she was elected general chairman of the annual convention of the California Federation of Colored Women's Clubs. But Anna Magruder did not confine her associations solely to black women's organizations. She campaigned for and endorsed local political candidates, worked for the San Francisco USO during the Second World War, was an active member of the NAACP, and later served on the board of directors of the Buchanan Street YMCA. Because Magruder had lived in San Francisco before the war, her background differed sharply from those of Thurman and Glover, who were both wartime migrants. Magruder represented both the views of the old elite, of which her husband had been a member, and the new elite, which included a larger number of professional women.[18]

In contrast to the role of black businessmen in many northern black communities, where they represented a significant sector of the new elite, few black businessmen assumed leadership roles in San Francisco's black community during the World War II era. Black migrants were more inclined to work in Bay Area shipyards, defense industries, government employment, and white-collar jobs than to work in business-related occupations. Heretofore, San Francisco's black population had not been sizable enough to support a class of black entrepreneurs, and few blacks had been successful in gaining white-collar jobs in major San Francisco businesses before 1940. Thus, with the exception of the black funeral director Cecil Finley and black businessman Jefferson Beaver (who later managed the Trans-Bay Savings and Loan Corporation), black businessmen did not play major roles in the new leadership class.[19]

Members of the new leadership differed from their predecessors in another important respect. They sought interracial alliances more zealously than had the old elite. These alliances reflected the confidence of black leadership in white liberals, whites' commitment to participate in the struggle for civil rights, and the perception by both groups that racial progress required multiracial coalitions. Curiously, San Francisco's old elite had not been as interested or as successful in establishing interracial alliances, although it would seem that such alliances would be even more necessary during periods when blacks were fewer in number and wielded far less power and influence. The new elite, however, seized the initiative and created several interracial organizations to address racial problems, including the Church for the Fellowship of All Peoples and the San Francisco Urban League. These two organizations, one religious, the other secular, were both headed by members of the new elite, and they revealed that blacks and whites were now more willing to cooperate to end racial discrimination.

The reasons that Howard Thurman resigned from his comfortable position as Dean of the Chapel and professor of Religion at Howard University were related directly to the need for an interracial alliance between black and white San Franciscans. In 1943, a progressive white faction spearheaded by Dr. Alfred G. Fisk, a Presbyterian clergyman and professor of philosophy at San Francisco State College, asked Thurman to recommend a minister for a proposed interracial church. Fisk was convinced that the liberal wartime atmosphere provided a unique opportunity to engage in a bold interracial experiment. Fisk envisioned an integrated church that would serve the spiritual needs of a broad spectrum of San Franciscans. "I am now serving and expect to become pastor of the new enterprise. But we don't want it to be in any sense run by whites for Negroes," Fisk wrote. Instead, he assured Thurman that "we are committed to a real equality between the races in all aspects of church organization" and thus, the "boards of the church, the choir, and the Sunday School, and its staff will all be of mixed character."[20]

Although acting under the pretense of seeking a recommendation for this novel undertaking, Fisk was cleverly encouraging Dr. Thurman to consider the position on his own accord. Two weeks after the initial correspondence, Fisk confronted Thurman directly: "I wish that I could enable you to see the challenge of this situation as I see it." San Francisco, he continued, "so it seems to me now, is doomed if you do not come. There is no one in the nation who could do what you could do here." Indeed, racial tensions had magnified as a result of the large black influx, but there was no indication that the situation had deteriorated to the point Fisk described as "tensions rising to the breaking point, the outbreak of violence in minor instances with more general rioting only averted by a hair's breadth." San Franciscans had not gone that far.[21]

Thurman accepted the challenge, even though it meant losing his professorship, uprooting his family, and accepting a cut in salary. His belief that God and destiny were both playing some part in the decision did not prevent Thurman from encouraging his contacts to use their influence to support this endeavor. He assured Fisk that "Dr. Channing Tobias and Mrs. Mary McLeod Bethune have offered to write to their friends around the Bay urging them to give every encouragement by attendance and in other ways to the project."[22]

Thurman too was convinced that an interracial church had unlimited potential. He maintained that the church "could provide a genuine source of religious experience and life for a group of interested and committed people." He applauded Fisk's "suggestion that we build our program around the cultural contributions of various groups in San Francisco." Yet several practical concerns weighed in the balance. Would Thurman's commitment be permanent? Or would he return to Howard University after the church was organized? Thurman wrote Fisk candidly, even before his arrival in San Francisco, that "my leave is for one year, but I do not see how I can escape the necessity for having it renewed." Apparently, Thurman had more than a temporary leave in mind, although he was careful to not sever his relations with Howard University.[23]

Thurman expressed another concern regarding his specific role within the church hierarchy: "It is important, it seems to me, to know how well and intimately two men of different races sharing common leadership of a church can work themselves into the life of a community made up of different races." Thurman did not wish to devote a disproportionate amount of his time to peripheral functions. "I do not want to seem to be some kind of ecclesiastical prima donna. Somewhere between these two extremes I hope to find a place of effective leadership."[24] Within six months, the multiracial experiment was officially launched and it met with enthusiasm. Officially named the Church for the Fellowship of All Peoples, it was the first "fully integrated" church in America, according to Thurman. Although that claim has never been proven, the Fellowship Church was at the very least a bold and unparalleled achievement in San Francisco's history.[25]

Fellowship Church established several multicultural programs, and these activities were a bridge into San Francisco's ethnic communities. The church sponsored weekly fellowship lunches with members of the congregation and monthly intercultural fellowship dinners, which celebrated the culture of different groups of church members. It also maintained a library, which collected and circulated materials about different races, religions, and cultures. Weekly forums, coffee hours, and intercultural workshops for children and adults were also part of Fellowship Church's multifaceted program. Howard Thurman believed that these experiences were absolutely essential if people were ever to learn respect for each other as human beings, irrespective of race, religion, and ethnicity. Thus underlying these programs was "a profound conviction that meaningful and creative experiences between people can be more compelling than all the ideas, concepts, faiths, fears, ideologies, and prejudices that divide them." Thurman was optimistic that Christian fellowship under the proper circumstances could erode decades of misconceptions, stereotypes, and racial disharmony.[26]

Despite Thurman's optimism and dedication, Fellowship Church had only a marginal impact on San Francisco's race relations. His church never attracted a large segment of the black community. The church's congregation was predominantly white and it is doubtful whether these white members were exposed to the city's working class blacks. Fellowship Church catered to San Francisco's black elite, and black professionals like D. Donald Glover and Clarence Johnson, a prominent attorney, served on the church's board of directors. Within a decade, Thurman moved the church out of the black community altogether, for fear that it "would become a Negro church in a comparatively short time or disappear entirely."[27]

Thurman's experiment in religious fellowship did not fail, but it achieved only limited success. The church did not accelerate the pace of equality in housing or employment, and Thurman's work in the church kept him from playing more than a peripheral role in the black community. Yet Howard Thurman and Fellowship Church should not be faulted for failing to eradicate racial discrimination single-handedly. The interaction between members of various races was an achievement, though an intangible one. But the multicultural programs, teas, coffee hours, and dinners were small measures, considering the magnitude of the problem. Fellowship Church did succeed in diversifying San Francisco's black ministerial class, for Thurman, unlike his black ministerial colleagues who served the black community exclusively, made a successful entry into the city's multiracial communities and attracted a number of whites to his church.[28]

Fellowship Church was only one of many attempts at interracial unity and cooperation during the 1940s by San Francisco's new elite. Myriad ad hoc and formal interracial committees and organizations were established to address the numerous wartime and postwar racial challenges. The creation of a San Francisco Urban League branch was indicative of this commitment.[29] The 1940s was not the first time local leaders rallied for the establishment of a San Francisco Urban League branch. The formative struggle had been waged almost two decades earlier, but neither the National Urban League office nor influential white civic leaders were convinced that San Francisco's small black community required an Urban League branch during the 1920s. Consequently, the movement was abandoned. But several urgent wartime and postwar problems, particularly the declining postwar economic status of black workers and the adjustment of black migrants, rekindled the drive for a local Urban League.[30]

A small group of black and white leaders led by Dr. Daniel A. Collins worked together to form an Urban League in San Francisco. During the spring of 1944, Collins informed National Urban League Field Secretary Reginald A. Johnson that a "committee of responsible citizens had formed themselves into a sponsoring committee to establish a local Urban League Branch." After obtaining approval from the national office, Collins attempted to persuade a broad sector of business and civic leaders of the necessity for a local branch. He proceeded judiciously to establish a network of supporters. Since Collins already had a firm foothold in the black community through his affiliation with the Booker T. Washington Community Center, the NAACP, and several fraternal organizations, gaining the support of local blacks posed few problems. Moreover, Collins made inroads into several interracial societies, including Fellowship Church, the newly established Council for Civic Unity, and the Commonwealth Club of America.[31]

Obtaining a broad-based constituency was essential, because Urban League branch presidents were as often white as black, executive directors and field secretaries were typically black, and the Boards of Directors were multiracial. Thus, it came as no surprise when Reginald Johnson told Collins that his local committee should be interracial and "if it is not I would suggest that representative key white persons be added."[32] The National Urban League office also believed that a San Francisco branch could establish a stronger program financially if it was multiracial. This would certainly be true in the initial fund-raising campaigns but also as local Urban League officials attempted to build a harmonious relationship with the private sector. The national office indicated that a local branch required "from $7,000 to $8,000 to establish an Urban League in a community." Consequently, the cooperation and financial support of business, civic, and community leaders of all races were fundamental to the success of this endeavor.[33]

With these precautions in mind, the San Francisco Urban League Sponsoring Committee worked closely with Eva Hance, director of the social planning department of the San Francisco Community Chest. Reginald Johnson felt that Hance was "well acquainted with the Urban League program" and that her strategic position on the agency that funded most local programs was a potential boon to local leaders. Hence, Reginald Johnson's carefully worded advice to Collins: that Eva Hance "will be in [an] excellent position to advise your committee on its relationship with the Community Chest." Johnson, who planned to visit the Bay Area in order to assist the sponsoring committee, recommended that the two organizations work closely together "in order that your mutual efforts will dovetail."[34]

By the end of the year, Daniel Collins had secured enough interracial community support to make a formal request for funding to the local community chest. The sponsoring committee included, among others, Harry L. Kingman, FEPC regional director, Joseph James, NAACP president, Alfred G. Fisk, professor of philosophy at San Francisco State College and organizer of Fellowship Church, Reverend A. Morgan Tabb, Rector of St. Cyprians Episcopal Church, Robert Flippin, director of the Booker T. Washington Community Center, and Reverend Francis Drescher of St. Benedict the Moor Catholic Church. Collins could not have orchestrated a more prestigious and broad-based committee.[35]

Despite these optimistic signs, the sponsoring committee seemed, at first, to accomplish little beyond its initial meeting. Keeping the National Urban League office abreast of the committee's progress, Collins reported that "there has been no meeting of the Board of Directors since the first organizational meeting." Collins seems to have waved a red flag prematurely, because the committee progressed considerably within the course of a year. Problems of a far more serious nature arose from critics in the black community. Robert Flippin opposed the Urban League because he wished to expand his power as executive director of the Booker T. Washington Community Center. He tried to convince black leaders that the community center could also serve as an employment agency under his jurisdiction. But the center was in no position to function as an Urban League. It lacked the funds, expertise, and personnel.[36]

The National Urban League office was not concerned with Flippin's ploy. Reginald Johnson described the "recent flare-up" as "merely a repeat of several self-seeking interests that should cause only temporary. delay in the establishment of a league unit there." In his characteristically confident tone, Johnson informed National Urban League executive director, Eugene Kinckle Jones, that he expected a budget within the "next few weeks." But Johnson also warned Collins that the national office might look favorably upon the reorganization of the Booker T. Washington Community Center and the strengthening of its program along with the establishment of an Urban League branch. In his attempt to lessen Collins's apprehension, Johnson confided, "There is plenty of room and need for a strong center and a strong league branch, and they will both need each other."[37] The National Urban League office eventually rejected Flippin's suggestion to strengthen the community center. Instead, it granted a charter to the San Francisco Urban League branch.

The San Francisco Urban League achieved few significant breakthroughs for black workers during its first decade. Rather, it focused on maintaining the employment gains blacks had achieved during World War II. Seaton W. Manning and D. Donald Glover established a broad network of business and industrial contacts throughout the San Francisco Bay Area and encouraged them to continue hiring black workers in semiskilled, skilled, white-collar, and professional jobs. Manning believed that blacks must continue to make progress in jobs that were under the jurisdiction of organized labor, particularly the AFL. The Urban League's executive secretary was well aware that opportunities within the ranks of organized labor had been slow in coming for black San Franciscans, and he was equally aware that many labor unions still excluded blacks because of their race after 1945. By 1950, Manning informed Lester B. Granger that limited breakthroughs had been achieved for blacks as bank tellers, salesmen, clerks, and secretaries. And while the San Francisco Urban League could not take complete credit for these achievements, Manning wrote that "we have sound reason to believe that their action has been stimulated by the [Urban] League's persistent pecking and the Damoclean horrors of an FEP [Fair Employment Practices] law."[38]

The new black leaders and their respective organizations profoundly improved San Francisco's race relations in both tangible and intangible ways. Although few concrete gains were realized immediately, the numerous interracial forums, meetings, and workshops they sponsored committed San Franciscans to the ideals of racial equality and equal opportunity who might otherwise have been unaffected. They also alerted black San Franciscans that more whites than ever before were committed to equal opportunity for blacks. And even though they challenged the old elite for status and leadership positions, their presence was not perceived as a threat to the existing leadership. The continuity of their racial strategies with those of the old elite made the transition in black leadership a relatively smooth process in San Francisco during the Second World War era.

11

THE GROWTH AND FLOWERING
OF INTERRACIAL ORGANIZATIONS

The Second World War accelerated interracial activism in San Francisco, as it did in many cities between 1940 and 1945. The new interracial leadership was buttressed by an impressive number of broad-based organizations and committees, many of which were a direct result of the large-scale influx of black migrants during World War II. Deeply conscious of their city's national image, these men and women expanded the activities of existing protest and civil rights organizations and established new challenges and priorities in their quest to improve the city's racial climate and to procure access to jobs and housing for black San Franciscans. They attempted to end racial discrimination in almost every area of the city. Relishing their role as San Francisco's new interracial leadership class, these individuals dominated the executive committees and the boards of directors of almost every major civil rights organization. Their organizations also attracted professional men and women of all races, who often worked closely with a diversity of civil rights leaders. Moreover, both the old black elite and the new elite welcomed the forging of interracial coalitions.[1]

At the outbreak of World War II, the San Francisco branch of the NAACP was still the preeminent civil rights organization in the city. Although it drew its membership from a broad sector of San Francisco society and had not forsaken the interracial leanings of its forebears, its small core of active leadership remained predominantly black. Between 1940 and 1943, however, the San Francisco NAACP experienced dissension, strife, and leadership disputes. Consequently, the branch's energy, resources, and creativity were too frequently expended attempting to settle internal conflicts rather than serving the local community.[2]

In light of the NAACP's disunity, black and white leaders established several organizations to curb discrimination and to offer leadership and direction in race relations. The Bay Area Council against Discrimination (BACAD) was the prototype for the interracial societies established during the Second World War. Committed to solving a broad spectrum of racial problems and attracting an impressive group of multiracial leaders, the organization began its full-fledged program in 1942. The Council's leadership was drawn not only from San Francisco, but also from the surrounding cities of Oakland, Berkeley, Richmond, and Alameda. The BACAD sought to construct a multiethnic coalition, and many racial and ethnic groups were represented within the organization.[3]

Prominent East Bay black attorney Walter Gordon served as the BACAD's first chairman. By the Second World War, Gordon had emerged as one of the most respected and influential black leaders in the state. Born in Atlanta, Georgia, Gordon migrated to Riverside, California, with his family at the age of ten and subsequently completed high school in this Southern California community. Gordon entered the University of California, Berkeley in 1914, but made his most memorable contributions in athletics. He excelled in the boxing ring and on the gridiron and was selected to Walter Camp's prestigious All-American Football team in 1918.[4]

Gordon's postcollegiate career was equally impressive. After completing his law degree at the University of California's Boalt Hall, Gordon joined the Berkeley police force. While working as a full-time policeman and practicing law simultaneously, Gordon took active leadership roles in many community organizations. As president of the Alameda County chapter of the NAACP for fourteen years, Gordon solidified his leadership position among East Bay blacks. His subsequent election to the Commonwealth Club of California, the executive board of the University of California YMCA, and the Lawyers' Guild of San Francisco strengthened his position among Bay Area white liberals as well. Gordon's rising stature was undoubtedly an important factor in his selection by Governor Earl Warren as a member of California's Board of Prison Terms and Paroles in 1943. Warren thought so highly of Gordon that he appointed him to head the new California Adult Authority in 1945. Gordon later served as both governor and as U.S. district judge for the Virgin Islands.[5]

Despite his stature in the community, Gordon did not have a marked influence on the BACAD's policy. He was largely a figurehead, since the BACAD's executive committee, rather than an autocratic leader, directed the organization's focus. In addition, numerous subcommittees were established in potentially controversial areas, such as labor and housing. Hence, members worked through the varied subcommittees, contributing to the BACAD in their areas of interest or expertise. As a result, an outstanding labor leader such as C. L. Dellums could put the weight and financial status of his union, the Oakland division of the Brotherhood of Sleeping Car Porters, behind the BACAD's program.[6]

The BACAD worked diligently to ally itself with established organizations and institutions. Thus, within the formative months of the organization, the temporary executive committee recommended that membership should be open to both individuals and organizations. But attracting a broad spectrum of organizations did not appear to be a particularly pressing concern for the BACAD. Representatives from organizations like the Jewish Survey Council, the Brotherhood of Sleeping Car Porters, the California CIO, the Marine Cooks and Stewards, and the War Manpower Commission were active. Within two years, the BACAD was composed of representatives from more than seventy organizations. It had become the Bay Area's premier omnibus organization.[7]

The BACAD's avowed purpose was to end discrimination against all racial, ethnic, and religious groups. It devised an ambitious program, which included legislation against discrimination in housing, employment, and public accommodations. The BACAD's labor subcommittee also worked closely with the War Manpower Commission to press for an end to racial discrimination in the hiring, promotion, and upgrading policies of organized labor.[8]

The BACAD pushed with equal vigor in the housing arena. It published pamphlets that informed the public about housing laws and worked with organizations such as the San Francisco Housing and Planning Association. The BACAD's housing subcommittee also spearheaded a drive to introduce a bill in the California State Assembly banning restrictive covenants and strengthening the state's civil rights statute. Understandably, the BACAD took a keen interest in public hearings conducted by the San Francisco Board of Supervisors regarding housing discrimination.[9]

As blacks increasingly reported "difficulties in renting private housing, and their inability to secure housing in public housing projects other than the [integrated] Westside Court project," the BACAD presented a far-reaching plan, which it urged the San Francisco city fathers to adopt. First, the BACAD advocated a policy of nondiscrimination and nonsegregation for the San Francisco Housing Authority. It also demanded that the emergency War Housing Center, created to address the serious wartime housing shortage, make referrals to private housing without discrimination. Finally, the BACAD asked the San Francisco Board of Supervisors to adopt a general public policy of nondiscrimination. These were ambitious goals under the best of circumstances, but reaching these goals in a city racked by wartime dislocation, overcrowding, and increasing racial tensions would be a monumental achievement.[10]

When the BACAD was not locked in a struggle against Jim Crow, the organization urged prestigious national organizations like the FEPC and the War Manpower Commission to take a more aggressive posture in fighting racial discrimination. The War Manpower Commission's national director, for example, could not have been pleased when the BACAD's monthly newsletter reported that "the War Manpower Commission in its Washington, regional and local offices still have failed to come to grips with the problem of discrimination" and that the agency "has not yet undertaken any positive activity to meet the problem." The BACAD also criticized the FEPC. "Although the crippled Committee on Fair Employment Practice is still continuing to function," the BACAD wrote, "its status is unclear, its power uncertain." However, the BACAD commended the FEPC when a regional office opened in San Francisco in September 1943 and Harry L. Kingman was appointed regional director.[11]

Although the two organizations worked closely between 1943 and 1944 investigating alleged complaints of racial, ethnic, and religious discrimination throughout the San Francisco Bay Area, the BACAD could not compete with the federally funded FEPC. The BACAD's expenses for its first year of operation were a mere $1,700. Although the organization attempted to raise $10,000 to hire a full-time director and simultaneously expand its program, it never succeeded. The BACAD's treasury contained less than $1000 by the end of 1943. Thus, the organization relied on volunteers to sustain its programs, many of whom were employed in demanding jobs and also had commitments to other agencies. The lack of both resources and a full-time staff proved to be the BACAD's Achilles' heel.[12]

The BACAD never achieved its goal of eliminating all racial discrimination in the Bay Area, but it did make progress in that direction. Since the BACAD was largely a pressure group and a fact-finding agency, its concrete achievements are difficult to measure. The organization took partial credit, however, for the hiring of the first black motorman on the San Francisco Municipal Railway system, though it had little impact in the employment gains of black workers. The BACAD's major achievement was the pressure that it exerted on city officials, the business community, and trade unions. It opened the lines of communication between the races and pushed vigorously for uniform policies of nondiscrimination.[13] At the same time, it succeeded in creating an atmosphere of egalitarianism and good will among a much wider group of individuals in the

Bay Area. Yet its concrete achievements were modest, and its major goals were never realized. It would take much more than an interracial committee of distinguished Bay Area leaders to end racial discrimination.[14]

The BACAD faded quietly from the scene in mid-1944 because of apathy and the lack of resources. In a matter of months, however, the San Francisco Council for Civic Unity (CCU) was organized, and the CCU became the most ambitious interracial organization in the city. Councils for Civic Unity were established in many American cities during the Second World War in an effort to improve the racial climate after the large wartime migration of blacks. In its scope, funding, and longevity, San Francisco's CCU far exceeded its predecessor, the BACAD. Within two years the CCU blossomed as the major interracial society in San Francisco, rivaling the local chapter of the NAACP.[15]

The CCU's ambitious program was attributed in large measure to its second executive director, a young white liberal named Edward Howden. A native of Oakland, Howden grew up in the Bay Area and attended the University of California, Berkeley. As an undergraduate philosophy major, Howden was active in campus affairs, including Stiles Hall, the campus YMCA. In this liberal environment, Howden also encountered a variety of racial problems and came under the influence of Harry L. Kingman, Stiles Hall's executive director. After Howden completed his military obligation in 1946, he was invited to apply for the CCU's top post by the Columbia Foundation's director, who knew of Howden's previous work in public housing as executive director of the California Housing and Planning Association. Heeding the foundation director's advice, Howden applied for the slot, which had been vacant for two years, and obtained the position.[16]

Howden's tenure as the CCU's executive director coincided with several significant developments for interracial societies in the San Francisco Bay Area. Prior to the Second World War, civil rights organizations in the San Francisco Bay Area were manned and run almost exclusively by blacks. Indeed, whites were allowed to become members and to participate in the general business affairs of organizations like the NAACP, but their membership was primarily symbolic. Whites were welcomed principally for their financial contributions and their status in the community. The Second World War, however, changed both the "complexion" of Bay Area civil rights organizations and the positions that whites were permitted to assume within these organizations. No longer were whites merely token executive board members and honorary lifetime members. Instead, men like Edward Howden and Harry L. Kingman were among the major figures who devised a good deal of the strategy and plotted the direction that their respective organizations and agencies would follow. Only the San Francisco branch of the NAACP and the National Urban League retained a consistent policy of electing black chief executives.[17]

Regardless of his race, the CCU's executive director would have his hands full in San Francisco. The city's black population had increased more than 600 percent in four short years, to over 32,000. Housing was in short supply, ghettoization was advancing, and the rapid postwar decline in defense industries spelled a high unemployment rate for black workers. Racial tensions were also increasing, and police brutality against Afro-Americans was on the rise. The national image of San Francisco's race relations was tarnished for the first time since the anti-Chinese campaigns of the late nineteenth century.[18]

Howden, along with his board of directors, plotted a strategy to address these problems. Howden stated years later that his method and priorities were quite simple: "I picked major issues and started slugging away at them. That was the only strategy I knew." Howden understated his ability to chart an agenda on sensitive racial issues, for he proved systematic and thorough in his quest to erode discriminatory barriers in San Francisco.[19]

Howden believed that the CCU's program was "similar to that of other organizations in the [civil rights] field." It sought to end discrimination in "housing, employment, health, recreation, welfare, and civil rights generally." In addition, the CCU ran an "active information-education program" to disseminate information and to increase public awareness of its activities. If the CCU had a philosophy, it was best expressed in the United States Constitution and the numerous natural rights pamphlets upon which the nation's heritage and freedoms were constructed. But in Howden's view, this philosophical foundation did not include segregation laws. Speaking at the Fifth Annual Fisk University Institute of Race Relations in Nashville, Tennessee, Howden remarked, "We must change existing practices and conditions of discrimination as rapidly as possible."[20] Choosing to underscore the moral and ethical implications of discrimination, Howden argued that "allowing persons of whatever group to take their places in the community on the basis of individual merit is not only essential to securing justice, but is of significant educational value for majority groups." Moreover, Howden believed that the dominant white population was "more or less neutral or only passively interested in the values for which we stand." Yet he remained optimistic and concluded that the "reservoir of good will" could be tapped through a sensitive program and the "proper techniques."[21]

The CCU succeeded in attracting a large membership and creating a strong financial base from the outset. At its peak, the membership roles of the CCU listed between 1700 and 1800 members, including many politically and socially prominent San Franciscans. Although only a small percentage of members participated actively in the organization, the majority, according to Howden, found "satisfaction in assisting and supporting the organization and in a general identification with its purposes and program." Yet Howden maintained that "strength of membership in numbers and prestige is extremely important," because an active membership gave the CCU the financial security that most civil rights organizations envied.[22]

The lion's share of the CCU's budget, however, came from contributions by local foundations. The Columbia and Rosenberg foundations, in particular, funded this maverick organization during its formative years. The CCU's annual budget, which ranged between $25,000 to $30,000, made it the best-endowed civil rights organization in Northern California. Annual memberships and fund raising drives were also important sources of funding, but they merely supplemented foundation support.[23]

The CCU's impact on San Francisco's race relations varied, but it did play an important role in the elimination of segregation in some of the city's hospitals. Even after 1940, black doctors were denied hospital privileges and barred from using the facilities of most of the city's public and private hospitals to treat their patients.[24] Moreover, some black patients were segregated in Jim Crow wards, along with other nonwhite patients. The CCU and San Francisco's interracial leadership worked to alter this policy, although it took more than five years of concerted pressure to eradicate the practice completely.[25]

The CCU also reported that black medical students had difficulty gaining entry to medical schools in San Francisco. Only two black students, reported the CCU, were enrolled in Bay Area medical schools in 1947. And although many black doctors had migrated to San Francisco during World War II, only one black physician for every 6,667 black residents practiced in San Francisco, in sharp contrast with the city-wide ratio of one doctor per 475 residents.[26] With few exceptions, then, San Francisco's small pool of black physicians had been trained in southern black medical schools.

Both the CCU and black leadership learned that these problems were not easily resolved and that racism was deeply rooted within San Francisco's white medical community. The number of black patients denied access to white medical institutions may never be known. The fact that one black woman was instructed by the nurse of a white physician that he did not "see or take Negro patients" may well have been a peculiarity of one doctor. On the other hand, the San Francisco County Medical Society informed Franklin Williams, the NAACP's regional director, that even though the majority of member physicians treat all patients, doctors "maintain the freedom of choice of patients in accordance with the American Medical Association Principles of Medical Ethics. A physician is free to choose whom he serves." Williams questioned whether this practice violated a physician's Hippocratic oath, but a county medical official maintained that "there is no infringement in the instance you cited." Unable to persuade the white medical establishment that its policies were inconsistent with the city's liberal postwar ideals, the CCU and black leadership would press the issue of equal access to hospitals and medical facilities into the next decade.[27]

Though the CCU did not succeed immediately in halting discrimination against black physicians and black patients, the organization was more successful in other areas. Edward Howden devised and orchestrated a wide-ranging program to end segregation in employment, public accommodations, housing, and urban redevelopment. The CCU lobbied both local and state officials to pass nondiscriminatory laws in these areas and to adopt a statewide FEPC. The CCU also attempted to heighten racial awareness by publishing periodic newsletters and reports. A monthly newsletter, "Among These Rights," summarized the CCU's activities, and comprehensive surveys in the areas of health and employment buttressed the organization's contention that discrimination was widespread throughout the city.[28]

Howden also used the radio airwaves effectively to push the CCU's program before the public. For six years he narrated the weekly radio program, "Dateline Freedom." The fifteen-minute program followed the Sunday-night news and was devoted exclusively to race relations. "Dateline Freedom" was the only program of its kind in California when it first aired in 1952. No other western state covered civil rights issues so extensively over a major radio network. Howden attributed the program's success to several factors. Many citizens of all races, he believed, were starved for racial information, and "Dateline Freedom" provided an analysis of race relations throughout the entire nation. Fortunately, the program initially followed the CBS Sunday-night news, which had a large radio audience during the 1950s, and Howden realized that the back-to-back scheduling of the two programs was an added drawing card. When the show was moved to a less popular Saturday night time slot, Howden confirmed that his listening audience declined. Furthermore, Howden acknowledged that the program's summary and analysis format, which he used to discuss racial issues, was tantamount to editorializing on the air but that it appealed to many people. Although the program aired for only fifteen minutes, its major segment was thirteen-and-a-half minutes of uninterrupted news. Howden was a forceful speaker and an accomplished interviewer, and he utilized this time wisely.[29]

"Dateline Freedom" was regularly excerpted in the black press, which heightened its popularity. The *Sun-Reporter* summarized the program's highlights in its weekly columns, illustrating the cooperation between black leadership and interracial organizations. Understandably, the weekly radio program and the corresponding news column became symbols of achievement for many San Franciscans. Whereas white liberals boasted that San Francisco confronted its racial problems squarely and sensitively, blacks took pride in knowing that a major network program discussed their plight. Howden recalled years later that people of all races would come up to him on the streets and express how much they missed his show and how well he informed them about race relations in the San Francisco Bay Area as well as on the national scene. These were the black community's "fireside chats," and the CCU struck a responsive multiracial chord in this pioneering venture.[30]

Despite the effectiveness of the San Francisco Council for Civic Unity, Howden and many other black and white leaders were unwilling to let racial issues fall entirely on the shoulders of one organization. By 1946, the San Francisco CCU worked closely with the NAACP, the American Council on Race Relations (ACRR), and the Pacific Coast Committee on American Principles and Fair Play to form a statewide interracial omnibus organization. Organizing a statewide federation of civic rights and civil liberties organizations was no easy task, but a group of interracial leaders, which included Ruth W. Kingman, Joseph James, and Laurence Hewes, seized the initiative.[31]

Ruth Kingman, the wife of the FEPC's West Coast regional director, Harry L. Kingman, was but one of a score of women who contributed to civil rights organizations. Even though she worked in the shadow of her husband much of her life, the Los Gatos, California, native did not shy away from controversial issues. A respected community activist whose father was a Methodist minister, Ruth Kingman was committed to racial equality. "At home, as a child, I wasn't raised with any degree of race prejudice of any kind. I think that if I had ever shown any degree of race prejudice I would have been punished," recalled Kingman, reflecting upon her upbringing.[32] As a student at San Francisco's Mission High School, Kingman "ran into many Orientals, but very few blacks."[33] Her early contact with Asians explains in part why she persuaded many business and civic leaders throughout the state to organize the Pacific

Coast Committee on American Principles and Fair Play. The Fair Play Committee, as it came to be known, attempted to obtain justice for the Japanese who were relocated during the war. When the Fair Play Committee's business abruptly came to an end in December 1945, Kingman and others realized that the "problems facing the Japanese Americans were not entirely distinct from those facing other racial groups." Consequently, several statewide organizing committees convened with the ACRR to form the California Council for Civic Unity (CCCU) in 1946. Ruth Kingman was elected the organization's first president, one of three female chief executives that the CCCU would elect during its first decade.[34]

Ruth Kingman acknowledged the role of several organizations that were instrumental in the CCCU's founding. None, however, was more critical than the ACRR. Kingman, on more than one occasion, stated that the "development of the CCCU would have been greatly retarded" without the support of ACRR's board of directors, which included Pearl S. Buck, Ralph J. Bunche, Marshall Field, and Charles S. Johnson. According to its bylaws, the organization was committed to rendering "assistance to local communities in organizing to meet their interracial problems where existing programs seem inadequate." In 1946, the ACRR established a Pacific Coast office based in San Francisco. Assisting local leaders to form the CCCU was one of its priorities.[35]

Within eighteen months after its inception, the CCCU emerged as a viable federation of interracial organizations. To be sure, the organization benefited from the atmosphere of postwar liberalism, for only four months after its incorporation, the CCCU claimed more than forty member organizations. Ruth Kingman reported that such diverse groups as the NAACP, the YWCA, the Jewish Survey, and the B'nai B'rith Committee applied for membership.[36] By virtue of its diverse member organizations, the CCCU attracted some of the most influential civic, community, and business leaders throughout the state.

The CCCU charted an ambitious course during its formative years. The organization claimed to serve as a "clearing house, consultant, coordinator, [and] statewide action group." The CCCU's board of directors adopted a series of goals and priorities consistent with the aims of its predecessors, the BACAD and the CCU. They included equal access to employment, public accommodations, public services, and private institutions. The organization addressed such diverse problems as discrimination in the insurance industry to discrimination in the California National Guard. The CCCU's board of directors affirmed "that all human relationships short of free and unsegregated living for all persons are contrary to American democracy."[37]

As the CCCU fought for recognition and legitimacy, it gradually severed its relationship with the ACRR. The CCCU's break with the ACRR was not the result of an ideological schism between the two organizations, but rather the ACRR's insistence that the CCCU assume its own identity, much like a young adult breaking away from its parents. Consequently, by the spring of 1947, the ACRR made plans to close its San Francisco office. Laurence J. Hewes, the ACRR's Pacific Coast director, affirmed that "it is the hope of the ACRR that a good many of its responsibilities to the community can be passed on to the CCCU."[38]

Hewes's suggestion that the CCCU become the successor agency to the ACRR troubled Ruth Kingman, who felt strongly that the ACRR's withdrawal from the Bay Area would "detract sharply from the effectiveness of the CCCU program." Nevertheless, ACRR president Louis Wirth was adamant, yet he assured Kingman that his agency would not pull out of the city immediately. He promised to keep the San Francisco office open on a "reduced basis" or "as long as is necessary" to meet current obligations.[39]

The CCCU's prospective autonomy probably frightened Kingman for several reasons. First, the ACRR would no longer provide financial support to her organization, which meant that Kingman would have to tap state foundations and private benefactors for funding. Moreover, Kingman might have doubted her ability to run the CCCU effectively without the ACRR's expertise. The ACRR's staff and board of directors, which included Louis Wirth as well as Lester Granger, executive director of the National Urban League, Charles S. Johnson, Walter White, and the novelist Richard Wright, were impressive. But autonomy did not require complete disassociation of the CCCU and the ACRR. The ACRR would continue to assist the CCCU in structuring its program and issue "advice and technical knowledge" as the occasion warranted.[40]

By summer, Ruth Kingman was much more confident. Resigned to the break, she began to prepare the CCCU's affiliates accordingly. Caroline MacChesney, Kingman's good friend and the future CCCU president, plotted her heretofore cautious friend's course in straightforward language: "Someone has to move in, concentrate on individual contacts and do the footwork. You and I recognized that necessity before." A month later, Kingman informed Louis Wirth that "you would be interested and pleased to see the manner in which the CCCU is rapidly achieving adulthood since my return from Chicago."[41] Kingman requested that the

CCCU's board of directors hold their annual meeting "at the earliest practicable date" to discuss the "changed relationship with the American Council on Race Relations."[42]

The break between the two organizations did not affect leadership or policy within the CCCU, and most Californians were probably unaware that a transition had occurred. With the exception of a name change the following year to the California Federation for Civic Unity (CFCU), this statewide coalition of interracial organizations continued to address racial issues in the broadest possible context.[43]

The number of interracial organizations established between 1942 and 1946 gave evidence of the San Francisco Bay Area's commitment to build a benign and nondiscriminatory racial order. San Francisco, by virtue of the creation of the BACAD, CCU, and CFCU, emerged as the center of interracial leadership in the state of California and throughout the Pacific Coast. (In contrast, Los Angeles, Seattle, and Portland failed to develop a comparably diverse group of interracial societies or the aggressive leadership that emerged in San Francisco.[44]) These multifaceted organizations were designed to eliminate racial discrimination totally, and never before in the city's history had so many San Franciscans of all races united for this purpose. Yet the concrete achievements of these organizations were modest, and numerous racial barriers in housing, employment, and public accommodations existed until the end of the decade. Interracial societies were most effective as fact-finding agencies and as forums for educating the public on the inherent contradictions of racial discrimination in an era when the nation was moving toward full equality for all of its citizens. Only the San Francisco CCU employed a direct action program to eliminate racial discrimination, and every agency underestimated the extent of discrimination against blacks. Additionally, the reliance on volunteers by some organizations made consistent and sustained programming difficult. Nonetheless, San Francisco went further than other American cities, such as Milwaukee, Detroit, Chicago, and Evansville, but it was still not quite ready to guarantee blacks full participation in the city's burgeoning opportunities.[45]

12

POSTWAR EMPLOYMENT: GAINS AND LOSSES

Postwar employment progress proceeded slowly for black San Franciscans. To be sure, blacks had made impressive wartime employment gains, but many areas remained restricted because of race. Between 1945 and 1954, blacks continued to work with white allies to crush every remaining vestige of racial discrimination in employment. These campaigns achieved only mixed success, however, as San Franciscans were not entirely ready to ignore race when making employment decisions. Black workers had a particularly difficult time making the transition from defense employment to permanent employment in the private sector, and black women continued to face even greater obstacles because of their gender. Yet black workers slowly began to integrate many businesses and corporations that had hired few blacks either before or during the war. Moreover, black professionals would be hired to teach in the San Francisco Unified School District for the first time since the nineteenth century. San Francisco, despite its unwillingness to eradicate all racial barriers in employment, would be far more open and integrated on the eve of the historic 1954 *Brown v. the Board of Education of Topeka, Kansas* decision than at any previous time in the city's history.

Instead of a large postwar out-migration, San Francisco's black population continued to grow between 1945 and 1950. The 1950 federal census reported 43,460 blacks in San Francisco, a staggering 904 percent increase from the 1940 population. The Urban League's executive director, Seaton W. Manning, informed Lester B. Granger in 1950 that the "migration of Negroes into San Francisco and the Bay Area is still continuing," and "I find it hard to believe that there are any Negroes left in Texas and Louisiana." While the local branch of the NAACP reported that the black populace had swelled to 55,000 by 1951, the black population had not in fact registered another phenomenal increase in the space of a year. Instead, its growth had begun to slow by the early 1950s, at least by the standards of the previous decade, and its demographic pattern would become more typical of black urban communities.[1]

As early as 1944, black migrants had shown an inclination to remain in the Bay Area, when a northern California industry survey revealed that only 15 percent of black workers expected to return home at the war's end. One-third of white workers surveyed indicated a desire to return to their former location. Though the survey did not reveal the black workers' reasons for wishing to remain in California, it is likely that the majority of black migrants believed they had found a better life for themselves and their children in California. Two-thirds of the black newcomers had migrated from southern states, where postwar economic opportunities were few, where segregation was sanctioned by state law, and where fear and racial violence had been an integral part of their world. Those memories were probably uppermost in their minds.[2]

Several additional factors stimulated the black community's postwar growth. Unlike the pre–World War II years, when black workers made only marginal progress in semiskilled and skilled jobs, blacks made relatively significant gains in organized labor between 1941 and 1950. Fred Stripp interviewed 205 Bay Area union officials affiliated with the American Federation of Labor and the Congress of Industrial Organizations and concluded that significant changes had occurred in the policies of many locals. More than nine thousand black workers, noted Stripp, composed 9 percent of seventy-six San Francisco locals. Many blacks were still employed in the service sector, but one-third of black union members now worked in the building trades, 26 percent in the food and clothing industry, and 14 percent in metal and machinery. Greater diversity was evident in the positions held by blacks in labor unions, and these gains were impressive when measured against the number of union locals that had reported black members before the war. Moreover, the eradication of segregated locals and auxiliaries accelerated during the 1940s, though discriminatory practices continued openly in a number of affiliates.[3]

Black occupational advances also occurred more frequently in white-collar, civil service, and professional jobs. Before 1940, blacks had either been excluded from these areas or employed in them sparingly. Yet according to the San Francisco Urban League, black workers gradually began to penetrate the private sector as clerks, stenographers, office personnel, and secretaries. Some banks, insurance companies, and corporations, such as the Pacific Gas and Electric Company (PG&E) and

Pacific Telephone and Telegraph (PT&T), were also lifting the racial veil that had excluded blacks from many white-collar jobs.[4]

The occupational gains by Bay Area black females, though less dramatic than those made by black men, were nonetheless significant. Although one study reported that only 18 percent of Bay Area black women reported domestic service as their occupation in 1948 (down from two-thirds in 1940), the 1950 federal census reported a much higher percentage. By 1950, 52 percent of black women in the San Francisco-Oakland metropolitan area were servants. Although black females still worked at

Table 12.1. Occupations by Race, Sex, and Ethnic Group,
San Francisco–Oakland Standard Metropolitan Area, 1950
(in percentage)

	White	Negro	Other races
Males			
Agriculture, forestry, fisheries	2.5	0.6	11.1
Mining	0.2	0.07	—
Construction	10.0	14.1	1.5
Manufacturing	23.6	17.3	9.4
Transportation	12.5	19.2	4.9
Wholesale and retail trade	22.0	9.8	36.9
Finance, insurance, and real estate	5.2	2.3	2.4
Business and repair services	4.0	2.7	1.4
Personal services	3.3	6.8	19.3
Entertainment and recreation	1.4	0.9	0.8
Professional	6.5	5.6	5.2
Public administration	7.9	19.4	5.9
Females			
Agriculture, forestry, fisheries	0.5	0.1	3.8
Mining	0.05	—	—
Construction	0.9	0.3	0.3
Manufacturing	14.2	6.9	17.2
Transportation	7.2	3.1	2.9
Wholesale and retail trade	26.1	12.1	20.9
Finance, insurance, and real estate	9.5	1.9	8.7
Business and repair services	2.0	0.4	1.1
Personal services	10.3	52.9	22.1
Entertainment and recreation	1.3	0.5	0.5
Professional	19.4	12.0	11.4
Public administration	6.8	8.6	9.3

Source: United States Bureau of the Census, Census of Population: 1950, vol. 2, Characteristics of the Population, pt. 5, California (Washington, D.C.: Government Printing Office, 1952), pp. 356–58. The 1950 census reported detailed occupation statistics by race and gender only for the San Francisco–Oakland Metropolitan area, rather than for San Francisco alone.

the lowest occupational levels, important strides had been made in many areas.[5] The Second World War may have not been a watershed for black female workers, as William Chafe and others have argued; nevertheless, a larger percentage of black women than ever before were employed as unskilled and semiskilled laborers, clerks, secretaries, managers, and professionals.

Black professionals, both male and female, also found fewer obstacles in their path during the 1940s. Blacks were more likely to gain employment as managers, proprietors, and professional workers than ever before. The San Francisco Unified School District had hired its first black teacher, Josephine Cole, in 1944, and several others, along with a black principal, would follow. Cole's breakthrough was an important achievement for black San Franciscans, for San Francisco had lagged behind Oakland, Los Angeles, Portland, and Seattle in hiring black teachers. Cole was the first black teacher employed by the school district since the 1870s, when several black teachers were hired to teach exclusively in the Jim Crow school that had been established for black children. Moreover, black policemen were just beginning to integrate San Francisco's police force during the postwar years, although Pittsburgh had already hired fifty black policemen and firemen by 1930 and Lincoln, Nebraska, had employed eight black police officers during the 1890s. San Francisco's fire department, however, did not hire a black fireman until 1955. The fire department's reluctance to integrate its ranks stemmed in part from the long-standing tradition of an all-white fire department in San Francisco and the revulsion of some white firemen to sharing their living facilities with blacks, a factor that the police department did not have to consider. The wartime migration also brought at least a dozen black physicians and attorneys to San Francisco, swelling the ranks of the black professionals and the new black elite.[6]

R. J. Reynolds and William McKinley Thomas were typical of this emerging black professional class during the postwar years. Reynolds, a black attorney, had served as president of the Topeka, Kansas, branch of the NAACP for a decade before migrating to San Francisco in 1946. What motivated Reynolds to move to San Francisco after practicing law for seventeen years in Topeka is unclear. Perhaps he sensed that the racial tide had changed enough during the war years to attempt a professional career in San Francisco. Yet Reynolds was not naive. "I can feel an undercurrent [of racial prejudice] and see the effect of subtle forces at work," he wrote in 1947.[7] Reynolds remained optimistic, though, and urged San Franciscans to keep the city a "citadel for minorities." He joined the NAACP and was elected branch president in 1951. Reynolds succeeded in gaining a position under the city's district attorney, Edmund G. Brown, the state's future governor, and he was later appointed by the city attorney as the first black deputy district attorney in San Francisco.[8]

The black physician William McKinley Thomas pursued an equally distinguished career as a public servant. Educated at Wiley College, Meharry Medical School, the Harvard School of Public Health, and the Army Medical Field Service School, Thomas, like Carlton Goodlett, was a committed community activist as well as a respected physician.[9] A proud "Alf Landon Republican," Thomas was a staunch defender of Republican party politics. While residing in Kansas during the 1930s, Thomas had been an alternate delegate to the 1936 Republican National Convention. Migrating to California did not change his political allegiance, for Thomas served as a member of the San Francisco County Republican Central Committee. Thomas also served as a housing authority commissioner from 1946 to 1950, the first black San Franciscan to hold this prestigious political post.[10]

Reynolds and Thomas were exceptional men by any standard, and their advancement illustrated the success of the new elite in obtaining political appointments during the postwar years. No longer were black leaders content to settle for positions as pages and messengers. The new elite demanded to share in San Francisco's decision making process at all levels, and with the enormous increase in the black voting population between 1940 and 1945, white politicians and policy makers were more willing to listen than ever before. The achievements of Reynolds and Thomas were also concrete evidence that black professionals could advance beyond their narrow, race-based constituency in the black community. Apparently, there really was room for more than one black professional in the white man's club in San Francisco. However, black female professionals did not advance as rapidly as their male counterparts. The plight of rank-and-file black workers was even less encouraging.

Black San Franciscans' perceptions of postwar economic opportunities were often skewed by the tremendous demand for black employment that existed during World War II. Since most blacks were wartime migrants and had not competed with whites for employment under normal circumstances, they underestimated employment discrimination in San Francisco. Thus, the rapid layoffs and the high black unemployment rate that followed the armistice were a rude awakening for many blacks. Bay Area shipyards reduced their work forces to a fraction of the peak wartime levels. The Kaiser shipyards alone, which employed more than 47,000 workers in late 1944, employed less than 9,000 by the spring of 1946.[11]

The reduction of the wartime labor force was catastrophic for black workers. Throughout the Bay Area, black workers suffered a disproportionately high unemployment rate between 1945 and 1950. As early as 1946, 20 percent of all persons receiving unemployment insurance were nonwhites, primarily blacks, though blacks accounted for only 5 percent of the Bay Area's population. A year later the California State Employment Service reported that the black unemployment rate was 30 percent. Similarly, a 1948 sample of the Bay Area's black labor force revealed that black males had an unemployment rate twice as high as the statewide level. The unemployment rate for black women, however, was six times as great as the statewide level. "Conservative estimates indicate that at least one third of all Negroes in the Bay Area labor force are unable to find jobs," noted sociologist Wilson Record. San Francisco may well have shown a "relatively civilized and tolerant attitude toward minority groups," as former FEPC regional director Harry L. Kingman suggested. Yet black workers were discovering that civility and toleration had little if any relationship to their postwar job prospects, which were growing increasingly worse as the 1940s drew to a close.[12]

Several factors contributed to the high black unemployment rate in San Francisco and throughout the Bay Area. Black workers had been less diversified in their employment than white workers during World War II. More than half of all blacks worked in either shipbuilding or government employment, and the precipitous declines in these two sectors resulted in widespread joblessness for many blacks. The leading industries in San Francisco employed only a small percentage of the total black work force. For example, 90 percent of all minority workers in San Francisco had been employed by only 10 percent of the 100 leading firms. Despite the wartime manpower shortages and the availability of black workers, forty of these firms employed no blacks whatsoever. Another factor also worked to the detriment of black workers: while most black shipyard and government workers had remained on the job for the war's duration, many white workers left the shipyards in favor of "more permanent work" in the private sector. These private firms were less likely to lay off white workers than black workers at the end of the war.[13]

Black San Franciscans were faced with a paradox during the postwar years. On the one hand, a broader spectrum of jobs was open to them than ever before. On the other hand, employment discrimination was widespread in both the public and the private sectors, preventing them, in effect, from gaining access to these jobs. Employment discrimination in San Francisco's private industry was not new. Blacks had complained for decades that they were denied employment opportunities solely because of their race. The FEPC corroborated these charges during the Second World War, as two-thirds of all employment discrimination complaints received in the FEPC's San Francisco office were filed against private businesses.[14]

Certainly not every private employer in San Francisco was guilty of employment discrimination. A major employer like PG&E began hiring black females as switchboard operators after some resistance.[15] Not all employers were as progressive as PG&E, however. Many refused even to consider black applicants in the absence of an FEPC. Some firms hired blacks, but only for menial positions. Thus, a major employer like Pacific Telephone & Telegraph felt no obligation to hire blacks beyond the level of maintenance workers, according to the FEPC. Black females, in particular, faced difficulties obtaining employment during the postwar era. When one black female lieutenant in the Women's Army Corp attempted to obtain a job at the local Veterans' Administration Hospital in San Francisco, she was denied the position in spite of her experience and qualifications. The FEPC never reported whether a more qualified candidate obtained the post. Although born and raised in California, the woman had to settle for employment at a Jim Crow hospital in North Carolina. Some black women were denied employment because employers felt that they were "diseased" and could not pass the Wasserman test to detect syphilis. Perhaps the opinion of one white physician that blacks were a "notoriously syphilis-soaked race" had influenced a sector of Bay Area whites as well.[16]

San Francisco's mayor and Board of Supervisors were also aware of employment discrimination. The Board of Supervisors learned through committee hearings in 1948 that 80 percent of all California State Employment Service work orders in San Francisco were discriminatory. The National Urban League placed the figure at 90 percent. Apparently, employment referrals that were made without regard to race by either the State Employment Service or private employers were the exception, as the local Urban League branch discovered to no avail. The question of whether blacks were qualified was not at issue, but whether or not private businesses and industry would break long-standing precedent and integrate their work forces in the absence of statutory pressure or coercion from the local, state, or federal government. Fearing low employee morale and adverse public opinion, many companies were reluctant to integrate. Others were satisfied to hire black workers only for menial jobs.[17]

The Board of Supervisors, conscious of preserving the city's liberal reputation in a national climate of postwar racial strife, debated the necessity of a local Fair Employment Practices ordinance in 1950. An FEPC ordinance had never been a popular issue in San Francisco and had met with disapproval on every occasion at either the local or state level. In 1943, for example, Mayor Roger D. Lapham failed to support a Board of Supervisors' resolution that endorsed a proposed FEPC bill. Lapham stated his opposition categorically: "I am against all discrimination or abridgment in employment or in union membership because of race, creed, color, national origin, or ancestry. But it is my conviction that man-made laws—the compulsory method—is not the right way to deal with a human relations problem of this kind. . . . It is my considered judgment that passage of antidiscrimination laws is not in the public interest or in the interest of any minority group. I do not believe that they can solve the always present and eternal problems of human relations by legislation." The bill was ultimately defeated.[18]

Several years later, FEPC bills were defeated again on the state level, though some San Franciscans actively pushed for their passage. The opposition, however, was formidable. California State Assembly committees, led by a strong agricultural lobby, crushed FEPC bills in the 1945, 1946, and 1949 legislative sessions. Another FEPC measure, Proposition 11, was placed before California voters in 1946. The proposition, if passed, would have created a full-time five-person commission appointed by the governor. The most controversial function of the commission was its broad, sweeping power over employment discrimination, including the authority to "receive, investigate, act in, and render decisions" on complaints that alleged discrimination in employment. The commission's duties would include keeping the state legislature abreast of fair employment matters and educating the public and employers about the insidious effects of employment discrimination. Sponsors of the proposition were some of the leading white liberals and civil rights organizations across the state, including Harry L. Kingman, former regional director of the FEPC; Monroe E. Deutsch, vice-president and provost of the University of California, Berkeley; and Hugh A. Donohoe, editor of the *Monitor*, a prominent Catholic newspaper. The CCU and the NAACP also pushed for a state commission, but the proposition was overwhelmingly defeated. California would not create a state fair employment commission until 1959, despite the existence of commissions in New York, Massachusetts, New Jersey, Wisconsin, and Indiana.[19]

In spite of the defeat of Proposition 11, the Board of Supervisors adopted a "voluntary" fair employment plan in 1950, in lieu of a fair employment commission with statutory power. Many supervisors shared the conviction that employment discrimination could be eliminated by a

"Gentleman's Agreement," without the cumbersome and costly bureaucracy of a formal commission. Civil rights organizations were far less optimistic. "The voluntary plan does not call for much in the way of commitment by anyone and it is the feeling (and hope) among most proponents of the mandatory measure that it will not work," reported Seaton W. Manning. Given the political climate of San Francisco in 1950 and the opposition to a state FEPC by the business community, a "voluntary plan" was the best that civil rights organizations could expect.[20]

Many local organizations, including the NAACP and the CCU, opposed the voluntary plan and pushed for the creation of a formal fair employment commission, but the most influential opponent of the voluntary plan was a coalition of prominent individuals and organizations, the San Francisco Citizens Committee for Equal Employment Opportunity. This interracial organization, whose membership read like a social and political register of San Francisco, was created for the sole purpose of defeating the voluntary plan. San Franciscans of all races and nationalities participated in the organization, including Carlton B. Goodlett, William McKinley Thomas and Seaton W. Manning, three newcomers whose affiliation with this influential committee reflected the prominence of recent black migrants in interracial leadership positions. Only one black committee member, Reverend F. D. Haynes, pastor of the largest black congregation in the city, had lived in San Francisco before the Second World War.[21]

The citizens committee criticized every facet of the voluntary plan and pronounced it a failure. "The voluntary plan has failed substantially to broaden job opportunities for minorities in San Francisco," the committee charged in its "Summary of Findings and Conclusions." It further maintained that employment discrimination "continues as widespread as before the adoption of the voluntary plan, though some of it is more subtle and devious." Consequently, blacks and other nonwhites were excluded from numerous occupations and relegated largely to unskilled jobs. These menial jobs offered fewer opportunities for advancement, paid lower wages, had less security, and reinforced in the public's mind that blacks were not capable of assuming responsible positions in the skilled, white-collar, or professional sectors.[22]

The citizens committee presented considerable evidence to support its charge that the voluntary plan had failed. Two dozen spokesmen presented testimony before the Board of Supervisors describing the prevalence of employment discrimination against racial, ethnic, and religious groups in San Francisco. What was particularly striking about this testimony, though, was not the insistence that employment discrimination existed—that was hardly a revelation in 1951. Much more revealing was the fact that many large private businesses had hired no blacks or non-whites whatsoever by 1951. Many other employers hired blacks in minuscule numbers. The citizens committee corroborated this evidence by conducting several informal employment surveys. In one instance, the committee surveyed thirty-one branches of a major bank and found that only one black female was employed in a staff of over 500 employees. Another survey revealed that blacks were not employed by many service stations and food chains. When the committee visited fourteen restaurants of a popular food chain, they noted that blacks were employed as kitchen helpers, dishwashers, and "cleanup men," but not as cooks and servers. An experienced black female secretary who was denied employment at a bank but asked if "she had considered domestic work or baby-sitting" confirmed that these attitudes and employment practices had little relationship to one's qualifications. Many employers had little respect for the intellect and capability of black workers and operated on the common premise that blacks were capable of performing only the most rudimentary tasks.[23]

Blacks were also denied the opportunity to train and acquire skills for many positions. Some secretarial training schools felt that black applicants would be wasting their time, since it would be difficult to place a skilled black secretary. "We don't have no rule against accepting Negroes," reported one secretarial school. But the manager "doesn't want to place a burden on the [black] student by taking her money and finding she can't place her." Another secretarial school stated bluntly, "We don't take Negroes because we feel it is part of our job to find employment for our students." This policy was typical, for only two of ten schools surveyed indicated an "unreserved acceptance of Negroes."[24] The white employer's insistence that blacks were unqualified, while primarily a smokescreen to avoid integration, would also become a self-fulfilling prophecy in respect to future employment.

Nor were black domestic and service workers protected from employment bias. "It is also a fact that with respect to employment of custodial service workers in hotels and apartment houses that our union hiring halls are every day asked to dispatch persons of a particular national group because the employer has certain policies," testified Richard Liebes, research director for the Building Service Employers Union in San Francisco.[25] Liebes's AFL-affiliated union represented almost 12,000 employees in the building service occupations, but he observed that only ten blacks were employed as elevator operators out of 800 employees in this job classification. Similarly, William Kilpatrick, secretary of the Cooks,

Pastry Cooks, and Assistants Union, testified that only one chain restaurant in San Francisco employed blacks as cooks.[26] Liebes and Kilpatrick both speculated that blacks were less likely to occupy positions that were "more in the public eye." In effect, a hierarchy of service work existed, with black workers at the bottom of the scale.[27]

Over and over, testimony revealed that the voluntary plan had failed. It did not curb employment discrimination in the private sector, private training schools, or employment agencies, though it did achieve one success: it eliminated racial, ethnic, and religious categories on employment forms. This was small consolation to blacks, given the reluctance of employers to hire them.[28]

No advocates of a compulsory fair employment ordinance were more critical of the voluntary plan than the National Urban League's executive director, Seaton W. Manning, and the CCU's executive director, Edward Howden. Manning and Howden had led their respective organizations since 1946 and had succeeded in influencing a wide sector of Bay Area liberal opinion. Manning's public pronouncements were far more moderate than Howden's. Perhaps Manning did not wish to antagonize the city's business community, which the Urban League depended upon for employment opportunities. Nonetheless, he had criticized the voluntary plan from its inception and presented testimony before the Board of Supervisors "on the nature and extent of employment discrimination." Manning wrote privately, "Actually, I do not believe that employers or unions will take the kind of concerted action which would guarantee the success of the voluntary plan." He referred to the policy as "really no plan at all" and wrote that "we cannot sit back on inert fannies waiting for a law to be passed." Yet Manning was also ambivalent about the practicality of a mandatory fair employment law. His correspondence to National Urban League executive director Lester B. Granger revealed his indecision. "But neither am I convinced of the efficacy of the law for the sake of law. We want more job opportunities. How we get them—by voluntary action or by mandate—is not of the moment."[29]

While Manning was indecisive about the need for a fair employment ordinance, Howden was adamant that nothing short of a compulsory law would gain employment opportunities for minorities. Howden had no confidence in the voluntary plan, but "stood ready to cooperate in any way possible." The CCU's expertise in race relations, however, was never sought by employers or by the business community. Instead, Howden inferred that the Employers Council, which had taken the responsibility for enforcing the voluntary plan, had no intention of honoring its pledge. Howden charged, among other things, that the city's employers did not even submit a report on "education of employees of private industry," as they had agreed, to help them understand the nuances of employment discrimination. Nor did the Employers Council submit a progress report to the Board of Supervisors regarding the gains in minority employment, although the report, Howden reminded the supervisors, was almost nine months overdue. "We have watched and we have waited. We are still watching and waiting as to a solid report of actual progress in hiring members of minority groups," Howden concluded.[30]

The Employers Council never satisfied the most basic conditions of the voluntary plan. Howden and others wondered how the Employers Council would promote fair employment if it was reluctant even to comply with the paperwork requirements of an earlier resolution. Howden also ridiculed a report issued by Almon Roth, attorney for the Employers Council, who had argued that minorities had indeed made progress since the voluntary plan had been put into place. "I think that we can only conclude if there had been remarkable progress, as Mr. Roth's report puts it," stated Howden, "the report itself constitutes a remarkable failure to document that progress." The voluntary plan was clearly not working.[31]

Despite the plan's effectiveness in curbing employment discrimination, neither the mayor nor the Board of Supervisors pushed for a compulsory fair employment law. Consequently, most discriminatory practices that had been cited by the citizens committee in 1951 continued unabated through much of the decade. A comprehensive survey of employment practices in San Francisco confirmed the persistence and the severity of employment discrimination in San Francisco. The survey, "Employment Practices in Private Industry in San Francisco Affecting Minority-Group Applicants," was the handiwork of the CCU. The data was compiled between 1954 and 1956, under the supervision of Edward Howden and Dr. Irving Babow. The report was ultimately published in 1958, under the title, *A Civil Rights Inventory of San Francisco, Part 1, Employment*. The CCU interviewed 100 private employers in San Francisco, thirty union officials, twenty-eight private employment agencies, and sixty-five staff members of the state department of employment in San Francisco. Sixty-five written questionnaires were also distributed to college placement personnel, yielding a response rate of 69 percent.[32]

The 350-page report remains one of the most comprehensive employment surveys of minority workers ever undertaken in San Francisco. The study made no attempt to compare the status of minorities in San Francisco with that of minorities in other cities. It dealt strictly with discrimination in private employment. The CCU presented many of the survey's findings before the Board of Supervisors in 1957, as the city fathers once again considered a fair employment ordinance. In the six year interim since Edward Howden had first presented testimony before the Board of Supervisors, little had changed in San Francisco's employment picture. Employment discrimination was still widespread, though blacks, through the prodding and vigilance of the CCU, the NAACP, and the Urban League, continued to make modest gains. Yet the *Civil Rights Inventory* concluded, "Employment opportunity in private industry in San Francisco is still widely restricted according to race. These restrictions are experienced most acutely by Negro members of the labor force, and less so by Orientals and other nonwhites of Asian background."[33]

Edward Howden, who had served as the CCU's executive director for more than a decade, presented the forty-three page summary report before the supervisors. His testimony, once again, was not encouraging, for it revealed how entrenched employment discrimination had become by the mid-1950s. Private employment agencies and job placement services were still reluctant to place qualified black workers. Dozens of agencies, in fact, reported that blacks were not requested by employers and that their opportunities for white-collar employment were still considerably fewer than those of whites. One employment agency manager stated that he could refer 75 percent of his white applicants, but only 5 percent of his black applicants with comparable qualifications. A black woman who had recently moved to San Francisco from New York recalled that after applying at eight or nine agencies she was still unemployed. Several agencies refused to permit her even to complete an application stating her qualifications. Although this practice was not the norm, Howden charged that 10-to-15 percent of the agencies refused "even to register nonwhite applicants." Hence, when one personnel official stated that "Negroes are wasting their time looking for office work," he was speaking for a number of employment agencies.[34]

Some of the jobs blacks were unable to get may indeed have been filled. In other cases, black workers may not have possessed the requisite education or practical work experience. Yet far too many educated and qualified blacks were turned away from entry level positions to ignore claims of discrimination altogether. "It is possible that this explanation was a subterfuge," reported one black woman after being informed that every job in her area had been filled. Consequently, black clerical workers were frequently underemployed and forced to settle for employment in domestic work or the service industry.[35]

Aspiring black teachers also found that placement offices were of little help in light of the resistance of many school districts to hiring blacks.

Some college placement services simply refused to refer prospective black teachers to school districts that had not hired Afro-Americans in the past. As late as 1954, San Francisco State College referred black teachers seeking employment only to school districts "where they know they will be hired." Franklin H. Williams wrote the California Commissioner of Education to clarify the legality of this practice. The state's assistant administrative advisor replied that "the governing board of a school district has complete discretion with respect to the hiring of certified employees." Moreover, she continued, "the governing board may thus impose qualifications other than educational qualifications." The state official discounted Williams's charge that the practice was either illegal or discriminatory. "To send to a prospective employer a candidate whom the employer stated he will not hire, would, we believe, be doing a disservice to the candidate by causing him needless embarrassment and expense, and at the same time risking the future effectiveness of the placement service by alienating the patronage of the governing boards through disregard of this institution," she concluded. Thus, some college placement offices would honor an all-white school district's wish to remain segregated in order to remain on good terms with the governing boards.[36]

The CCU was less optimistic than other civil rights organizations that blacks could make occupational progress throughout the 1950s. The organization concluded that blacks "are still found only in the lowest job levels and in those not entailing contact with the public." Moreover, the CCU took the Board of Supervisors to task for claiming that San Francisco's race relations were ahead of most major cities. "Certain occupations traditionally filled by Negroes in other regions of the country have not yet opened to them here," concluded the *Civil Rights Inventory.*[37] Blacks, for instance, were even excluded from driving cabs for white companies in San Francisco because employers feared that the public would resent the close physical contact. Howden, though reluctant to place the blame for the persistence of employment discrimination on any one sector, denounced the "widespread absence of affirmative action and meaningful policy" in general. He believed, as many civil rights leaders had long suspected, that "in the last analysis, management does play the decisive role—or can play the decisive role—in establishing and implementing merit employment, if it so chooses."[38]

The CCU's employment survey also revealed a gaping disparity between an employer's professed ideals and his actual employment practices. Almost 90 percent of all firms who had claimed to have a merit employment policy, for example, admitted later that they lacked a program to communicate this policy to their employees. Similarly, almost half of all employers who stated that their job orders to agencies were nondiscriminatory either "contradicted or modified" their policies later. Thus, Howden had to be somewhat skeptical at the results of another survey: it showed that 60 percent of supervisory and managerial personnel claimed they would hire nonwhite applicants if they were "the best qualified for a job."[39] Though the survey results seemed an encouraging sign, the CCU's exhaustive research revealed otherwise.

Black workers also lagged behind white workers and other nonwhite races in median income in San Francisco and throughout the state. The median income for blacks in California was $1,575 in 1949, compared with $2,234 for whites and $1,695 for other nonwhite races. In San Francisco, whites earned a median income of $2,545. Blacks earned $1,924 and other nonwhite races earned $2,050. San Francisco's black males earned considerably more than black females ($2,303 compared with $1,274), which reflected their ability to secure better jobs and their progress in gaining entry into labor unions. However, black males earned 73.3 percent of the median income of white male workers, but 7 percent above the median income of males of other nonwhite races. Black females, in contrast, earned only 64.9 percent of the median income of white female workers and 76.4 percent of the median income of females of other nonwhite races.[40]

These figures compare closely with those for the Los Angeles labor force, although black females fared much better there, relative to white females. Black males earned 70.4 percent of the median income of white males in Los Angeles, while black females earned 83.6 percent of the median income of white females. Yet female workers of other nonwhite races reported an income of $1,367, the highest median income for all women; this figure was 23 percent above the median income of black females and 8 percent above the median income of white females. The median incomes of black males and males from other nonwhite races were virtually identical, although males from other races held a slight edge. The median incomes of blacks in San Francisco, Los Angeles, and throughout the state confirm that the incomes of black workers were not keeping pace with those of white laborers or workers from other nonwhite races, and that the "Employment Practices Survey" and the *Civil Rights Inventory* were accurate in noting the disparity between the illusion of employment equality in San Francisco and the reality that black workers faced daily.[41]

In addition to their dismal reports of racial discrimination in hiring and inequities in pay, the "Employment Practices Survey" and the *Civil Rights Inventory* reported some encouraging signs. Some personnel directors admitted when queried that they wished to pursue merit or non-discriminatory hiring policies within their firms, but they were thwarted by supervisors or top management. Whether these employers were torn by the disparity between their openly avowed racism and the democratic creed, as Gunnar Myrdal had speculated more than a decade earlier, is subject to debate. Moreover, the surveys indicated that blacks had made progress in many areas. The deck, however, would continue to be stacked against black workers for the present.[42]

The obvious conclusion to be drawn from these surveys and San Francisco's postwar employment picture was not encouraging for black workers. "It remains that inequality of job opportunity because of color, creed, or ancestry is widespread and pervasive in private industry in San Francisco," lamented Edward Howden.[43] Without a local or state FEPC, civil rights organizations like the CCU, NAACP, and the National Urban League stood only a small chance of persuading employers to cease discriminatory policies. As a result, black San Franciscans lagged behind the employment gains of black workers in midwestern and eastern cities, where black workers were employed in higher percentages in the automobile industry and as semiskilled factory operatives. Stephan Thernstrom noted that black Bostonians nearly doubled their proportion of jobs as semiskilled operatives during the 1940s, as Boston's labor market experienced significant growth. Moreover, black workers continued to make gains in this area, as almost one-third of black laborers secured semiskilled jobs during the 1950s. "On the eve of World War II," wrote Thernstrom, "only 1 in 8 Negro males held such jobs." Similarly, the number of black Bostonians who held white-collar jobs between 1950 and 1970 doubled, and Boston's black professional class increased from 5 percent to 11 percent between 1940 and 1970. August Meier and Elliott Rudwick found a similar pattern in Detroit during the 1940s, as black workers increased their proportion in the auto industry from 5.5 percent in 1942 to 15 percent by the spring of 1945. Discrimination had not been eliminated altogether in the auto industry, particularly in the skilled crafts, such as tool-and-die making. Yet "in Detroit by mid-century," concluded Meier and Rudwick, "the blacks' position in semi-skilled jobs was secure." On the other hand, black workers fared as well economically in San Francisco as in other large California urban centers by 1950. San Francisco's employment practices might well have been unethical and contrary to the image that the city portrayed to the nation, but employment discrimination was neither the exception nor illegal in San Francisco the year that the historic *Brown* decision was handed down by the United States Supreme Court.[44]

13

THE MATURATION OF BLACK
SAN FRANCISCO: HOUSING,
AUTONOMY, AND POLITICS

San Francisco's black community had undergone a metamorphosis by 1950. Once small and struggling, it was now bustling with vigor, and the Fillmore district, which Urban League Director Seaton Manning described as like New York's Harlem, had become the hub of the black population.[1] Though blacks were generally optimistic about equal opportunity in San Francisco, they were also critical of San Francisco's inconsistent commitment to civil rights. Few denied that racial discrimination was still a barrier in their quest for jobs or housing. "Job discrimination based on color, is, in my opinion, more vicious in the city of San Francisco than it is in other parts of the South," wrote Thomas Fleming, managing editor of the *Sun-Reporter*. The Reverend Hamilton T. Boswell wrote that "western racial segregation is a subtle contrivance. You are up to your neck before you become aware of its enclosure." Similarly, Joseph Kennedy, Northern California NAACP president, stated that "as a matter of fact, we all tend to make the South the scapegoat for the nation's sins. People who live in segregated glass houses shouldn't throw stones. The people of the North, Midwest and Far West are in no position to jeer too loudly at the undemocratic practices in the South." These observations were typical of black leaders who challenged racial discrimination between 1950 and 1954.[2] San Francisco's black leaders fought every remaining vestige of legal and de facto segregation and attempted, through their press, protest organizations, and the local government to mold San Francisco into a city that would be more responsive to their needs. They focused their greatest energy in the areas of improving housing, gaining greater autonomy within their community, and organizing the black vote.[3]

Housing remained a top priority for black leaders, as they challenged the high percentage of substandard housing in their community, residential segregation, and the severe shortage of housing in general. Not only was housing in short supply, but residential restrictions excluded blacks from many neighborhoods. Seaton Manning was so distressed over his personal housing situation that he threatened to resign as executive director of the Urban League and return to Boston. "After two full years," Manning wrote Lester Granger, "we have been unable to find a house or apartment in San Francisco. The housing shortage of course is acute. . . . Anything that is any good is restricted." The Urban League's executive director lived in a "war housing project twelve miles out of the city." NAACP West Coast Regional Director Franklin H. Williams also decried the rampant housing discrimination in San Francisco: "It is a gross overstatement for some people to say in San Francisco Negroes have a fair or equal opportunity to obtain jobs or housing."[4] The problem had grown increasingly severe by the 1950s, affecting blacks in all social and economic classes.

Black leaders believed that the housing shortage could be rectified in part by the construction of permanent low-income housing projects. After 1946, the San Francisco Housing Authority proceeded with their pre–World War II plans and constructed six additional housing developments.[5] These housing projects would have provided relief for several hundred black low-income families, but the local Housing Authority excluded blacks from all but one project that was located in a densely populated black neighborhood. The Housing Authority had adopted a resolution in 1942 by unanimous vote that was straightforward on this matter: "In the selection of tenants for the projects of this Authority, this Authority shall act with references to the established usages, customs and traditions of the community." Nor would the Housing Authority, "insofar as possible, enforce the commingling of races, but shall insofar as possible maintain and preserve the same racial composition which exists in the neighborhood where a project is located."[6]

Black leadership organized to overturn the "neighborhood pattern," as the policy became known. William McKinley Thomas, a member of the Housing Authority commission, led the opposition and worked toward the policy's abolition. Thomas criticized the Housing Authority's blatant disregard of an antidiscrimination resolution that the Board of Supervisors had passed in 1949. He believed that the Housing Authority could carry on their segregated policy indefinitely. Departing from the protocol that was characteristic of commissioners, Thomas publicly criticized the commission's chairman, E. N. Ayer, for being "derelict in his duties." Thomas later entertained a motion to put the Housing Authority on record opposing segregation in its developments. His motion failed to receive a second. It is doubtful whether Thomas believed that he could change the positions of his fellow commissioners single-handedly. Although he did not bring a single commissioner into his camp, he placed his own position firmly in the public record.[7]

Despite public pressure from local civil rights organizations, including the CCU and the NAACP, the San Francisco Housing Authority was committed to maintaining its "neighborhood policy." In 1952, the bubble burst. The "neighborhood policy" was a decade old when the NAACP supported the challenge of Mattie Banks and her husband, James Charley, Jr., to obtain admission to the North Beach housing project. The 101-unit development opened in 1952, and the Housing Authority commissioners were adamant that tenant selection would reflect the community's existing racial and ethnic composition. Few blacks resided in this community, which was in close proximity to Fisherman's Wharf. This case had the potential of testing the legality of the Housing Authority's policy for all nonwhite tenant selection.[8]

The NAACP's battery of attorneys consisted of Loren Miller, Terry Francois, and Nathaniel Colley. Miller had already become one of the most respected black attorneys in the state. This son of a former slave was active in black journalism, the Los Angeles NAACP, and would appear before the United States Supreme Court on many occasions, arguing civil rights cases in the area of housing discrimination.[9]

Miller, perhaps mindful of local custom and judicial protocol, decided to defer to his less experienced black colleague, Terry Francois. Francois was a young black attorney who had earned an undergraduate degree at Xavier University in New Orleans and a master's degree in business administration from Atlanta University. He had migrated to San Francisco after World War II. He attended the Hastings Law School in San Francisco and upon graduation, established a legal practice in the Western Addition's bustling black community. Despite his growing prominence in the black community, this was Francois's first major civil rights case. Little did he know in 1952 that the stakes were much higher than the admittance of three blacks to a segregated housing project. His participation in this case would enhance his status among his NAACP cohorts and in the larger black community. It would also be an important factor in his later election to the San Francisco Board of Supervisors.[10]

The attorneys for Mattie Banks challenged the legality of the "neighborhood policy." Though the policy had never been tested in court, Francois and Miller believed that California's courts would strike down an avowed policy of segregation in public housing. Proving that the Housing Authority maintained a Jim Crow policy was the least of their problems.

"At present, Negroes are admitted only to Westside Courts," testified Housing Authority Commissioner John W. Beard in San Francisco Superior Court.[11] Before 1952, Beard denied publicly that the Housing Authority discriminated in its selection and placement of nonwhite tenants. Although he never explained the ambiguity of his earlier position, Beard made no pretense in open court concerning the Housing Authority's policy in 1952 toward nonwhites.

Although the Housing Authority admitted that its "neighborhood policy" discriminated against blacks, it denied that Mattie Banks and her husband were barred from the North Beach project because of their race. Instead, Beard argued that the reprehensible moral character of these individuals was the reason for their exclusion. He referred to James Charley, Jr., as a "burglar on probation" who refused to pay his debts and criticized Mattie Banks in similar language. Beard also testified that Banks was not eligible for veteran's preference for public housing because her husband had committed polygamy. The commissioner charged, finally, that Banks had understated her income and had bought an expensive television set, apparently signs, insofar as Beard was concerned, of Banks's irresponsibility, deceit, and frivolous spending.[12] Terry Francois took issue with Beard's character assassination of his clients and established the fact that neither the credit backgrounds nor the personal spending habits of white tenants were criteria for their admittance into the North Beach project. "These people would not have been considered under any circumstances, because they are non-whites, is that correct?" Francois challenged Beard during the trial proceedings. Beard's affirmation was devastating to the Housing Authority's case. He finally admitted that the "neighborhood pattern rule was designed to localize Negroes to occupancy in the Westside Courts project."[13]

During the course of the trial, San Francisco Superior Court Judge Melvyn I. Cronin offered to set aside 20 of the 101 housing units for prospective black tenants, "pending [a] decision on whether Negroes should be admitted there." Francois agreed, and the Housing Authority, though reluctant, also consented. While this gesture did not necessarily guarantee blacks entrance into the disputed housing project, it represented an important psychological shift in the trial.[14]

Cronin's demeanor throughout the trial gave blacks hope, and their optimism was not in vain. On September 1, 1952, Cronin ruled that the "neighborhood pattern" was "illegal and void" and in "unlawful violation of the Fourteenth Amendment and the laws and general public policy of the State of California and the City and County of San Francisco."[15] Black San Franciscans were jubilant, and the Housing Authority commissioners were stunned. Since the adoption of the "neighborhood pattern" in 1942, the Housing Authority had grown complacent and smug, but also arrogant about the necessity of confining all nonwhites to segregated developments. No longer could the Housing Authority claim that it had both the court's stamp of approval and racial custom as justifications for its policy.

The superior court's decision had important implications for black low-rent housing opportunities. The federal government had always maintained a neutral position on the issue of segregation in federally financed public housing, viewing the question as "purely a matter of local concern."[16] At least one superior court judge, however, was disturbed over the city's professed liberalism and its practice of residential segregation in public housing and ordered a halt to the long-standing policy. Not all San Franciscans were in agreement with Judge Cronin's decision. Three weeks after his decision, Cronin received a death threat, in which he was called, among other things, "a traitor to our white race."[17] This was apparently part of the price that a white liberal judge had to pay in San Francisco.

The Housing Authority promptly appealed the decision. Commissioner John Beard, still denying that racial discrimination had anything to do with Mattie Banks's exclusion, maintained that wholesale white flight would result if San Francisco's public housing projects were integrated. This may well have been true, and indeed by the early 1960s Beard's comment would prove prophetic.[18] Yet in 1952, with the exception of the Hunter's Point temporary housing project, large-scale residential integration had been the exception in San Francisco. Hence, the integration of permanent housing projects would be an experiment, and John Beard could not point to any precedent when he suggested that integration would prompt white families to flee from public housing. The district court of appeals upheld the superior court's ruling in 1953, and when the United States Supreme Court refused to hear the case, the Housing Authority's back was finally broken.[19] The Supreme Court's refusal to review the case, wrote former judge and legal historian Loren Miller, "was taken to mean that the separate-but-equal rule had no application to public housing."[20]

The Banks decision did not create a housing bonanza for the thousands of low-income black families in San Francisco. But blacks were now free to compete with whites for these scant public dwellings, rather than forced to wait for the modest turnover in the Westside Courts development. Hence, the court's decision did raise the expectations of many blacks who were living in substandard housing. The city, however, could

not satisfy the demand for low-income housing in 1952. Nor did the
Banks decision influence the pace of residential integration in the private housing sector. The *New York Times* accurately appraised the decision's impact when it wrote, "Despite this decision, racial residential
segregation is the general rule in all cities and towns of the Far West."
San Francisco, however, did not follow the familiar pattern of stopping
.the construction of public housing once these units became integrated.
Rather, as late as 1964, San Francisco's electorate approved Proposition
H, a ballot measure which provided 2,500 additional public housing units
for senior citizens and low-income families.[21]

Banks v. the San Francisco Housing Authority was important from
another vantage point. The NAACP defended the case and, in the process, regained some of the prestige and influence that it had lost to the
CCU. Though the NAACP and the CCU were never at odds over ideological or organizational issues, the numerous factional disputes within the
NAACP's San Francisco branch permitted the CCU to play the predom-
inant role in civil rights struggles throughout the 1940s. The NAACP's
success in the Banks case, however, signaled that the pioneering civil
rights organization was once again ready to play the role of the preeminent protest organization in the Bay Area communities. Even the CCU
praised the NAACP's renewed vigor and activism. "The NAACP is already making most of the reportable news which comes to our attention—we refer to the Association more frequently than to any other organization," wrote Edward Howden.[22] Hence, after years of intermittent
strife, a housing discrimination case provided the catalyst that unified
the San Francisco branch.

The NAACP's zeal in defending Mattie Banks was evidence of the emerging political energy in the black community during the 1950s, as civil
rights organizations pushed more vigorously than ever before to eradicate racial caste and de facto discrimination in employment and housing.
San Francisco's black leadership no longer had to be cautious for fear of
offending civic leaders or the business community, because San Francisco
was more committed than ever before to providing equal opportunity for
blacks. Black leaders now saw their struggle for racial equality as part of
a larger mosaic that kept civil rights in the national spotlight. Franklin
H. Williams, executive director of the NAACP's West Coast regional office, was typical of this aggressive leadership. Williams assumed the
position as director of the West Coast regional office in October 1950
after serving for five years as a legal assistant for Thurgood Marshall in

the NAACP's Legal Defense Fund. Although he occasionally locked horns with Thurgood Marshall over the informal manner in which Marshall ran the Legal Defense Fund's office, the black honors graduate from Fordham Law School would emerge as one of the unsung leaders in NAACP circles.[23]

Williams, although only thirty-three years of age when he occupied his post, showed the maturity and polish that the National NAACP office desired in their representatives in the important West Coast region. At the urging of Roy Wilkins, Williams replaced Noah Griffin, who had served as director of the regional office between 1944 and 1950. Although he disliked being demoted, Griffin willingly took a back seat to Williams. Apparently the "tall, handsome, and glib" Williams, who had rubbed shoulders with Walter White and earned his admiration, was ideal for this position. The new West Coast regional director launched a successful career as an NAACP executive and later, as assistant district attorney for civil rights in the state attorney general's office. Williams would later become the United States ambassador to Ghana and executive director of the Phelps-Stokes Fund.[24]

Operating out of the San Francisco headquarters and coordinating the activities of all NAACP branches in the seven-state West Coast region, Williams proved an efficient executive. Williams's primary function was public relations. He made hundreds of speeches each year promoting the NAACP and served as a liaison between the national office and the branches under his jurisdiction. The young executive refused few requests for his services, and in the process, he helped to enhance the West Coast region's image and boosted the membership in the West Coast NAACP branches after the sharp postwar decline.[25]

Even though his hands were full with the day-to-day affairs of the West Coast region, Williams also monitored the association of radical groups with the NAACP's program. Fear that Communist influence existed in the San Francisco branch had surfaced after the Second World War, a concern that had not existed before 1941. "It is my opinion that a definite check will be made against further [Communist] infiltration," Noah Griffin assured Walter White in 1946.[26] Infiltration was one thing, but could the NAACP demand that the Communist party abandon the cause of civil rights? White apparently thought not and devised a different strategy. When the NAACP's chief executive learned that a local Communist party organization, the John Brown Club, picketed a San Francisco theater that refused to hire blacks, he did not object publicly to the picketing. Rather, White urged the San Francisco branch to take the lead and be "the originator of the plan to be followed, or it should very definitely be in on the ground floor with those making the plans."[27] White believed that as long as the NAACP remained in the vanguard, the alignment of their causes with the Communists, though undesirable, was tolerable.

Despite a concerted attempt to keep Communist organizations at a distance, the NAACP never succeeded in ridding itself completely of this stigma. The association, however, singled out numerous alleged "Communist-Front" organizations, including the California Labor School, the Civil Rights Congress, and the National Negro Labor Council. In addition, several newspapers, including the *Militant, Political Affairs,* and the *Daily People's World,* were labeled subversive, and NAACP branches within the West Coast region were instructed to avoid interaction with these publications.[28] The NAACP's West Coast Regional Conference in 1947 had passed a resolution condemning Communist party attempts "to secure control of our branches outright, or to use the branches as sounding boards for political and other ideas." Roy Wilkins was not only pleased with this resolution, but he also personally informed William L. Patterson, executive secretary of the Civil Rights Congress, that the Communist party was involved in civil rights merely as a "secondary consideration." The NAACP, he concluded, had no immediate plans for forging an alliance with the Civil Rights Congress. "We want none of that unity today," affirmed Wilkins.[29]

The NAACP's concern with being linked with Communism stemmed, in part, from the postwar hysteria that was gripping the nation but also from the knowledge that linking an organization with the Communists was a tactic used by racists to discredit the civil rights movement. The NAACP simply could not risk an association with Communist organizations at this critical juncture in its history when it was challenging racial discrimination in the courts. The insinuation that the NAACP was being infiltrated by Communists might also discourage influential white supporters and philanthropists at the very time that the association's membership was suffering a sharp postwar decline.[30]

After weighing these issues, the NAACP's 1950 annual convention adopted a resolution that permitted the national office to "expel any unit that had," in the judgment of the board of directors, "come under communist or other political control." The resolution was overwhelmingly adopted by a vote of 309 to 57.[31] A year later, the NAACP amended its constitution at the forty-second annual convention to prevent Communists from becoming members. The amendment, which was adopted by the NAACP's board of directors, restricted membership to "those who support the principles and program of the NAACP [and] these principles include opposition to Communist infiltration and control." Roy Wilkins supported the controversial amendment by publishing an article in the *American* magazine, where he referred to the Communist party's failure to recruit blacks as "Stalin's Greatest Defeat."[32]

The NAACP had shifted its national policy on the Communist party in the space of two years. When the *Crisis* magazine wrote an editorial, "The NAACP and the Communists," in March 1949 regarding the misrepresentation of the NAACP in the *Daily Worker*, the NAACP exhibited toleration. Although the association was not in agreement with Communism, it conceded nonetheless that the Communist party did "constitute a political party and have rights under the Constitution as do other parties." The *Crisis* concluded that "these rights must be maintained." By 1951, the Communist party may have still possessed rights under the United States Constitution, but those rights did not include membership in the NAACP.[33]

These exclusionary policies were effective in barring openly avowed Communists and radicals from the NAACP, and they prevented radical groups from assuming leadership roles within the organization. However, they did not prevent any left-wing or progressive organization from taking an active interest in civil rights. But that was not enough. Roy Wilkins and Franklin Williams would have preferred that the Communist party stay out of civil rights issues altogether, but that was unrealistic given the Communist party's revised postwar platform, which included efforts to improve the lowly status of blacks. The NAACP's anti-Communist policies may have also hurt the broad spectrum of civil rights and progressive movements in the late 1940s and early 1950s, as William Chafe concluded about the postwar anticommunist hysteria. The NAACP's criticism may have deterred these organizations from pursuing civil rights more vigorously than they did, and the anti-Communist campaign made alliances between Communist leaders and mainstream civil rights organizations virtually impossible.[34]

Franklin Williams attempted to discourage any relationship between the NAACP and the Communists. Yet, whereas Walter White had been cautious and diplomatic in his approach to this volatile issue, Williams was abrupt and abrasive. He informed Walter White and Roy Wilkins that he was confident that the West Coast region could control "Communist and Front organizations," and that "I am fortunate enough to have a fairly reliable pipeline into Communist plans for [the] NAACP here in the West." In reality, Williams was deeply troubled and he conceded later that "it is a most serious situation."[35]

Apparently concerned because the NAACP throughout California was on the United States' subversives list, Williams compiled a "subversives list" of his own and publicly denounced organizations that were "attempting to mislead the Negro community."[36] Two left-wing newspapers, the *Militant* and the *Daily People's World*, were singled out by Williams, and he campaigned to discredit both in the eyes of the NAACP hierarchy and the black community. Williams demanded, among other things, that both papers cease publishing news concerning NAACP activities. True, neither Williams nor any other NAACP official was in a position to demand censorship. The editors of both papers, George Breitman and Al Richmond, were nonetheless infuriated at this suggestion and were unsparing in denouncing Williams. Breitman reminded Williams that the *Militant* had been fighting for civil rights long before the West Coast regional office came into existence. Moreover, Breitman insisted that the *Militant* opposed the Stalinists. Though the NAACP had heretofore denounced the attorney general's "subversives list" as "violations of democratic rights and traditions," wrote Breitman, the association now "imitates the McCarthyites." The *Militant*'s editor could not have chosen a more damning example.[37]

Similarly, Alexander Richmond, the executive editor of the *Daily People's World*, denounced Williams's demand to cease printing NAACP-related news. "We desire no quarrel with the NAACP. We would much prefer to expend our energies in battle against McCarthyism, jim crow, and reaction," wrote Richmond. Discounting a news boycott as "a prior censorship [and] completely destructive of the press," Richmond wrote that his paper would not cease reporting NAACP news "no more than we would consider a boycott on news about labor unions, progressive political groupings and other progressive organizations."[38]

Williams apparently ignored the olive branch that Richmond extended, and instead, used his influence within NAACP circles to discredit the *Daily People's World* at every opportunity. Williams refused to send Richmond NAACP press releases "unless ordered to do so by Walter White or the Board," and he referred to the paper privately to Henry Lee Moon, director of NAACP public relations, as "our West Coast Communist rag." On almost every occasion, Williams criticized the paper. "We do not consider the *People's World* as a newspaper at all, but rather consider it merely an organ of the Communist Party," he mused. Although Williams took personal delight in these pejorative comments, he ultimately conceded that the *People's World* has "damaged us severely."[39]

The NAACP's attempt to discredit left-wing organizations also reflected the hegemony that the West Coast regional office sought over most civil rights and progressive organizations. Franklin Williams, in particular, attempted to save the black community from itself by charting the proper course in the civil rights struggle and steering blacks away from alliances that were not in their interest. Williams, for instance, routinely asked many progressive and civil rights organizations throughout the Bay Area to clear any protest or news releases with his office. Some organizations, such as the San Francisco Miscellaneous Employees, consented willingly. "The union from now on before taking any action on civil liberty or discrimination cases must first clear with your organization," wrote the union's president, Helen Wheeler. Still others, like the Marine Cooks and Stewards, informed Williams that they had no intention of complying with this request.[40]

Williams proved unrelenting in his quest for civil rights supremacy, and he did not confine his suggestions to white organizations. He criticized the National Urban League branch in San Francisco on more than one occasion, because it had, in his opinion, overreached its primary mission as a social service agency and ventured into civil rights. Moreover, he refused to concede that the NAACP was responsible, even in part, for past dissension between the two organizations. "I have concluded that in most instances where cooperation does not exist the Urban League is primarily responsible," Williams wrote in a self-righteous tone. He also believed that "conflict and confusion arise from public misconceptions of the structure, function, and purposes of the two organizations." The National Urban League, concluded Williams, is a "social work agency" and the NAACP, "a mass membership direct action and propaganda agency," and "it is important that their functions be clearly understood."[41] By the time Franklin Williams left office in 1958, the West Coast regional office had achieved the status and hegemony that he desired.

By the early 1950s, San Francisco's black leaders were shedding the provincialism of earlier years, and they desired to be part of a community that was progressive and in the political mainstream. The black community's emerging maturity, between 1950 and 1954, was manifested in campaigns to rid black neighborhoods of vice and crime and in attempts at greater involvement in local and state politics. These activities illustrated the growing pride that blacks were taking in their community, but also that political power was needed if these problems were to be resolved. Black leaders no longer believed they were powerless to improve the quality of their lives, and they willingly shouldered a greater share of the burden of cleaning up their community and making progress.

San Francisco's black residents expressed growing dismay that the Fillmore district had become a cesspool of crime and vice. San Francisco's black community had avoided the reputation of being a crime-ridden population before 1945, but both black and white leaders believed that

illegal activities among blacks multiplied significantly after the Second
World War. This suspicion prompted San Francisco District Attorney
Edmund G. Brown to study "the Negro and his relationship to crime in
San Francisco." Brown had always enjoyed a good relationship with the
black community, and his appointment of black attorney Raymond J.
Reynolds to conduct the study solidified that relationship. Reynolds's
findings were submitted to the district attorney in a 1947 report, "The
Negro and Crime in San Francisco."[42]

Reynolds's conclusion, that blacks represented a disproportionate percentage of arrests in San Francisco, confirmed what many San Franciscans had suspected. Blacks were more likely to be arrested than
whites for vagrancy, gambling, narcotics violations, burglary, and homi-
cide. Reynolds also discovered that blacks were twice as likely to be
arrested for vagrancy as whites, and even more likely to be held over for
bail after an arrest. Moreover, Reynolds reported that most of the violent
crimes committed by blacks were perpetrated on other blacks. In an
attempt to explain the reasons for this upsurge in postwar criminal activity, Reynolds pointed to the large influx of southern blacks, many of
whom had difficulty adjusting, and the wide economic disparity between
black and white San Franciscans. "The Negro's over-proportion in the
crime of San Francisco is not a racial but a sociological or community
problem," he concluded. Reynolds was optimistic, however, that the over-
representation of blacks in serious crimes would "level off" after they
obtained better housing and employment and when their "adjustment to
this community has become more permanent."[43] Reynolds questioned the
arrests of the large percentage of blacks for vagrancy, casting doubt on
the objectivity of the police force as well as the courts, but he concluded
that San Francisco's criminal courts "dispense justice without regard to
race or color." Yet, he remained adamant that until blacks were better
integrated into San Francisco's employment and housing sectors, they
would continue to represent a disproportionate percentage of the city's
criminal element.[44]

Reynolds's report was not encouraging for blacks. He might have
added that blacks were also more likely to be victims of police brutality
than whites. Even the influential black editor and physician Carlton
Goodlett was victimized by police brutality on two occasions. Yet Reynolds had correctly identified a disturbing trend that appeared to be
accelerating. Black crime was indeed on the increase, and most of these
crimes were committed in the Fillmore district. The *Sun-Reporter*, disturbed with the waning reputation of the city's largest black neighborhood, launched a campaign to rid the Fillmore district of vice and crime.[45]

The editors of the *Sun-Reporter* attempted to expose every possible vestige of illegal activity. "For too long the Fillmore area has been a cesspool of crime," and "it is common knowledge that the Fillmore district is wide open," wrote the *Sun-Reporter*. The paper charged that many black businesses also served as fronts for illegal activities. "The pimping and prostitution situation has become so serious," wrote the editors, "that the wives and daughters of decent citizens are afraid to travel the streets without a male escort." The East Bay black congressman William Byron Rumford also stated that the drug problem in the Fillmore district was worse than in any other section of the Bay Area and represented a "serious problem." Apparently, the *Sun-Reporter* was not exaggerating these charges, because the series ran intermittently for more than a year and the editors received widespread support from their readers.[46]

The Chinese were frequently singled out by black readers and by black editors for operating gambling and lottery operations openly in the Fillmore. "We don't want the Chinaman taking over the Fillmore," wrote one angry reader. "How long do you think a Negro could run a dice game in Chinatown?" This anti-Chinese sentiment was typical and reflected an important shift in the attitude of black leaders toward their community. In an editorial entitled, "Get the Record Straight," the *Sun-Reporter* expressed a growing pride and ethnocentrism in the Fillmore district: "We are not berating the Chinese—we have great respect for them, but we are unalterably opposed to any group becoming a parasite on the lifeline of the community."[47]

Although gambling and Chinese lotteries did exist openly in the Fillmore, the black press erred in assuming that Chinese illegal activity was the heart of the problem. Blacks were arrested in disproportionate percentages for almost all crimes, with the exception of rape. Other nonwhite races had a relatively low incidence of arrests, and crime was virtually absent among the Japanese community in San Francisco. The Chinese were apparently scapegoats for black leaders as they attempted to search for solutions to this complex problem. (The use of the Chinese as scapegoats for black crime, however, was not a new tactic, for the *Los Angeles Eagle* had frequently published articles on this theme in the early decades of the twentieth century.)[48]

Some forms of criminal activity, such as gambling, crapshooting, bookmaking, and lotteries, had operated openly for decades in black communities throughout the nation without the stigma of hard-core criminal activity. Recent studies by Donn Rogosin, Jules Tygiel, Rob Ruck, and Janet Bruce have shown that black bookmakers were prominent figures in black baseball prior to the integration of the major leagues. The heavyweight champion Joe Louis also wrote fondly of a black bookmaker who helped him during the early stages of his career. The *Sun-Reporter*'s editor, Carlton Goodlett, purportedly won control of his paper in a card game.[49] Blacks were certainly aware that these activities were illegal and blemished the image of their community. Yet as long as these activities did not get out of hand, as they had in the Fillmore by 1951, black leaders, though critical, were often willing to view them as relatively harmless forms of recreation. The *Sun-Reporter* could even find humor in the midst of this controversy: "We heard of a possibility of forming the Lottery, Crapshooters, and Card Players Protective Association," the paper wrote.[50] Nonetheless, the black press continued to write scathing editorials urging blacks to rid the Fillmore of criminal activity and to strive to make their community a wholesome and respected environment.

As blacks took pride in cleaning up their community, they also began to take a keener interest in local and state politics. Black leaders had always expressed some interest in political issues, but never before had the black community been large enough to exert significant political leverage on white politicians. By 1950, however, when San Francisco's black population numbered 43,460, black leadership and some white politicians were more willing to concede that an organized black vote could indeed make a difference in local elections, and that white political officials should be more sensitive to the interests of black voters.

California's governor, Earl Warren, was regularly criticized in the black press in San Francisco and Los Angeles for his insensitivity to racial issues. Despite Warren's appointment of the prominent black leader, Walter Gordon, to the California Adult Authority, the state's chief executive and blacks had always had a lukewarm relationship. As a young politician, Warren had virtually no contact with blacks. When he became governor in 1943, he did little to court San Francisco's black community.[51] Perhaps Warren believed that the black vote in San Francisco was too small to justify granting political concessions to the black community. So, for the most part, he ignored blacks. Thomas Fleming, the *Sun-Reporter*'s political columnist and managing editor, criticized Warren's relationship with the black community. "He [Warren] has never made any gestures toward Negroes to cause any of them to think that he realizes that there are such people as Negroes," wrote Fleming.[52]

The *Sun-Reporter* also questioned Warren's civil rights record as governor. When the paper learned that Warren might become a candidate for president in 1952, it wrote, "We are not at all convinced that Warren understands, or even cares about, the Negro's problems."[53] Black leaders also criticized Warren because he refused to reopen the legal case of George Holman, a black man convicted of setting a grisly fire at the New Amsterdam Hotel in 1944 that killed twenty-two people. Although Holman affirmed his innocence and the testimony placing him at the scene of the crime was questionable, he was convicted of murder and sent to prison for life. The *San Francisco Chronicle* conducted its own investigation of the case and found several irregularities. Nonetheless, Warren denied Holman executive clemency.[54]

Despite these strained relations between Warren and black leaders, there were periodic attempts at fence mending between 1952 and 1954. Heretofore, Warren had been a paradox to black leaders. On the one hand, he had refused to end segregation in the California National Guard before 1949 or to endorse a state FEPC before 1951. Yet the governor refused to extradite to North Carolina a black youth who had fled the Tar Heel state while on probation. Warren intervened in this case, but never changed his mind about the guilt of George Holman. The *Sun-Reporter* concluded that Warren was insensitive to blacks and that "80 percent of the Negro voters of the state" opposed him.[55] The black press was no realistic barometer of black opposition to Warren, but San Francisco's black leaders were skeptical of Warren's commitment to civil rights on the eve of his appointment to the United States Supreme Court. President Dwight D. Eisenhower may well have been the most surprised person in America when he discovered Warren's belated liberalism as Chief Justice of the United States Supreme Court. But black San Franciscans were just as surprised, given Warren's record in racial matters.[56]

White city officials were more sensitive to the black community's request for political patronage, and black San Franciscans made some important political gains between 1950 and 1954. Black attorneys, Cecil Poole and Raymond J. Reynolds in particular, achieved unprecedented success in obtaining political appointments. Poole was appointed to head the Superior Court Trial Division of the District Attorney's office. A former president of the San Francisco branch of the NAACP, Poole was a graduate of the University of Michigan Law School. He had served as assistant district attorney since 1949 and commanded the acclaim of San Francisco District Attorney Thomas C. Lynch, who considered Poole "one of my most skillful trial lawyers."[57] By 1953, the San Francisco Chamber of Commerce and *Time* magazine selected Poole as one of a hundred "Newsmakers of Tomorrow." The *Sun-Reporter* even urged Governor Goodwin Knight to consider Poole as a municipal court judge. Although he was never a serious contender for a local judicial appointment, Poole was later nominated and confirmed as a United States Federal Judge in 1976.[58]

Poole was the most successful of the black attorneys to gain political favor, but several others, including Raymond J. Reynolds, also obtained pathbreaking political appointments. In 1954, Reynolds was appointed the first black deputy district attorney for San Francisco, a position that had been beyond the reach of black leaders five years earlier. James Stratten, one of the most influential black Republicans in San Francisco, served on the redevelopment commission. Several black law school students also cracked the color barrier as clerks in city government.[59] These appointments had been slow in coming, and capable young black attorneys such as McCants Stewart, Tabytha Anderson, and William L. Patterson had been unable to obtain them before 1940. Yet black San Franciscans had never before been in a position to demand anything from city officials. By 1954, not only had the times changed, but black leaders were beginning to reflect the political sophistication and maturity that had been evident for decades in northern black communities like Chicago and New York.

Organizing the black vote was one of the principal tasks of black leadership between 1950 and 1954, and these campaigns reflected a new-found political enthusiasm. The majority of black San Franciscans generally voted for Democratic party candidates in local, state, and national elections following the Second World War. Although a handful of prominent black Republicans, such as William McKinley Thomas and James Stratten, were highly visible figures in the black community, the *Sun-Reporter* wrote that most blacks were "registered Democrats." The black weekly endorsed Adlai Stevenson during the 1952 presidential election, and it criticized the prominent black writer, Zora Neale Hurston, for urging blacks to support Robert Taft. Black leaders also criticized the civil rights record of the Republican party and their indifference to black political appointments. The *Sun-Reporter* urged blacks to consolidate their vote, as John Pittman had urged two decades earlier, and elect white candidates who were sensitive and responsive to racial issues. Although an endorsement from the black press did not guarantee a victory at the polls, it made a difference in closely contested elections. When the *Sun-Reporter* endorsed the reelection of Elmer E. Robinson for mayor of San Francisco in 1951 and Thomas C. Lynch for district attorney, the endorsements not only aligned numerous black leaders with the candidates, but also swayed many black voters. Robinson, a Republican, won a closely contested mayoral race with widespread support from the Fillmore and the Hunter's Point districts, both heavily populated black neighborhoods. The *Sun-Reporter* noted that the election marked a rare occasion where black voters "swung away from the leading Democratic candidate."[60]

By the early 1950s, black leaders were demanding that white politicians state their position openly on racial issues, for their political fortunes could well hinge on the support of black voters in close elections. "We can no longer afford to settle for the vague, implied support of the gradualists. For it has proven time and time again that many of these men who say they are in favor of gradual change are really hoping that this eventual moment will never fall within their lifetime," wrote the *Sun-Reporter*. The editors advised blacks, "If we want equality, we must support the men and women who are standing straight up and exclaiming that they are ready to do something about our getting those opportunities."[61] An aspiring white candidate like Philip Burton apparently grasped this message early in his political career and endorsed a wide spectrum of civil rights issues. Similarly, Republican supervisor George Christopher became much more conciliatory to the black community after suffering the wrath of black voters in 1951. The black press had criticized Christopher's hiring policies in his local milk business and did not support him in the 1951 mayoral election. The black press, however, endorsed his successful mayoral campaign in 1956.[62]

Black political power, however, was more shadow than substance between 1950 and 1954. No black candidate came close to winning a citywide election. The campaign of the Reverend F. D. Haynes to secure a seat on the San Francisco Board of Supervisors was typical. The influential black pastor of the Third Baptist Church, which had a congregation of over 4,000 members, had lived in San Francisco for almost two decades when he ran for political office. As did his black ministerial counterpart in New York, Adam Clayton Powell, Jr., Haynes used his influence as both a minister and a community leader to push his candidacy. "Minority people should have representation in every election campaign," he declared emphatically in 1951.[63] Haynes had forged an impressive interracial coalition throughout San Francisco. He had been president of the San Francisco black Ministerial Alliance for seven years, grand chaplain of the Prince Hall Masonic Lodge, and an active member of both the Urban League and the NAACP. His appointments to the Mayor's Committee for Civic Unity and the San Francisco Citizens Committee, which proposed a mandatory FEPC ordinance for San Francisco, were indicative of his biracial support.[64]

The black community, however, was the principal force behind Haynes's candidacy. Some of the city's leading black businessmen and professionals, including Cecil Poole, Carlton Goodlett, Howard Thurman, and Robert Flippin, supported Haynes. Haynes, however, received only 36,000 votes, not nearly enough to win in a city-wide election. Yet this showing was impressive for a black candidate in the early 1950s, and some whites also voted for Haynes. His defeat was discouraging to his political supporters, and other black candidates met similar fates. More than a decade passed before a black person served on the San Francisco Board of Supervisors.[65]

By 1954, black leaders believed that they had made a number of significant political changes. In the course of a decade, white politicians had begun courting the black vote, and political appointments were granted more frequently. Political concessions of any sort represented a major departure from the past, when the black vote and black leaders had been taken for granted. Black San Franciscans were now demanding to be part of the decision-making process at all levels; they were no longer content to remain quietly on the periphery or to seek only menial political posts. During the 1950s, black leadership increasingly advocated the ballot as the most effective tool for extracting political favors. Black leaders had not, however, suggested forging coalitions with other racial, ethnic, or special interest groups in San Francisco in order to bolster their political clout. Nonetheless, black San Franciscans had matured politically since the World War II migration, and race relations, though strained on occasion, had progressed, primarily through the efforts of black protest organizations and interracial committees. (These changes were also evident in a western urban center like Phoenix, Arizona, where black and white leaders joined forces during the 1950s and 1960s and pushed more vigorously for civil rights in a number of areas).[66] Despite this progress and optimism, many problems remained unresolved in San Francisco's black community. Residential segregation continued to plague blacks and adequate housing was in short supply. Police brutality was on the increase, and the high number of blacks arrested for vagrancy was indicative of economic deprivation and police harassment. Although the number of black voters had increased almost tenfold since 1940, no black candidate could be elected to city-wide office. Blacks still enjoyed a greater measure of equality in 1954 than at any previous time in the city's history. But Franklin Williams's observation that "the West Coast has not kept pace with the rest of the country in improving the conditions of civil rights" was accurate in some areas and further proof that San Francisco had neither totally eliminated racial caste nor lived up to its liberal image. Full equality in employment and housing was still beyond the grasp of many black San Franciscans.

EPILOGUE:
THE DREAM AND THE REALITY

By 1954, blacks had lived in San Francisco for more than a century and had made considerable progress socially, politically, and economically. The *Sun-Reporter* was optimistic that the landmark *Brown v. the Board of Education, Topeka* decision would accelerate the pace of racial progress in San Francisco and throughout the nation. "This is a year of momentous decision and harmony in human relations as well as unity of action is absolutely imperative if victory is to crown our ultimate purpose," wrote the black weekly.[1]

Yet black San Franciscans made few gains economically or politically during the remaining years of the decade, and they continued to occupy a large percentage of San Francisco's substandard housing. Herb Caen, San Francisco's liberal columnist, no longer boasted that the city was in the racial vanguard, and in 1965 he openly criticized San Francisco's race relations:

The Negro 'problem' is very much with the city, too. The Negro population has grown tenfold since World War II, but San Francisco, for all its vaunted tolerance, has moved slowly to meet the challenge that this presents. The Negro, now representing one-tenth of the city's population, is largely restricted to a single section of substandard old housing—centering on, and radiating from, Fillmore Street—and the ills implicit in such a situation are clearly to be seen: de facto segregation in the schools, inequitable job opportunities, crime out of proportion to the population, mass picketing and demonstrations.[2]

Caen admitted in 1965 what numerous black and some white leaders had argued for decades. San Francisco's liberal image was largely a facade, and despite the efforts of interracial leaders and the civility of whites, the Golden Gate City's race relations represented a striking ambiguity. On the one hand, blacks had integrated many areas of San Francisco, including public accommodations, schools, labor unions, and public housing, and organizations like the NAACP, National Urban League, and the CCU continued to push for full equality in private housing and employment. Though blacks and whites took pride in these accomplishments, the black San Franciscans' struggle also illustrated the limits of race liberalism as a strategy to achieve equality in employment and housing. In some respects, as Herb Caen had written, the gap between blacks and whites had grown wider by the 1960s, rather than narrower. Franklin H. Williams "singled out San Francisco as an example of the slow progress of full civil rights for minorities."[3]

Residential segregation had become a particularly odious problem by the mid-1950s. Seaton Manning wrote that "it is not necessarily by choice that Negro families live in the Western Addition."[4] Despite the Banks decision, which outlawed segregation in San Francisco's public housing projects, blacks continued to have difficulty renting and purchasing private dwellings. Franklin Williams charged that banks and financial agencies discriminated "in the extension of credit for the purchase of homes by Negroes [and] private builders and owners openly discriminate in the sale or rental of homes."[5] Williams confirmed the conclusion of historian Kenneth T. Jackson that blacks as well as blue-collar workers and immigrants were discriminated against in the loan application process by Federal Housing Administration guidelines and officials.[6] When the young black baseball player Willie Mays was initially denied the opportunity to purchase a home in an exclusive San Francisco neighborhood solely because of his race in 1957, he was reminded that neither his status nor his class mattered as much as the color of his skin. "What happened in Mays' case is dramatically enacted daily by hapless Negro families whose lack of prominence does not command the attention of the press and officials of San Francisco," wrote the San Francisco NAACP.[7] The *Pittsburgh Courier* was even more pointed in its remarks. "Willie Mays has been reminded that he is still a Negro," wrote the influential black weekly.

This episode confirmed the persistence of racial caste in the minds of whites and the necessity for blacks to gain political power so they could prevent recurrences. Though this incident did not necessarily indict the entire city, it typified the unwillingness of whites to break down racial barriers unless they were compelled to do so. By 1960, Tarea Hall Pittman, who succeeded Franklin Williams as acting director of the

NAACP's West Coast region, testified before the United States Commission on Civil Rights that "residential segregation based on race is the general rule in the towns and cities in the West."[8] Despite San Francisco's attempt to promote civility and live up to its egalitarian image, its housing patterns by the mid-1960s resembled a northern city like Chicago, which had a well-defined black ghetto. San Francisco's reputed liberalism in matters of race was belied by its inability to deal satisfactorily with this problem.[9]

Economic opportunity for blacks continued to lag behind the economic opportunity available to whites throughout the 1950s, despite the creation of a local FEPC in 1958 and a statewide agency in 1959. By the late 1950s, employment discrimination based on race was so entrenched in many industries, reported the CCU, that blacks were still overwhelmingly employed as domestics and unskilled workers. Franklin Williams's glum forecast, that the "employment outlook is bleak for the Negro in the Western states," had a ring of authenticity that few black San Franciscans would deny.[10]

It would be inaccurate to ignore the progress that had been made or to portray San Francisco as a racially stagnant city. Blacks had made important gains in white-collar jobs, the professions, semiskilled labor, and skilled jobs between 1940 and 1960. Black women were also breaking the vicious cycle of domestic work, as more were hired by banks, department stores, schools, insurance companies, and large corporations. But as the CCU's employment survey had revealed in 1958, San Francisco's race relations were not superior to those of most major cities, and racial discrimination continued to be practiced widely in both public and private employment. Again, San Francisco was not the open and progressive city that it was purported to be.

Black San Franciscans made only marginal political progress between 1954 and 1965. After years of lobbying and political organizing by black leaders, John W. Bussey, a black attorney, was appointed to the San Francisco Municipal Court in 1958. Three years later, James Stratten was appointed to the board of education and, in 1964, the Reverend Hamilton T. Boswell was appointed as a commissioner to the local housing authority. That same year, Terry Francois was appointed to the Board of Supervisors by Mayor John Shelley, and a black migrant from Mineola, Texas, Willie L. Brown, Jr., was elected to the California State Assembly, running in the Western Addition's predominantly black congressional district. Brown's election reflected both the degree to which black leaders had organized the black vote successfully by 1964 and their increasing ghettoization in the Western Addition. Brown's political acu-

men would later earn him chairmanship of the powerful House Ways
and Means Committee, and, more recently, Speaker of the Assembly.
Cecil Poole would also climb rapidly up the political ladder, first as the
United States Attorney for Northern California, and then as a United
States Federal Judge. Poole was later named to the United States Appel-
late Court under President Carter.[11]

These isolated achievements, however noteworthy, obscure the fact
that San Francisco never came to grips with racial discrimination in
many areas and that the black community had grown increasingly frustrated by the mid-1960s with the lack of progress. Blacks' frustration
culminated in a race riot in 1966. The riot erupted after a white policeman killed a black teenager who had allegedly stolen an automobile.
When news of the slaying was reported by black Hunter's Point residents
and the local media, the entire city exploded for five days.[12] The riot
seemed to take many white San Franciscans by surprise, for they had
grown complacent and ignored the disparity between themselves and the
black community. The city had, in fact, become less open by 1960 as
ghettoization accelerated. Many white businesses left the Fillmore district in the wake of arson and looting, while others operated with such
tight security that conducting business in a normal fashion became almost impossible. By the late 1960s, the Fillmore district had become the
same kind of institutional and physical ghetto that had emerged in Chicago and Cleveland during the First World War. San Francisco's image as
a racially progressive city bore little relationship to the status of most
blacks by the 1960s.

How, then, did the experiences of black San Franciscans compare to
blacks and racial minorities in other western cities? This is a particularly
difficult question to evaluate, because no other western city has produced
a book about its black community, and only one scholar to date has
written a comparative study of blacks and another racial minority in a
western urban center.[13] Moreover, the scant literature on blacks in the
twentieth century urban West rarely extends beyond 1940, making com-
parisons between San Francisco and other western black communities
virtually impossible after World War II. My research, however, reveals
that the struggle of black San Franciscans for racial equality was similar
to the struggle of their counterparts in Oakland, Richmond, Los Angeles,
Portland, Seattle, and Phoenix.[14] Black populations in these cities, with
the exception of Los Angeles, were relatively small before 1940, and
World War II also had a "transforming" effect on these black communities. The war increased defense spending in all seven of these cities,

resulting in a dramatic rise in their black population. Blacks in these cities also formed interracial organizations, such as NAACP, Civic Unity Councils, and Urban Leagues, and pushed for greater access to jobs in both the public and private sectors. The greatest employment gains were registered by black males, as black female workers were unable to keep pace with the progress of white females or black males, either before or after World War II. Black women did not succeed in breaking the familiar pattern of domestic and unskilled menial labor until the 1960s. "The vast majority of black female wage earners were barred from peacetime factory labor and from the traditional (white) female occupations of secretarial and sales work until well into the 1960s," wrote Jacqueline Jones in her history of black female workers and the black family. San Francisco's black female workers would certainly agree with this conclusion, but so would black female laborers in Oakland, Los Angeles, Portland, Seattle, and Phoenix. Employment opportunities for these women were also restricted because of their race and gender, and they would be largely excluded from the occupational breakthroughs that many black males experienced after 1940.[15]

The employment gains that black workers, male and female, made after 1940 were striking when compared to the pre–World War II era. Fewer blacks worked in unskilled menial jobs after 1940, and a considerable number joined AFL or CIO unions, gaining union wages, job security, and seniority for the first time. Similarly, the black professional and white-collar classes also increased in western cities after 1940, and blacks in a suburban community like Orange County, California, could take advantage of a "continuously growing job market" to make impressive economic gains between 1950 and 1980. Yet Orange County blacks, like blacks in San Francisco and Los Angeles, also experienced increasing ghettoization by the 1960s, for almost 73 percent of the county's black residents lived in two cities. "The city of Santa Ana, with 11 percent of the county's population," wrote Lawrence B. de Graaf, "had over 66 percent of its blacks."[16] The "limited assimilation" of Orange County blacks was similar to the experience of black San Franciscans with one exception: blacks in Orange County were far more likely to own their homes than black San Franciscans during the postwar era.[17]

The employment gains that black westerners achieved were also consistent with the findings of Stephan Thernstrom, who concluded that black Bostonians made striking employment gains relative to whites after 1940 in semiskilled and skilled jobs. The proportion of black professionals in Boston's black labor force increased from 5 percent to 11 percent between 1940 and 1970, although the proportion of professionals within the white labor force almost tripled during these years. Even though the rise in the black professional class admittedly did not keep pace with an even greater increase in the ranks of white professionals, these were impressive gains that could not have been made before 1940.[18]

Thernstrom's research on black Bostonians offers another useful comparison. The occupational progress that Boston blacks made between 1940 and 1970, he concludes, "does not seem to have yielded a similar narrowing of the income gap between the races." In 1950, the median income of black male workers in Boston was 71.9 percent of the white median, similar to the percentage (73.3 percent) in San Francisco. By 1960, however, the median income of black males in Boston had actually declined relative to white (66.2 percent). And although black workers recovered some of these gains between 1960 and 1970, they still earned less than three-quarters of what white males earned in 1970.[19]

Thernstrom's explanation for this "seeming paradox" in Boston also helps us understand the disparity in median income between blacks and whites in San Francisco, Oakland, and Los Angeles in 1950. Black Bostonians moved into occupations between 1940 and 1970, wrote Thernstrom, "in which the racial gap in income was widest." Thus blacks, ironically, were more likely to earn an income similar to whites in unskilled jobs than as semiskilled factory operatives, skilled craftsmen, white-collar workers, or professionals. Black professionals in Boston, in fact, earned only 66 percent of the median income of white professionals in 1970, while black unskilled laborers earned 95 percent of the median income of whites in unskilled jobs.[20] The lesson for blacks in Boston and San Francisco was clear. The upward movement of blacks into white-collar, professional, semiskilled, and skilled jobs was no assurance that they would earn the same wages of whites in these job categories for similar work.

Civil rights activity was evident in many western cities, including San Francisco, during the 1940s and 1950s. This activity had first been apparent in the early 1940s, when black leaders in Oakland, Los Angeles, and Portland worked fervently to end the segregated auxiliary unions that operated in the wartime shipyards.[21] Yet an interior western city such as Phoenix, Arizona, also showed considerable interracial activism during these years. Whether other interior western cities such as Denver, Albuquerque, and Reno also organized interracial coalitions to push harder for racial equality is not known. It is reasonable to assume, however, as Gerald D. Nash does, that "wartime conditions accelerated the breakdown of discrimination patterns and crystallized conditions that generated the civil rights movement just a decade later."

Thus World War II had a profound effect on black San Franciscans and, for that matter, on every western black community. The racial campaigns that black and white leaders waged in these cities differed only in degree. Whether blacks resided in San Francisco, Los Angeles, Orange County, Portland, Seattle, or Phoenix, they continued to struggle for equal opportunity in employment and housing and attempted to break down pernicious white attitudes that had historically viewed blacks as an inferior and unassimilable racial caste, both in western cities and throughout much of the nation. To be sure, the persistent and determined struggle had not achieved racial equality for black San Franciscans or black westerners by the mid-1960s. De facto housing and employment discrimination existed throughout the 1970s and the early 1980s to some degree, as the black Congressman Willie L. Brown, Jr., discovered when he attempted to rent an apartment in a fashionable area of San Francisco. Brown's travails were similar to those of Willie Mays almost three decades earlier—a disturbing sign that San Francisco had not resolved all of its racial problems by the 1980s. Not all black San Franciscans lived to see the dream of racial equality realized, but they never ceased working to make the dream of a multiracial, integrated society a reality.[22]

NOTES

INTRODUCTION

1. Gilbert Osofsky, *Harlem: The Making of a Ghetto: Negro New York, 1890–1930*, 2d. ed. (New York: Harper and Row, 1971); Allan H. Spear, *Black Chicago: The Making of a Negro Ghetto, 1890-1920* (Chicago: University of Chicago Press, 1967); David M. Katzman, *Before the Ghetto: Black Detroit in the Nineteenth Century* (Urbana: University of Illinois Press, 1973); Constance McLaughlin Green, *The Secret City: A History of Race Relations in the Nation's Capital* (Princeton, N.J.: Princeton University Press, 1967); Kenneth L. Kusmer, *A Ghetto Takes Shape: Black Cleveland, 1870—1930* (Urbana: University of Illinois Press, 1976); Howard N. Rabinowitz, *Race Relations in the Urban South, 1865–1890* (New York: Oxford University Press, 1978); August Meier and Elliott Rudwick, *Black Detroit and the Rise of the UAW* (New York: Oxford University Press, 1979); Thomas C. Cox, *Blacks in Topeka, Kansas, 1865–1915: A Social History* (Baton Rouge: Louisiana State University Press, 1982); John Bodnar, Roger Simon, and Michael P. Weber, *Lives of Their Own: Blacks, Italians, and Poles in Pittsburgh, 1900–1960* (Urbana: University of Illinois Press, 1982); James Borchert, *Alley Life in Washington: Family, Community, Religion, and Folklore in the City, 1850-1970* (Urbana: University of Illinois Press, 1980); Joe William Trotter, Jr., *Black Milwaukee: The Making of an Industrial Proletariat, 1915–1945* (Urbana: University of Illinois Press, 1985); George C. Wright, *Life behind a Veil: Blacks in Louisville, Kentucky, 1865–1930* (Baton Rouge: Louisiana State University Press, 1985); Darrel E. Bigham, *We Ask Only a Fair Trial: A History of the Black Community of Evansville, Indiana* (Bloomington: Indiana University Press, 1987); Nicholas Lemann, *The Promised Land: The Great Migration and How It Changed America* (New York: Knopf, 1990). For a comprehensive summary and analysis of books and articles on blacks in cities, consult Kenneth L. Kusmer, "The Black Urban Experience in American History," in Darlene Clark Hine, ed., *The State of Afro-American History: Past, Present, and Future* (Baton Rouge: Louisiana State University Press, 1986), pp. 91–122.

2. Gerald D. Nash, *The American West in the Twentieth Century: A Short History of an Urban Oasis* (Englewood Cliffs, N.J.: Prentice Hall, 1973), p. 8.

3. Quintard Taylor, "Black Urban Development—Another View: Seattle's Central District, 1910–1940," *Pacific Historical Review* 58 (November 1989): 429–48; Lawrence B. de Graaf, "Recognition, Racism, and Reflections on the Writing of Western Black History," *Pacific Historical Review* 44 (February 1975): 42; Lawrence B. de Graaf, "Negro Migration to Los Angeles, 1930–1950," Ph.D. dissertation, University of California, Los Angeles, 1962.

4. Quoted in William Issel and Robert W. Cherny, *San Francisco, 1865–1932: Politics, Power, and Urban Development* (Berkeley: University of California Press, 1986), p. 33.

5. Ibid., pp. 33–39.

6. See Rudolph Lapp, *Blacks in Gold Rush California* (New Haven, Conn.: Yale University Press, 1977); Douglas Henry Daniels, *Pioneer Urbanites: A Social and Cultural History of Black San Francisco* (Philadelphia: Temple University Press, 1980).

7. Lawrence B. de Graaf, "The City of Black Angels: Emergence of the Los Angeles Ghetto, 1890–1930," *Pacific Historical Review* 39 (August 1970): 323–52.

8. Daniels, *Pioneer Urbanites*, chs. 2–3. Herb Caen has done more to perpetuate the image of San Francisco as a liberal, tolerant, and romantic city than perhaps any other writer. The best source to consult is Caen's daily column in the *San Francisco Chronicle*. See also Herb Caen, *The San Francisco Book* (Boston: Houghton Mifflin, 1948); Herb Caen, *Baghdad-by-the-Bay* (New York: Doubleday, 1954); Herb Caen, *Only in San Francisco* (New York: Doubleday, 1960); Herb Caen and Dong Kingman, *San Francisco: City on Golden Hills* (Garden City, N.Y.: Doubleday, 1967). See also Oscar Lewis, *This Was San Francisco* (New York: David McKay, 1962).

9. Daniels, *Pioneer Urbanites*, passim.

10. Stephan Thernstrom, *The Other Bostonians: Poverty and Progress in the American Metropolis, 1880–1970* (Cambridge, Mass.: Harvard University Press, 1973).

11. Lawrence B. de Graaf, "Negro Migration," p. 242; Quintard Taylor, "The Emergence of Black Communities in the Pacific Northwest: 1865–1910," *Journal of Negro History* 64 (Fall 1979): 342–54; Quintard Taylor, Jr., "A History of Blacks in the Pacific Northwest, 1788–1970," Ph.D. dissertation, University of Minnesota, 1977, pp. 128, 162, 165, 172, 187, 195, 216.

12. Meier and Rudwick, *Black Detroit and the Rise of the UAW*, passim.

13. de Graaf, "The City of Black Angels," 323–52; Taylor, "Black Urban Development—Another View," pp. 429–48.

14. Quintard Taylor, "Blacks and Asians in a White City: Japanese Americans and African Americans in Seattle, 1890–1940," *Western Historical Quarterly* 22 (November 1991): 401–29.

15. Gunther Barth, *Bitter Strength: A History of the Chinese in the United States* (Cambridge, Mass.: Harvard University Press, 1964).

16. Trotter, *Black Milwaukee*, pp. 147–219; Bigham, *We Ask Only a Fair Trial*, pp. 217–34.

17. Arnold R. Hirsch, *Making the Second Ghetto: Race and Housing in Chicago, 1940–1960* (New York and London: Cambridge University Press, 1983); Lemann, *The Promised Land*.

18. Gerald D. Nash, *The American West Transformed: The Impact of the Second World War* (Bloomington: Indiana University Press, 1985).

19. On the use of the racial caste model in a northern city, consult Katzman,

Before the Ghetto, pp. 81-103; Jacqueline Jones, *Labor of Love, Labor of Sorrow: Black Women, Work, and the Family from Slavery to the Present* (New York: Basic Books, 1985); Lawrence B. de Graaf, "Race, Sex, and Region: Black Women in the American West, 1850–1920," *Pacific Historical Review* 49 (May 1980): 285–313.

20. William H. Chafe, *Civilities and Civil Rights: Greensboro, North Carolina, and the Black Struggle for Freedom* (New York: Oxford University Press, 1980), p. 8; George C. Wright, *Life Behind a Veil.*

21. W. E. B. Du Bois, *The Souls of Black Folk* (reprint ed., New York: New American Library, 1982), p. 54.

CHAPTER 1. THE GROWTH AND DEVELOPMENT
OF SAN FRANCISCO'S BLACK COMMUNITY, 1900–1930

1. Roger W. Lotchin, *San Francisco, 1846–1856: From Hamlet to City* (New York: Oxford University Press, 1974); Judd Kahn, *Imperial San Francisco: Politics and Planning in an American City, 1877–1906* (Lincoln: University of Nebraska Press, 1974), pp. 5–7; J. S. Holliday, *The World Rushed In: The California Gold Rush Experience* (New York: Simon and Schuster, 1981).

2. Lotchin, *San Francisco,* p. 30.

3. Ibid.

4. Kahn, *Imperial San Francisco,* pp. 6–7; William Issel and Robert W. Cherny, *San Francisco, 1865–1932: Politics, Power, and Urban Development* (Berkeley: University of California Press, 1986), p. 24.

5. Issel and Cherny, *San Francisco, 1865–1932,* p. 25; Kahn, *Imperial San Francisco,* pp. 7–11.

6. Issel and Cherny, *San Francisco, 1865–1932,* pp. 25–26.

7. Peter R. Decker, *Fortunes and Failures: White Collar Mobility in Nineteenth Century San Francisco* (Cambridge, Mass.: Harvard University Press, 1978), pp. 247–48, 260.

8. Kahn, *Imperial San Francisco,* pp. 81–84; Issel and Cherny, *San Francisco, 1865 1932,* pp. 109 11.

9. Kevin Starr, *Americans and the California Dream, 1850–1915* (New York: Oxford University Press, 1975), pp. 288–306; Decker, *Fortunes and Failures,* pp. 231–45; Kahn, *Imperial San Francisco,* pp. 80–102.

10. For early labor relations in San Francisco and the rest of the state, see Lucile Eaves, *A History of California Labor Legislation* (Berkeley: University of California Press, 1910); Issel and Cherny, *San Francisco, 1865–1932,* p. 80.

11. Issel and Cherny, *San Francisco, 1865–1932,* pp. 81-85.

12. Ibid., pp. 84–85.

13. See Fred Stripp, "The Treatment of Negro-American Workers by the AFL and the CIO in the San Francisco Bay Area," *Social Forces* 28 (March 1950): 330–32; Stripp, "The Relationship of the San Francisco Bay Area Negro-American Worker with the Labor Unions Affiliated with the American Federation of Labor and the Congress of Industrial Organizations," Th.D. thesis, Pacific School of Religion, Berkeley, 1948.

14. Decker, *Fortunes and Failures,* p. 239.

15. Ibid., pp. 60–86, 215, 237–60; Lotchin, *San Francisco,* pp. 45-82. To compare San Francisco with other cities during the nineteenth century, see Stephan Thernstrom, *Poverty and Progress: Social Mobility in a Nineteenth Century City*

(Cambridge, Mass.: Harvard University Press, 1964); Stephan Thernstrom and Richard Sennett, eds., *Nineteenth-Century Cities: Essays in the New Urban History* (New Haven, Conn.: Yale University Press, 1969), and Thernstrom, *The Other Bostonians: Poverty and Progress in the American Metropolis, 1880–1970* (Cambridge, Mass.: Harvard University Press, 1973).

16. *Proceedings of the First State Convention of the Colored Citizens of the State of California*, Sacramento, 1855; Starr, *Americans and the California Dream*, p. 76.

17. *Frederick Douglass' Paper*, December 11, 1851, October 30, 1851.

18. Mifflin W. Gibbs, *Shadow and Light: An Autobiography* (Washington, D.C., 1902, reprint ed., New York: Arno Press, 1968), pp. 44–45.

19. Gibbs, *Shadow and Light*, p. 44; Decker, *Fortunes and Failures*, pp. 118–20, 295; Rudolph M. Lapp, *Blacks in Gold Rush California* (New Haven, Conn.: Yale University Press, 1977), 95–102; James A. Fisher, "The California Negro, 1860: An Analysis of State Census Returns," African-American Historical and Cultural Society Monograph, San Francisco, n.d; Lotchin, *San Francisco*, p. 133.

20. Douglas H. Daniels, *Pioneer Urbanites: A Social and Cultural History of Black San Francisco* (Philadelphia: Temple University Press, 1980), pp. 33–41.

21. *California Legislature, Third Session*, 1852, Petition from San Francisco Residents Concerning Negro Testimony in Judicial Cases, March 22, 1852; *Proceedings of the First State Convention of the Colored Citizens of the State of California*, Sacramento, 1855; *San Francisco Pacific Appeal*, April 5, April 12, April 19, April 26, 1862; *San Francisco Elevator*, November 10, May 26, 1865; James A. Fisher, "The Struggle for Negro Testimony in California, 1851–1863," *Southern California Quarterly* 51 (December 1969): 313–34; Charles W. Wollenberg, *All Deliberate Speed: Segregation and Exclusion in California Schools, 1855–1975* (Berkeley: University of California Press, 1977), pp. 8–27; *Pleasant v. North Beach and Mission Railway Company*, 1867, California State Archives; *Charlotte L. Brown vs. the Omnibus Railway Company*, April 17, 1863, California Historical Society, San Francisco.

22. Lotchin, *San Francisco*, p. 131. On the plight of blacks in other western towns and cities, consult Eugene H. Berwanger, *The Frontier against Slavery: Western Anti-Negro Prejudice and the Slavery Extension Controversy* (Urbana: University of Illinois Press, 1967); W. Sherman Savage, *Blacks in the West* (Westport, Conn.: Greenwood Press, 1976); Thomas C. Cox, *Blacks in Topeka, Kansas: A Social History* (Baton Rouge: Louisiana State University Press, 1982); Ronald G. Coleman, "A History of Blacks in Utah, 1825–1910," Ph.D. dissertation, University of Utah, 1980; Lawrence B. de Graaf, "Recognition, Racism, and Reflections on Western Black History," *Pacific Historical Review* 44 (February 1975): 22–51. The best study of white attitudes toward blacks through the nineteenth century remains George C. Fredrickson, *The Black Image in the White Mind: The Debate on Afro-American Character and Destiny, 1817–1914* (New York: Harper and Row, 1971). To examine the status of the Irish and the Chinese in San Francisco, consult Robert A. Burchell, *The San Francisco Irish, 1848–1880* (Berkeley: University of California Press, 1980): Gunther Barth, *Bitter Strength: A History of the Chinese in the United States, 1850–1870* (Cambridge, Mass.: Harvard University Press, 1964); Alexander Saxton, *The Indispensable Enemy: Labor and the Anti-Chinese Movement in California* (Berkeley: University of California Press, 1971). On blacks in Evansville, Indiana, see Darrel E. Bigham, *We Ask Only a Fair Trial: A History of the*

Black Community of Evansville, Indiana (Bloomington: Indiana University Press, 1987); Kenneth L. Kusmer, *A Ghetto Takes Shape: Black Cleveland, 1870–1930* (Urbana: University of Illinois Press, 1976), pp. 3–31; David M. Katzman, *Before the Ghetto: Black Detroit in the Nineteenth Century* (Urbana: University of Illinois Press, 1973).

23. Philip Montesano, "San Francisco's Black Community, 1849–1890: The Quest for Equality before the Law," Ph.D. dissertation, University of California, Santa Barbara, 1974; James A. Fisher, "A History of the Political and Social Development of the Black Community in California, 1850–1950," Ph.D. dissertation, State University of New York at Stony Brook, 1971; Katzman, *Before the Ghetto*, pp. 81–84.

24. *San Francisco Elevator*, March 27, 1868; Lapp, *Blacks in Gold Rush California*, pp. 95–99, 272.

25. *San Francisco Pacific Appeal*, July 27, 1863.

26. *Pacific Appeal*, January 9, 1864, June 24, 1865; *Elevator*, August 11, 1865, June 12, 1868, May 10, 1873; *San Francisco Sentinel*, September 20, 1890.

27. *California Legislature, Third Session, 1852*, Petition from San Francisco Residents Concerning Negro Testimony in Judicial Cases, March 22, 1852; Gibbs, *Shadow and Light*, p. 47; Lotchin, *San Francisco, 1846–1856*, pp. 131–32, *Proceedings of the First State Convention of the Colored Citizens of the State of California, Held at Sacramento, November 20th, 21st, 22nd in the Colored Methodist Church*, Sacramento, 1855; *Pacific Appeal*, April 12, April 19, April 26, April 5, 1862; Herbert Aptheker, ed., *A Documentary History of the Negro People in the United States* (New York: Citadel Press, 1951), p. 416; Fisher, "The Struggle for Negro Testimony," pp. 313–24; Lapp, *Blacks in Gold Rush California*, pp. 205–209.

28. *Elevator*, April 21, 1865, September 20, 1867, February 21, 1868; *Pacific Appeal*, August 22, 1863, October 26, 1867; Kusmer, *A Ghetto Takes Shape*, pp. 7–8; Gilbert Osofsky, *Harlem: The Making of a Ghetto, 1890–1930* (New York: Harper and Row, 1963), pp. 35–36.

29. *Elevator*, November 10, May 26, 1865: Brainerd Dyer, "One Hundred Years of Negro Suffrage," *Pacific Historical Review* 41 (February 1968): 1–20. For a general treatment of black suffrage during Reconstruction, see Leslie H. Fishel, Jr., "Northern Prejudice and Negro Suffrage, 1865–1870," *Journal of Negro History* 39 (January 1954): 8–26; Forrest G. Wood, *Black Scare: The Racist Response to Emancipation and Reconstruction* (Berkeley: University of California Press, 1968); Eugene Berwanger, *The West and Reconstruction* (Urbana: University of Illinois Press, 1981), pp. 158–84; Eric Foner, *Reconstruction: America's Unfinished Revolution, 1863–1877* (New York: Harper and Row, 1988), pp. 291, 314, 446–49, 518–19.

30. *Pacific Appeal*, April 26, 1862; *Elevator*, June 21, 1865; *Frederick Douglass' Papers*, September 22, 1854; *New York Anglo-African*, March 1859, pp. 80–83. For early examples of segregation in the California public schools, see Nicholas C. Polos, "Segregation and John Swett," *Southern California Quarterly* 46 (March 1964): 69–82. Some Catholic schools also segregated blacks. See Ann Curry, *Mother Teresa Comer Ford, Foundress of the Sisters of the Presentation* (San Francisco, n.p., n.d.); Wollenberg, *All Deliberate Speed*; Leonard P. Curry, *The Free Black in Urban America, 1800–1850: The Shadow of the Dream* (Chicago: University of Chicago Press, 1981), pp. 147–73; Lotchin, *San Francisco*, p. 320; *Elevator*, March 26, 1869; *Manual of the Board of Education of the City and County of San Francisco, 1860 and 1861* (San Francisco: Towne and Bacon,

1860), copy in the Jeremiah Burke Sanderson Papers, Bancroft Library, University of California, Berkeley; *Pacific Appeal*, November 19, 1871; Carleton Mabee, *Black Education in New York State, from Colonial to Modern Times* (New York: Syracuse University Press, 1979).

31. *San Francisco Municipal Reports, 1861–1862*, pp. 202, 204; *Pacific Appeal*, June 12 and June 19, 1875, May 27, 1870. During the 1850s, a larger proportion of blacks attended school than whites. By the 1860s, however, the trend had been reversed. See Lotchin, *San Francisco*, p. 320.

32. *Pacific Appeal*, November 25, 1871, March 15, May 17, August 30, November 15, and November 22, 1873.

33. "Testimony of Mary Francis Ward," Mary Francis Ward Papers, California Historical Society, San Francisco; Speech from Hon. J. F. Cowdery of San Francisco, "The Word White in California School Laws," January 30, 1874, House of Assembly, Sacramento, California, January 3, 1874; *Dwinelle's Argument on the Rights of Negroes in California to the Supreme Court of California, on the Rights of Colored Children to be Admitted to the Public Schools*, California Historical Society, San Francisco; *Pacific Appeal*, January 9, August 7, and July 10, 1875; *Ward v. Flood, California Reports* (1874), vol. 48, pp. 36–57; *Statutes of California, 1880*, p. 142. For evidence of the persistence of segregation in California's schools, see Charles Wollenberg, "Mendez vs. Westminister: Race, Nationality, and Segregation in California Schools," *California Historical Society Quarterly* 53 (Winter 1974): 317–32, and Wollenberg, *All Deliberate Speed*, pp. 21–27.

34. *Pacific Appeal*, July 10, August 7, 1875; Wollenberg, *All Deliberate Speed*, pp. 25–26.

35. *Pacific Appeal*, May 24, 1862, March 4 and July 4, 1863; *Pleasant v. North Beach and Mission Railway Company*, California State Archives, Sacramento, 1867; W. Sherman Savage, "Mary Ellen Pleasant," in *Notable American Women, 1607–1950* (Cambridge, Mass.: Belknap Press of Harvard University Press, 1971), pp.75–77; *Charlotte L. Brown v. the Omnibus Railway Company*, April 17, 1863, California Historical Society.

36. Lapp, *Blacks in Gold Rush California*, pp. 106, 208–09, 268–69; Gibbs, *Shadow and Light*, p. 46; Lotchin, *San Francisco*, pp. 130–33; *Pacific Appeal*, April 5, 1862, September 28, 1867; *Elevator*, September 13, 1873; Decker, *Fortunes and Failures*, p. 120.

37. Daniels, *Pioneer Urbanites*, pp. 36–42.

38. Issel and Cherny, *San Francisco, 1865–1932*, pp. 81, 125–26. On the growth of the Chinese community in San Francisco, see Saxton, *The Indispensable Enemy*; pp. 3–7.

39. U.S. Bureau of the Census, *Population of the United States at the Eleventh Census: 1890*, pt. 1 (Washington, D.C.: Government Printing Office, 1895), p.404; U.S. Bureau of the Census, *Twelfth Census of the United States, 1900*, vol. 1, pt. 1, *Population* (Washington, D.C.: Government Printing Office, 1901), p. 531; U.S. Bureau of the Census, *Thirteenth Census of the United States* (Washington, D.C.: Government Printing Office, 1913), p. 593; U.S. Bureau of the Census, *Fourteenth Census of the United States*, vol. 2, *Population* (Washington, D.C.: Government Printing Office, 1922), pp. 116–17, 127, 304; U.S. Bureau of the Census, *Fifteenth Census of the United States, Population*, vol. 3, pt. 1, *Reports by States* (Washington, D.C.: Government Printing Office, 1933), pp. 61, 69, 285–87; U. S. Bureau of the Census, *Sixteenth Census of the United States*, vol. 2, pt. 1, *Characteristics of the Population, Reports by States* (Washington, D.C.: Government Printing Office, 1943), pp. 621, 660.

40. *Fourteenth Census of the United States*, vol. 2, *Population*, pp. 116–17, 127, 304; *Fifteenth Census of the United States, Population*, vol. 3, pt. 1, *Reports by States*, pp. 61, 69, 285–87; *Sixteenth Census of the United States*, vol. 2, pt. 1, *Characteristics of the Population, Reports by States*, pp. 621, 660.

41. Allan H. Spear, *Black Chicago: The Making of a Negro Ghetto, 1890–1920* (Chicago: University of Chicago Press, 1967), pp. 129–146; Kusmer, *A Ghetto Takes Shape*, pp. 157–173; Lawrence B. de Graaf, "Negro Migration to Los Angeles, 1930–1950," Ph.D. dissertation, University of California, Los Angeles, 1962; Osofsky, *Harlem*; W. E. B. Du Bois, *The Philadelphia Negro* (Philadelphia: University of Pennsylvania Press, 1899); James R. Grossman, "The Great Migration: A Leaderless Movement?" paper presented at the American Historical Association Annual Meeting, December 1983. Peter Gottlieb examines the importance of kinship networks as a factor in northern migration in *Making Their Own Way: Southern Blacks' Migration to Pittsburgh, 1916–30* (Urbana: University of Illinois Press, 1987).

42. *Oakland, California, Sunshine*, April 28, 1906; *San Francisco Examiner*, April 19, 1906; *Official Memorial Souvenir, San Francisco Earthquake*, April 18, 1906 (Los Angeles: Radial, 1906).

43. Spear, *Black Chicago*, p. 140; Bigham, *We Ask Only a Fair Trial*, p. 108; Joe William Trotter, *Black Milwaukee: The Making of an Industrial Proletariat, 1915–1945* (Urbana: University of Illinois Press, 1985), p. 41.

44. Florette Henri, *Black Migration: Movement North, 1900–1920* (Garden City, N.Y.: Anchor Press, 1975), p. 66; Spear, *Black Chicago*, pp. 129, 134–36. Emory Tolbert discusses the growth of Los Angeles' black community between 1910 and 1930 and the ease with which blacks were able to purchase property in some areas of Los Angeles. See Emory Tolbert, *The UNIA and Black Los Angeles: Ideology and Community in the American Garvey Movement* (Los Angeles: Center for Afro-American Studies, 1980), pp. 88–93.

45. Horace Cayton and St. Clair Drake, *Black Metropolis*, vol. 2 (New York: Harcourt, Brace, and World, 1945); John Daniels, *In Freedom's Birthplace* (Boston: Houghton Mifflin, 1914); Mary White Ovington, *Half a Man: The Status of the Negro in New York* (New York: Longmans, Green, 1911); Du Bois, *The Philadelphia Negro*; Daniel Patrick Moynihan, "The Negro Family in America: The Case for National Action," reprinted in Lee Rainwater and William Yancey, eds., *The Moynihan Report and the Politics of Controversy* (Cambridge, Mass.: M.I.T. Press, 1967); E. Franklin Frazier, *The Negro Family in Chicago* (Chicago: University of Chicago Press, 1932); E. Franklin Frazier, *The Negro Family in the United States* (Chicago: University of Chicago Press, 1939); Herbert Gutman, *The Black Family in Slavery and Freedom, 1750–1925* (New York: Pantheon Books, 1976); Andrew Billingsley, *Black Families in White America* (Englewood Cliffs, N.J.: Prentice-Hall, 1968); Robert Staples, *The Black Family, Essays and Studies: Sex, Marriage, and Family* (Chicago: Nelson-Hall, 1975); Staples, "The Myth of the Black Matriarchy," *Black Scholar* (January/February, 1970): 8–16. Osofsky, *Harlem*, pp. 138–143, 151–155.

46. Philip M. Montesano, "The 1900 Census: Data on Black Families in San Francisco," pp. 75–77, *Proceedings of the Bicentennial Symposium, Historical Perspectives on the Family and Society*, October 21, 1975, Stanford University; *Fifteenth Census of the United States*, vol. 6, *Families*, pp. 82, 168; Gutman, *The Black Family in Slavery and Freedom*, pp. 432–56.

47. *Fifteenth Census of the United States*, vol. 6, *Families*, p. 82.

48. Ibid., p. 163.

49. Ibid., p. 82.

50. Ibid., p. 108; *Sixteenth Census of the United States, 1940*, vol. 4, *Characteristics by Age*, p. 657; Lawrence B. de Graaf, "Race, Sex, and Region: Black Women in the American West, 1850–1920," *Pacific Historical Review* 49 (May 1980): 287–89; interviews with Alfred Butler, November 5, December 10, 1976, San Francisco; interview with Katherine Stewart Flippin, February 17, 1976, San Francisco.

51. *Fourteenth Census of the United States, 1920*, vol. 2, *Population*, pp. 116–17; *Thirteenth Census of the United States, 1910*, p. 593; *Fifteenth Census of the United States, 1930*, vol. 3, *Reports by States*, p. 61; *Sixteenth Census of the United States, 1940*, vol. 2, pt. 1, pp. 115–16; *Special Census of San Francisco, California*, August 1, 1945 (Washington, D.C.: Government Printing Office, 1945); *1950 Census of Population*, vol. 2, *Characteristics of the Population*, pt. 5 (Washington, D.C.: Government Printing Office, 1952), pp. 5–207; Bigham, *We Ask Only a Fair Trial*, p. 24.

52. *Fifteenth Census of the United States, 1930*, vol. 3, pt. 1, *Reports by States* (Washington, D.C.: Government Printing Office, 1933), p. 69; Mabee's *Black Education in New York State* also examines a black population with a high rate of literacy. On literacy in Cleveland's black community, see Kusmer, *A Ghetto Takes Shape*, p. 211.

53. *Sixteenth Census of the United States, 1940*, vol. 2, *Characteristics of the Population*, p. 660. For the shortcomings of black education in the South, see Henry Allen Bullock, *A History of Negro Education in the South, from 1619 to the Present* (New York: Praeger, 1970); Louis R. Harlan, *Separate and Unequal: Public School Campaigns and Racism in the Southern Seaboard States, 1901–1915* (New York: Atheneum, 1969); James D. Anderson, *The Education of Blacks in the South, 1860–1935* (Chapel Hill: University of North Carolina Press, 1988).

54. William H. Hollinger, "Health of the Negro in San Francisco," M. A. thesis, Stanford University, 1948, pp. 12–28, 35, 56; interview with Seaton Manning, president of the San Francisco Urban League, 1945–1960, June 17, 1976, San Francisco; interview with Edward Howden, June 7, 1983, San Francisco; *The Annual Reports of the San Francisco Health Department from 1897–1945* were also consulted and were important in corroborating Hollinger's findings. See also *Mortality Statistics 1935: 36th Annual Report* (Washington, D.C.: Government Printing Office, 1937), p. 104; *Annual Reports of the San Francisco Health Department, Division of Statistics, 1914–1953* (San Francisco: City and County of San Francisco); Drake and Cayton, *Black Metropolis*, vol. 1, pp. 204–5; Osofsky, *Harlem*, pp. 151–55.

55. Delilah L. Beasley, *The Negro Trail Blazers of California* (Los Angeles: Times Mirror Printing, 1919), pp. 105–6; *San Francisco Call*, April 27, 1889, p. 5; interview with Josephine Cole, December 9, 1976, San Francisco.

56. *San Francisco Police Department Annual Reports, 1940–1945*; Du Bois, *The Philadelphia Negro*, pp. 235–68; Herbert Asbury, *The Barbary Coast: An Informal History of the San Francisco Underworld* (New York: Capricorn, 1968); Ruth Rosen, *The Lost Sisterhood: Prostitution in America, 1900–1918* (Baltimore, Md.: Johns Hopkins University Press, 1982); de Graaf, "Race, Sex, and Region," pp. 285–313. For a broader survey of western black women and crime, consult Anne M. Butler, "Still in Chains: Black Women in Western Prisons, 1865–1910," *Western Historical Quarterly* 20 (February 1989): 18–35; Issel and Cherny, *San Francisco*, p. 71; Barth, *Bitter Strength*, p. 85.

57. *Statistical Report of the San Francisco Juvenile Court, 1927, 1929, 1932, 1938* (San Francisco: City and County of San Francisco); *Youth in a Changing World: San Francisco Juvenile Court Annual Report, 1944* (San Francisco: City and County of San Francisco), p. 37.

58. Ovington, *Half a Man*; Du Bois, *The Philadelphia Negro*, p. 195; Ricardo Romo, *East Los Angeles, History of a Barrio* (Austin: University of Texas Press, 1983), pp. 66–67.

59. Interview with Alfred Butler, November 5, 1976, San Francisco; interview with F. L. Ritchardson, September 13, 1976, San Francisco.

60. Loren Miller, *The Petitioners: The Story of the Supreme Court of the United States and the Negro* (New York: Pantheon Books, 1966), p. 246; Roger L. Rice, "Residential Segregation by Law, 1910–1917," *Journal of Southern History* 31 (May 1968): 179–99; Lawrence B. de Graaf, "The City of Black Angels: Emergence of the Los Angeles Ghetto, 1890–1930," *Pacific Historical Review* 39 (August 1970): 352; Spear, *Black Chicago*, pp. 147–66; Kusmer, *A Ghetto Takes Shape*, pp. 167–71; Dominic J. Capeci, Jr., *Race Relations in Wartime Detroit: The Sojourner Truth Housing Controversy of 1942* (Philadelphia: Temple University Press, 1984).

61. All information concerning residential characteristics was taken from the United States printed censuses, "Population by Assembly Districts," and checked to ascertain street boundaries by using the assembly district maps in the San Francisco Archives, City Hall, San Francisco. I consulted San Francisco assembly district maps for 1902, 1904, 1907, 1912, 1916, 1926, 1929, 1932, and 1938.

62. *San Francisco Spokesman*, November 22, 1933, p. 6; interviews with Alfred Butler, November 5, 1976, and F. L. Ritchardson, September 13, 1976. Both lived in the Fillmore district before the Second World War. Consult the *Spokesman* between 1932 and 1935 for a representative list of black business establishments during the 1930s. City directories were of little value in locating black businesses.

63. Compiled from printed United States censuses, 1910–1940; San Francisco assembly district maps, 1902, 1916, 1929, 1938, San Francisco City Archives. An Oakland printer, Charles Tilghman, undertook a personal census of black San Franciscans between 1916 and 1917. His results, though not comprehensive, were representative of black residential patterns for the entire city. See *Tilghman's Directory of the Leading Cities of Northern California 1916–1917* (Oakland, Calif.: Tilghman Printing, 1917).

64. U.S. Bureau of the Census, *Fifteenth Census of the United States, 1930*, vol. 6, *Families*, p. 161; Montesano, "The 1900 Census," pp. 57–77; John Bodnar, Roger Simon, and Michael Weber, *Lives of Their Own: Blacks, Italians, and Poles in Pittsburgh, 1900–1960* (Urbana: University of Illinois Press, 1982) pp. 255–57.

65. *1939 Real Property Survey, San Francisco, California* (San Francisco: City and County of San Francisco, 1941), pp. 6, 7–9, 24–30; *Housing Authority of the City and County of San Francisco, California, Annual Report for the Year Ending April 18, 1939*, pp. 3–4. To compare the substandard housing of black San Franciscans with housing in another city during the 1930s, see Raymond A. Mohl, "Trouble in Paradise: Race and Housing in Miami during the New Deal Era," *Prologue* 19 (Spring 1987): 7–21.

66. *1939 Real Property Survey*, pp. 4–10, 26–27; *San Francisco Housing Authority, First Annual Report*, pp. 1–5.

67. Issel and Cherny, *San Francisco, 1865–1932.*
68. Issel and Cherny, *San Francisco, 1865–1932*, pp. 56, 70–71; Willard B. Farwell, *The Chinese at Home and Abroad* (San Francisco: A. L. Bancroft, 1885), pp. 5–8.
69. U.S. Bureau of the Census, *Twelfth Census of the United States, 1900*, vol. 1, pt. 1, *Population*, pp. 531, 610; Ophelia Davison to Stuart Davison, November 21, 1918, Stuart T. Davison Papers, African American Historical and Cultural Society, San Francisco; *San Francisco Housing Authority, Second Annual Report, April 18, 1940*, p. 15; *San Francisco Board of Supervisors, Journal of Proceedings, 1938–1940*; *Langley's San Francisco City Directory 1935*, pp. 406, 602; interviews with Josephine Cole, daughter of Joseph Foreman, December 9, 1976, San Francisco; and Mrs. Emma Scott Jones, daughter of Mrs. Emma Scott, June 15, 1976, San Francisco; "Financial Record and Membership Record of San Francisco Branch, NAACP," January 1, 1926, Stewart-Flippin Papers, Moorland-Spingarn Research Center, Howard University (hereafter cited as Stewart-Flippin Papers); *Thirteenth Census of the United States, 1910*, p. 186.
70. *Oakland Sunshine*, December 21, 1907; California Assembly Bill 1057, January 21, 1927, introduced by Fred Roberts (original copy in San Francisco Branch files, NAACP Papers, Library of Congress, Washington, D.C., hereafter cited as SFBF, NAACP Papers); director of NAACP Branches to secretary [Lena] Parker, June 17, 1927, SFBF, NAACP Papers; *Western American*, March 18, 1927.
71. *Divisadero District Advocate*, October 10, 1924; *Spokesman*, May 17, 1934, p. 6; "Financial and Membership Records of the San Francisco Branch, NAACP," May 12, 1924 and October 13, 1924, Stewart-Flippin Papers.
72. Interviews with F. L. Ritchardson, September 13, 1976, and February 15, 1977, San Francisco.
73. *Divisadero District Advocate*, October 10, 1924. Blacks in Los Angeles experienced similar problems. See de Graaf, "The City of Black Angels," 348–49.
74. Interview with F. L. Ritchardson, September 13, 1976, San Francisco. This story was confirmed by Katherine Stewart Flippin in an interview on February 17, 1976, in San Francisco. Mrs. Flippin's mother, Mary McCants Stewart, was a cofounder of the Booker T. Washington Community Center. Edward Mabson to Robert Bagnall, October 7, 1924, SFBF, box 23, NAACP Papers; *Divisadero District Advocate*, October 10, 1924.
75. *History of Booker T. Washington Community Center, 1921–1971*; Mabson to Bagnall, October 7, 1924, SFBF, box 23, NAACP Papers; interview with F. L. Ritchardson, September 13, 1976, San Francisco; "Annual Report of the Booker T. Washington Community Center, 1929," Stewart-Flippin Papers; "Preliminary Report on the Booker T. Washington Community Center" [1938–1939], 25 p., Stewart-Flippin Papers.
76. *1939 Real Property Survey*, p. 32.
77. Alma Taeuber and Karl Taeuber, *Negroes in Cities: Residential Segregation and Neighborhood Change* (Chicago: Aldine Publishing, 1965), pp. 40–44; See Curry, *The Free Black in Urban America*, pp. 54–56, regarding the difficulty of measuring residential segregation. See also Kusmer, *A Ghetto Takes Shape*, p. 52, concerning the residential segregation index of San Francisco before 1930. Kusmer states, but offers no evidence, that the residential segregation index was relatively low in San Francisco before 1930 compared to most northern cities. In their study the Taeubers computed the residential segregation index for San Francisco and numerous northern cities between 1940 and 1960, sug-

gesting increasing ghettoization of black San Franciscans and a change in the residential segregation index between 1930 and 1940. Darrel E. Bigham's study of Evansville, Indiana, offers a useful comparison with San Francisco. See Bigham, *We Ask Only a Fair Trial*, pp. 21–34, 114–16; Trotter, *Black Milwaukee*, pp. 21–25, 180–82.

78. de Graaf, "The City of Black Angels," pp. 323–352; *1939 Real Property Survey*, p. 35; Charles S. Johnson, *The Negro War Worker in San Francisco* (San Francisco: n.p., 1944), p. 3; E. Franklin Frazier, *The Negro in the United States* (New York: Macmillan, 1957), pp. 270–71.

CHAPTER 2. EMPLOYMENT AND ENTERPRISE, 1900–1930

1. Carey McWilliams, *California: The Great Exception* (New York: Current Books, 1949); Ira Cross, *A History of the Labor Movement in California* (Berkeley: University of California Press, 1935); Lucile Eaves, *A History of California Labor Legislation* (Berkeley: University of California Press, 1910); U.S. Bureau of the Census, *Twelfth Census of the United States, 1900: Occupations* (Washington, D.C.: Government Printing Office, 1904), pp. 720–24; U.S. Bureau of the Census, *Fifteenth Census of the United States, 1929: Manufacturers* (Washington, D.C.: Government Printing Office, 1933), pp. 74–75; San Francisco *Labor Clarion*, August 29, 1919.

2. *Fifteenth Census of the United States, 1930*, vol. 3, pt. 2, *Occupations, Reports by States*, pp. 208–10.

3. Kusmer, *A Ghetto Takes Shape: Black Cleveland, 1870–1930* (Urbana: University of Illinois Press, 1976), pp. 275–79; *Western Appeal*, June 22 and November 2, 1921; Joe W. Trotter, Jr., *Black Milwaukee: The Making of a Black Proletariat, 1915–1945* (Urbana: University of Illinois Press, 1985); John Bodnar, Roger Simon, and Michael P. Weber, *Lives of Their Own: Blacks, Italians, and Poles in Pittsburgh, 1900–1960* (Urbana: University of Illinois Press, 1982), pp. 58–65.

4. J. Alexander Somerville, *Man of Color* (Los Angeles: L. L. Morrison, 1949), pp. 26–55; Max J. Williams and Rene A. Hewlett, eds., *Negro Who's Who in California*, 1948 ed. (Negro Who's Who in California Publishing Company), p. 10; "C. L. Dellums, International President of the Brotherhood of Sleeping Car Porters and Civil Rights Leader," interview conducted by the Bancroft Regional Oral History Office, University of California, Berkeley, 1973, pp. 4–8 (hereafter cited as "C. L. Dellums Interview"); *Oakland Sunshine*, May 29, January 2, 1915; *San Francisco Spokesman*, March 5, 1932, p. 1, January 20, 1934, p. 6.

5. "C. L. Dellums Interview," p. 6; interview with F. L. Ritchardson, February 15, 1976, San Francisco; interview with Revels Cayton, October 21, 1976, San Francisco; *San Francisco Examiner*, November 15, 1978.

6. Information concerning occupations was taken from published censuses of occupations, 1900–1930. See *Twelfth Census of the United States, 1900: Occupations*, pp. 720–24.

7. *Twelfth Census of the United States, 1900: Occupations*, pp. 720–24; U.S. Bureau of the Census, *Thirteenth Census of the United States*, vol. 4, *Occupations* (Washington, D.C.: Government Printing Office, 1913), pp. 600–601; U.S. Bureau of the Census, *Women in Gainful Occupations, 1870 to 1920*, Census Monograph 9 (Washington, D.C.: Government Printing Office, 1929), pp. 8–13; David Katzman, *Seven Days a Week: Women and Domestic Service in Industri-

alizing America (New York: Oxford University Press, 1978), pp. 184–222; See the *San Francisco Examiner,* November 15, 1978, p. A-2, regarding the attitude of a black woman toward economic opportunity in San Francisco; David A. Gerber, *Black Ohio and the Color Line, 1860–1915* (Urbana: University of Illinois Press, 1976), pp. 68–69; Kusmer, *A Ghetto Takes Shape,* pp. 84–85; Glenda Riley, "American Daughters: Black Women in the West," *Montana, the Magazine of Western History* 38 (Spring 1988): 14–27; Sandra L. Myres, *Westering Women: The Frontier Experience, 1800–1915* (Albuquerque: University of New Mexico Press, 1982), pp. 85–86.

8. *Thirteenth Census of the United States,* vol. 4, *Occupations,* pp. 600–601; Kusmer, *A Ghetto Takes Shape,* pp. 80–81; Albert S. Broussard, "McCants Stewart: The Struggles of a Black Attorney in the Urban West," *Oregon Historical Quarterly,* 89 (Summer 1988): 159–79; William L. Patterson, *The Man Who Cried Genocide* (New York: International Publishers, 1971), pp. 39–46.

9. *Thirteenth Census of the United States, 1910,* vol. 4, *Occupations,* pp. 600–601; Darlene Clark Hine, *Black Women in White: Racial Conflict and Cooperation in the Nursing Profession, 1890–1950* (Bloomington: Indiana University Press, 1989), pp. 87–107; Trotter, *Black Milwaukee,* pp. 93, 96–97; Darrel E. Bigham, *We Ask Only a Fair Trial: A History of the Black Community of Evansville, Indiana* (Bloomington: Indiana University Press, 1987), pp. 165–66; Leonard Curry, *The Free Black in Urban America, 1800–1850: The Shadow of the Dream* (Chicago: University of Chicago Press, 1981), pp. 146–68.

10. U.S. Bureau of the Census, *Fourteenth Census of the United States, 1920,* vol. 2, *Population* (Washington, D.C.: Government Printing Office, 1922), pp. 1226–30; *Fifteenth Census of the United States, 1930,* vol. 3, pt. 2, *Occupations, Reports by States,* pp. 208–10; Berlinda Davison, "Educational Status of the Negro in the San Francisco Bay Region," M.A. thesis, University of California, Berkeley, 1921, pp. 10, 19–20; Robert Coleman Francis, "A Survey of Negro Business in the San Francisco Bay Region," M.A. thesis, University of California, Berkeley, 1928, pp. 46–47; interview with Katherine Stewart Flippin, July 19, 1986, San Francisco, regarding her mother, Mary McCants Stewart. Unlike Kenneth L. Kusmer, who placed black barbers and hairdressers in the category of skilled workers, I have left them in the category of domestic and personal service workers, for these individuals did not have the wealthy white clientele in San Francisco that Kusmer found common among black barbers in Cleveland. See Kusmer, *A Ghetto Takes Shape,* pp. 277–79.

11. San Francisco *Sun-Reporter,* April 26, 1975; U.S. Bureau of the Census, *Special Census of San Francisco, California, Population by Age, Color, and Sex, for Census Tracts, August 1, 1945* (Washington, D.C.: Government Printing Office, 1945). Peter Gottlieb and Joe William Trotter provide excellent examples of how industrial jobs attracted black migrants to Pittsburgh and Milwaukee. See Gottlieb, *Making Their Own Way: Southern Blacks' Migration to Pittsburgh, 1916–30* (Urbana: University of Illinois Press, 1987); Trotter, *Black Milwaukee.*

12. *Fourteenth Census of the United States, 1920,* vol. 2, *Population,* pp. 1227–28. The 1910 census did not separate occupations by race other than "white" and "nonwhite." Thus, the changes in occupational patterns for blacks in San Francisco can only be measured over the intervals from 1900 to 1920, and 1920 to 1930. On information regarding black seamen, see *Crocker-Langley's San Francisco City Directory,* (San Francisco: R. L. Polk, 1931), p. 1802; interview with Revels Cayton, November 11, 1976, San Francisco. Cayton was a former black seaman and an officer within the seamen's union. Quintard Taylor, Jr., "A His-

tory of Blacks in the Pacific Northwest, 1788–1970," Ph.D. dissertation, University of Minnesota, 1977, p. 183; "Valenti Angelo, Arts and Books: A Glorious Variety," interview conducted by the Bancroft Regional Oral History Office, 1977–1979, University of California, Berkeley, p. 71; Trotter, *Black Milwaukee*, pp. xii, 47, 53; George C. Wright, *Life Behind a Veil: Blacks in Louisville, Kentucky, 1865–1930* (Baton Rouge: Louisiana State University Press, 1985), pp. 77, 214, 216; Bodnar, Weber, and Simon, *Lives of Their Own*, pp. 58–65; Howard N. Rabinowitz, *Race Relations in the Urban South, 1865–1890* (New York: Oxford University Press, 1978), pp. 66–67.

13. Delilah L. Beasley, *The Negro Trail Blazers of California* (Los Angeles: Times Mirror Printing, 1919), p. 149; *Spokesman*, May 17, April 5, and October 12, 1934, February 22 and February 27, 1935. Leland Hawkins to Walter White, March 11, 1933; and William Pickens to Leland Hawkins, October, 1934, San Francisco Branch files, NAACP Papers, Library of Congress, Washington, D.C. (hereafter referred to as SFBF, NAACP Papers); August Meier and Elliott Rudwick, *Black Detroit and the Rise of the UAW* (New York: Oxford University Press, 1979), pp. 3–33.

14. *San Francisco Labor Clarion*, August 29, 1919, September 10, 1915, October 10, 1919; *Report of the Proceedings of the Thirty-Seventh Annual Convention of the American Federation of Labor,* (Washington, D.C.: Law Reporter Printing, 1917), pp. 349–50; William H. Harris, *The Harder We Run: Black Workers since the Civil War* (New York: Oxford University Press, 1982), pp. 42–44, 48; Michael Paul Rogin and John L. Shover, *Political Change in California: Critical Elections and Social Movements, 1890–1966* (Westport, Conn.: Greenwood Press, 1970), pp. 68–69; Walter White to William L. Green, October 3, 1933; Assistant Secretary, NAACP to Horace Cayton, October 29, 1934, Labor, Series C, NAACP Papers.

15. Victor Anthony Walsh, "The International Longshoreman's Association: The Rebirth of a Union," M.A. thesis, San Francisco State University, 1971, pp. 168–69; *Spokesman*, May 19 and August 9, 1934.

16. John W. Blassingame, *Black New Orleans, 1860–1880* (Chicago: University of Chicago Press, 1973), pp. 64–65; Robert Coleman Francis, "A History of Labor on the San Francisco Waterfront," Ph.D. dissertation, University of California, Berkeley, 1934, p. 103, 161, 171–72, 182–83; David M. Katzman, *Before the Ghetto: Black Detroit in the Nineteenth Century* (Urbana: University of Illinois Press, 1973), pp. 106, 118–120, 125; *San Francisco Sun-Reporter*, May 10, 1975; Fred Stripp, "The Relationship of the San Francisco Bay Area Negro-American Worker with the Labor Unions Affiliated with the American Federation of Labor and the Congress of Industrial Unions," Th.D. thesis, Pacific School of Religion, Berkeley, Calif., 1948; Stuart T. Davison, "Membership Card, Waterfront Employee's Union," August 3, 1920, Davison Papers, African American Historical and Cultural Society, San Francisco.

17. "T. Arnold Hill Survey," National Urban League Papers, San Francisco Affiliate files, Library of Congress, Washington, D.C.; "C. L. Dellums Interview," pp. 6–8; William Muraskin, *Middle-Class Blacks in a White Society: Prince Hall Freemasonry in America* (Berkeley: University of California Press, 1975), pp. 89–90; Quintard Taylor, "Blacks and Asians in a White City: Japanese Americans and African Americans in Seattle, 1890–1940," *Western Historical Quarterly* 22 (November 1991): 404; *San Francisco Sun-Reporter*, May 24, 1975.

18. Interview with Naomi Johnson regarding her father, Orval Anderson, September 30, 1976, San Francisco; interview with Alfred Butler, a former

railroad employee and relative of Walter Maddox, November 5, 1976, San Francisco; Stuart T. Davison to his mother, April 27, 1916, Davison Papers, African-American Historical and Cultural Society, San Francisco; Lawrence P. Crouchett, *William Byron Rumford: The Life and Public Services of a California Legislator* (El Cerrito, Calif.: Downey Place Publishing, 1984), pp. 10–16; A. Philip Randolph to C. L. Dellums, May 11 and June 14, 1928, Brotherhood of Sleeping Car Porters Papers, Bancroft Library, University of California, Berkeley; William H. Harris, *Keeping the Faith: A. Philip Randolph, Milton P. Webster, and the Brotherhood of Sleeping Car Porters, 1925–1937* (Urbana: University of Illinois Press, 1977), p. 41; Grossman, *Land of Hope*, pp. 129, 139. See the membership lists in the Brotherhood of Sleeping Car Porters Papers at both the Bancroft Library and the Library of Congress for the names and addresses of Bay Area black railroad workers. Most of these workers resided in Oakland, rather than San Francisco.

19. For the early struggles of the Brotherhood of Sleeping Car Porters for recognition, see Jervis Anderson, *A. Philip Randolph: A Biographical Portrait* (New York: Harcourt, 1973); William H. Harris, *Keeping the Faith*, passim; "C. L. Dellums Interview," pp. 13–15; William H. Harris, *The Harder We Run: Black Workers since the Civil War* (New York: Oxford University Press, 1982), pp. 77–94.

20. Albert S. Broussard, "Carlotta Stewart Lai, a Black Teacher in the Territory of Hawai'i," *Hawaiian Journal of History* 24 (1990): 129–54.

21. *Western Appeal*, October 14, 1920; interview with Josephine Cole, December 9, 1976, San Francisco; interview with Naomi Johnson, September 30, 1976, San Francisco; interview with F. L. Ritchardson, February 15, 1976, San Francisco. Although blacks worked in the post office in every northern city, no scholar has documented the practice of dismissing black workers after a specified period in order to avoid granting permanent status and seniority.

22. Florence P. Kahn to C. L. Synder, June 23, 1930; Walter A. Butler to William T. Andrews, December 11, 1930; John T. Doyle to Andrews, December 8, 1930, all from the SFBF, NAACP Papers. Information on Richard Williamson can also be found in the "Financial Record and Membership Record of the San Francisco Branch, NAACP," January 1, 1926, Stewart-Flippin Papers, Moorland-Springarn Research Center, Howard University.

23. "William Byron Rumford, Legislator for Fair Employment, Fair Housing and Public Health," Bancroft Regional Oral History Office, University of California, Berkeley, 1973, pp. 5–9; *Spokesman*, June 22, 1933; Lawrence P. Crouchett, *William Byron Rumford: The Life and Public Services of a California Legislator*, pp. 22–24. For Rumford's opinion of job discrimination within the Civil Service, consult the interview conducted by the Bancroft Regional Oral History Office of twenty-four people who knew Walter Gordon. See "Walter Gordon, Athlete, Office in Law Enforcement and Administration, Governor of the Virgin Islands" (1976–1979), pp. 174–177. Kusmer also found Civil Service discrimination in his study of blacks in Cleveland. See Kusmer, *A Ghetto Takes Shape*, p. 79.

24. Taylor, "Blacks and Asians," pp. 412–15; Willard B. Gatewood, *Aristocrats of Color: The Black Elite, 1880–1920* (Bloomington: Indiana University Press, 1990).

25. Patterson, *The Man who Cried Genocide*, pp. 40–41.

26. McCants Stewart to Katherine Stewart, March 10, March 24, March 31, December 11, 1917, Stewart-Flippin Papers; interviews with Katherine Stewart

Flippin, the daughter of McCants Stewart, February 17, 1976, and July 19, 1986, San Francisco. A reprinted copy of the suicide note is located in box 97-4 of the Stewart-Flippin Papers.

27. Patterson, *The Man Who Cried Genocide*, pp. 44–45; interview with Naomi Johnson, September 30, 1976, San Francisco (Mrs. Johnson is the surviving sister of the black female attorney Tabytha Anderson). The letters of black attorney S. L. Mash are also revealing in illustrating the difficulties of black attorneys. See S. L. Mash to Most Reverend P. W. Riordan, February 28, 1914, Chancery Archives, Colma, Calif.: See Dan T. Carter, *Scottsboro: A Tragedy of the American South* (Baton Rouge: Louisiana State University Press, 1979), pp. 147–48, concerning Patterson's involvement with the Communist party. Charles H. Martin, "The International Labor Defense and Black America," *Labor History* 26 (Spring 1985); 165–94.

28. Hine, *Black Women in White*, pp. 6, 26–62; Mitchell F. Rice, "The Decline of the Black Hospital," paper presented at the annual meeting of the Association for the Study of Afro-American Life and History, October 18, 1986, Houston, Tex.; Kusmer, *A Ghetto Takes Shape*, p. 61.

29. Director of Highland Hospital to George H. Johnson, n.d., Northern California Branch files, NAACP Papers, Library of Congress, Washington, D.C.; interview with Naomi Johnson, September 30, 1976, San Francisco (one of Mrs. Johnson's sisters was San Francisco's first black nurse); interview with Mary Neyland, a former black nurse at Stanford Hospital in San Francisco, February 2, 1976, San Francisco; Crouchett, *William Byron Rumford*, p. 24; *San Francisco Chronicle*, December 1, 1947, p. 3; William H. Hollinger, "The Health of the Negro in San Francisco," M. A. thesis, Stanford University, 1948, pp. 35–36; interview with Seaton Manning, June 17, 1976, San Francisco. Stuart T. Davison was one of the few black doctors who practiced in San Francisco. Information on his early medical career can be found in the Davison Papers. Kusmer, *A Ghetto Takes Shape*, pp. 60–61; Hine, *Black Women in White*, p. 27.

30. Interview with Dr. Earl T. Leaner, December 10, 1976, Berkeley; *Spokesman*, May 21, 1932, p. 4; *San Francisco Chronicle*, January 18, 1922.

31. Interview with Ferdonia Baquie, the daughter of the late Reverend E. J. Magruder, November 2, 1976, San Francisco; interview with an anonymous family member of the late Reverend F. D. Haynes, Sr., pastor of the Third Baptist Church, December 2, 1976, San Francisco; *California Eagle*, January 22 and August 12, 1943. Additional information on Reverend Magruder was obtained from the scrapbook of his wife, S. Anna Duncan Magruder, East Bay Negro Historical Society, Oakland, and the *Portland Advocate*, May 5, May 19, June 23, July 14, and August 18, 1923.

32. Interview with Mrs. Ferdonia Baquie, November 2, 1976, San Francisco; *Fifteenth Census of the United States, Occupations*, p. 209; *Census of Religious Bodies: 1926*, vol. 1, *Summary and Detailed Tables* (Washington, D.C.: Government Printing Office, 1930), pp. 536–37; C. Eric Lincoln and Lawrence H. Maniya, *The Black Church in the African American Experience* (Durham, N.C.: Duke University Press, 1990), pp. 115–26.

33. The advertisements that black businessmen ran in San Francisco's black press, including the *Western Outlook*, *Western Appeal*, and *Spokesman*, reveal that the majority of these establishments were located in the Western Addition, where most blacks resided. See also Charles Tilghman, *Tilghman's Colored Directory of the Leading Cities of Northern California, 1916–1917* (Oakland, Calif.: Tilghman Publishing, 1917). Interview with E. A. Daly, November 3,

1976, Oakland. Daly was the former editor and owner of the *Oakland Voice*; Robert Coleman Francis, "A Survey of Negro Business in the San Francisco Bay Region," M.A. thesis, University of California, Berkeley, 1928, pp. 24–27; *Colored American Magazine* 9 (November 1905): 648–50. Black businesses were much more successful in cities with large black communities between 1900 and 1930. See Wright, *Life Behind a Veil*, pp. 220–28; Kusmer, *A Ghetto Takes Shape*, pp. 192–95, 243–44; Allan H. Spear, *Black Chicago: The Making of a Negro Ghetto, 1890–1920* (Chicago: University of Chicago Press, 1967), pp. 181–86; Walter B. Weare, *Black Business in the New South: A Social History of the North Carolina Mutual Life Insurance Company* (Urbana: University of Illinois Press, 1973).

34. *Spokesman*, March 2 and December 28, 1933; interviews with Alfred Butler, one of the surviving brothers of John Howard Butler, on November 5, 1976 and December 10, 1976, San Francisco. For information on Luther Hudson and Cecil Finley, consult Rene A. Hewlett and Max J. Williams (eds.), *Negro Who's Who in California*, 1948, ed., pp. 14, 55, 84; Taylor, "Blacks and Asians," pp. 413–14.

35. Kusmer, *A Ghetto Takes Shape*, pp. 83–84; Francis, "A Survey of Negro Business," pp. 24–27; John Pittman to Noel Sullivan, November 5, 1931, Noel Sullivan Papers, Bancroft Library, University of California, Berkeley; Gilbert Osofsky, *Harlem: The Making of a Ghetto, 1890–1930*, 2d ed. (New York: Harper and Row, 1971), pp. 93–104; James R. Grossman, *Land of Hope: Chicago, Black Southerners, and the Great Migration* (Chicago: University of Chicago Press, 1989), 123–40.

36. Gerber, *Black Ohio and the Color Line*, pp. 310–18; Spear, *Black Chicago*, pp. 181–85; Kusmer, *A Ghetto Takes Shape*, pp. 192–95.

37. Carleton Mabee, *Black Education in New York State, from Colonial to Modern Times* (Syracuse, N.Y.: Syracuse University Press, 1979); Grossman, *Land of Hope*, pp. 254–56; Lawrence P. Crouchett, Lonnie G. Bunch, and Martha Kendall Winnacker, *Visions toward Tomorrow: The History of the East Bay Afro-American Community, 1852–1977* (Oakland: Northern California Center Afro-American History and Life, 1989), p. 19.

38. Kusmer, *A Ghetto Takes Shape*, p. 182.

39. Trotter, *Black Milwaukee*, pp. 39–66.

40. George M. Fredrickson, *The Black Image in the White Mind: The Debate on Afro-American Character and Destiny, 1817–1914* (New York: Harper and Row, 1971), pp. 320–25.

41. Taylor, "Blacks and Asians," p. 407; Stephan Thernstrom, *The Other Bostonians: Poverty and Progress in the American Metropolis, 1880–1970* (Cambridge, Mass.: Harvard University Press, 1973), pp. 196–97.

CHAPTER 3. CLASS, STATUS, AND SOCIAL LIFE

1. Milton M. Gordon, *Social Class in American Society* (Durham, N.C.: Duke University Press, 1958), p. 253; Robert Bierstedt, "An Analysis of Social Power," *American Sociological Review* 15 (December 1950): 730–38.

2. Horace Cayton and St. Clair Drake, *Black Metropolis: A Study of Negro Life in a Northern City*, vol. 2, rev. ed. (New York: Harcourt, Brace, and World, 1970), pp. 661–63; E. Franklin Frazier, *The Negro in the United States* (New York: Macmillan, 1957), pp. 279–305; Andrew Billingsley, *Black Families in White America* (Englewood Cliffs, N.J.: Prentice-Hall, 1968), pp. 122–46.

3. Booker T. Washington Country Club, Articles of Incorporation, California State Archives, Sacramento. Consult the society pages of the *Spokesman, Western American*, and the *Western Appeal* regarding the elitism of black social clubs. Kenneth L. Kusmer, *A Ghetto Takes Shape: Black Cleveland, 1870-1930* (Urbana: University of Illinois Press, 1976), p. 100.

4. See the invitations and Christmas greetings from prominent white city officials in the Edward Mabson Papers, African-American Historical and Cultural Society, San Francisco; Herb Caen, *Baghdad-by-the-Bay* (New York: Doubleday, 1954), pp. 111–12, 211; Kusmer, *A Ghetto Takes Shape*, pp. 100-101; Willard B. Gatewood, *Aristocrats of Color: The Black Elite, 1880–1920* (Bloomington: Indiana University Press, 1990).

5. Ophelia Davison to Stuart Davison, November 14, 1918, May 22, 1916, July 6, 1922, Stuart T. Davison Papers, African-American Historical and Cultural Society, San Francisco; Berlinda Davison, "The Educational Status of the Negro in the San Francisco Bay Region", M.A. thesis, University of California, 1922; University of California Medical School, *Bulletin* 12 (February 1919): 73; Lawrence P. Crouchett, Lonnie G. Bunch, and Martha Kendall Winnacker, *Visions toward Tomorrow: The History of the East Bay Afro-American Community, 1852–1977* (Oakland: Northern California Center for Afro-American History and Life, 1989), pp. 26–27.

6. Berlinda Davison to Ophelia Davison, April 30, 1923, Davison Papers. Also see the extensive collection of post cards from Berlinda Davison's trip around the world in the Davison Papers.

7. Ophelia Davison to Stuart Davison, May 22, 1916, November 12, November 14, December 2, and December 11, 1918, Davison Papers.

8. These names were taken from the society columns of the *Western Appeal, Western American, Western Outlook, Spokesman, California Voice, Oakland Sunshine*, and from interviews with longtime San Francisco residents. A special note of gratitude to Mrs. Josephine Cole for her insights and cooperation.

9. San Francisco *Elevator*, August 31, 1872, February 12, 1869; San Francisco *Pacific Coast Appeal*, April 23, 1904; *Western Outlook*, January 2, 1915.

10. Iantha Villa Mays, *History of the California Association of Colored Women's Clubs, 1908–1955* (Oakland, Calif.: East Bay Negro Historical Society, n.d.); *Spokesman*, December 1, 1932, p. 1, February 27, 1932, p. 1, March 9, 1932, p. 1; interview with Josephine Cole, December 9, 1976, San Francisco; interview with F. L. Ritchardson, September 13, 1976, San Francisco. New York also established homes to provide lodging, information, and protection for young black women. See Nancy J. Weiss, *The National Urban League, 1910–1940* (New York: Oxford University Press, 1974), pp. 15–20.

11. Interview with Katherine Stewart Flippin, July 7, 1986, San Francisco.

12. Scrapbook of the Anderson family, in the possession of Naomi Johnson, sister of Tabytha Anderson. I also conducted two interviews with Naomi Johnson, September 16 and September 30, 1976, in San Francisco. William Pickens to Secretary Garrard, San Francisco Branch files, NAACP Papers, Library of Congress, Washington, D.C. (hereafter cited as SFBF, NAACP Papers); *Western Appeal*, June 8, 1921, p.1.

13. Walter White to the Anderson family, August 2, 1935, letter of condolence in the Anderson family scrapbook; *Spokesman*, March 15, 1935, p. 1 and July 12, 1935, p. 1; Tabytha Anderson to Executive Board, San Francisco Branch, NAACP, September 30, 1928, Stewart-Flippin Papers. Most of the materials in

the Stewart-Flippin Collection are housed at the Moorland-Spingarn Research Center at Howard University.

14. *Langley's San Francisco City Directory* (San Francisco: R. L. Polk, 1928), pp. 245, 759, 1202; *1935 City Directory,* pp. 406, 602; interview with Naomi Johnson, September 16, 1976, San Francisco.

15. Selected papers and scrapbooks of Robert Flippin, in the possession of his widow, Katherine Flippin. Interviews with Katherine Flippin, February 17, 1976, July 19, 1986, San Francisco.

16. J. J. Byers to E. K. Jones, August 14, 1926, National Urban League Papers, San Francisco Affiliate files, Library of Congress; *Spokesman,* April 16, 1932, p. 1.

17. See the *Spokesman's* society pages for 1932 concerning the numerous social affairs hosted by black San Franciscans and the accolades they received for acting as gracious hosts.

18. Douglas H. Daniels, "Afro-San Franciscans: A Social History of Pioneer Urbanites, 1860–1930," Ph.D. dissertation, University of California, Berkeley, 1975, p. 136. The San Francisco press reported on the trial of Lester Mapp in November–December, 1921. Kusmer also noted that in Cleveland blacks who made money in illegitimate activities were ostracized. Kusmer, *A Ghetto Takes Shape,* pp. 147, 220.

19. Cayton and Drake's *Black Metropolis,* vol. 2, was the forerunner of later attempts to document black class structure. They concluded that church affiliation was often a good indicator of class status. More recent studies by Kenneth L. Kusmer and Allan H. Spear have utilized the Cayton-Drake model, although they have failed to produce any hard evidence, such as church membership lists. Scholars should not be content merely to rest their conclusions on these highly impressionistic and superficial analyses, but should strive for more concrete information. Unfortunately, those sources were not available in San Francisco. See Kusmer, *A Ghetto Takes Shape,* pp. 92–96, 209; Allan H. Spear, *Black Chicago: The Making of a Negro Ghetto, 1890–1920* (Chicago: University of Chicago Press, 1967), pp. 92–96.

20. San Francisco *Examiner,* December 7, 1961, p. 33; interview with Alfred Butler, a close personal friend of Walter Sanford, December 10, 1976, San Francisco.

21. 1934 Tax Receipt, Mabson Papers; Mayor James Rolph, Jr., to Edward Mabson, December 1932 and January 10, 1932, Mabson Papers; Judge Franklin A. Griffin to Edward Mabson, December 1932, Mabson Papers; Matthew Brady, District Attorney, to Edward Mabson, Mabson Papers; *San Francisco Chronicle,* January 18, 1922, p. 15; Spear, *Black Chicago,* pp. 51–70; Kusmer, *A Ghetto Takes Shape,* pp. 116–36; David M. Katzman, *Before the Ghetto: Black Detroit in the Nineteenth Century* (Urbana: University of Illinois Press, 1973), pp. 160–62.

22. *Spokesman,* February 13, 1932, p. 4; *Western Appeal,* June 8, 1921.

23. Invitation, Christmas morning buffet breakfast, San Francisco YWCA, December 25, 1937, Davison Papers; interview with Josephine Cole, December 9, 1976, San Francisco; Gatewood, *Aristocrats of Color,* pp. 54–55, 80–86.

24. *Spokesman,* May 14, 1932, p. 4; interview with Mrs. Katherine Flippin, February 17, 1976, San Francisco; "Board Members of Cosmos," May 14, 1943, and "Cosmos Social Club Program," February 17, 1929, Stewart-Flippin Papers; *Western Outlook,* February 26, 1927.

25. *Spokesman,* February 13, 1932, p. 4, February 27, 1932, p. 4, February 23, 1933, pp. 1, 3.

26. Herb Caen, *Only in San Francisco* (New York: Doubleday, 1960), p. 142; Caen, *Baghdad-by-the-Bay*, pp. 111–12; *Argonaut*, March 4, 1955.

27. Interview with Josephine Cole, Joseph Foreman's surviving daughter, December 9, 1976, San Francisco; interview with Katherine Flippin, February 17, 1976, San Francisco.

28. For a representative review of the literature on black class structure in northern cities, see Cayton and Drake, *Black Metropolis*, vol. 2, chs. 19–22; Frazier, *The Negro in the United States*, pp. 273–305; Kusmer, *A Ghetto Takes Shape*, ch. 5; W. E. B. Du Bois, *The Philadelphia Negro* (Philadelphia: University of Pennsylvania Press, 1899), pp. 309–321; Spear, *Black Chicago*, pp. 51–89; David A. Gerber, *Black Ohio and the Color Line, 1860–1965* (Urbana: University of Illinois Press, 1976), pp. 93–139. The occupations of middle-class blacks were determined by taking a sample of names from the society pages of three black weeklies and cross-checking them in city directories. Personal interviews were also utilized to confirm occupations of selected individuals. The society page of black newspapers described the social activities of middle-class blacks as well as elite blacks.

29. Interviews with Alfred Butler, November 5 and December 10, 1976, San Francisco.

30. Interview with Alfred Butler, December 10, 1976, San Francisco.

31. Cayton and Drake, *Black Metropolis*, vol. 2, pp. 668–69, 688–89.

32. *Spokesman*, February 13, 1932, p. 4, May 21, 1932, p. 4.

33. Ibid., February 13, 1932, pp. 4-6, April 30, 1932, p. 4.

34. Ibid., February 13, 1932, p. 7, February 20, 1932, p. 6.

35. Ibid., May 21, 1932, p. 1, February 20, 1932, p. 4.

36. Information on social events sponsored by black churches in San Francisco is scattered throughout the pages of the black press. The San Francisco *Spokesman*, 1932–1935, provided the most complete description of church activities. See also the scrapbook of S. Anna Duncan Magruder, wife of Reverend E. J. Magruder, East Bay Negro Historical Society, Oakland. Interview with Ferdonia Baquie, November 2, 1976, San Francisco; *Third Baptist Church, 1852–1952, Anniversary Souvenir Program and Honor Roll* (San Francisco, n.p., 1962); *Third Baptist Church, More Than a Century of Witnessing through Spiritual Involvement* (San Francisco, n.p., 1967).

37. "Report of the Dance Hall Committee," *Survey*, July 1924, copy in the San Francisco League of Women Voters Papers, California Historical Society, San Francisco. The social custom of close supervision at parties and dances was confirmed in many personal interviews with black women, such as Josephine Cole, Katherine Flippin, and Naomi Johnson.

38. *Prince Hall Masonic Directory*, January 31, 1954; *Souvenir Program, 1855–1955, Most Worshipful Prince Hall Grand Lodge*; *San Francisco City Directory*, 1860–1861, p. 449; *San Francisco City Directory*, 1867, pp. 687–88, all from the California Historical Society in San Francisco. William H. Grimshaw, *A History of Freemasonry among the Colored People in North America* (reprint ed., New York: Arno Press, 1969), pp. 217–19.

39. Membership lists, 1930–1939, SFBF, NAACP Papers; William Muraskin, "Black Masons: The Role of Fraternal Orders in the Creation of a Middle-Class Black Community," Ph.D. dissertation, University of California, Berkeley, 1970.

40. Muraskin, "Black Masons," pp. 275–80.

41. Gatewood, *Aristrocrats of Color*, pp. 45–46; William Muraskin, *Middle*

Class Blacks in a White Society: Prince Hall Freemasonry in America (Berkeley: University of California Press, 1975).

42. The material in this section was gathered through two separate interviews with Mr. Solomon, July 5 and July 8, 1976, San Francisco, California.

43. Ibid.

44. Ibid.

45. Kusmer, *A Ghetto Takes Shape,* pp. 99–105.

46. James Borchert, *Alley Life in Washington: Family, Community, Religion, and Folk-Life in the City, 1850–1970* (Urbana: University of Illinois Press, 1980), pp. 100–142.

47. Interviews with F. L. Ritchardson, September 13, 1976, February 13, 1977, San Francisco. For patterns of black street-corner life in northern cities, see Elliot Liebow, *Tally's Corner: A Study of Negro Streetcorner Men* (Boston: Little, Brown, 1967). For a comparative ethnic approach, consult William Whyte, *Street Corner Society: The Social Structure of an Italian Slum* (Chicago: University of Chicago Press, 1943) and Herbert Gans, *The Urban Villagers: Group and Class in the Life of Italian Americans* (New York, Free Press of Glencoe, 1962); James Borchert, *Alley Life in Washington;* James O. Horton and Lois E. Horton, *Black Bostonians: Family Life and Community Struggle in the Antebellum North* (New York: Holmes and Meier, 1979), pp. 36–37. On the significance of the saloon as an informal social club, see Jon M. Kingsdale, "The Poor Man's Club: Social Functions of the Urban Working-Class Saloon," *American Quarterly* 25 (October 1973): 472–89.

48. Roger Lotchin, *San Francisco, 1846–1856: From Hamlet to City* (New York: Oxford University Press, 1974), pp. 276–88; interview with Katherine Stewart Flippin, July 7, 1986, San Francisco; interview with Josephine Cole, December 9, 1976, San Francisco; Spear, *Black Chicago,* pp. 201–14; William M. Tuttle, Jr., *Race Riot: Chicago in the Red Summer of 1919* (New York: Atheneum, 1974), pp. 32–33.

49. *Spokesman,* April 30, 1932, p. 7, May 7, 1932, p. 6, March 12, 1932, p. 6; Chris Mead, *Champion: Joe Louis, Black Hero in White America* (New York: Charles Scribner's Sons, 1985).

50. *Spokesman,* May 14, 1932, p. 6, February 13, 1932, p. 2; interview with F. L. Ritchardson, former director of boys' programs at the Booker T. Washington Community Center, September 13, 1976, San Francisco.

51. *Spokesman,* April 16, 1932, p. 6, March 19, 1932, p. 6. See also Donn Rogosin, *Invisible Men: Life in Baseball's Negro Leagues* (New York: Atheneum, 1983).

52. Janet Bruce, *The Kansas City Monarchs: Champions of Black Baseball* (Lawrence: University Press of Kansas, 1985), p. 28.

53. Rob Ruck, *Sandlot Seasons: Sport in Black Pittsburgh* (Urbana: University of Illinois Press, 1987), p. 3. On the positive role of sports in an immigrant community, see Gary Ross Mormino, "The Playing Fields of St. Louis: Italian Immigrants and Sports, 1925–1941," *Journal of Sport History* 9 (Summer 1982): 5–19.

54. *Spokesman,* April 25, 1932, p. 4, March 25, 1932, pp. 4–6.

55. Oakland *Sunshine,* January 2, 1915; *Spokesman,* April 25, 1932, p. 5.

56. *Spokesman,* March 26, 1932, p. 1; interview with Dr. Earl T. Leaner, December 10, 1976, Berkeley; interviews with Alfred Butler, November 5 and December 10, 1976, San Francisco.

57. Lotchin, *San Francisco,* pp. 276–302; Gunther Barth, *City People: The*

Rise of Modern City Culture in Nineteenth-Century America (New York: Oxford University Press, 1980), pp. 192–228; Robert C. Toll, *Blacking Up: The Minstrel Show in Nineteenth-Century America* (New York: Oxford University Press, 1974), pp. 195–229.

58. Russell Hartley, "The Black Dancer on the San Francisco Stage," San Francisco Dance Archives, San Francisco. For images of blacks in American society, see George Fredrickson, *The Black Image in the White Mind: The Debate on Afro-American Character and Destiny* (New York: Harper and Row, 1971), and I. A. Newby, *Jim Crow's Defense: Anti-Negro Thought in America, 1900–1930* (Baton Rouge: Louisiana State University Press, 1965).

59. Assorted clippings and programs of black entertainers on the San Francisco Stage, San Francisco Dance Archives.

60. Ann Charters, *Nobody: The Story of Bert Williams* (New York: Macmillan, 1970), p.13; interview with Alfred Butler, December 10, 1976, San Francisco.

61. Assorted clippings and programs, San Francisco Dance Archives; Sylvia Dannett, *Profiles of Negro Womanhood* (New York: Yonkers Educational Heritage, 1964–1966).

62. Charles S. Johnson, *The Negro War Worker in San Francisco* (San Francisco, n.p., 1944).

63. Interview with Josephine Cole, December 9, 1976, San Francisco; Kusmer, *A Ghetto Takes Shape*, pp. 90–112; Gerber, *Black Ohio and the Color Line*, pp. 93–139; Spear, *Black Chicago*, 51–89; George C. Wright, Life Behind a Veil: Blacks in Louisville, Kentucky, *1865–1930* (Baton Rouge: Louisiana State University Press, 1985), pp. 135–39; Gatewood, *Aristocrats of Color*, pp. 39–138.

CHAPTER 4. PROTEST ORGANIZATIONS, 1915–1930

1. For the membership and activities of the Negro Welfare League, see Charles Tilghman, *Tilghman's Colored Directory of the Leading Cities of Northern California, 1916-1917* (Oakland, Calif.: Tilghman Printing, 1917), p. 139. For a list of officers in the Negro Equity League, consult the *San Francisco Chronicle*, May 1, 1920.

2. See Charles Flint Kellogg, *NAACP: A History of the National Association for the Advancement of Colored People* (Baltimore: Johns Hopkins University Press, 1967). The importance of moral reform in the black community is examined in August Meier, *Negro Thought in America, 1880–1915: Racial Ideologies in the Age of Booker T. Washington* (Ann Arbor: University of Michigan Press, 1963); Louis R. Harlan, *Booker T. Washington, The Wizard of Tuskegee, 1901–1915* (New York: Oxford University Press, 1983), pp. 32–62, 359–378; Gilbert Osofsky discusses the issue of Progressive reform in the black community in *Harlem: The Making of a Ghetto, Negro New York, 1890-1930* (New York: Harper and Row, 1963), pp. 53–67. For similar treatments, see Mary White Ovington, *Half a Man: The Status of the Negro in New York* (New York: Longmans, Green, 1911); John Daniels, *In Freedom's Birthplace* (Boston: Houghton, Mifflin, 1914).

3. Membership rolls for 1916–1919, Northern California Branch files, NAACP Papers, Library of Congress (hereafter cited as NCBF, NAACP Papers); W. E. B. Du Bois, "Colored Californians," *Crisis* 5 (August 1913): 192–96.

4. Thomas Cripps, "The Reaction of the Negro to the Motion Picture *Birth of a Nation*, in August Meier and Elliott Rudwick, eds., *The Making of Black America*, vol. 2 (New York: Atheneum, 1969), pp. 150–153; Everett Carter, "Cul-

tural History Written with Lightning: The Significance of the Birth of A Nation," *American Quarterly* 12 (Fall 1960): pp. 347–57.

5. Cripps, "The Reaction of the Negro," pp. 151–53; Carter, "Cultural History Written with Lightning," pp. 347–50.

6. *Oakland Sunshine*, February 20 and June 25, 1915.

7. *Western Appeal*, June 8, 1921; scrapbook of Tabytha Anderson, in the possession of Tabytha's surviving sister Naomi Johnson. I also conducted two personal interviews with Johnson on September 16 and September 30, 1976, in San Francisco.

8. John Drake to San Francisco Mayor James Rolph, June 3, 1921, NCBF, NAACP Papers.

9. Frank C. Jordan, secretary of state, to John Drake, May 19, 1921, NCBF, NAACP Papers; San Francisco Board of Supervisors, *Journal of Proceedings, 1922*, pp. 410, 445, 449.

10. Walter A. Butler to Mayor James Rolph, February 26, 1915; Eva B. Jones to Governor Hiram A. Johnson, May 26, 1915, NAACP Papers.

11. Frank K. Mott to Walter A. Butler, May 10, 1915, NAACP Papers.

12. Mary Ashe Miller to Northern California Branch, March 2, 1915, NAACP Papers; *Oakland Sunshine*, March 29, 1915; Cripps, "The Reaction of the Negro," pp. 152–55.

13. Walter A. Butler to May Childs Nerney, April 2, 1915, NCBF, NAACP Papers; Western Union day letter, Nerney to Butler, April 5, 1915; San Francisco Moving Picture Censor Board to Butler, March 2, 1915; Butler to Nerney, May 19, 1915, NAACP Papers.

14. William M. Tuttle, Jr., *Race Riot: Chicago in the Red Summer of 1919* (New York: Atheneum, 1970); Allan H. Spear, *Black Chicago: The Making of a Black Ghetto, 1890-1920* (Chicago: University of Chicago Press, 1967); Mary Frances Berry, *Black Resistance, White Law: A History of Constitutional Racism in America* (New York: Appleton, Century, Crofts, 1971); Elliott Rudwick, *Race Riot in East St. Louis, July 2, 1917* (Carbondale: Southern Illinois University Press, 1964); *The Negro in Chicago: A Study of Race Relations and a Riot in 1919* (Illinois: Chicago Commission on Race Relations, 1922); *Opinions of the San Francisco City Attorney, 1912–1916* (San Francisco: San Francisco City and County, [1917]) pp. 931–33.

15. San Francisco Board of Supervisors, *Journal of Proceedings: 1922*, (San Francisco: City and County of San Francisco), pp. 203, 221, 445, 459–460.

16. NAACP press release, "Birth of Nation Stopped in California," July 8, 1921, NAACP Papers. The film was later shown in San Francisco in 1930, despite black protests. See John Howard Butler to Walter White, September 5, 1930, Stewart-Flippin Papers, Moorland-Spingarn Research Center, Howard University.

17. For membership figures and specific names, consult the NCBF, 1915–1923, NAACP Papers. The growth of individual branches is also discussed in Kellogg, *NAACP*, pp. 117–37.

18. Original charter of the Northern California Branch, copy in the NCBF, NAACP Papers.

19. NAACP Press Release, "Birth of A Nation Stopped in California," NAACP Papers.

20. John Howard Butler to Walter White, September 5, 1930, Stewart-Flippin Papers.

21. "Secretary's Report," annual meeting, San Francisco NAACP, November 18, 1928, Stewart-Flippin Papers.

22. "Executive Board Minutes," August 22, 1930, San Francisco NAACP, Stewart-Flippin Papers.

23. Ibid.

24. "Executive Board Minutes," August 31, 1930, San Francisco NAACP, Stewart-Flippin Papers.

25. Walter White to John Howard Butler, September 2, 1930, Stewart-Flippin Papers.

26. Ibid.

27. "Annual Report," November 20, 1930, San Francisco NAACP, Stewart-Flippin Papers.

28. Butler to White, September 5, 1930, Stewart-Flippin Papers.

29. Ibid.

30. On the earlier alliance between black leaders in San Francisco and Oakland, see Albert S. Broussard, "Organizing the Black Community in the San Francisco Bay Area, 1915–1930," *Arizona and the West* 21 (Winter 1981): 339–45. The Northern California Branch changed its name officially to the Oakland Branch in 1933. See Alberta Martin to Walter White, August 28, 1933, box 20, NCBF, NAACP Papers.

31. For information on the San Francisco Executive Committee, see *San Francisco Mirror of the Times*, August 22, 1857, and December 12, 1857; *San Francisco Pacific Appeal*, June 25, 1868, and December 13, 1873.

32. "Executive Board Minutes," San Francisco Branch, NAACP, June 24, 1923, Stewart-Flippin Papers.

33. "Executive Board Minutes," San Francisco Branch, NAACP, February 9, 1928, Stewart-Flippin Papers.

34. "Executive Board Minutes," San Francisco Branch, NAACP, March 1, 1928, Stewart-Flippin Papers. E. Burton Ceruti to James Weldon Johnson, October 29, 1920 and Memorandum from Walter White, "California Branches Win Important Civil Rights Case," February 1921, both from the San Francisco Branch Files (hereafter cited as SFBF), NAACP Papers.

35. "Executive Board Minutes," June 11, July 30, 1923, San Francisco Branch, NAACP, Stewart-Flippin Papers.

36. Annual Reports of branch activities for the San Francisco Branch, 1930–1939, SFBF, NAACP Papers; "Executive Board Minutes," San Francisco Branch, 1923, 1927, 1928, Stewart-Flippin Papers; "Financial Record and Membership Record of San Francisco Branch, NAACP," September 10, October 13, and November 18, 1924, Stewart-Flippin Papers.

37. Secretary De Hart to James Weldon Johnson, November 17, 1917, NAACP Papers. Undated news clippings regarding the East St. Louis riots; annual reports of branch activities, April 14, 1927, both from SFBF, NAACP Papers; Rudwick, *Race Riot at East St. Louis.*

38. Robert Bagnall to Lena Parker, October 9, October 23, and November 9, 1927; Mrs. L. E. Davis and M. Robinson to Lena Parker, February 13, 1928, all from the Stewart-Flippin Papers. *Western American*, March 28, 1928; *Oakland Voice*, May 18, 1929.

39. Alberta Morton to Mary White Ovington, July 24, 1933, SFBF, NAACP Papers. On the efforts of East Bay blacks, see the two folders on the Scottsboro Defense League, NAACP administrative files, California, NAACP Papers. For a

detailed history of this case, consult Dan T. Carter, *Scottsboro: A Tragedy of the American South*, rev. ed. (Baton Rouge: Louisiana State University Press, 1979).

40. See B. Joyce Ross, *J. E. Spingarn and the Rise of the NAACP, 1911–1939* (New York: Atheneum, 1972); "Financial Record and Membership Record of the San Francisco Branch, NAACP," October 19, 1926, Stewart-Flippin Papers; "Executive Board Minutes," NAACP, San Francisco Branch, June 16, 1928– December 4, 1930, Stewart-Flippin Papers.

41. H. L. Richardson to Mary White Ovington, December 27, 1926, NAACP Papers; Eldridge Ross to Mary White Ovington, January 20, 1927, NAACP Papers.

42. National Chairman to Secretary De Hart, January 17, 1927; National Chairman to John Drake, n.d.; John Drake to James Weldon Johnson, January 13, 1927, and January 10, 1927; James Weldon Johnson to Mary White Ovington, January 14, 1927, all from the NCBF, NAACP Papers.

43. J. A. Dennis to James Weldon Johnson, March 26, 1918; Marguerite Evans to NAACP National Office, April 16, 1918, both from the NAACP Papers.

44. *San Francisco Chronicle*, January 18, 1922, p. 14; "Edward Mabson, Candidate for Assemblyman" and "Edward Mabson for Associate Justice of the Supreme Court," November 7, 1922, California Historical Society, San Francisco; "Financial and Membership Record of the San Francisco Branch," August 19, 1926, Stewart-Flippin Papers.

45. Negro Equity League to Fred R. Johnson, September 27, 1920; Edward Mabson to Robert Bagnall, April 9, 1923, and October 7, 1924; Robert Bagnall to Edward Mabson, April 25, 1923, all from the San Francisco Branch files, NAACP Papers.

46. Robert Bagnall to Edward Mabson, April 25, 1923; Bagnall to H. P. Peterson, July 10, 1923, both from Howard University, Washington, D.C. An application for a San Francisco charter was approved and signed on July 9, 1923 by the National Office. A copy of the charter is in the SFBF, NAACP Papers, and also in the Stewart-Flippin Papers. *Forty-Seventh Annual Convention, NAACP, 1909-1956, June 26-July 1*, p. 22; "Annual Report of Branch Activities," April 14, 1927, SFBF, NAACP Papers; Walter White to Forrest C. Bailey, American Civil Liberties Union, SFBF, NAACP Papers; "Annual Report of San Francisco Branch," December 19, 1929, Stewart-Flippin Papers; "Financial Report of San Francisco Branch," January 1–December 31, 1926, Stewart-Flippin Papers; "Financial and Membership Record of the San Francisco Branch, NAACP," March 5, March 12, March 19, May 6 and May 15, 1923, and April 14, 1924, Stewart-Flippin Papers.

47. Tony Martin, *Race First: The Ideological and Organizational Struggles of Marcus Garvey and the Universal Negro Improvement Association* (Westport, Conn.: Greenwood Press, 1976); Lawrence W. Levine, "Marcus Garvey and the Politics of Revitalization," in John Hope Franklin and August Meier, eds., *Black Leaders of the Twentieth Century* (Urbana: University of Illinois Press, 1982); E. David Cronon, *Black Moses: The Story of Marcus Garvey and the Universal Negro Improvement Association* (Madison: University of Wisconsin Press, 1955); Theodore Vincent, *Black Power and the Garvey Movement* (San Francisco: Ramparts Press, 1972), pp. 267–68; Amy Jacques Garvey, ed., *Philosophy and Opinions of Marcus Garvey*, 2 vols. (New York: Atheneum, 1970); *New York Negro World*, July 24, 1926, August 14, 21, and 28, 1926, September 4, 1926; *Western American*, February 24, 1928; Robert A. Hill, ed., *The Marcus Garvey and Uni-*

versal Negro Improvement Association Papers, 2 vols. (Berkeley: University of California Press, 1983); Judith Stein, *The World of Marcus Garvey: Race and Class in Modern Society* (Baton Rouge: Louisiana State University Press, 1986).

48. Secretary De Hart to Robert Bagnall, July 26, 1922, NCBF, NAACP Papers.

49. *Western American,* March 9, 1928.

50. *California Voice,* February 18 and May 23, 1930; *New York Negro World,* September 29, 1926, February 5 and February 19, 1927.

51. *Western Appeal,* September 29, 1926, February 5, 1921; *Western Outlook,* April 9, 1922. See Emory Tolbert, *The UNIA and Black Los Angeles* (Los Angeles: Center for Afro-American Studies, 1980), regarding the activities of a UNIA local on the Pacific Coast. *Western American,* March 16, 1928; Quintard Taylor, "A History of Blacks in the Pacific Northwest, 1788–1970," Ph.D. dissertation, University of Minnesota, 1977, p. 191.

52. Tolbert, *The UNIA and Black Los Angeles,* pp. 81–82.

53. Edward Mabson to Robert Bagnall, April 9, 1923, SFBF, NAACP Papers; "Executive Board Minutes," September 5, 1928, April 7, 1931, NAACP, San Francisco Branch, Stewart-Flippin Papers; C. Eric Lincoln and Lawrence H. Mamiya, *The Black Church in the African American Experience* (Durham, N.C.: Duke University Press, 1990), p. 117–22.

54. *Tentative Findings of the Survey of Race Relations* (Stanford: Stanford University Press, 1925); Robert E. Park, "Behind Our Masks," *Survey* 56 (May 1926): 135–39; Park, "Our Racial Frontier on the Pacific," *Survey* 56 (May 1926): 192–96. The Park survey records I consulted are located at the Hoover Institution, Manuscripts Division, Stanford University.

55. J. J. Byers to E. K. Jones, August 14, 1926, National Urban League Papers, San Francisco Affiliate files, Library of Congress, Washington, D.C. (hereafter cited as SF Affiliate files, Urban League Papers); journal of T. A. Hill, November 18, 1926, SF Affiliate files, Urban League Papers (hereafter cited as T. A. Hill Journal). Helen Swett Artieda to T. Arnold Hill, October 28, 1932; Miss Lesznski to T. Arnold Hill, November 9, 1926, both from the SF Affiliate files, Urban League Papers; *Oakland Voice,* January 25, 1929.

56. E. B. Gray to T. Arnold Hill, November 30, 1928, SF Affiliate files, Urban League Papers.

57. T. A. Hill Journal; D. L. Beasley to National Urban League, July 28, 1930; Ruth Moore to T. A. Hill, January 27 and May 18, 1929, all from the SF Affiliate files, Urban League Papers.

58. T. A. Hill Journal; "Survey of Economic and Social Conditions of Bay Area Negroes," T. A. Hill, n.d., SF Affiliate files, Urban League Papers (hereafter cited as T. A. Hill Survey).

59. T. A. Hill Journal; SF Affiliate files, Urban League Papers.

60. T. A. Hill Survey; Irving Stone, *There Was Light: Autobiography of a University, Berkeley, 1868–1968* (New York: Doubleday, 1970), pp. 249–66; Lawrence P. Crouchett, Lonnie G. Bunch, and Martha Kendall Winnacker, *Visions toward Tomorrow: The History of the East Bay Afro-American Community, 1852–1977* (Oakland: Northern California Center for Afro-American History and Life, 1989), p. 19.

61. T. A. Hill Survey; T. A. Hill to William G. Matthews, March 3, 1927; Associated Charities to E. K. Jones, September 2, 1926; Helen Swett Artieda to T. A. Hill, October 28, 1933, all from the SF Affiliate files, Urban League Papers. *California Voice,* January 25, 1929.

62. *Opportunity* 21 (January 1943): 22–23, and 24 (April–June 1946): 95; Lawrence B. de Graaf, "Negro Migration to Los Angeles, 1930–1950," Ph.D. dissertation, University of California, Los Angeles, 1962; interview with Seaton Manning, June 17, 1976, San Francisco (Manning was the first president of the San Francisco Urban League and served in that post from 1946 to 1960).

63. T. A. Hill Survey, SF Affiliate files, Urban League Papers; *Oakland Sunshine*, June 6, 1915. Despite relatively small black populations, Urban League branches were organized in Milwaukee and Seattle. See Joe W. Trotter, Jr., *Black Milwaukee: The Making of a Black Proletariat, 1915–1945* (Urbana: University of Illinois Press, 1985), pp. 53–54, 57–58, 65–66; Quintard Taylor, "Black Urban Development—Another View: Seattle's Central District, 1910–1940," *Pacific Historical Review* 58 (November 1980): 443.

64. *Tilghman's Directory, 1916–1917* contains the names of several black political organizations. See also the *San Francisco Chronicle*, January 18, 1922, p. 14; interview with A. P. Alberga, member and organizer of the Negro Welfare League, November 8, 1976, Oakland. The exact number of black political leagues is impossible to determine because of the short life spans of these organizations, the lack of surviving records, and the periodic gaps in the black press. The black press remains the major source of information on these organizations.

65. Booker T. Washington Community Center, Articles of Incorporation, California State Archives, Sacramento; interview with Mrs. Katherine Flippin, February 17, 1976, San Francisco (Flippin's mother was one of the founders of the community center). See "Victory Club Minutes, 1919–1920," Stewart-Flippin Papers; *History of the Booker T. Washington Community Center, 1920–1970* (San Francisco, n.p., 1971). Ann Scott evaluates the significance of these organizations and the contributions that both black and white women have made. See Anne Scott, "Making the Invisible Woman Visible: An Essay Review," *Journal of Southern History* 38 (1972): 632; and Scott, "Most Invisible of All: Black Women's Voluntary Associations," *Journal of Southern History* 56 (February 1990): 3-22. See also Gerda Lerner, "Community Work of Black Club Women," *Journal of Negro History* 59 (April 1979):158–67. For an excellent discussion of the role of black women in social service organizations in the South, see Cynthia Neverdon-Morton, *Afro-American Women of the South and the Advancement of the Race, 1895–1925* (Knoxville: University of Tennessee Press, 1989).

66. *Booker T. Washington Community Center Annual Reports, 1926–1930*, Bancroft Library, University of California, Berkeley.

67. *Spokesman*, May 7, 1932, p. 1; "Annual Report of the Booker T. Washington Community Center," 1929; "Survey of the Booker T. Washington Community Center," June 1, 1934; "Preliminary Report on the Booker T. Washington Community Center," [1938–1939]; "Booker T. Washington Study Committee Meeting," May 7, 1940, all contained in the Stewart-Flippin Papers. Rob Ruck, *Sandlot Seasons*, p. 208.

68. *Booker T. Washington Community Center, Annual Reports, 1926-1930*; *History of the Booker T. Washington Community Center, 1920-1970*; "Executive Board Minutes," NAACP, 1928–1931, Stewart-Flippin Papers.

69. Interview with Seaton Manning, June 17, 1976, San Francisco. See Nancy Weiss's insightful study, *The National Urban League, 1910–40* (New York: Oxford University Press, 1974), p. 305; Ralph J. Bunche, "The Programs, Ideologies, Tactics, and Achievements of Negro Betterment and Interracial Organizations," microfilm of unpublished monograph in the Schomburg Collection, New York Public Library, June 1940, pp. 765–71. John Hope Franklin emphasized

the importance of black institutions in his introduction to Emma Lou Thornbrough's biography of T. Thomas Fortune. See Emma Lou Thornbrough, *T. Thomas Fortune: Militant Journalist* (Chicago: University of Chicago Press, 1972), pp. vii–viii.

CHAPTER 5. POLITICS, PROTEST,
AND RACE RELATIONS, 1920–1940

1. Fred L. Israel, *The State of the Union Messages of the Presidents*, vol. 3 (New York: Chelsea House, Robert Hector Publishers, 1966), pp. 2648–49, 2688–89, 2702; Donald R. McCoy, *Calvin Coolidge: The Quiet President* (New York: Macmillan, 1967), pp. 125, 200, 328–29. For a general discussion of the executive branch's response to discrimination during the 1920s and 1930s, consult Richard B. Sherman, *The Republican Party and Black America: From McKinley to Hoover, 1896–1933* (Charlottesville: University Press of Virginia, 1973); Richard B. Sherman, "The Harding Administration and the Negro, An Opportunity Lost," *Journal of Negro History* 49 (July 1964): 151–168; Robert K. Murray, *The Harding Era: Warren G. Harding and His Administration* (Minneapolis: University of Minnesota Press, 1969), pp. 54, 125, 397, 402; Donald J. Lisio, *Hoover, Blacks and Lily-Whites: A Study in Southern Strategies* (Chapel Hill: University of North Carolina Press, 1985); Rayford W. Logan, *The Betrayal of the Negro: from Rutherford B. Hayes to Woodrow Wilson* (New York: Collier Books, 1964); Leslie A. Fishel, Jr., "The Negro in Northern Politics, 1870–1900," *Mississippi Valley Historical Review* 42 (December 1955): 466–89; Nancy J. Weiss, *Farewell to the Party of Lincoln: Black Politics in the Age of FDR* (Princeton, N.J.: Princeton University Press, 1983); Darrel E. Bigham, *We Ask Only a Fair Trial: A History of the Black Community of Evansville, Indiana*, (Bloomington: Indiana University Press, 1987), pp. 87–100. There are only scattered references to black politics in San Francisco newspapers prior to the 1920s. Large gaps in the Bay Area black press make it almost impossible to reconstruct the political affairs of blacks in San Francisco between 1900 and 1920.

2. Emma Lou Thornbrough, *T. Thomas Fortune: Militant Journalist* (Chicago: University of Chicago Press, 1972), pp. 105–16; Thornbrough, "The National Afro-American League, 1887–1908," *Journal of Southern History* 27 (November 1961): 494–512; Harr Wagner, ed., *Notable Speeches by Notable Speakers of the Greater West* (San Francisco: Whitaker and Ray, 1902), pp. 323–34; *San Francisco City Directory*, 1890, p. 971.

3. *First Meeting of the Afro-American Congress of California* (San Francisco: n.p., 1895). This brief history of the Congress also contains a history of the San Francisco Afro-American League. *Vindication of Hon. M. M. Estee, Address by T. B. Morton, President of the San Francisco Afro-American League* (San Francisco: Valleau and Oliver, 1894); Wagner, ed., *Notable Speeches*, pp. 324–25.

4. *First Meeting of the Afro-American Congress*.

5. Wagner, ed., *Notable Speeches*, pp. 324–25; Thornbrough, *T. Thomas Fortune*, pp. 119–22.

6. J. B. Wilson to George C. Pardee, August 28, October 31, and November 6, 1902, George C. Pardee Papers, Bancroft Library, University of California, Berkeley; Committee of Arrangements to Pardee, October 21, 1902, Pardee Papers; F. P. Henry to Pardee, April 28, 1903, Pardee Papers; James Alexander

to Pardee, September 25, 1903, Pardee Papers; Afro-American Congress to Frank P. Flint, February 23, 1904, Pardee Papers.

7. J. B. Wilson to Governor George C. Pardee, July 2, 1906, Pardee Papers.

8. *Western Appeal*, October 14, 1920. It is virtually impossible to determine the political affiliation of blacks during this period, because the black populace was simply too small, barely 1 percent of even the most heavily populated black assembly districts. However, the black press, though a poor gauge of voting behavior, indicates that more blacks were switching to the GOP by 1934. It is not possible to determine the exact year that a majority of black San Franciscans switched to the Democratic party. See Nancy J. Weiss, "Fighting Wilsonian Segregation," *Political Science Quarterly* 84 (March 1969): 61–79; Weiss, *Farewell to the Party of Lincoln*, p. 180.

9. *Notary Public Appointments*, 15 vols. 1862–1924, California State Archives, Sacramento; State Papers, administration of Governor George Stoneman, *Notarial Applications, 1883–1886*, p. 38; Colored American Employees Association, Articles of Incorporation, California State Archives, Sacramento; interview with Alfred Butler, November 30, 1976, San Francisco; *San Francisco Examiner*, December 7, 1961, p. 33; recommendation of W. H. Blake for notary public commission to George Stoneman, from the Colored Citizens Committee, California State Archives; *Pacific Coast Appeal*, January 4, 1902, April 23, 1904; *Oakland Sunshine*, January 2, 1915; McCants Stewart to Harry Jones, October 5, 1918, Stewart-Flippin Papers, Howard University; *San Francisco Chronicle*, January 18, 1922, p. 14; interview with Josephine Cole, December 9, 1976, San Francisco.

10. Original political tract published during the Hoover campaign, in the author's possession, a gift from E. A. Daly; interview with E. A. Daly, November 3, 1976, Oakland; *Spokesman*, August 27, 1932, p. 2, October 30, 1932, p. 2. For John Howard Butler's political activities, including his association with the NAACP, see J. H. Butler to Lena M. Parker, September 5, 1927; Butler to Mayor James Rolph, Jr., November 23, 1927; Butler to Samuel M. Shortridge, n.d.; Walter White to Butler, September 2, 1930; Butler to White, September 5, 1930; Butler to Executive Board, San Francisco Branch, NAACP, October 8, 1930, all from the Stewart-Flippin Papers.

11. Wesley C. Peoples to Earl Warren, February 4, 1936, Earl Warren Papers, California State Archives, Sacramento.

12. Chairman, Republican State Central Committee to Wesley C. Peoples, February 6, 1936; Warren to Peoples, February 4, 1936, both from the Earl Warren Papers. San Francisco Registrar of Voters, "Register of Votes Cast and Number of Precincts at Each Election since 1878," County Clerk's Office, San Francisco City Hall.

13. Telegram, Paul H. Davis to A. M. Curtis, August 25, 1936; Republican National Committee for California to A. M. Curtis, September 8, 1936; Wesley C. Peoples to Herbert C. Hoover, February 4, 1936; Republican National Committee to A. M. Curtis, October 3, 1936; Charles D. Heywood to Earl Warren, n.d.; Pacific-West-California Situation, Voters of African Descent, n.d., all from the Earl Warren Papers.

14. Interview with A. P. Alberga, November 8, 1976, Oakland.

15. Wesley C. Peoples to Earl Warren, March 14, 1936; Republican National Committee to A. M. Curtis, October 3, 1936, both from the Earl Warren Papers. Interview with A. P. Alberga, November 8, 1976, Oakland.

16. Message from Walter Gordon, July 20, 1936, California State Colored

Republican League, Earl Warren Papers, California State Archives, Sacramento. Telegram, Paul H. Davis to A. M. Curtis, August 25, 1936; Betty Hill to Earl Warren, March 9, 1936; Tracy Mitchell to Warren, September 23, 1936; National Republican Committee to Tracy Smith, September 29, 1936, all from the Earl Warren Papers. Iantha Villa Mays, *History of the California Association of Colored Women's Clubs 1906–1955* (Oakland, Calif.: East Bay Negro Historical Society, n.d.), pp. 6–8, 12; *Spokesman*, April 30, 1932, p. 8, April 6, 1933, p. 6, March 1, 1934, p. 6; *Western American*, October 5, 1928; *Western Appeal*, February 1, 1922; "Executive Board Minutes," 1928 and 1931, San Francisco Branch, NAACP, Stewart-Flippin Papers.

17. *Western American*, May 28, 1926.

18. *California Voice*, July 4, 1930.

19. Interview with E. A. Daly, November 3, 1976, Oakland.

20. Ibid.

21. *Western American*, May 27, 1927.

22. *San Francisco Chronicle*, January 18, 1922, p.14. Consult the *Spokesman*, 1932–1935, for W. J. Wheaton's regular political column. The *California Eagle* published a political column by Wheaton between 1943 and 1945.

23. John Pittman, "Railroads and Negro Labor," M.A. thesis, University of California, Berkeley, 1930; telephone interview with Tarea Hall Pittman, September 16, 1976, Berkeley, California.

24. See Emma Lou Thornbrough, *T. Thomas Fortune*; Peter Gilbert, ed., *John Edward Bruce: Militant Black Journalist* (New York: Arno Press, 1971); and Andrew Buni, *Robert L. Vann of the Pittsburgh Courier* (Pittsburgh: University of Pittsburgh Press, 1974). For the founding of the *Spokesman* and its early struggles, see John Pittman to Noel Sullivan, November 22, 1931, and February 25, 1932, Noel Sullivan Papers, Bancroft Library, University of California, Berkeley. "Disbursements—First Six Issues of *Spokesman*," [1931]; Pittman to Herman Barnett, July 20 and July 24, 1932; Pittman to Sullivan, September 3, 1932, all from the Sullivan Papers. See *People's World*, 1938–1945, a communist party paper that Pittman later cofounded and edited, and *Freedomways* (Spring and Fall 1961). Pittman to Doctor Byers, February 25, 1932; Pittman to Noel Sullivan, June 14, 1932, and March 12, 1934, all from the Sullivan Papers. Gunnar Myrdal, *An American Dilemma: The Negro Problem and Modern Democracy*, vol. 2 (New York: Harper and Row, 1944), p. 783.

25. *Spokesman*, February 20, 1932, p. 8, July 9, 1932, p. 8, March 12, 1932, p. 8, May 24, 1932, p. 8; Pittman to Richard E. Doyle, November 5, 1931; "Plan for Negro-Democrat Alliance" [1931-32], 5 p., Sullivan Papers.

26. *Spokesman*, March 12, 1932, p. 8; Pittman to Sullivan, February 29, 1932; Pittman to James D. Meredith, February 29, 1932; Pittman to Sullivan, October 23, 1932, all from the Sullivan Papers. *Spokesman*, May 24, 1932, p. 8, July 2, 1932, p. 8, October 30, 1932, p. 8, June 25, 1932, p. 8.

27. *Spokesman*, November 2, 1933, p. 6; interview with E. A. Daly, November 3, 1976, Oakland; membership lists, July 11, 1932, San Francisco Branch files, NAACP Papers, Library of Congress, Washington, D.C. (hereafter cited as SFBF, NAACP Papers). Interview with Ferdonia Baquie, November 2, 1976, San Francisco; interview with A. P. Alberga, November 8, 1976, Oakland; Moses Rischin, "Sunny Jim Rolph: The First Mayor of All the People," *California Historical Society Quarterly* 53 (Summer 1974): 165–72; Herman G. Goldbeck, "The Political Career of James Rolph, Jr.: A Preliminary Study," M.A. thesis, University of California, 1936.

28. *Spokesman*, December 1, 1932, p. 8, November 21, 1933, p. 6.

29. Ibid., November 21, 1933, p. 6, December 7, 1933, p. 6; interview with E. A. Daly, November 3, 1976, Oakland. See also *New York Times*, December 4, 1933; *New York Herald Tribune*, November 28, 1933.

30. Leland Hawkins to William Pickens, April 3, 1934, SFBF, NAACP Papers; Walter White to Leland Hawkins, November 27, 1933, SFBF, NAACP Papers.

31. *Spokesman*, June 7, 1934, p. 1; Leland Hawkins to Walter White, November 27, 1933, SFBF, NAACP Papers.

32. *Spokesman*, March 5, 1932, p. 8, April 23, 1932, p. 8, November 3, 1932, p. 8; *Western Appeal*, September 8, 1921; *Spokesman*, June 14, 1934, p. 6.

33. *Western Appeal*, February 18, 1922; *Spokesman*, November 3, 1933, p. 6.

34. *Western Appeal*, October 26, 1928; California *Voice*, August 6, 1926.

35. Leland Hawkins to Mayor Angelo J. Rossi, June 2, 1934, SFBF, NAACP Papers. For a thorough review of the NAACP's antilynching stance, see Charles Flint Kellogg, *NAACP: A History of the National Association for the Advancement of Colored People* (Baltimore: Johns Hopkins University Press, 1967); Raymond Wolters, *Negroes and the Great Depression: The Problem of National Recovery* (Westport, Conn.: Greenwood, 1970); James Weldon Johnson, *Along This Way* (New York: Viking Press, 1933); B. Joyce Ross, *J. E. Spingarn and the Rise of the NAACP, 1911–1939* (New York: Atheneum, 1972); Robert Zangrando, *The NAACP Crusade against Lynching, 1909–1950* (Philadelphia: Temple University Press, 1980). National NAACP secretary to San Francisco Branch president Leland Hawkins, February 23 and April 14, 1934; Leland Hawkins to Mayor Angelo J. Rossi, June 21, 1934; Tabytha Anderson to Walter White, April 28, 1935, all from the SFBF, NAACP Papers.

36. Lelia Flippin to Walter White, December 5, 1932, SFBF, NAACP Papers; Zangrando, *The NAACP Crusade against Lynching*, pp. 98–165; Robert L. Zangrando, "The NAACP and a Federal Antilynching Bill, 1934–1940," *Journal of Negro History* 50 (April 1965): 106–17.

37. *Western American*, October 5, 1928, May 6, 1927.

38. Ibid., October 26, 1928; *Spokesman*, October 30, 1932, p. 2, November 3, 1932, p. 3.

39. Lelia Flippin to William Pickens, November 24, 1932, SFBF, NAACP Papers. San Francisco City Hall, Registrar of Voters, "Register of Votes Cast and the Number of Precincts at Each Election since 1878"; Weiss, *Farewell to the Party of Lincoln*, pp. 209–35.

40. *Western Appeal*, April 8, 1927, April 15, 1929; *Oakland Sunshine*, May 12, 1928; interview with E. A. Daly, November 3, 1976, Oakland.

41. *Spokesman*, November 10, 1932, p. 8, May 14, 1932, p. 8, February 27, 1932, p. 8.

42. Ibid., October 26, 1933, p. 6, December 1, 1933, p. 6, December 15, 1932, p. 1.

43. Ibid., February 8, 1934, p. 6, October 26, 1933, p. 1, February 27, 1932, p. 8.

44. Ibid., February 22, 1934, p. 6.

45. Ibid., June 14, 1934, p. 6, February 8, 1934, p. 6, July 27, 1933, p. 6, April 5, 1934, p. 6, January 18, 1934, p. 6, June 7, 1934, p. 6.

46. Ibid., January 27, 1932, p. 8, August 20, 1932, p. 8, March 5, 1932, p. 8, May 14, 1932, p. 8, May 21, 1932, p. 8, July 16, 1932, p. 8, November 10, 1932, p. 8.

47. Ibid., October 30, 1932, p. 8.

48. Ibid., July 6, 1933, p. 1, July 4, 1933, p. 1, June 7, 1934, p. 6, August 30, 1934, p. 6, August 3, 1933, p. 6.

49. Telephone interview with Tarea Hall Pittman, September 16, 1976; Tarea Pittman, a long-time Bay Area civil rights activist, is no relation to John Pittman; interview with A. P. Alberga, November 8, 1976, Oakland; interview with E. A. Daly, November 3, 1976, Oakland, California.

50. *Spokesman*, May 29, 1935, p. 1; Al Richmond, *A Long View from the Left* (New York: Dell, 1972), p. 289; John Pittman, "The Negro People Spark the Fight for Peace," *Political Affairs* 25 (August 1946). For the fate of two black Communists, see Nell Irvin Painter, *The Narrative of Hosea Hudson: His Life as a Negro Communist in the South* (Cambridge, Mass.: Harvard University Press, 1979); Charles H. Martin, *The Angelo Herndon Case and Southern Justice* (Baton Rouge: Louisiana State University Press, 1976). Mark Naison's recent study of the Communist party in Harlem during the 1930s is also useful in reconstructing the relationship between blacks and Communists during these years. See Mark Naison, *Communists in Harlem during the Depression* (Urbana: University of Illinois Press, 1983).

51. Rudolph Lapp, *Afro-Americans in California* (San Francisco: Boyd and Fraser, 1979), pp. 40, 54–55; Lawrence P. Crouchett, *William Byron Rumsford: The Life and Public Services of a California Legislator* (El Cerrito, Calif.: Downey Place, 1984). For a comparison of San Francisco's black community with those of Oakland and Berkeley, consult Lawrence P. Crouchett, Lonnie G. Bunch III, Martha Kendall Winnacker, *Visions toward Tomorrow: The History of the East Bay Afro-American Community, 1852–1977* (Oakland: Northern California Center for Afro-American History and Life, 1989).

52. Richard L. Watson, "The Defeat of Judge Parker: A Study in Pressure Group Politics," *Mississippi Valley Historical Review* 50 (September 1963): 213–34; Irving Bernstein, *The Lean Years: A History of the American Worker, 1920–1933* (Boston: Houghton Mifflin, 1972), pp. 406–9.

53. John Howard Butler to Samuel M. Shortridge, n.d. [1930], Stewart-Flippin Papers; telegrams, Samuel M. Shortridge to John Howard Butler, April 2 and April 24, 1930, Stewart-Flippin Papers.

54. Butler to Shortridge, n.d. [1930], Stewart-Flippin Papers.

55. Watson, "The Defeat of Judge Parker," pp. 213, 218, 230; Harvard Sitkoff, *A New Deal for Blacks: The Emergence of Civil Rights as a National Issue: The Depression Decade* (New York: Oxford University Press 1978), pp. 85–86; John Hope Franklin, *From Slavery to Freedom*, 6th ed. (New York: Knopf, 1988), pp. 344, 362; William H. Harris, *The Harder We Run: Black Workers since the Civil War* (New York, 1982), pp. 88–89.

56. Assistant Secretary, NAACP, to Horace Cayton, October 29, 1934, box 322, NAACP Papers.

57. Telegram, Walter White to William Green, October 3, 1933, box 322, NAACP Papers; Assistant Secretary, NAACP, to Horace Cayton, October 29, 1934, box 322, NAACP Papers; *Report of Proceedings of the Fifty-Fourth Annual Convention of the American Federation of Labor*, San Francisco, Oct. 1–12, 1934 (Washington, D.C.: Law Reporter Printing Company) p. 255.

58. Harris, *The Harder We Run*, pp. 44–45, 88–91; Philip S. Foner, *Organized Labor and the Black Worker, 1619–1973* (New York: International Publishers, 1976), pp. 204–14; *Report of Proceedings of the Fifty-Fourth Annual Convention of the American Federation of Labor*, pp. 255, 705–6.

59. San Francisco *Spokesman*, April 5, September 20, October 4, and October 12, 1934.

60. William Pickens to Leland Hawkins, October 27, 1934, box 24, SFBF, NAACP Papers.

61. Fred Stripp, "The Relationship of the San Francisco Bay Area Negro-American Worker with the Labor Unions Affiliated with the American Federation of Labor and the Congress of Industrial Organizations," Th.D. thesis, Pacific School of Religion, Berkeley, 1948.

62. Walter Maddox to Frederick M. Roberts, February 9 [1931], Stewart-Flippin Papers; Walter Maddox to William Pickens, February 9 [1931], Stewart-Flippin Papers.

63. *Crisis* 43 (August 1936): 250.

64. Interview with Ferdonia Baquie, November 2, 1976, San Francisco; interview with Katherine Flippin, February 17, 1976, San Francisco.

65. John W. Blassingame, *Black New Orleans, 1860-1880* (Chicago: University of Chicago Press, 1973), p. 173.

66. *Spokesman*, June 5, 1933, p. 2, September 7, 1933, p. 1, May 17, 1934, p. 1.

67. Ibid., July 13, 1933.

68. Ibid., May 31, 1933, p. 4, January 18, 1935, p. 1, December 1, 1932, p. 2; "Executive Committee Minutes," April 7, 1931, San Francisco Branch, NAACP, Stewart-Flippin Papers; Howard Thurman, *Footprints of a Dream: The Story of the Church for the Fellowship of All Peoples* (New York: Harper Brothers, 1959), p. 120.

69. Interview with Alfred Butler, December 19, 1976, San Francisco; interview with Earl T. Leaner, December 10, 1976, Berkeley; *Spokesman*, March 26, 1932, and June 15, 1933.

70. Ibid., November 17, 1932, and February 1, 1934.

71. Ibid., December 1, 1932.

72. Ibid., November 17, December 8, and December 15, 1932; "Before the Police Commission of the City and County of San Francisco, State of California," December 1932, Noel Sullivan Papers, Bancroft Library.

73. "Before the Police Commission," pp. 2-3, Sullivan Papers.

74. Ibid., p. 3.

75. Leland Hawkins to Walter White, December 23, 1932, Box 24, SFBF, NAACP Papers; "Statement of Activities for the Year Ending January 11, 1934," box 24, SFBF, NAACP Papers.

76. *Spokesman*, December 1, December 8, and December 15, 1932, January 27, 1933.

77. Ibid., June 29, 1933.

78. Pauli Murray, *States' Laws on Race and Color*, pp. 55-56. For the demise of California's antimiscegenation law, consult the *American Civil Liberties Union News*, November 1948.

79. *Spokesman*, February 6, 1932, and July 16, 1933; interview with E. A. Daly, November 3, 1976, Oakland (Daly was the former owner and editor of the *Oakland Voice*). *San Francisco Chronicle*, January 18, 1922, p. 14, April 8, 1922, p. 17, April 9, 1930, p. 26, April 14, 1930, p. 20, October 2, 1936, January 15, 1938, January 22, 1938, August 11, 1939.

80. *Spokesman*, January 12, 1939, p. 16, January 25, 1939, p. 4, November 18, 1910, p. 14. I also consulted the Chester H. Rowell Papers at the Bancroft

Library, University of California, Berkeley, but they were not useful in illustrating Rowell's philosophy on blacks or race relations.

81. Carey McWilliams, *California: The Great Exception* (New York: Current Books, 1949), p. 76; Delilah L. Beasley to William Pickens, January 26, 1931, series D, box 350, NAACP Papers; *Oakland Tribune*, January 21, 1931, p. 1; William Pickens to Laura Davis, February 2, 1931, Stewart-Flippin Papers.

82. "Executive Board Minutes," August 9 and August 10, 1929, San Francisco NAACP, Stewart-Flippin Papers.

83. "Executive Board Minutes," August 12, August 19, and September 3, 1929, Stewart-Flippin Papers.

84. "Statement of Activities," April 12, 1935, box 24, San Francisco Branch files, NAACP Papers.

85. George C. Wright, *Life behind A Veil: Blacks in Louisville, Kentucky, 1865–1930*, (Baton Rouge: Louisiana State University Press, 1985), pp. 254–56; Howard N. Rabinowitz, "The Conflict between Blacks and Police in the Urban South, 1865–1900," *Historian* 39 (November 1976): 62–76; August Meier and Elliott Rudwick, "Negro Retaliatory Violence in the Twentieth Century," *New Politics* 5 (Winter 1966): 41–51; Kenneth L. Kusmer, *A Ghetto Takes Shape: Black Cleveland, 1870–1930* (Urbana: University of Illinois Press, 1976), p. 178; Constance M. Green, *The Secret City: A History of Race Relations in the Nation's Capitol* (Princeton, N.J.: 1967), pp. 128, 226, 265, 288–89, 335; George C. Wright, "The Billy Club and the Ballot: Police Intimidation of Blacks in Louisville, Kentucky, 1880–1930," *Southern Studies* 23 (Spring 1984): 20–41; Eugene J. Watts, "The Police in Atlanta, 1890–1905," *Journal of Southern History* 39 (May 1973): 165–82.

86. Allan H. Spear, *Black Chicago: The Making of a Negro Ghetto, 1890–1920*, (Chicago: University of Chicago Press, 1969) pp. 201–22; Kusmer, *A Ghetto Takes Shape*, pp. 174–89.

CHAPTER 6. THE WORST OF TIMES:
BLACKS DURING THE GREAT DEPRESSION
AND THE NEW DEAL, 1930–1940

1. No scholar has evaluated the Great Depression's impact on a western black community, but numerous studies have surveyed the impact of both the Depression and the New Deal on blacks in northern, midwestern, and southern cities. See Raymond Wolters, *Negroes and the Great Depression: The Problem of National Recovery* (Westport, Conn.: Greenwood, 1970); Harvard Sitkoff, *A New Deal for Blacks, The Emergence of Civil Rights as a National Issue* (New York: Oxford University Press, 1978); St. Clair Drake and Horace Cayton, *Black Metropolis: A Study of Negro Life in a Northern City*, rev. ed. (New York: Harcourt, 1970); Robert Austin Warner, *New Haven Negroes: A Social History* (New Haven: Yale University Press, 1940), pp. 253–54, 266; Richard E. Sterner, *The Negro's Share: A Study of Income, Consumption, Housing, and Public Assistance* (New York: Harper, 1943); Constance McLaughlin Green, *The Secret City: A History of Race Relations in the Nation's Capital* (Princeton, N.J.: Princeton University Press, 1967), pp. 218–49; Leslie H. Fishel, Jr., "The Negro in the New Deal Era," in Barton J. Bernstein and Allen J. Matusow, eds., *Twentieth Century America: Recent Interpretations* (New York: Harcourt, 1969), pp. 288–300; Gun-

nar Myrdal, *An American Dilemma: The Negro Problem and Modern Democracy* (New York: Harper and Row, 1944); John B. Kirby, *Black Americans in the Roosevelt Era: Liberalism and Race* (Knoxville: University of Tennessee Press, 1980); Christopher G. Wye, "The New Deal and the Negro Community: Toward a Broader Conceptualization," *Journal of American History* 59 (December 1972): 621–39; August Meier and Elliott Rudwick, *Black Detroit and the Rise of the UAW* (New York: Oxford University Press, 1979), pp. 21–67; William H. Harris, *The Harder We Run: Black Workers since the Civil War* (New York: Oxford University Press, 1982), pp. 89–113; John Bodnar, Roger Simon, and Michael P. Weber, *Lives of Their Own: Blacks, Italians, and Poles in Pittsburgh, 1900–1960* (Urbana: University of Illinois Press, 1982), pp. 217–18, 227–28, 243, 248; Nancy J. Weiss, *Farewell to the Party of Lincoln: Black Politics in the Age of FDR* (Princeton, N.J.: Princeton University Press, 1983); George C. Wright, *Life behind a Veil: Blacks in Louisville, Kentucky, 1865–1930* (Baton Rouge: Louisiana State University Press, 1985), pp. 218, 227, 230; Joe William Trotter, Jr., *Black Milwaukee: The Making of an Industrial Proletariat, 1915–45* (Urbana: University of Illinois Press, 1985), pp. 147–65; Darrel E. Bigham, *We Ask Only a Fair Trial: A History of the Black Community of Evansville, Indiana* (Bloomington: Indiana University Press, 1987), pp. 217–24; Earl Lewis, "At Work and at Home: Blacks in Norfolk, Virginia, 1910–1945," Ph.D. dissertation, University of Minnesota, 1984, pp. 249–80.

2. David S. Lavender, *California: A Bicentennial History* (New York: W. W. Norton, 1976), pp. 179–82.

3. There is no satisfactory history of San Francisco during the Great Depression and New Deal era, but most histories of California evaluate the Depression's impact on the major urban centers in the state. See Warren A. Beck and David A. Williams, *California: a History of the Golden State* (New York: Doubleday, 1972), pp. 390–406; Walton Bean, *California, An Interpretative History* (New York: McGraw, 1968), pp. 409–25; Andrew F. Rolle, *California: A History,* 2d ed. (New York: Crowell, 1969), pp. 529–48. The records of the California State Relief Administration provide the most complete statistical information on the decline of California's economic activity during the 1930s. See *Review of the Activities of the State Relief Administration of California, 1933–35* (Sacramento: California State Printing Office, 1936); and Paul N. Woolf, *Economic Trends in California* (Sacramento: California State Printing Office, 1935). For a general survey of San Francisco during the 1930s, consult John B. McGloin, *San Francisco: The Story of a City* (San Rafael, Calif.: Presidio, 1978), pp. 303–19.

4. John W. Caughey, *California: A Remarkable State's Life History,* 3d ed. (Englewood Cliffs, N.J.: Prentice-Hall, 1970), p. 454; Beck and Williams, *California: A History of the Golden State,* p. 391; "James Rolph," *Dictionary of American Biography,* vol. 21, supplement 1 (New York: Scribner's, 1944), pp. 638–39; Herman G. Goldbeck, "The Political Career of James Rolph, Jr.: A Preliminary Study," M.A. thesis, University of California, 1936, pp. 159–68; Sister Clementia Maria Fisher, "James Rolph, Jr., 1869–1934: An Estimate of His Influence on San Francisco's History," M.A. thesis, University of San Francisco, 1965; David W. Taylor, *The Life of James Rolph, Jr.* (San Francisco: Committee for Publication of James Rolph, Jr., 1934); Moses Rischin, "Sunny Jim Rolph: The First Mayor of All the People," *California Historical Society Quarterly* 53 (Summer 1974): 65–72; William Issel and Robert W. Cherney, *San Francisco, 1865–1932: Politics, Power, and Urban Development* (Berkeley: University of California Press, 1986), pp. 165, 176–77, 198–99.

5. Rolle, *California: A History*, p. 532.

6. Richard Lowitt and Maurine Beasley, eds., *One Third of a Nation: Lorena Hickok Reports on the Great Depression* (Urbana: University of Illinois Press, 1981), pp. 308–9.

7. U. S. Bureau of the Census, *Final Report on Total and Partial Unemployment, 1937*, vol. 1, *Census of Partial Employment, Unemployment, and Occupations* (Washington, D.C.: Government Printing Office, 1938), p. 330; U.S. Bureau of the Census, *Report on the Progress of the Works Program to January, 1938* (Washington, D.C., Government Printing Office, n.d.), introduction, unpaged.

8. *Final Report on Total and Partial Unemployment, 1937*, pp. 319, 327–28, 353.

9. Ibid., p. 330.

10. Jacqueline Jones, *Labor of Love, Labor of Sorrow: Black Women, Work, and the Family from Slavery to the Present* (New York: Basic Books, 1978), pp. 184–222.

11. Woolf, *Economic Trends in California*, pp. 1–4.

12. Ibid., p. 5.

13. Kenneth L. Kusmer, *A Ghetto Takes Shape: Black Cleveland, 1870–1930* (Urbana: University of Illinois Press, 1976), pp. 190–205; Trotter, *Black Milwaukee*, pp. 47, 53–56; Bodnar, Simon and Weber, *Lives of Their Own*, pp. 227–28, 243, 248; Lewis, "At Work and at Home," p. 254; Wright, *Life behind a Veil*, pp. 44–46.

14. Trotter, *Black Milwaukee*, p. 151; *Review of the Activities of the State Relief Administration of California*, pp. 72–73; "Migratory Labor in California," California State Relief Administration, July 1936; and H. Dewey Anderson, "Who Are on Relief in California, 1939," California State Relief Administration, both from the Stewart-Flippin Papers, Moorland-Spingarn Research Center, Howard University.

15. Interview with Katherine Flippin, July 19, 1986, San Francisco.

16. "Tarea Hall Pittman, NAACP Official and Civil Rights Worker," interview conducted by the Bancroft Regional Oral History Office, 1974, pp. iii, 1–4, 17–22, 29–32. Information on Tarea and William Pittman was also provided in a telephone interview on September 16, 1976, and by the University of California Alumni Office, Records Division, University of California, Berkeley, July 16, 1986.

17. Tarea Hall Pittman to Noel Sullivan, January 19, 1932, Noel Sullivan Papers, Bancroft Library, University of California, Berkeley.

18. Pittman to Sullivan, April 7, April 15, and June 21, 1931, Sullivan Papers. The Sullivan Papers did not reveal whether Tarea Pittman received the loan she requested.

19. Albert S. Broussard, "Organizing the Black Community in the San Francisco Bay Area, 1915–1930," *Arizona and the West* 23 (Winter 1981): 341–43; interviews with Alfred Butler, November 5 and December 10, 1976, San Francisco.

20. Interviews with Alfred Butler, November 5 and December 10, 1976, San Francisco.

21. Interview with Katherine Stewart Flippin, July 19, 1986, San Francisco. For the various ways that black families managed scant resources during difficult times, consult Jones, *Labor of Love, Labor of Sorrow*, p. 230; Carol B. Stack, *All Our Kin: Strategies for Survival in the Black Community* (New York: Harper,

1974); Arthur E. Hippler, *Hunter's Point: A Black Ghetto* (New York: Basic Books, 1974); Herbert G. Gutman, *The Black Family in Slavery and Freedom, 1750–1925* (New York: Vintage, 1976), pp. 432–75.

22. U.S. Bureau of the Census, *Fifteenth Census of the United States, 1930*, vol. 6, *Families* (Washington, D.C.: Government Printing Office, 1933), p. 166; Jones, *Labor of Love, Labor of Sorrow*, pp. 266–31.

23. *Fifteenth Census of the United States, United States Summary*, p. 82.

24. *Sixteenth Census of the United States*, vol. 3, pt. 2, *The Labor Force* (Washington, D.C.: Government Printing Office, 1943), p. 205.

25. *Fifteenth Census*, vol. 6, *Families*, pp. 158, 164–66.

26. *Sixteenth Census of the United States, 1940*, vol. 4, *Characteristics of the Population*, p. 657.

27. Anderson, "Who Are on Relief in California," Stewart-Flippin Papers; *Review of the Activities of the State Relief Administration of California*, pp. 67–73; Burke, *Olson's New Deal for California*, p. 78.

28. *Review of the Activities of the State Relief Administration of California*, pp. 22–27; Anderson, "Who Are on Relief in California," Stewart-Flippin Papers; Robert E. Burke, *Olson's New Deal for California* (Berkeley: University of California Press, 1953), p. 78.

29. Anderson, "Who Are on Relief in California," Stewart-Flippin Papers; *Review of the Activities of the State Relief Administration of California*, pp. 67–73; Burke, *Olson's New Deal for California*, p. 78.

30. *Final Report on Total and Partial Unemployment 1937*, vol. 1, pp. 327–28, 330; Richard Sterner, *The Negro's Share*, pp. 239–53.

31. *Sixteenth Census of the United States*, vol. 3, pt. 2, *The Labor Force*, p. 205.

32. *Final Report on Total and Partial Unemployment, 1937*, vol. 1, p. 330.

33. Ibid.; Harris, *The Harder We Run*, p. 106. Robert Austin Warner (*New Haven Negroes*, p. 266) also noted that blacks in New Haven improved their economic status in many respects during the Depression as a result of federal New Deal programs and government regulation.

34. *Report on the Progress of the Works Program to January, 1938*, introduction, unpaged; Robert Wayne Burns to Mary McLeod Bethune, October 10, 1940, C. L. Dellums Papers, Bancroft Library, University of California, Berkeley; *Final Report*, National Youth Administration, Division of Negro Affairs, National Youth Administration Papers, National Archives (hereafter cited as NYA Papers).

35. "Number and Location of Negroes in NYA Projects," November 30, 1940, May 31, February 28, March 31, April 30, June 30, and August 31, 1941, Dellums Papers; "Negro Youth on the National Youth Administration Program in California," n.d., Division of Negro Affairs, NYA Papers.

36. *Final Report*, Division of Negro Affairs, NYA Papers; B. Joyce Ross, "Mary McLeod Bethune and the National Youth Administration: A Case Study of Power Relationships in the Black Cabinet of Franklin D. Roosevelt," *Journal of Negro History* 60 (January 1975): 1–28; Joanna Schneider Zangrando and Robert L. Zangrando, "ER and Black Civil Rights," in Joan Hoff-Wilson and Marjorie Lightsman, eds., *Without Precedent: The Life and Career of Eleanor Roosevelt* (Bloomington: Indiana University Press, 1984), pp. 88–106; Weiss, *Farewell to the Party of Lincoln*, pp. 139–49; Rackham Holt, *Mary McLeod Bethune* (Garden City, N.Y.: Doubleday, 1964).

37. Ross, "Mary McLeod Bethune and the National Youth Administration," 15–16.

38. "Report on the Status of California State Advisory Committee," May 5, 1941, Records of the National Advisory Committee; "NYA for California," n.d. [1941]; "California State Advisory Committee," July 15, 1941; Aubrey Williams to W. G. Frischknecht, August 28, 1942; Robert Wayne Burns to S. Burns Weston, October 23, 1941; "Minutes of the State Advisory Committee"; "A Special Report to the State Advisory Committee," October 28, 1941; and "NYA for California," November 14, 1941, all from the NYA Papers.

39. "Proceedings of the State Negro Advisory Board," February 12, 1941; Robert Wayne Burns to S. Burns Weston, March 31, 1941, both from the NYA Papers.

40. Molly Yard to Robert Wayne Burns, April 24, 1941, NYA Papers.

41. Burns to Weston, March 31, 1941, NYA Papers.

42. Ibid.

43. "NYA for California," State Advisory Committee, n.d. [1941]; "California State Advisory Committee," July 15, 1941, both from the NYA Papers.

44. C. L. Dellums to Robert Wayne Burns, September 20, 1941, Dellums Papers.

45. Ibid.

46. Dellums to Aubrey Williams, December 1, 1941; Dellums to Franklin D. Roosevelt, November 28, 1941, both from the Dellums Papers.

47. Robert E. Brown to Dellums, June 18, 1941, Dellums Papers; "Proceedings of the State Negro Advisory Board," February 12, 1941, NYA Papers; Brown to Dellums, September 18, 1941, Dellums Papers.

48. Interview with Vivian Osborne Marsh, June 8, 1976, Berkeley; *California Voice*, October 7, 1938; *Who's Who in Colored America, 1928–29*, 2d ed. (New York: Who's Who in Colored America Corporation, 1929), p. 257; Vivian Costroma Osborne Marsh, "Types and Distribution of Negro Folklore in America," M.A. thesis, University of California, 1922.

49. Vivian Osborne Marsh to Mary McLeod Bethune, n.d. [1939]; Marsh to Bethune, April 20, 1939; "California Report," October 1937; "California Report," January [1939], all from the Division of Negro Affairs, NYA Papers.

50. Marsh to Bethune, April 20, 1939; Bethune to Anne de G. Treadwell, March 1, 1939, "Negro Youth on the National Youth Administration Program in California," n.d.; "Report on the NYA in California," June 14, 1939, all from the Division of Negro Affairs, NYA Papers. "Census and Employment Questionnaire," NYA, Division of Negro Affairs, copy in the author's possession, a gift from Vivian Osborne Marsh.

51. San Francisco *Spokesman*, June 14, 1934, April 26, 1935, June 7, 1934; Charles H. Taylor to Roy Wilkins, April 3, 1934, series C, NAACP Papers, Library of Congress; Robert Fechner to Thomas L. Griffith, Jr., September 21, 1935, series C, NAACP Papers; John A. Salmond, *The Civilian Conservation Corps, 1933–1942* (Durham, N.C.: Duke University Press, 1967), pp. 91, 93; Salmond, "The Civilian Conservation Corps and the Negro," *Journal of American History* 52 (June 1965): 75–88; Calvin W. Gower, "The Struggle of Blacks for Leadership in the Civilian Conservation Corps, 1933–1942," *Journal of Negro History* 61 (April 1976): 123–35.

52. *Spokesman*, June 14, 1934, August 2, 1935; "C. L. Dellums, International President of the Brotherhood of Sleeping Car Porters and Civil Rights Leader,"

interview conducted by Bancroft Regional Oral History Office, University of California, 1973, pp. 77–79.

53. C. L. Dellums to Sheridan Downey, October 9, 1939; Dellums to Congressman John H. Tolan, June 27, 1939; Dellums to Mandell, September 8, 1939; Dellums to Augustus Hawkins, November 7, 1939; Dellums to Mary McLeod Bethune, June 17, 1940; Bethune to Dellums, October 29, 1940, all from the Dellums Papers.

54. Interview with Vivian Osborne Marsh, June 8, 1976, Berkeley; Ross, "Mary McLeod Bethune and the NYA," pp. 15–16; Dellums to Augustus Hawkins, June 17, 1940, Dellums Papers; Marsh to Bethune, n.d. [1939], Division of Negro Affairs, NYA Papers. Dellums to Clarence R. Johnson, June 26, 1940; Dellums to Hawkins, June 22, 1940; Dellums to Robert E. Brown, December 4, 1940; Dellums to Robert E. Brown, December 4, 1940, all from the Dellums Papers. See also the "Open Letter," June 15, 1940, by Vivian Osborne Marsh in the Dellums Papers.

55. Dellums to John Tolan, June 26, 1940; Clarence R. Johnson to Dellums, June 27, 1940; Johnson to Dellums, June 14, 1940; Robert Wayne Burns to Bethune, May 21, 1940, all from the Dellums Papers. "C. L. Dellums, International President of the Brotherhood of Sleeping Car Porters and Civil Rights Leader," p. 79.

56. *Spokesman*, January 13 and December 15, 1932, January 27, 1933; Rolle, *California: A History*, p. 498.

57. Leland Hawkins to Walter White, March 11, 1933, San Francisco Branch files, NAACP Papers, Library of Congress, Washington, D.C. (hereafter SFBF, NAACP Papers); Wolters, *Negroes and the Great Depression*, pp. 199–200.

58. San Francisco Branch Executive Board to Walter White, June 26, 1934, SFBF, NAACP Papers; Leland Hawkins to Walter White, November 27, 1933, SFBF, NAACP Papers; *Spokesman*, February 13, 1932.

59. Leland Hawkins to Walter White, June 26, 1934; "Statement of Activities," 1932, both from the SFBF, NAACP Papers; *Spokesman*, April 16, May 14, September 16, June 25, and July 2, 1932.

60. *Spokesman*, November 23, November 30, and December 1, 1933.

61. *Spokesman*, January 14, 1934, October 30, 1932, November 30, 1933. John Pittman was far more critical of New Deal programs than most Bay Area black leaders. Interviews with E. A. Daly, November 3, 1976, Oakland, and Vivian Osborne Marsh, June 8, 1976, Berkeley.

62. Wolters, *Negroes and the Great Depression*, p. 170.

63. Victor Anthony Walsh, "The International Longshoreman's Association: The Rebirth of a Union," M.A. thesis, San Francisco State University, 1971, pp. 168–69; *Waterfront Worker*, October 3, 1933, May 21 and August 28, 1934; Charles P. Larrowe, *Harry Bridges: The Rise and Fall of Radical Labor in the United States*, 2d rev. ed. (Westport, Conn.: Lawrence Hill, 1977).

64. *Spokesman*, May 10 and May 17, 1934.

65. Ibid., August 9 and September 20, 1934.

66. Ibid., June 8, 1935.

67. Trotter, *Black Milwaukee*, pp. 158, 166–68; Lawrence B. de Graaf, "Negro Migration to Los Angeles, 1930–1950," Ph.D. dissertation, University of California, Los Angeles, 1962, pp. 102–30. Several scholars have argued that the New Deal programs were not successful in the state of California. See Richard Lowitt, *The New Deal and the West* (Bloomington: Indiana University Press, 1984), pp. 174, 189; Burke, *Olson's New Deal for California*, pp. 230–33.

CHAPTER 7. THE GROWTH
OF BLACK SAN FRANCISCO, 1940–1945

1. U.S. Bureau of the Census, *Special Census of San Francisco, California, Population by Age, Color, and Sex, for Census Tracts,* August 1, 1945 (Washington, D.C.: Government Printing Office, 1945); U.S. Bureau of the Census, *1950 Census of Population,* vol. 2, pt. 5, *Characteristics of the Population* (Washington, D.C.: Government Printing Office, 1952), pp. 5–207. On San Francisco's first population explosion, see Roger Lotchin, *San Francisco, 1846–1856: From Hamlet to City* (New York: Oxford University Press, 1974), pp. 3–30.

2. "1942 Annual Survey of Business Conditions in San Francisco," San Francisco Chamber of Commerce, January 29, 1943, and "1943 Economic Survey," Research Department, San Francisco Chamber of Commerce, n.d., p. 15, United Church Board for Homeland Ministries Archives, Amistad Research Center, Tulane University, New Orleans.

3. "1942 Annual Survey of Business Conditions in San Francisco," and "Population of San Francisco as of December 1, 1942," San Francisco Chamber of Commerce, Industrial Department, n.d., Homeland Ministries Archives; Eugene T. Broderick, Chief, Air Raid Warden Service, "Instructions to Block Wardens," n.d. L. Deming Tilton to R. W. Hawksley, January 12, 1943; and Harold J. Boyd, Controller, to R. W. Hawksley, January 12, 1943, both from the Homeland Ministries Archives.

4. Davis McEntire to Ruth Kaiser, May 5, 1949, California Federation for Civic Unity Papers, Bancroft Library, University of California, Berkeley; Davis McEntire, "California Population Problems: A Progress Report," September 30, 1943; and Davis McEntire, "Supplement 2: The Negro Population in California," both from the Commonwealth Club of California, Homeland Ministries Archives. See also Davis McEntire, *The Labor Force in California: A Study of Characteristics and Trends in Labor Force, Employment, and Occupations in California, 1900–1950* (Berkeley: University of California Press, 1952), and Davis McEntire, *The Population of California: A Report of the Research Study Made by the Authorization of the Board of Governors of the Commonwealth Club of California* (San Francisco: Parker Printing, 1946).

5. McEntire, "California Population Problems: A Progress Report," Homeland Ministries Archives.

6. Raymond Wolters, *Negroes and the Great Depression: The Problem of National Recovery* (Westport, Conn.: Greenwood Publishing, 1970); Lawrence B. de Graaf, "Negro Migration to Los Angeles, 1930–1950," Ph.D. dissertation, University of California, Los Angeles, 1962. See chapter five for a description of the poor economic conditions in the South for black farmers and sharecroppers.

7. Interviews with Sue Bailey Thurman, June 9, 1982, and July 26, 1982, San Francisco.

8. *Special Census of San Francisco, California,* August 1, 1945.

9. Ibid.

10. McEntire, "California Population Problems, A Progress Report"; U.S. Bureau of the Census, *Special Census of Richmond, California, Population by Age, Race, and Sex, by Census Tracts,* September 23, 1947 (Washington, D.C.: Government Printing Office, 1948); U.S. Bureau of the Census, *Special Census of Oakland, California,* October 9, 1945 (Washington, D.C.: Government Printing Office, 1946); U.S. Bureau of the Census, *Special Census of Los Angeles, California, Population by Age, Race and Sex,* February 28, 1946 (Washington,

D.C.: Government Printing Office, 1946); U.S. Bureau of the Census, *Special Census of Berkeley, California*, April 12, 1944 (Washington, D.C.: Government Printing Office, 1944); de Graaf, "Negro Migration to Los Angeles," p. 242.

11. McEntire, "California Population Problems, A Progress Report"; McEntire, "Supplement II—The Negro Population in California."

12. Charles S. Johnson, *The Negro War Worker in San Francisco* (San Francisco, n.p., 1944). "Memorandum on the Study of the Negro Population," n.d.; "Tentative Working Plan of Study," n.d.; "Report of the Interim Steering Committee of the Johnson Survey," June 30, 1944, all from the Homeland Ministries Archives.

13. "Report of the Interim Steering Committee of the Johnson Survey."

14. "Volunteer Interviewers," n.d., Homeland Ministries Archives. A list of sponsors appears opposite the table of contents in *The Negro War Worker in San Francisco*. See Josephine Whitney Duveneck, "Working for a Real Democracy with Children and Other Minority Groups," interview conducted by the Bancroft Regional Oral History Office, 1976, Bancroft Library, University of California, Berkeley, pp. 54–55.

15. "Report of the Interim Steering Committee of the Johnson Survey."

16. Charles S. Johnson and Herman H. Long, *People vs. Property: Race Restrictive Covenants in Housing* (Nashville, Tenn.: Fisk University Press, 1947), preface.

17. Johnson, *The Negro War Worker in San Francisco*, pp. 4–5, 13–15.

18. Ibid., pp. 12, 79. The 1950 census material is quoted from de Graaf, "Negro Migration to Los Angeles," pp. 132, 134–35, 185. Cy Record, "Willie Stokes at the Golden Gate," *Crisis* 56 (June 1949): 176. Record conceded that "no recent conclusive studies of states of origin of the present Negro population in the Bay Area have been done." But a study of unemployed blacks in Richmond, California, after the war revealed that 30 percent had migrated from rural areas and 70 percent from urban areas.

19. Johnson, *The Negro War Worker in San Francisco*, pp. 7, 80.

20. Ibid., pp. 5–6, 10, 12.

21. Ibid., p. 5.

22. *Special Census of San Francisco, California*, August 1, 1945.

23. Johnson, *The Negro War Worker in San Francisco*, pp. 7–8.

24. Ibid., p. 8.

25. Ibid., pp. 9–10, 12.

26. James R. Grossman, *Land of Hope: Chicago, Black Southerners, and the Great Migration* (Chicago: University of Chicago Press, 1989), p. 106.

27. Johnson, *The Negro War Worker in San Francisco*, pp. 12–13; Herbert Gutman found a high incidence of relatives residing with black migrant families in New York City following the World War I migration. See Herbert Gutman, *The Black Family in Slavery and Freedom, 1750–1925* (New York: Vintage Books, 1976), pp. 454–56, 515–17.

28. For information concerning the recruitment of labor to the San Francisco Bay Area, see "Meeting of the San Francisco Council for Civic Unity," December 20, 1944, Stewart-Flippin Papers, Moorland-Spingarn Research Center, Howard University; National Defense Migration, *First Interim Report of the Select Committee Investigating National Defense Migration*, 77th Congress, 1st session, October 21, 1941, pp. 4–6; Carey McWilliams, "Report on Importation of Negro Labor to California," August 10, 1942, Department of Industrial Rela-

tions, Division of Immigration and Housing; McEntire, "California Population Problems, A Progress Report."

29. Douglas H. Daniels, *Pioneer Urbanities: A Social and Cultural History of Black San Francisco* (Philadelphia: Temple University Press, 1980), p. 165; National Defense Migration, *First Interim Report*, pp. 4–5.

30. Interview with Sarah Lane Hastings, February 1, 1976, San Francisco.

31. Johnson, *The Negro War Worker in San Francisco*, p. 80. Johnson noted in his survey of black war workers that 20 percent either owned homes or were in the process of buying property. National Defense Migration, *First Interim Report*, p. 5; Record, "Willie Stokes at the Golden Gate," pp. 176–79.

CHAPTER 8. WORLD WAR II, FAIR EMPLOYMENT, DISCRIMINATION, AND BLACK OPPORTUNITY

1. Davis McEntire, "A Study of California Population Problems, Progress Report," September 30, 1943, Commonwealth Club of California, Race Relations Department, American Missionary Association Papers, United Church Board for Homeland Ministries Archives, Amistad Research Center, Tulane University, New Orleans; Charles S. Johnson, *The Negro War Worker in San Francisco: A Local Self Survey* (San Francisco: n.p., 1944), pp. 9–14.

2. Carl Abbott, *The New Urban America: Growth and Politics in Sunbelt Cities*, rev. ed. (Chapel Hill: University of North Carolina Press, 1987), pp. 102–3; Richard M. Bernard and Bradley R. Rice, eds., *Sunbelt Cities: Politics and Growth since World War II* (Austin: University of Texas Press, 1983); Gerald D. Nash, *The American West Transformed: The Impact of the Second World War* (Bloomington: Indiana University Press, 1985), pp. 17–55.

3. Davis McEntire, "The Negro Population in California," supplement 2, Commonwealth Club of California, Homeland Ministries Archives.

4. Ibid.

5. Clifton Jones, "California Report, Minorities Committee, California C.I.O. Council," October 1943, Homeland Ministries Archives; interview with Matt Crawford, n.d., conducted by the staff of Charles S. Johnson, Homeland Ministries Archives; C. L. Dellums to Matt Crawford, June 26, 1940 and John P. Davis to Matt Crawford, October 3, 1939, C. L. Dellums Papers, Bancroft Library, University of California.

6. McEntire, "The Negro Population in California," Supplement 2, Homeland Ministries Archives.

7. McEntire, "A Study of California Population Problems," Homeland Ministries Archives.

8. "Summary of Minorities Committee Survey on Union Membership and Employment of Minorities in California," California CIO Minorities Committee, n.d., Homeland Ministries Archives. McEntire, *The Negro Population in California*, supplement 2; *Fair Employment Practices Committee* [FEPC], *Final Report* (Washington, D.C.: Government Printing Office, 1947), p. 78.

9. "Summary, Labor, Industry and the Negro Worker," California CIO, n.d.; Homeland Ministries Archives.

10. *FEPC, Final Report*, pp. 77–81.

11. "Summary, Labor, Industry and the Negro Worker," Homeland Ministries Archives.

12. Louis Ruchames, *Race, Jobs, and Politics: The Story of FEPC* (New York: Columbia University Press, 1953), p. 22; Herbert Garfinkel, *When Negroes March: The March on Washington Movement in the Organizational Politics for FEPC* (New York: Atheneum, 1969).

13. *Fair Employment Practices Committee, First Report* (Washington, D.C.: Government Printing Office, 1945), pp. 5–7.

14. Ibid., pp. 7, 140–43. For an account of the demise of formal segregation in the military, see Richard M. Dalfiume, *Fighting on Two Fronts: Desegregation of the U.S. Armed Forces, 1939–1953* (Columbia: University of Missouri Press, 1969); Bernard Nalty, *Strength for the Fight: A History of Black Americans in the Military* (New York: Free Press, 1986), pp. 235–69.

15. Ruchames, *Race, Jobs, and Politics*, pp. 137–39, 142.

16. Harry L. Kingman to Joe W. Ervin, April 1, 1945, Harry L. Kingman Papers, Bancroft Library, University of California; *The International Year Book and Statesmen's Who's Who, 1959; International Who's Who, 1968*, p. 156; Harry Lees Kingman, "Citizenship in a Democracy," interview conducted by the Bancroft Regional Oral History Office, 1973, Bancroft Library, University of California, pp. 1–6, (hereafter BROHO); Ruth W. Kingman, "The Fair Play Committee and Citizen Participation," interview conducted by the BROHO, 1973, p. 4. Additional information concerning Kingman's years in China can be found in the Kingman Papers.

17. Kingman to Robert Gordon Sproul, December 5, 1940; Robert B. Stone to Sproul, December 5, 1940; Kingman to Yori [Wada], August 13, 1942; Kingman to John McCloy, Assistant Secretary of War, February 5, 1943, all from the Kingman Papers. *The International Year Book and Statesmen's Who's Who, 1959* can also be found in the biographical section of the Kingman Papers.

18. Kingman to Paul C. Smith, editor, *San Francisco Chronicle*, December 10, 1945; Kingman to Clarence Mitchell, September 28, 1945; Kingman to Jefferson Beaver, April 19, 1944; Kingman to George M. Johnson, July 29, July 16, and July 23, 1943; Kingman to Anson S. Blake, January 15, 1944, all from the Kingman Papers.

19. Kingman to Will Maslow, November 11 and December 19, 1944; Kingman to Jefferson Beaver, April 19, 1944; Kingman to Joseph James and Jefferson Beaver, January 30, 1945; Kingman to Clarence Mitchell, January 4 and September 28, 1945, all from the Kingman Papers; *Who Was Who in America*, vol. 8, *1982–1985* (Chicago: Marquis Who's Who, 1985), p. 285.

20. *Fair Employment Practices Committee, First Report*, pp. 21–22; Ruchames, *Race, Jobs, and Politics*, p. 142.

21. Virginia R. Seymour to Kingman, January 4, April 18, and September 9, 1944; Kingman to Eugene Davison, April 18, 1944, all from the Kingman Papers. *FEPC, First Report*, p. 10.

22. Kingman to Johnson, February 9, 1945; Seymour to Kingman, January 19, 1945, both from the Kingman Papers.

23. Seymour to Kingman, September 9, 1944, Kingman Papers.

24. R. P. Wiggins to Franklin D. Roosevelt, October 30, 1943; unsigned letter, August 6, 1942, to President Franklin D. Roosevelt, both in Region 12, FEPC Papers.

25. Kingman to Supervisor Don Fazackerley, December 26, 1949, Kingman Papers.

26. Kingman to Fazackerley, December 19, 1949, Kingman Papers.

27. Kingman to Will Maslow, June 28, 1944, Kingman Papers; United States

Employment Service, Report 150, "Report of Discriminatory Hiring Practices, Kelling Nut Company, San Francisco," n.d., War Manpower Commission Papers, National Archives; Kingman to Fazackerley, December 19, 1949, Kingman Papers.

28. Kingman to Dr. J. J. Rourke, January 26, 1944; Kingman to F. S. Durie, Superintendent, University of California Hospital, January 26, 1944; Kingman to Durie, February 23, 1944; Kingman to Sam Kagel, March 7, 1944; Kingman to Will Maslow, June 28, 1944, all from the Kingman Papers. August Meier and Elliott Rudwick, *Black Detroit and the Rise of the UAW* (New York: Oxford University Press, 1979), pp. 19–20.

29. Frank S. Pestana to Sam Kagel, March 10, 1944; Pestana to Home Laundry Company, June 7, 1944; Telegram, Kingman to Maslow, January 19, 1945, all from the Kingman Papers. R. P. Wiggins to Franklin D. Roosevelt, October 30, 1943, Region 12, FEPC Papers, National Archives.

30. A. F. Mueller to Sam Kagel, January 11, 1944; Mueller to Edward Rutledge, January 25, 1944, both from Region 12, FEPC Papers.

31. Interview with John Pittman, conducted by Herman H. Long, n.d., Homeland Ministries Archives; *People's World,* October 6, 1945.

32. Sam Kagel to Rutledge, n.d., Case No. 12-BR-409; Kingman to Maslow, December 6, 1944; C. L. Dellums to Bernard Ross, October 6, 1945, all from Region 12, FEPC Papers.

33. Kingman to Maslow, December 6, 1944; Dellums to Ross, October 6, 1945; statement from Jessa Mae Janice, April 10, 1945; R. E. Hambrook to Edward Rutledge, March 5, 1945; Kagel to Rutledge, n.d., Case No. 12-BR-409, all from Region 12, FEPC Papers.

34. Final Disposition Report No. 12-BR-205, February 12, 1944, Field-Ernst Envelope Company, San Francisco; Edward Rutledge to president of Field-Ernst Envelope Company, January 17, 1944, both from Region 12, FEPC Papers. See interview with Harry L. Kingman, n.d., in the Homeland Ministries Archives. For a general discussion of black female workers and discrimination during World War II, see Karen Tucker Anderson, "Last Hired, First Fired: Black Women Workers during World War II," *Journal of American History* 69 (June 1982): 82–97; David M. Katzman, *Seven Days a Week: Women and Domestic Service in Industrializing America* (New York: Oxford University Press, 1978), ch. 5. To place black women within the context of all working women during World War II, see Karen Anderson, *Wartime Women: Sex Roles, Family Relations, and the Status of Women during World War II* (Westport, Conn.: Greenwood Press, 1981).

35. Final Disposition Report No. 12-BR-159, February 17, 1944, Fleishacker Box Company, San Francisco,Retion 12, FEPC Papers.

36. Kingman to Clarence Mitchell, March 15, 1945; unsigned complaint to FEPC Regional Office, October 26, 1944, Region 12, FEPC Papers.

37. Franklin O. Nichols to Floyd Covington, February 6, 1942; Covington to C. L. Dellums, March 31, 1942, Dellums Papers. *American Civil Liberties Union News,* February and April 1942; Alexander Richmond, *Ten Years: the Story of a People's Newspaper* (San Francisco: Daily People's World, 1948), pp. 15–16.

38. Dellums to Covington, February 17, 1942, Dellums Papers. Kingman to Elmer Henderson, March 19, 1944; telegram, Kingman to St. Claire Bourne, November 28, 1944; Kingman to William Scott, December 29, 1944, all from the Kingman Papers. Interview with Naomi Johnson, September 30, 1976, San Francisco. Mrs. Johnson's husband mentioned casually during the course of my

interviews with his wife that he was the second black driver employed by the San Francisco Municipal Railway System. Unlike Audley Cole, Mr. Johnson experienced no difficulty, and he drove San Francisco's buses and streetcars until he retired.

39. "First Progress Report of the Bay Area Council against Discrimination," August 1942, Dellums Papers. For a comprehensive account of the civil rights activities see the minutes for 1942 of the Bay Area Council against Discrimination, in the Dellums Papers.

40. *People's World,* January 1 and January 3, 1938; Richmond, *Ten Years: The Story of a People's Newspaper,* pp. 15–16; Al Richmond, *A Long View from the Left: Memoirs of an American Revolutionary* (New York: Dell, 1972), p. 289; C. L. Dellums to John Pittman, March 8, 1945, Dellums Papers.

41. Interview with John Pittman, conducted by Herman H. Long, n.d., Homeland Ministries Archives; *People's World,* October 2 and December 2, 1943. Pittman and *People's World* would also press for the eradication of the segregated auxiliaries in Bay Area unions. See *People's World,* November 24, November 26, November 29, and December 1, 1943.

42. Interview with Matt Crawford, conducted by the staff of Charles S. Johnson, n.d., Homeland Ministries Archives.

43. Clifton Jones, "California Report," October 1943, Minorities Committee, California CIO Council, Homeland Ministries Archives; interview with Richard Lynden, conducted by the staff of Charles S. Johnson, n.d., Homeland Ministries Archives.

44. Final Disposition Report No. 12-UR-612, July 17, 1945, Region 12, FEPC Papers; interview with Richard Lynden, Homeland Ministries Archives.

45. Final Disposition Report No.12-UR-213, December 23, 1943, Region 12, FEPC Papers.

46. Interview with Richard Lynden, conducted by the staff of Charles S. Johnson, Homeland Ministries Archives; interview with Matt Crawford, conducted by the staff of Charles S. Johnson, Homeland Ministries Archives.

47. Interview with Richard Lynden, Homeland Ministries Archives.

48. Interview with John Pittman, conducted by Herman H. Long, n.d., Homeland Ministries Archives.

49. "Summary, Labor, Industry, and the Negro Worker"; "Summary of Minorities Committee Survey on Union Membership and Employment of Minorities in California," both from the California CIO Minorities Committee, n.d., Homeland Ministries Archives. Frank S. Pestana to A. Guy Robinson, March 9, 1944, Kingman Papers.

50. Davis McEntire, "The Negro Population in California," supplement 2, Homeland Ministries Archives. The quotation by Selvin is from McEntire's report.

51. Interview with Matt Crawford, Homeland Ministries Archives.

52. "Report of Discriminatory Hiring Practices," November 24, 1943, Region 12, FEPC Papers; "Questionnaire Forms for Labor Union Head, Shipyard and Marine Shop Laborers," folder 17, Homeland Ministries Archives.

53. Kingman to Maslow, October 27, 1944, Kingman Papers; interview with C. L. Dellums, conducted by the staff of Charles S. Johnson, Homeland Ministries Archives.

54. Final Disposition Report No. 12-UR-658, July 15, 1945; "Report of Discriminatory Hiring Practices," November 24, 1943, both from Region 12, FEPC Papers.

55. "Summary, Labor, Industry, and the Negro Worker," Homeland Ministries Archives; Johnson, *The Negro War Worker in San Francisco*, pp. 71–74.

56. McEntire, "The Negro Population in California," supplement 2; "Summary, Labor, Industry, and the Negro Worker"; C. L. Dellums interview, all from the Homeland Ministries Archives. Kingman to Louise Douglas, February 2, 1942, Kingman Papers; interview with Richard Lynden, Homeland Ministries Archives; C. L. Dellums to Ben O'Brien, June 20, 1944, Dellums Papers.

57. "Summary, Labor, Industry and the Negro Worker"; interview with Richard Lynden, both from the Homeland Ministries Archives.

58. Mrs. Joseph James listed her address as 1865 Pine Street when she took out a membership in the San Francisco branch of the NAACP. See Matalize Hutchinson to San Francisco Branch, April 28, 1943, San Francisco Branch files, NAACP Papers, Library of Congress (hereafter cited as SFBF, NAACP Papers). Interview with John Pittman, Homeland Ministries Archives. Alberta James also served as a volunteer for the study of black wartime workers conducted by Charles S. Johnson. See "Volunteer Interviewers," Alberta James, folder 20, Homeland Ministries Archives; Charles Wollenberg, "James vs. Marinship: Trouble on the New Black Frontier," *California History* 60 (Fall 1981): 269; David F. Selvin to Walter White, January 19, 1944, Dellums Papers.

59. Interview with Edward Rainbow, conducted by the staff of Dr. Charles S. Johnson, November 2, 1943, Homeland Ministries Archives. Rainbow, President of the Boilermakers' Union Local No. 6, stated that James started as a trainee before moving to journeyman and finally leaderman. Charles Wollenberg notes that James started as a welder's helper before advancing to journeyman. See Wollenberg, "James vs. Marinship," p. 269; Joseph James, "Against the Setting Up of Auxiliary Unions for Negroes (specifically, Boilermakers' Local 6)," n.d., Homeland Ministries Archives (a copy of this report can also be found in the FEPC Papers for Region 12); "Minutes from Sunday Meeting," November 28, 1943, Homeland Ministries Archives. The following year Eugene Small killed himself as well as his wife and child. See *San Francisco Reporter*, April 16, 1945; and testimony of Joseph James, [September 13, 1943], 6 p., Region 12, FEPC Papers. At the time this interview was conducted by the staff of the FEPC's Regional Office, James worked as a journeyman welder in the Flying Squad, a group of highly trained welders who worked on special projects whenever there was a production bottleneck. He noted in the interview that he could become a leaderman only if he was willing to take an all black work crew.

60. James, "Against the Setting Up of Auxiliary Unions for Negroes"; Joseph James to Harry Kingman and Edward Rutledge, October 18, 1943; complaint by James, June 11, 1943, and September 27, 1943; testimony of Joseph James [September 13, 1943], 6 p., all from the Region 12 FEPC Papers.

61. Malcolm Ross to Boilermakers Union Local No. 6, n.d., Region 12, FEPC Papers. George E. Bodle to A. A. Liveright, November 29, 1943; Thomas F. Neblett to William H. Davis, November 29, 1943; Neblett to Joseph James, December 1, 1943, all from the War Manpower Commission Papers, National Archives Regional Office, San Bruno (hereafter WMC Papers); Joseph James to Chairman, FEPC, February 29, 1944, Region 12, FEPC Papers; "On the Scene of the Walkout at Marinship," November 27, 1943, clipping in the Homeland Ministries Archives; *San Francisco Chronicle*, November 30, 1943, p. 10.

62. Kingman to George M. Johnson, November 30, 1943, Region 12, FEPC Papers; *News from the Bay Area Council against Discrimination*, December 1942; petition by the "Shipyard Workers Committee against Discrimination,"

n.d., Kingman Papers. Regarding James's association with the San Francisco Branch of the NAACP, see Berlinda Davison to editor, *NAACP Bulletin*, August 7, 1941. Ella J. Baker to D. W. Ruggles, February 16, 1944; Thurgood Marshall to Walter White, July 5, 1944; Joseph James to Roy Wilkins, August 21, 1944; telegrams, Josephine Jones to Roy Wilkins, November 7 and November 9, 1944, all from the SFBF, NAACP Papers.

63. James to Sheridan Downey, November 22, 1943; David Selvin to David Donovan, n.d., Region 12, FEPC Papers.

64. Telegram, Ray Thompson, chairman of the Shipyard Workers Committee against Discrimination, n.d.; George M. Johnson to David Selvin, August 6, 1943, both from Region 12, FEPC Papers. *News from the Bay Area Council against Discrimination*, December 1943; Neblett to William H. Davis, November 29, 1943, both from the WMC Papers. George Johnson to Francis J. Haas, September 2, 1943, Region 12, FEPC Papers. Alonzo Smith and Quintard Taylor, "Racial Discrimination in the Workplace: A Study of Two West Coast Cities during the 1940's," *Journal of Ethnic Studies* 8 (Spring 1980): 36–54.

65. Interview with Edward Rainbow, conducted by the staff of Charles S. Johnson, November 2, 1943, Homeland Ministries Archives; Wollenberg, "James vs. Marinship," p. 271.

66. Wollenberg, "James vs. Marinship," p. 271; testimony of Joseph James [September 13, 1943], 6 p., Region 12, FEPC Papers.

67. Katherine Archibald, *Wartime Shipyards: A Study in Social Disunity* (Berkeley: University of California Press, 1947), pp. 61–64.

68. Quoted in Wollenberg, "James vs. Marinship," p. 267; James to Stanley White, March 13, 1944, Region 12, FEPC Papers.

69. Wollenberg, "James vs. Marinship," pp. 271–74.

70. Memo, Thurgood Marshall to Walter White, July 5, 1944, SFBF, NAACP Papers; *James v. Marinship Corp.* 25 Cal.2d (December 30, 1944), 724.

71. Kingman to George M. Johnson, January 7 and February 17, 1944, Kingman Papers; Malcolm Ross to Boilermakers Union Local No. 6, n.d., Region 12, FEPC Papers; Kingman to Will Maslow, March 29, 1944, Kingman Papers.

72. Quoted in Wollenberg, "James vs. Marinship," p. 274.

73. *James v. Marinship Corp.*, pp. 730–31, 739.

74. Ibid., pp. 741, 745.

75. William H. Harris, *The Harder We Run: Black Workers since the Civil War* (New York: Oxford University Press, 1982), p. 121; Wollenberg, "James vs. Marinship," p. 276.

76. Wollenberg, "James vs. Marinship," p. 277; Fred Stripp, "The Relationship of the San Francisco Bay Area Negro-American Worker with the Labor Unions Affiliated with the American Federation of Labor and the Congress of Industrial Organizations," Th.D. thesis, 1948, Pacific School of Religion, Berkeley. Although dated, the Stripp thesis remains the most comprehensive account of the black workers' relationship to Bay Area unions after World War II.

77. Harris, *The Harder We Run*, p. 121; Lawrence B. de Graaf, "Negro Migration to Los Angeles, 1930–1950," Ph.D. dissertation, University of California, Los Angeles, 1962, pp. 117–119, 190; John Bodnar, Roger Simon, and Michael P. Weber, *Lives of Their Own: Blacks, Italians, and Poles in Pittsburgh, 1900–1960* (Urbana: University of Illinois Press, 1982), pp. 242–54; William H. Chafe, *Women and Equality: Changing Patterns in American Culture* (New York: Oxford University Press, 1977), p. 85; Darrel E. Bigham, *We Ask Only a Fair Trial: A History of the Black Community of Evansville, Indiana* (Bloomington: Indiana

University Press, 1987), pp. 226–34; Joe William Trotter, Jr., "Unemployment, Relief, and the Struggle for Fair Employment in Defense Industries: Black Milwaukee, 1933–1945," paper presented at the annual conference of the Association for the Study of Afro-American Life and History, Baltimore, Md., 1982, pp. 28–29; Joe William Trotter, Jr., *Black Milwaukee: The Making of an Industrial Proletariat, 1915–45* (Urbana: University of Illinois Press, 1985), pp. 165–75.

CHAPTER 9. WARTIME TENSIONS AND
THE STRUGGLE FOR HOUSING

1. Few scholars have examined the impact of the World War II black migration on northern or western urban centers. See Douglas H. Daniels, *Pioneer Urbanites: A Social and Cultural History of Black San Francisco* (Philadelphia: Temple University Press, 1980), ch. 10; Lawrence B. de Graaf, "Negro Migration to Los Angeles, 1930–1950," Ph.D. dissertation, University of California, Los Angeles, 1962; Quintard Taylor, Jr., "A History of Blacks in the Pacific Northwest, 1788–1970," Ph.D. dissertation, University of Minnesota, 1977; Charles S. Johnson, *The Negro War Worker in San Francisco* (San Francisco: n.p., 1944); Joe William Trotter, Jr., "Unemployment, Relief, and the Struggle for Fair Employment in Defense Industries: Black Milwaukee, 1922–1945," paper presented at the annual conference of the Association for the Study of Afro-American Life and History, Baltimore, Md., 1982; Alonzo N. Smith "Black People in the Los Angeles Area during the 1940s," paper presented at a conference of the Association for the Study of Afro-American Life and History, 1982; St. Clair Drake and Horace Cayton, *Black Metropolis: A Study of Negro Life in a Northern City,* 2 vols., rev. ed. (New York: Harcourt, Brace and World, 1970). A recent monograph by Jimmie Lewis Franklin, *Journey toward Hope: A History of Blacks in Oklahoma,* (Norman: University of Oklahoma Press, 1982), traces the black experience in Oklahoma from the antebellum era to the present. In *Black Detroit and the Rise of the UAW* (New York: Oxford University Press, 1979), August Meier and Elliott Rudwick examine the relation between the UAW and a major northern city during the Great Depression and the early years of the Second World War. See also Edward E. France, "Some Aspects of the Migration of the Negro to the San Francisco Bay Area since 1940," Ph.D. dissertation, University of California, Berkeley, 1962.

2. Robert Flippin, "The Negro in San Francisco [1943]," Stewart-Flippin Papers, Moorland-Spingarn Research Center, Howard University; interview with Josephine Cole, December 9, 1976, San Francisco. See also the interview with Cole conducted by the San Francisco Black Oral History Project, 1978, San Francisco. Transcripts of interviews with Cole and twenty other subjects are located in the African-American Historical and Cultural Society, San Francisco. For an overview of racial violence during World War II, consult Harvard Sitkoff, "Racial Militance and Interracial Violence in the Second World War," *Journal of American History* 58 (December 1971): 661–81.

3. *Christian Science Monitor,* July 27, 1943, pp. 1–2.

4. *San Francisco Reporter,* October 1, 1943, copy in the Stewart-Flippin Papers; Clifton Jones, "California Report, October 1943," United Church Board for Homeland Ministries Archives, Amistad Research Center, Tulane University, New Orleans; *American Civil Liberties Union News,* March 1944; Davis

McEntire, "Supplement 2—The Negro in California," Homeland Ministries Archives.

5. Leonard Brinson to Earl Warren, November 22, 1943, Earl Warren Papers, California State Archives.

6. Edwina Robbins to Earl Warren, January 10 and January 31, 1944, Warren Papers.

7. See postcard signed "Black and Black" to Earl Warren, May 20, 1945, Warren Papers.

8. J. F. Anderson to Earl Warren, December 9, 1944, Warren Papers.

9. George Backester to Earl Warren, August 11, 1945; John Stillions to Warren, November 1, 1943, both in the Warren Papers.

10. Mrs. Powell to Earl Warren, September 14, 1943, Warren Papers.

11. Marcelle Dean Poole to C. L. Dellums, September 13, 1945, C. L. Dellums Papers, Bancroft Library, University of California, Berkeley; *American Civil Liberties Union News*, March 1944; *News from the Bay Area Council against Discrimination*, October 1943; Robert B. Powers, "Law Enforcement, Race Relations, 1930–50," interview conducted by the Bancroft Regional Oral History Office, 1971, Bancroft Library, University of California, Berkeley; McEntire, "Supplement 2—The Negro in California," all in the Homeland Ministries Archives.

12. *American Civil Liberties Union News*, April, June, July, September, October, November, and December, 1944; "Meeting of the San Francisco Council for Civic Unity," October 10, 1945, Stewart-Flippin Papers; [Joseph James] to Robert W. Kenny, June 6, 1946, Robert Kenny Papers, Bancroft Library, University of California, Berkeley.

13. C. L. Dellums to Will Connolly, December 19, 1941, Dellums Papers; Oscar Jonness to Robert Flippin, December 18, 1944, Stewart-Flippin Papers.

14. McEntire, "Supplement 2—The Negro in California," Homeland Ministries Archives.

15. "An Appeal to the Publishers of the Bay Area Newspapers," September 3, 1943, Dellums Papers; McEntire, "Supplement 2—The Negro in California," Homeland Ministries Archives.

16. C. L. Dellums to Mattie Van Dyke, August 13, 1942, Dellums Papers.

17. William and Adde Critz to National Office, NAACP, January 14, 1944, San Francisco Branch Files, NAACP Papers, Library of Congress, Washington, D.C. (hereafter cited as SFBF, NAACP Papers); Grossman, *Land of Hope*, pp. 151–54.

18. Robert Flippin, "Welcome, the California Advocate," August 10, 1942, Stewart-Flippin Papers.

19. Charles S. Johnson, *The Negro War Worker in San Francisco* (San Francisco: n.p., 1944), pp. 92–93; Quintard Taylor, "The Great Migration: The Afro-American Communities of Seattle and Portland during the 1940s," *Arizona and the West* 23 (Summer 1981): 109.

20. Johnson, *The Negro War Worker in San Francisco*, p. 93.

21. "Meeting of the San Francisco Council for Civic Unity," December 20, 1944, Stewart-Flippin Papers.

22. "Minutes of the San Francisco Council for Civic Unity," June 21, 1945, Stewart-Flippin Papers; Mrs. Harold MacChesney to editor, *San Francisco Chronicle*, June 23, 1943, Stewart-Flippin Papers; Davis McEntire, "A Study of California Population Problems, Progress Report," September 30, 1943, Commonwealth Club of California, Homeland Ministries Archives.

23. Bernard Taper, *San Francisco Housing*, vol. 3 (San Francisco: n.p., 1941), p. 30. *1939 Real Property Survey, San Francisco, California* (San Francisco: City and County of San Francisco, 1940), p. 24; Johnson, *The Negro War Worker*, p. 22; U.S. Bureau of the Census, *Sixteenth Census of the United States, 1940, Housing Block Statistics* (Washington, D.C.: Government Printing Office, 1942), pp. 20–23; Herman H. Long, "San Francisco Self-Survey in Race Relations-Racial Problems in Housing, 1944," Homeland Ministries Archives (hereafter cited as "San Francisco Self-Survey").

24. McEntire, "Supplement 2—The Negro in California," Homeland Ministries Archives.

25. James Brury to C. L. Dellums, August 25, 1944, Dellums Papers.

26. "Report on the Conference of California Councils of Civic Unity," July 6, 1945, California Federation for Civic Unity Papers, Bancroft Library, University of California, Berkeley.

27. Johnson, *The Negro War Worker*, pp. 30–32.

28. *News from the Bay Area Council against Discrimination*, July 1943. For a discussion of white attitudes toward blacks in white neighborhoods, see Luigi Laurenti, *Property Values and Race: Studies in Seven Cities* (Berkeley: University of California Press, 1960), and Davis McEntire, *Residence and Race, Final and Comprehensive Report to the Commission on Race and Housing* (Berkeley: University of California Press, 1960).

29. *1939 Real Property Survey*, passim; J. C. Geiger to Thomas Brooks, June 30, 1943, Stewart-Flippin Papers; *Christian Science Monitor*, July 27, 1943; *San Francisco Chronicle*, June 26, 1943; McEntire, "Supplement 2—The Negro in California," Homeland Ministries Archives.

30. *San Francisco Reporter*, July 28, 1944; Taper, *San Francisco Housing*, vol. 3, pp. 6, 8, 19, 30–32.

31. Johnson, *The Negro War Worker*, p. 26; *People's World*, October 2, 1943; *1939 Real Property Survey*, pp. 24–28.

32. Long, "San Francisco Self-Survey," Homeland Ministries Archives; *1939 Real Property Survey*, p. 31.

33. Johnson, *The Negro War Worker*, pp. 24–27.

34. San Francisco Council for Civic Unity, "Agenda of the Board of Directors Meeting," January 18, 1945; memo, Harold J. Boyd to executive officers and directors of the Council for Civic Unity, November 2, 1944; Maurice E. Harrison to San Francisco Housing Authority, January 29, 1945; "Meeting of the Council for Civic Unity," April 15, 1944; Alice Griffith, "A Review of the Proceedings of the Housing Authority of San Francisco, April 17, 1938–August 17, 1943," all from the Stewart-Flippin Papers. *Hunter's Point Beacon*, September 1 and October 22, 1943, February 1, April 15, May 12, and August 28, 1944, March 9, 1945.

35. William and Adde Critz to National Office, NAACP, January 14, 1944, SFBF, NAACP Papers; John W. Beard to Maurice E. Harrison, August 12, 1945; "Second Regular Meeting of the Council for Civic Unity"; Maurice E. Harrison to San Francisco Housing Authority, January 29, 1945; Mayor's Committee on Civic Unity to Mayor Roger D. Lapham, March 15, 1945, all in the Stewart-Flippin Papers.

36. Interview with John Beard, conducted by Herman H. Long, n.d., copy in the Homeland Ministries Archives. John Beard to Maurice Harrison, August 2, 1945; Mayor's Committee on Civic Unity to Mayor Roger D. Lapham, March 15, 1945, both from the Stewart-Flippin Papers.

37. Meeting of the Council for Civic Unity, January 17, 1945, Stewart-Flippin Papers.

38. Alma Taeuber and Karl Taeuber, *Negroes in Cities* (Chicago: Aldine, 1965), pp. 40, 44.

39. Alice Griffith, "A Review of the Proceedings of the San Francisco Housing Authority," Stewart-Flippin Papers; *Road to the Golden Age: A Report of the First Twenty Years of Operation—1940 to 1960—by the Housing Authority of the City and County of San Francisco, California; Annual Report for 1938–39* (San Francisco: City and County of San Francisco, 1940); *Second Annual Report of the San Francisco Housing Authority, April 18, 1940* (San Francisco: City and County of San Francisco, 1940).

40. *San Francisco Housing Authority Sixth Annual Report, 1944* (San Francisco: City and County of San Francisco, 1944), p. 9; Horace Cayton to Frank S. Horne, May 14, 1942, Stewart-Flippin Papers; interview with Katherine Flippin, February 17, 1976, San Francisco. Robert Flippin's San Francisco Housing Authority pay stubs for 1943, Stewart-Flippin Papers. "Application by Robert Flippin to the San Francisco Housing Authority," n.d.; Sydney S. Clark to Robert Flippin, April 1943; Edward J. Wren to Robert Flippin, January 5, 1945; 1946 diary calendar of Robert Flippin, all contained in the Stewart-Flippin Papers. See also the obituary of Robert Flippin in the *San Francisco Sun-Reporter*, September 14, 1963.

41. Interview with John Beard, Homeland Ministries Archives.

42. Ibid.

43. *San Francisco Housing Authority Sixth Annual Report, 1944;* Clarence R. Johnson to C. L. Dellums, January 2, 1941, Dellums Papers; *Road to the Golden Age.* For specific reference to the Housing Authority's policy of tenant selection, see "Resolution No. 287," adopted unanimously at the Housing Authority commission meeting on May 28, 1942, copy in the West Coast Regional Files of the NAACP Papers, Bancroft Library, University of California, Berkeley.

44. Alice Griffith, "A Review of the Proceedings of the San Francisco Housing Authority," Stewart-Flippin Papers.

45. Clarence R. Johnson to C. L. Dellums, January 2, 1941, and Dellums to Johnson, February 27, 1941, Dellums Papers; Taeuber and Taeuber, *Negroes in Cities*, p. 20.

46. Interview with Edward Howden, June 7, 1983, San Francisco; Alice Griffith, "A Review of the Proceedings of the San Francisco Housing Authority," Stewart-Flippin Papers.

47. Clarence R. Johnson to C. L. Dellums, January 2, 1941, Dellums Papers.

48. Long, "San Francisco Self-Survey"; McEntire, "Supplement 2—The Negro in California," both in Homeland Ministries Archives.

49. For the NAACP's legal assault on the San Francisco Housing Authority's "neighborhood policy," see *Mattie Banks vs. Housing Authority of the City and County of San Francisco* (1952). A copy of the brief and testimony is located in the West Coast Regional Files of the NAACP Papers.

50. Dominic J. Capeci, Jr., *Race Relations in Wartime Detroit: The Sojourner Truth Housing Controversy of 1942* (Philadelphia: Temple University Press, 1984).

51. Ibid., pp. 75–80, 135–36, 142–47.

52. Johnson, *The Negro War Worker*, p. 28; NAACP Annual Report of the San Francisco Branch for 1945, SFBF, NAACP Papers.

53. Johnson, *The Negro War Worker*, p. 83.

54. McEntire, "Supplement 2—The Negro in California," Homeland Ministries Archives.

55. Interview with Marion Beers Howden, conducted by the Charles S. Johnson research team, n.d., Homeland Ministries Archives.

56. "Report on the Activities of the San Francisco Branch of the NAACP," April 3, 1943, SFBF, NAACP Papers; *News from the Bay Area Council against Discrimination*, December 1942, February, March, May, July, and November 1943, and April, 1944.

57. "Council Presents Plan to End Discrimination," n.d., "Minutes of the Fourth Meeting of the Bay Area Council against Discrimination," March 26, 1942; "Minutes of the Fifth Meeting of the Bay Area Council against Discrimination," April 2, 1942; "Statement of the San Francisco Housing Authority," May 1943; "Summary of Bay Area Council Legislative Proposals," n.d., all from the Dellums Papers; *News from the Bay Area Council against Discrimination*, July 1943. For information concerning the early campaigns of the San Francisco Council for Civic Unity against housing discrimination, see "Council for Civic Unity Construction and By-Laws," n.d.; "Council for Civic Unity Committee on Housing," n.d.; "Summary of the Work of the Council for Civic Unity, December 1, 1944 to June 1, 1945"; Maurice E. Harrison to San Francisco Housing Authority, January 29, 1945, all contained in the Stewart-Flippin Papers.

58. Long, "San Francisco Self-Survey."

59. *Christian Science Monitor*, July 27, 1943, pp. 1–2; Arnold R. Hirsch, *Making the Second Ghetto: Race and Housing in Chicago, 1940–1960* (Cambridge, Mass.: Cambridge University Press, 1983), pp. 1–36; John Bodnar, Roger Simon, and Michael P. Weber, *Lives of Their Own: Blacks, Italians, and Poles in Pittsburgh, 1900–1960* (Urbana: University of Illinois Press, 1982), pp. 192, 196–97, 216, 224.

CHAPTER 10. WORLD WAR II AND THE
NEW BLACK LEADERSHIP

1. The terms "new elite" and "old elite" are used in this chapter to describe both a change of personnel and, as Kenneth L. Kusmer noted in his study of blacks in Cleveland, "a social and psychological grouping in the black community." See Kenneth L. Kusmer, *A Ghetto Takes Shape: Black Cleveland, 1870–1930* (Urbana: University of Illinois Press, 1976), pp. 115–16.

2. Kusmer, *A Ghetto Takes Shape*, pp. 115–16, 236–43; Allan H. Spear, *Black Chicago: The Making of a Negro Ghetto, 1890–1920* (Chicago: University of Chicago Press, 1969), pp. 51–89; David A. Gerber, *Black Ohio and the Color Line: 1860–1915* (Urbana: University of Illinois Press, 1976), pp. 371–416. On the impact of World War II on blacks, consult Darlene Clark Hine, "Mabel K. Staupers and the Integration of Black Nurses into the Armed Forces," in John Hope Franklin and August Meier, eds., *Black Leaders of the Twentieth Century* (Urbana: University of Illinois Press, 1982), pp. 241–57; Richard M. Dalfiume, "The Forgotten Years of the Negro Revolution," *Journal of American History* 55 (June 1968): 90–106; Dalfiume, *Fighting on Two Fronts: Desegregation of the U.S. Armed Forces, 1939–1953* (Columbia: University of Missouri Press, 1969); Charles E. Silberman, *Crisis in Black and White* (New York: Random House, 1964), pp. 60, 65; Harvard Sitkoff, "Racial Militancy and Interracial Violence in the Second World War," *Journal of American History* 58 (December 1971): 661–

81; Gunnar Myrdal, *An American Dilemma: The Negro Problem and Modern Democracy*, vol. 2 (New York: Harper and Row, 1944), p. 997; John Hope Franklin, *From Slavery to Freedom*, 5th ed. (New York: Knopf, 1980), pp. 450–51; Raymond Gavins, *The Perils and Prospects of Southern Black Leadership: Gordon Blaine Hancock, 1884–1970* (Durham, N.C.: Duke University Press, 1977), pp. 100–127; William H. Chafe, *Civilities and Civil Rights, Greensboro, North Carolina, and the Black Struggle for Freedom* (New York: Oxford University Press, 1980), ch. 1; Robert H. Brisbane, *The Black Vanguard: Origins of the Negro Social Revolution, 1900–1960* (Valley Forge, Pa.: Judson Press, 1970), pp. 161–83; Lee Finkle, "The Conservative Aims of Militant Protest: Black Protest during World War II," *Journal of American History* 60 (December 1973): 692–713; Charles S. Johnson, *To Stem This Tide: A Survey of Racial Tension Areas in the United States* (Boston: Pilgrim Press, 1943); Herbert Garfinkel, *When Negroes March: The March on Washington Movement in the Organizational Politics for FEPC* (reprint ed. New York: Atheneum, 1968).

3. Charles S. Johnson, *The Negro War Worker in San Francisco* (San Francisco: n.p., 1944), pp. 4–5, 13–15. I constructed profiles of fifty members of the new elite by consulting the *San Francisco Sun-Reporter* from 1951–1964, the records of the NAACP, National Urban League, National Council of Negro Women, San Francisco Council for Civic Unity, Bay Area Council against Discrimination, and California Federation for Civic Unity. I also conducted personal interviews with surviving members of this new leadership class.

4. Johnson, *The Negro War Worker in San Francisco*, pp. 5–6, 10, 12; interview with Seaton W. Manning, June 12, 1976, San Francisco; interviews with Revels Cayton, October 21 and November 11, 1976, San Francisco; interview with Josephine Cole, December 9, 1976, San Francisco.

5. Interview with Seaton W. Manning, June 17, 1976, San Francisco; *Who's Who in Colored America*, 7th ed. (Yonkers-on-Hudson, N.Y.: Christian E. Burkel and Associates, 1950), pp. 117, 109, 352, 504; *Who's Who among Black Americans, 1980–81*, 3rd ed. (Northbrook, Ill.: Who's Who among Black Americans Publishing, 1981), p. 302; *Howard University Directory of Graduates, 1870–1976* (White Plains, N.Y.: Bernard C. Harris Publishing, 1977), p. 183; Charles Wollenberg, "James vs. Marinship: Trouble on the New Black Frontier," *California History* 60 (Fall 1981): 269; *Sun-Reporter*, October 27, 1951, September 18 and November 21, 1953, December 14, 1957.

6. "Cosmos Club, Paid Up Adult Members," March 17, 1944; "Board Members of the Cosmos [Club]," May 14, 1943, both from the Stewart-Flippin Papers, Moorland-Spingarn Research Center, Howard University; *Sun-Reporter*, March 17, 1951, April 5, 1952, June 6, 1953, March 6, 1954; interview with Josephine Cole, December 9, 1976, San Francisco. Cole stated that even though the Cosmos Club continued to hold its annual ball during the 1940s, there was less of a need for it by the early 1950s. She explained that integration and racial advancement in many areas prompted some blacks to question the necessity of an exclusive social organization.

7. *Who's Who in Colored America*, 7th ed., 1950, p. 504; *Sun-Reporter*, May 22, May 29, October 16, and November 6, 1954; "Biographical Information for Listing of Members of Urban League Boards," October 6, 1948, San Francisco Urban League, National Urban League Papers, Library of Congress (hereafter cited as SFUL Papers); *Who's Who in Colored America*, 7th ed., p. 117.

8. *Who's Who among Black Americans, 1980–81*, 3d ed., p. 302; *Howard University Directory of Graduates, 1870–1976*, p. 183; Donna Barnhill, "The Sun

Reporter: Its Role as a Negro Weekly in the San Francisco Bay Area Negro Community," M.A. thesis, San Francisco State College, 1965, pp. 25–29; Carlton B. Goodlett, "The Role of the Black Physician," *Freedomways* 9 (Fall 1969): 373–84; James Summerville, *Educating Black Doctors: A History of Meharry Medical College* (Tuscaloosa: University of Alabama Press, 1983). For Goodlett's role in the local NAACP, consult the San Francisco Branch files of the NAACP Papers from 1946 to 1950 at the Library of Congress, Washington, D.C. (hereafter cited as SFBF, NAACP Papers).

9. Howard Thurman, *With Head and Heart: The Autobiography of Howard Thurman* (New York: Harcourt Brace Jovanovich, 1979), pp. 25, 33, 40–41, 84–85, 131–34; *Life Magazine*, April 6, 1953, pp. 127–33.

10. Los Angeles, *California Eagle*, May 13, July 8, August 12, and October 21, 1943.

11. For background on Reverend Boswell, consult the *California Eagle*, November 24, December 2, and December 23, 1943, January 25, and February 1, 1945; *Sun-Reporter*, May 1, May 22, and October 16, 1954.

12. Interview with Seaton W. Manning, June 17, 1976, San Francisco; *Who's Who in Colored America*, 7th ed., 1950, p. 352.

13. *Sun-Reporter*, October 6, 1956; Resumé of D. Donald Glover, n.d.; "Index of Minutes, Second Annual Meeting," October 18–19, 1947, p. 15; Board of Directors, 1948 and 1950, all from California Federation for Civic Unity Papers, Bancroft Library, University of California, Berkeley (hereafter cited as CFCU Papers).

14. *Who's Who in Colored America*, 7th ed., 1950, pp. 490–91; biographical clipping of James Stratten, n.d., in the West Coast Regional Files, NAACP Papers, Bancroft Library (hereafter WCRF, NAACP Papers); *Sun-Reporter*, May 8, May 29, and June 5, 1954.

15. Matalize Hutchinson to secretary, San Francisco NAACP, April 28, 1943; Conference Assessment for San Francisco Branch, n.d.; Joseph James to Roy Wilkins, August 21, 1944; telegrams to Joseph James, November 7 and November 9, 1944; telegram, Wilkins to James, December 8, 1944; James to Wilkins, December 8, 1944; Ella J. Baker to Nellie Bonner, February 23, 1945, all from the SFBF, NAACP Papers. Memo, Thurgood Marshall to Walter White, July 5, 1944; James to Wilkins, March 12, 1945; Leaflet, San Francisco Branch, Public Meeting for State FEPC, February 26, 1945, SFBF, NAACP Papers; *James v. Marinship Corp. 25 Cal. 2d* (December 30, 1944), 721–45; *People's World*, November 24, November 26, and November 29, 1943; Wollenberg, "James vs. Marinship," p. 269. Thurgood Marshall to Mr. and Mrs. Joseph James, December 7, 1944; Wilkins to White, November 28, 1944, both from the SFBF, NAACP Papers.

16. Bettye Collier-Thomas, *N.C.N.W., 1935–1980* (Washington, D.C., National Council of Negro Women, 1981), pp. 1–6; telephone interview with Sue Bailey Thurman, July 26, 1982; Darlene Clark Hine, *When the Truth Is Told: A History of Black Women's Culture and Community in Indiana, 1875–1950* (Indianapolis: The National Council of Negro Women Indianapolis Section, 1981); Cynthia Neverdon-Morton, *Afro-American Women of the South and the Advancement of the Race, 1895–1925* (Knoxville: University of Tennessee Press, 1989); Jeanetta Welch Brown to Gertrude Barnes, January 6, 1943, National Council for Negro Women's Papers, Washington, D.C. (hereafter cited as NCNW Papers): *Sun-Reporter*, June 9, 1951; *Aframerican Woman's Journal* 1 (Spring 1940); Thurman, *With Head and Heart*, pp. 84–85, 131–34. The best sources on the founding

of the San Francisco chapter of NCNW are the NCNW Papers, located at the Black Women's Archives in Washington, D.C. These records are indispensable in reconstructing the chapter's activities. For example, see Gertrude Barnes to Mary McLeod Bethune, February 9, 1944, and December 30, 1943; Jeanetta Welch Brown to Barnes, February 15, 1944, all from the NCNW Papers. *Women United, Souvenir Year Book, Sixteenth Anniversary,* 1951, Mary Church Terrell Papers, Library of Congress, Washington, D.C. Sue Bailey Thurman was also instrumental in organizing a visit to Haiti for a delegation of black women in 1941. The trip was cancelled, however, as a result of our "defense program" during World War II. See Sue Bailey Thurman to Mary Church Terrell, April 24, July 14, and August 7, 1941; see also Thurman to Haitian-Seminar Delegation, July 21, 1941, Terrell Papers.

17. "Membership Report," November 1950; "Membership Report," August 5, 1954, NCNW Papers; *Sun-Reporter,* October 31 and November 21, 1953, December 21, 1957.

18. Scrapbook of S. Anna Duncan Magruder, East Bay Negro Historical Society, Oakland.

19. *Sun-Reporter,* May 29, June 5, August 7, and August 28, 1954; *Who's Who in Colored America,* 7th ed., 1950, p. 26. Jefferson Beaver was later indicted on three felony counts of "making and accepting illegal loans." See *Sun-Reporter,* December 7, 1963.

20. Thurman, *With Head and Heart,* pp. 137–62; Alfred Fisk to Howard Thurman, October 15, 1943, quoted from Howard Thurman, *First Footprints: The Dawn of the Idea of the Church for the Fellowship of All Peoples* (San Francisco: Howard Thurman, 1975). The most thorough account of the events that led to the founding of Fellowship Church is Howard Thurman, *Footprints of a Dream: The Story of the Church for the Fellowship of All Peoples* (New York: Harper and Brothers, 1959).

21. Alfred Fisk to Howard Thurman, October 30, 1943, in *First Footprints.*

22. Thurman to Fisk, December 1 and December 28, 1943, in *First Footprints;* Thurman, *With Head and Heart,* pp. 140–42.

23. Thurman to Fisk, November 12, 1943, June 2, 1944, in *First Footprints.*

24. Thurman to Fisk, January 3, 1944, in ibid.

25. Thurman, *With Head and Heart,* pp. 142–43; telephone interviews with Sue Bailey Thurman, June 9 and July 26, 1982.

26. Thurman, *With Head and Heart,* pp. 146–48; Thurman, *Footprints of a Dream,* pp. 29–53, 109.

27. Thurman, *Footprints of a Dream,* pp. 8, 43–44.

28. Ibid., pp. 43–44.

29. See chapter eleven for a detailed discussion and analysis of the interracial organizations and committees that were established in the San Francisco Bay Area during the World War II era.

30. For an analysis of black protest organizations in the San Francisco Bay Area before 1940, see Albert S. Broussard, "Organizing the Black Community in the San Francisco Bay Area, 1915–1930," *Arizona and the West* 23 (Winter 1981): 335–54; Weiss, *The National Urban League, 1910–1940,* pp. 299–302.

31. *Who's Who in Colored America,* 7th ed., 1950, p. 117; "Biographical Information for Listing of Members of Urban League Boards," October 6, 1948, SFUL Papers; Reginald A. Johnson to Eva Hance, March 24, 1944, SFUL Papers.

32. Reginald A. Johnson to Daniel Collins, March 24, 1944, SFUL Papers.

33. Johnson to Collins, March 24, 1944, SFUL Papers.

34. Johnson to Eva Hance, May 24, 1944; Johnson to Collins, March 24, 1944; Johnson to Jefferson Beaver, November 10, 1944; Johnson to Collins, November 10, 1944, all from the SFUL Papers.

35. Collins to Johnson, April 7, 1944, SFUL Papers. An obituary on Alfred Fisk appeared in the *Sun-Reporter*, April 11, 1959.

36. Collins to Johnson, January 23, 1945, SFUL Papers; C. L. Dellums to Matt Crawford, executive secretary, National Negro Congress, June 26, 1940, Dellums Papers, Bancroft Library; Joshua R. Rose to Reginald A. Johnson, April 4, 1944; George L. P. Weaver, June 15, 1945, both from the SFUL Papers. Jefferson Beaver to Reginald A. Johnson, October 3, 1944; Johnson to Daniel Collins, April 23, 1945; Johnson to George L. P. Weaver, June 15, 1945, all from the SFUL Papers. Interview with F. L. Ritchardson, September 13, 1976, San Francisco; *History of the Booker T. Washington Community Center, 1920–1970* (San Francisco, n.p., 1970); "Booker T. Washington Community Center Annual Reports, 1926–1930," Bancroft Library, University of California, Berkeley; Collins to Johnson, December 15, 1944, SFUL Papers. I obtained additional biographical information on Robert Flippin in interviews with his widow, Katherine Flippin, on February 17, 1976, and July 19, 1986, in San Francisco. She also allowed me to see family scrapbooks and photographs.

37. Reginald A. Johnson to Eugene K. Jones, April 23, 1945; Johnson to Collins, December 20, 1944, both from the SFUL Papers. Johnson to Collins, March 24, 1940, SFUL Papers; interview with Seaton Manning, June 17, 1976, San Francisco; *Who's Who in Colored America*, 7th ed., 1950, p. 352. For an analysis of the successes and failures of the National Urban League, see Weiss, *The National Urban League*, passim; Arvarh E. Strickland, *History of the Chicago Urban League* (Urbana: University of Illinois Press, 1966), evaluates the activities of an Urban League branch on the local level in a major urban center from 1915 to 1965.

38. D. Donald Glover, "Community Planning in Industrial Relations," October 25, 1950; Seaton W. Manning to Lester B. Granger, June 15, 1950; "Employment and Counseling Activities," San Francisco Urban League, November 28, 1952; "Officers and Directors, San Francisco Urban League, 1946–1953"; "Report of the Activities of the San Francisco Urban League for the Year 1948"; "Fourth Annual Report," December 31, 1949, San Francisco Urban League, all from the SFUL Papers. *Folio*, February and August 1947, February and May 1948.

CHAPTER 11. THE GROWTH AND FLOWERING
OF INTERRACIAL ORGANIZATIONS

1. Only a few studies have examined the dynamics between black and interracial leadership during the World War II era. See William H. Chafe, *Civilities and Civil Rights: Greensboro, North Carolina, and the Black Struggle for Freedom* (New York: Oxford University Press, 1980), pp. 13–41.

2. For a representative view of the dissension within the San Francisco NAACP branch, see memo, Roy Wilkins to Walter White, May 1, 1940; Roy Wilkins to the Committee on Administration, "Digest of the Conflict within the San Francisco Branch," April 30, 1940; Edward Mabson to George Johnson, May 31, 1940, San Francisco Branch Files, NAACP Papers, Library of Congress.

3. "First Progress Report of the Bay Area Council against Discrimination,"

August 1942; "Minutes of the Fifth Meeting of the Bay Area Council against Discrimination," April 2, 1942, San Francisco, C. L. Dellums Papers, Bancroft Library, University of California, Berkeley.

4. "Walter Gordon: Athlete, Officer in Law Enforcement and Administration, Governor of the Virgin Islands," interviews conducted by the Bancroft Regional Oral History Office, 1976–1979, Bancroft Library, University of California, Berkeley; *News from the Bay Area Council against Discrimination*, December 1943; *Sun-Reporter*, January 26, 1956; *San Francisco Chronicle*, December 15, 1939.

5. "Walter Gordon," Bancroft Regional Oral History Office.

6. "Minutes of the Fifth Meeting of the Bay Area Council against Discrimination," August 1942; C. L. Dellums to David F. Selvin, December 24, 1943; Berlinda Davison to C. L. Dellums, February 26, 1944, all from the Dellums Papers. The best source of information regarding the life and influence of C. L. Dellums is a lengthy interview conducted by the Bancroft Regional Oral History Office, "C. L. Dellums, International President of the Brotherhood of Sleeping Car Porters and Civil Rights Leader," University of California, 1973; William H. Harris, *Keeping the Faith: A. Philip Randolph, Milton P. Webster, and the Brotherhood of Sleeping Car Porters, 1925–1937* (Urbana: University of Illinois Press, 1977), pp. 41, 111, 129, 152, 183, 216.

7. "Minutes of the Third Meeting of the Bay Area Council against Discrimination," March 19, 1942; "Minutes of the Fourth Meeting of the Bay Area Council against Discrimination," March 26, 1942; open letter from John D. Barry, May 8, 1942; "Bay Area Council against Discrimination Trade Union Sub-Committee," n.d.; Aubrey Grossman to C. L. Dellums, April 14, 1942, all from the Dellums Papers. *News from the Bay Area Council against Discrimination*, March 1944.

8. "First Progress Report of the Bay Area Council against Discrimination," August 1942; Berlinda Davison to C. L. Dellums, February 26, 1944; "Council Presents Plan to End Discrimination," n.d.; "An Appeal to the Publishers of the Bay Area Newspapers," September 3, 1943; David F. Selvin to C. L. Dellums, May 20, 1943; Selvin to Walter White, January 19, 1943, all from the Dellums Papers. For a partial review of the Bay Area Council's achievements, see *News from the Bay Area Council against Discrimination*, January 1943, February 1943, December 1942.

9. *News from the Bay Area Council against Discrimination*, February, March, and July 1943, February and April 1944; "Minutes of the Fourth Meeting of the Bay Area Council against Discrimination," March 26, 1942, Dellums Papers.

10. "Minutes of the Fifth Meeting of the Bay Area Council against Discrimination," April 2, 1942; "Resolution on Discrimination in and Expansion of War Production Training Facilities," n.d.; "Statement to San Francisco Housing Authority," May 14, 1943, all from the Dellums Papers.

11. "Resolution on U.S. Employment Service," n.d., Dellums Papers; *News from the Bay Area Council against Discrimination*, May 1943, September 1943. Harry L. Kingman to George M. Johnson, July 29, 1943; Kingman to Anson S. Blake, January 15, 1944, Harry L. Kingman Papers, Bancroft Library, University of California, Berkeley.

12. *News from the Bay Area Council against Discrimination*, October 1943, December 1943, January 1944, May 1944.

13. "First Progress Report of the Bay Area Council against Discrimination," August 1942; "Council Presents Plan to End Discrimination," n.d., both from

Dellums Papers. See also C. L. Dellums to Franklin D. Roosevelt, August 13, 1943, Dellums Papers.

14. *News from the Bay Area Council against Discrimination*, August, September, and October 1943.

15. Interview with Edward Howden, June 10, 1982, San Francisco; *Social Planning*, September 1944, copy in National Urban League Papers, San Francisco Affiliate, Library of Congress (hereafter cited as NUL Papers); Josephine Whitney Duveneck, "Working for a Real Democracy with Children and Other Minority Groups," interview conducted by the Bancroft Regional Oral History Office, 1976, pp. 44–45, 56; Jefferson Beaver to Reginald A. Johnson, October 3, 1944, NUL Papers; Edward Howden, "Program, Techniques, and Problems of the Council for Civic Unity of San Francisco," July 14, 1948, California Federation for Civic Unity Papers, Bancroft Library, University of California, Berkeley (hereafter cited as CFCU Papers).

16. Interview with Edward Howden, June 10, 1982, San Francisco; *Sun-Reporter*, August 16, 1959. Biographical material concerning Howden is scattered throughout the *San Francisco Sun-Reporter* between 1952 and 1959.

17. Neither the San Francisco branch of the NAACP nor the local National Urban League Chapter elected a white president or executive director within the time framework of this study, but a number of whites were elected to the executive committees and the boards of directors of both organizations. For a thorough account of Harry L. Kingman's influence on the Bay Area's liberal community, see Harry L. Kingman, "Citizenship in a Democracy," interview conducted by the Bancroft Regional Oral History Office, 1973.

18. U.S. Bureau of the Census, *Special Census of San Francisco, California, Population by Age, Color, and Sex, for Census Tracts*, August 1, 1945 (Washington, D.C.: Government Printing Office, 1945); Charles Wollenberg, "James vs. Marinship: Trouble on the New Black Frontier," *California History* 60 (Fall 1981): pp. 262–79.

19. Interview with Edward Howden, June 10, 1982, San Francisco.

20. Howden, "Program, Techniques, and Problems"; Charles S. Johnson, *The Negro War Worker in San Francisco* (San Francisco: n.p., 1944).

21. Howden, "Program, Techniques, and Problems."

22. Interview with Edward Howden, June 10, 1982, San Francisco.

23. Ibid.

24. Interview with Seaton Manning, June 17, 1976, San Francisco; *San Francisco Chronicle*, December 1, 1947; Edward Howden to Harry L. Kingman, May 13, 1946, CFCU Papers.

25. *Chronicle*, December 1, 1947.

26. Ibid.

27. Feliza Williams to Franklin H. Williams, November 22, 1950; Allen T. Hinman to Franklin H. Williams, December 13, 1956; Williams to Hinman, December 21, 1950; Franklin H. Williams to San Francisco Medical Society, December 5, 1950, all in West Coast Regional Files, NAACP Papers, Bancroft Library, University of California, Berkeley. *Folio*, February 1947; "Report of the Activities of the San Francisco Urban League for the Year 1948," n.d.; *Folio*, February 1947, February 1948, all in NUL Papers.

28. Interview with Edward Howden, June 10, 1982, San Francisco; Irving Babow and Edward Howden, *A Civil Rights Inventory of San Francisco*, vol. 1, *Employment* (San Francisco: Council for Civic Unity, 1958); Howden, "Program, Techniques, and Problems." *Among These Rights*, the San Francisco Council for

Civic Unity's monthly newsletter, has not been collected or preserved by any major California library, but periodic issues have survived in the personal correspondence of Edward Howden and several larger collections. See *Among These Rights*, September 1948.

29. Interview with Edward Howden, June 10, 1982, San Francisco: The best source for following the weekly format of "Dateline Freedom" was the San Francisco *Sun-Reporter*, a weekly black newspaper that began publishing excerpts from the program in 1953. See *Sun-Reporter*, January 17, 1953. The black press continued its coverage until the demise of "Dateline Freedom" in 1958; *Sun-Reporter*, May 24, 1958.

30. Although it is impossible to measure the popularity of "Dateline Freedom," the periodic letters and editorials in the black press praising both Edward Howden and the program suggest that Howden was performing a valuable community service. See *Sun-Reporter*, January 31 and September 5, 1958, September 12, 1959, and August 16, 1958.

31. Articles of Incorporation, California Federation for Civic Unity, April 23, 1946, California State Archives. (A copy is also available in the CFCU Papers). Dorothy Handy to Laurence J. Hewes and Ruth Kingman, September 1946, CFCU Papers.

32. Ruth W. Kingman, "The Fair Play Committee and Citizen Participation," interview conducted by the Bancroft Regional Oral History Office, 1973, p. 2.

33. Ibid., p. 3.

34. Ruth Kingman to Robert Kenny, January 31, April 25, September 11, and October 25, 1944; Ruth Kingman, "The Fair Play Committee," pp. 24–25; Ruth Kingman to Robert Kenny, June 20, 1945, June 25, 1945, all in Robert Kenny Papers, Bancroft Library, University of California, Berkeley.

35. Ruth Kingman to Laurence Hewes, September 19, 1946; Louis Wirth to board of directors of the American Council on Race Relations, March 7, 1947; Dorothy Handy to Laurence J. Hewes and Ruth Kingman, September 1946; Ruth Kingman to Hewes, September 19, 1946; Kingman to Louis Wirth, June 12, 1947, all in the CFCU Papers.

36. Laurence Hewes to William C. Robinson, September 10, 1946; Hewes to Hilda Heifetz, May 7, 1946; "List of Members," California Council for Civic Unity, April 20, 1946, all from the CFCU Papers.

37. Edward Howden to Harry L. Kingman, May 13, 1946; Laurence J. Hewes to Joseph Sullivan, April 30, 1946; "Blueprint for Action, Automobile Insurance," 3 p., n.d.; "Report of Investigations of Racial Discrimination in Automobile Insurance," August 8, 1948; Margaret Rohrer, "Automobile Insurance Regulation Rate Discrimination," April 20, 1949; "American Civil Liberties Union Press Release," September 11, 1947; "Policy Statement of California Council for Civic Unity," March 17, 1946; "Press Release," California Federation for Civic Unity, February 13, 1950; Ruth Kingman to Earl Warren, September 24, 1947; "Proceedings for the Fourth Annual Convention," February 20, 1950, all from the CFCU Papers.

38. Laurence J. Hewes to Caroline MacChesney, March 31, 1947, CFCU Papers.

39. Ruth Kingman to Louis Wirth, April 24, 1947; Hewes to Wirth, April 24, 1947; Wirth to Ruth Kingman, May 19, 1947, all from the CFCU Papers.

40. Caroline MacChesney to Lowell Pratt, June 17, 1947, CFCU Papers. A detailed analysis of the CFCU's financial structure can be obtained from the grant applications and accounts books in the CFCU Papers. See "Account Book,

Cash, 1948"; "Journal, CFCU, Cash Received from March 12, 1948"; "Receipts of Contributing Members," [1954–1955].

41. MacChesney to Kingman, May 11, 1947; Ruth Kingman to Louis Wirth, June 12, 1947, both from the CFCU Papers.

42. Kingman to Board of Directors, August 3, 1947, CFCU Papers.

43. MacChesney to Remington Stone, September 26, 1947; MacChesney to Harry S. Scott, October 21, 1947, both from the CFCU Papers.

44. Taylor, "The Great Migration: The Afro-American Communities of Seattle and Portland during the 1940s," pp. 109–26; Elizabeth McLagan, *A Peculiar Paradise: A History of Blacks in Oregon, 1788–1940*, (Portland, Ore.: Georgian Press, 1980), pp. 173–82; de Graaf, "Negro Migration to Los Angeles," pp. 179–216; Quintard Taylor, "A History of Blacks in the Pacific Northwest, 1788–1970," Ph.D. dissertation, University of Minnesota, 1977, pp. 274–85.

45. Joe William Trotter, *Black Milwaukee: The Making of an Industrial Proletariat, 1915–1945* (Urbana: University of Illinois Press, 1985), pp. 171–88; Dominic J. Capeci, *Race Relations in Wartime Detroit: The Sojourner Truth Housing Controversy of 1942* (Philadelphia: Temple University Press, 1984), pp. 146–70; Darrel E. Bigham, *We Ask Only A Fair Trial: A History of the Black Community of Evansville, Indiana* (Bloomington: Indiana University Press, 1987), pp. 232–37; Arnold R. Hirsch, *Making the Second Ghetto: Race and Housing in Chicago, 1940–1960* (Cambridge, Mass.: Cambridge University Press, 1983), pp. 171–211.

CHAPTER 12. POSTWAR EMPLOYMENT:
GAINS AND LOSSES

1. *1950 Census of Population, Characteristics of the Population*, Part 5, vol. 2 (Washington, D.C.: Government Printing Office, 1952), p. 207; Seaton W. Manning to Lester B. Granger, June 15, 1950, National Urban League Papers, Library of Congress, Washington, D.C. (hereafter cited as NUL Papers); *NAACP, Annual Report of the West Coast Regional Office, 1951*, p. 8, West Coast Regional Files, NAACP Papers, Bancroft Library, University of California, Berkeley (hereafter cited as WCRF, NAACP Papers); R. J. Reynolds, "The Negro and Crime in San Francisco, 1947," WCRF, NAACP Papers.

2. *Fair Employment Practices Committee, Final Report* (Washington, D.C.: Government Printing Office, 1947), pp. 78–79; Cy Record, "Willie Stokes at the Golden Gate," *Crisis* 56 (June 1949), 175–76. On racial violence in the South, see George C. Wright, *Racial Violence in Kentucky, 1865–1940: Lynchings, Mob Rule, and "Legal Lynchings"* (Baton Rouge: Louisiana State University Press, 1990).

3. Stripp, "The Relationship of the San Francisco Bay Area Negro American Worker with the Labor Unions Affiliated with the American Federation of Labor and the Congress of Industrial Organizations," Th.D. thesis, Pacific School of Religion, 1948, pp. 272–76; "Report of the Activities of the San Francisco Urban League for the Year 1948"; Manning to Granger, June 15, 1950, both from the NUL Papers; *Folio*, May 1948. The San Francisco Urban League's newsletter, *Folio*, illustrated the employment achievements of the Urban League. Fred Stripp, "The Treatment of Negro-American Workers by the AFL and the CIO in the San Francisco Bay Area," *Social Forces* 28 (March 1950): 330–32. For a broader discussion of black workers' progress in labor unions during the 1940s,

consult William H. Harris, *The Harder We Run: Black Workers since the Civil War* (New York: Oxford University Press, 1982), pp. 123–41; Philip S. Foner, *Organized Labor and the Black Worker, 1619–1973* (New York: Praeger, 1976); Sterling D. Spero and Abram L. Harris, *The Black Worker,* reprint (New York: Atheneum, 1968).

4. "NAACP Monthly Report, 1946," WCRF, NAACP Papers; *Folio,* February 1948 and May 1948. "Report of the Activities of the San Francisco Urban League for the Year 1948"; Manning to Granger, June 15, 1950, both from NUL Papers; interview with Josephine Cole, December 9, 1976, San Francisco; G. James Fleming and Christian E. Burckel, eds., *Who's Who in Colored America,* 7th Ed., 1950 (Yonkers-on-Hudson, N.Y.: Christian E. Burckel, 1950), p. 109; Davis McEntire and Julia R. Tarnopol, "Postwar Status of Negro Workers in the San Francisco Area," *Monthly Labor Review* 70 (June 1950): 614–15; "NAACP West Coast Regional Conference," March 7–8, 1947, San Francisco, p. 3, C. L. Dellums Papers, Bancroft Library, University of California, Berkeley.

5. McEntire and Tarnopol, "Postwar Status of Negro Workers," p. 614. Karen Tucker Anderson argues that black women throughout the nation did not significantly alter their status during the decade of the 1940s. See Karen Tucker Anderson, "Last Hired, First Fired: Black Women Workers during World War II," *Journal of American History* 69 (June 1982): 82–97; William H. Chafe, *The American Woman: Her Changing Social, Economic, and Political Role, 1920–1970* (New York: Oxford University Press, 1972), pp. 142–43.

6. McEntire and Tarnopol, "Postwar Status of Negro Workers," p. 615; interview with Josephine Cole, December 9, 1976, San Francisco; *San Francisco Call,* February 2, 1945; *Sun-Reporter,* September 25, 1954, September 10, 1955, January 18, 1958, January 23, 1958; John Bodnar, Roger Simon and Michael P. Weber, *Lives of Their Own: Blacks, Italians, and Poles in Pittsburgh, 1900–1960* (Urbana: University of Illinois Press, 1982), p. 242; Mary E. Davies and Genevieve Marsh, "A Study of the Negro in Lincoln," M.A. thesis, University of Nebraska, 1904.

7. "NAACP Press Release," April 29, 1947, WCRF, NAACP Papers; Franklin H. Williams to Gloster Current, February 19, 1951, San Francisco Branch files, NAACP Papers, Library of Congress (hereafter cited as SFBF, NAACP Papers).

8. Reynolds to Roy Wilkins, July 21, 1953, SFBF, NAACP Papers; R. J. Reynolds, "The Negro and Crime in San Francisco," WCRF, NAACP Papers; *Sun-Reporter,* March 6, 1954, and May 1, 1954.

9. *Who's Who in Colored America,* 7th ed., p. 504.

10. *Sun-Reporter,* May 22, May 29, October 16, and November 6, 1954, March 5, 1955, July 28, 1956; "San Francisco Housing Authority Commission Minutes, 1946," San Francisco Housing Authority, San Francisco; interview with Edward Howden, June 7, 1983, San Francisco; interview with Seaton W. Manning, June 17, 1976, San Francisco; "NAACP Monthly Report," April 1946, WCRF, NAACP Papers.

11. *FEPC, Final Report,* p. 78; Record, "Willie Stokes," p. 177.

12. "Community Planning in Industrial Relations," October 25, 1950, NUL Papers; *Folio,* May 1948; Harry L. Kingman to Supervisor Don Fazackerley, December 19, 1949, Harry L. Kingman Papers, Bancroft Library, University of California, Berkeley; R. J. Reynolds, "The Negro and Crime in San Francisco, 1947," p. 10. The San Francisco Department of Public Health estimated San Francisco's black population at 50,000 in 1947; however, most scholars reject that estimate. See McEntire and Tarnopol, "Postwar Status of Negro Workers,"

p. 616; Ottole Krebs, "The Post-War Negro in San Francisco," senior thesis, Mills College, 1949; Record, "Willie Stokes," p. 175.

13. *FEPC, Final Report*, pp. 78–81; Kingman to Fazackerley, December 19, 1949, Kingman Papers.

14. Kingman to Fazackerley, December 26, 1949, Kingman Papers; *FEPC, Final Report*, p. 81.

15. "NAACP West Coast Regional Conference," San Francisco, March 28, 1947, p. 3, Dellums Papers; *FEPC, Final Report*, p. 80; Anderson, "Last Hired, First Fired: Black Women Workers during World War II," pp. 89–90.

16. *FEPC, Final Report*, p. 80; James Jones, *Bad Blood: The Tuskegee Syphilis Experiment* (New York: Free Press, 1981), p. 27.

17. Kingman to Fazackerley, December 19 and December 26, 1949, Kingman Papers; "Community Planning in Industrial Relations," October 25, 1950, NUL Papers; *Folio*, February and August, 1947; "Report of the Activities of the San Francisco Urban League for the Year 1948," NUL Papers; *FEPC, Final Report*, pp. 79–80; "Employment Practices in Private Industry in San Francisco Affecting Minority-Group Applicants," pp. 26–28, Testimony before the San Francisco Board of Supervisors, January 30, 1957, WCRF, NAACP Papers.

18. Roger D. Lapham to San Francisco Board of Supervisors, May 23, 1943, Stewart-Flippin Papers, Moorland-Spingarn Research Center, Howard University; interview with Edward Howden, June 7, 1983, San Francisco.

19. "Resolution Favoring State FEPC," June 17, 1945, SFBF, NAACP Papers; Joe James to Roy Wilkins, June 21, 1945, SFBF, NAACP Papers; *Among These Rights*, October 26, 1945; "State FEPC Laid to Rest This Session," Blueprint for Action, California Federation for Civic Unity, 1949, California Federation for Civic Unity Papers, Bancroft Library; Michael Tobriner, "The California Fair Employment Practices Commission: Its History, Accomplishments, and Limitations," M.A. thesis, Stanford University, 1963.

20. "Fair Employment for San Francisco? Voluntary Plan vs. FEPC," transcript of testimony presented to the Board of Supervisors, City and County of San Francisco, May 14, 1951, WCRF, NAACP Papers (hereafter cited as "Fair Employment for San Francisco"); interview with Seaton W. Manning, June 17, 1976, San Francisco.

21. Manning to Lester Granger, June 15, 1950, NUL Papers; testimony of R. J. Reynolds, president of the San Francisco Branch, NAACP, "Fair Employment for San Francisco," WCRF, NAACP Papers; *Sun-Reporter*, October 19, 1957.

22. Summary of Findings and Conclusions, "Fair Employment for San Francisco," WCRF, NAACP Papers.

23. List of Members, "Fair Employment for San Francisco," pp. 2–3, 6, WCRF, NAACP Papers. The best studies of white attitudes toward black intellect remain George M. Fredrickson, *The Black Image in the White Mind: The Debate on Afro-American Character and Destiny, 1817–1914* (New York: Harper and Row, 1971), and I. A. Newby, *Jim Crow's Defense: Anti-Negro Thought in America, 1900–1930* (Baton Rouge: Louisiana State University Press, 1965). To date, no study has examined white attitudes toward black intellect and character during the 1940s and 1950s.

24. "Fair Employment for San Francisco," pp. 6–7, WCRF, NAACP Papers. The historian William H. Harris argues that the inability to gain access to training programs remained a critical problem of black workers into the 1970s. See Harris, *The Harder We Run*, pp. 187–88.

25. "Fair Employment for San Francisco," pp. 12–13, WCRF, NAACP Papers.

26. Ibid., p. 6.

27. Ibid., pp. 13–14, 16.

28. Ibid., p. 22.

29. Manning to Granger, June 15, 1950, NUL Papers. For a broader discussion of the National Urban League's relationship with the business community, consult Nancy Weiss, *The National Urban League, 1910–1940* (New York: Oxford University Press, 1974). Arvarh E. Strickland examines the role of a local Urban League during the postwar years. See Strickland, *History of the Chicago Urban League* (Urbana: University of Illinois Press, 1966).

30. "Employment Practices in Private Industry," pp. 19–22, WCRF, NAACP Papers.

31. Ibid., pp. 24–25.

32. Edward Howden to Herman H. Long, October 13, 1954, Race Relations Department; Long to Howden, October 25, 1954, both from the Homeland Ministries Archives, Amistad Research Center, Tulane University, New Orleans; "Employment Practices in Private Industry," pp. 5–7, WCRF, NAACP Papers; Irving Babow and Edward Howden, *A Civil Rights Inventory of San Francisco, Part 1, Employment* (San Francisco, 1958), p. 1.

33. "Employment Practices in Private Industry," pp. 37–38, WCRF, NAACP Papers; Babow and Howden, *A Civil Rights Inventory of San Francisco,* pp. 303–04.

34. Ibid., pp. 25–28.

35. Ibid., pp. 25–28.

36. "Fourth Annual Report of the San Francisco Urban League, for the Year Ending December 31, 1949," NUL Papers; interview with Josephine Cole, December 9, 1976, San Francisco; interview with Katherine Flippin, February 17, 1976, San Francisco. "Employment Practices in Private Industry," pp. 31–32; Franklin H. Williams to [Education] Commissioner of California, February 9, 1954; J. Burton Vasche to Franklin H. Williams, February 17, 1954; Lucile Conrey to Franklin H. Williams, March 16, 1954, all from the WCRF, NAACP Papers. In a related case, the San Francisco Civil Service Commission disqualified all but three black colleges, Fisk, Talledega, and Howard, from consideration on job applications that required college degrees. The San Francisco branch of the NAACP appealed the ruling and subsequently overturned the decision in the First Appellate Division of the District Court of Appeals. See undated typescript in the SFBF, NAACP Papers during the 1950s. See also *Sun-Reporter,* February 9, 1952.

37. "Employment Practices in Private Industry," p. 37, WCRF, NAACP Papers; Babow and Howden, *A Civil Rights Inventory of San Francisco,* p. 304; *Sun-Reporter,* June 4, June 16, and August 6, 1955, March 3, 1956, August 3 and August 10, 1957. The Yellow Cab Company in San Francisco did not hire its first black cab driver until August 1957. "NAACP Monthly Report," June 8 and July 24, 1955, WCRF, NAACP Papers.

38. "Employment Practices in Private Industry," p. 40, WCRF, NAACP Papers.

39. Ibid., pp. 37–38; *A Civil Rights Inventory of San Francisco,* p. 149.

40. *1950 Census of Population, Detailed Characteristics of the Population, California,* pp. 5-463, 5-466.

41. Ibid., p. 5-463.

42. "Employment Practices in Private Industry," p. 325; Gunnar Myrdal, *An American Dilemma: The Negro Problem and Modern Democracy*, 2 vols. (New York: Harper and Row, 1944); memorandum, Seaton W. Manning to Lester B. Granger, n.d., NUL Papers; Babow and Howden; *A Civil Rights Inventory of San Francisco*, pp. 305–06.

43. "Employment Practices in Private Industry," pp. 42–43, WCRF, NAACP Papers.

44. August Meier and Elliott Rudwick, *Black Detroit and the Rise of the UAW* (New York: Oxford University Press, 1979), pp. 207–15; Stephan Thernstrom, *The Other Bostonians: Poverty and Progress in the American Metropolis, 1880–1970* (Harvard University Press, 1973), pp. 197–203.

CHAPTER 13. THE MATURATION OF BLACK SAN FRANCISCO: HOUSING, AUTONOMY, AND POLITICS

1. Seaton Manning to Lester B. Granger, June 15, 1950, National Urban League Papers, Library of Congress, Washington, D.C. (hereafter cited as NUL Papers); Los Angeles, *California Eagle*, September 10, 1942, February 10, March 3, March 24, May 27, July 1, July 8, July 29, and September 23, 1943, January 18, 1945.

2. *Sun-Reporter*, April 7, 1951, January 16, 1954, September 11, 1954.

3. "Annual Report," n.d., [1953–1954], San Francisco Branch files, NAACP Papers, Library of Congress, Washington, D.C. (hereafter cited as SFBF, NAACP Papers); *Sun-Reporter*, May 1, 1954.

4. Seaton Manning to Lester B. Granger, January 28, 1948; Granger to Manning, January 28, 1948; Manning to Granger, January 2, 1948, all in the NUL Papers; *Sun-Reporter*, January 16, 1954. See also Kenneth T. Jackson, "Race, Ethnicity, and Real Estate Appraisal: The Home Owners Loan Corporation and the Federal Housing Administration," *Journal of Urban History* 6 (August 1980): 419–52.

5. U.S. Bureau of the Census, *United States Census of Population, 1950, Bulletin P-D49* (Washington, D.C.: Government Printing Office, 1952), pp. 7–9; Ottole Krebs, "The Post-War Negro in San Francisco," senior thesis, Mills College, 1949, pp. 568–71.

6. Alice Griffith, "A Review of the Proceedings of the Housing Authority of San Francisco, April 17, 1938–August 17, 1943," Stewart-Flippin Papers, Moorland-Spingarn Research Center, Bancroft Library, University of California, Berkeley; "Resolution No. 287," resolution declaring policy of selection of tenants re: "All Projects," May 28, 1942, West Coast Regional Files, NAACP Papers, Bancroft Library University of California, Berkeley (hereafter cited as WCRF, NAACP Papers).

7. *Sixth Annual Report of the San Francisco Housing Authority, 1944*, San Francisco Housing Authority, San Francisco; interview with Edward Howden, June 7, 1983, San Francisco; NAACP, "Monthly Report," November, 1945, April 1946, May, 1949, January, 1950, WCRF, NAACP Papers.

8. "Resolution No. 287," WCRF, NAACP Papers.

9. Loren Miller, *The Petitioners: The Story of the Supreme Court of the United States and the Negro* (Cleveland: World, 1966); Richard Kluger, *Simple Justice: The History of Brown v. Board of Education and Black America's Struggle for*

Equality (New York: Alfred A. Knopf, 1975), pp. 312, 317, 803, 808–9; G. James Fleming and Christian E. Burckel, eds., *Who's Who in Colored America*, 7th ed., 1950, p. 374.

10. "Open Letter," Terry A. Francois, November 17, 1959, C. L. Dellums Papers, Bancroft Library, University of California, Berkeley. *San Francisco Chronicle*, December 19, 1955; *San Francisco News Call*, August 26, 1964; *Chronicle*, July 9 and July 10, 1963. Biographical information on Francois may also be found in the biographical index of the San Francisco Public Library, Special Collections.

11. *Chronicle*, October 3, 1952; interview with John Beard, conducted by Herman H. Long., n.d., Homeland Ministries Archives, Amistad Research Center, Tulane University; *Examiner*, October 8 and September 11, 1952.

12. *Examiner*, October 8, 1952.

13. Ibid.; *Chronicle*, October 9, 1952; excerpts from reporter's transcript, *Banks v. Housing Authority*, n.d., WCRF, NAACP Papers; petition in the Superior Court of California, *Mattie Banks v. the Housing Authority of the City and County of San Francisco*, 1952, copy in WCRF, NAACP Papers.

14. *Examiner*, September 11, 1952. Almon E. Roth represented the San Francisco Housing Authority at the trial proceedings. Roth had been a prominent figure in the San Francisco Employers Council, which opposed a mandatory Fair Employment Practices Commission for San Francisco. Consult "Fair Employment for San Francisco? Voluntary Plan vs. FEPC," transcript of testimony presented to the Board of Supervisors, City and County of San Francisco, May 14, 1951, WCRF, NAACP Papers.

15. *San Francisco News*, October 1, 1952; *Mattie Banks v. San Francisco Housing Authority*, "Statement of the Court"; affidavit of Mattie Banks, No. 15685; *Banks v. San Francisco Housing Authority*, "Findings of Fact and Conclusions of Law," November 7, 1952, all from the WCRF, NAACP Papers.

16. "Answer of Respondents," *Banks v. San Francisco Housing Authority*, WCRF, NAACP Papers.

17. *Chronicle*, October 21, 1952.

18. Robert Pitts to Franklin H. Williams, September 12, 1952, WCRF, NAACP Papers. By the early 1960s, the public housing projects had become segregated largely along racial lines.

19. "Affidavit in Support of Motion That Appeal Not Operate to Stay Execution and That the Matter Be Retained on Calendar for Further Proceedings," *Banks v. San Francisco Housing Authority*, October 17, 1952; *Banks v. San Francisco Housing Authority in the Supreme Court, State of California*, October 14, 1953; Terry A. Francois to San Francisco Housing Authority, February 6, 1953; Lester P. Bailey to Franklin H. Williams, April 13, 1954, all from WCRF, NAACP Papers.

20. Miller, *The Petitioners*, pp. 328–29.

21. Consult the annual reports of the San Francisco Housing Authority to see the demand for low-income housing in San Francisco between 1940 and 1965. Interview with Edward Howden, June 7, 1983, San Francisco; "Racial Distribution of Public Housing Units," n.d., WCRF, NAACP Papers; *New York Times*, February 27, 1955; *San Francisco Housing Authority, Twenty-Seventh Annual Report, 1964–65* (San Francisco: City and County of San Francisco, 1965).

22. Terry Francois to Franklin H. Williams, June 22, 1954; Edward Howden to Franklin H. Williams, March 20, 1953, both from WCRF, NAACP Papers; interview with Edward Howden, June 7, 1983, San Francisco; Gloria Harrison,

"The NAACP in California," M.A. thesis, Stanford University, 1949. Harrison's thesis is useful in examining broad issues within NAACP branches throughout California, even though she minimizes the dissension within the San Francisco branch and did not consult the San Francisco branch files for the 1940s.

23. Kluger, *Simple Justice*, p. 249, 272–74, 342–44. Franklin Williams to Peter Straus, April 8, 1955; Williams to Sam Chassler, September 24, 1958, and Chassler to Williams, September 22, 1958; Williams to editor, *Sun-Reporter*, March 30, 1959, all from the WCRF, NAACP Papers.

24. Interview with Mrs. Noah Griffin, June 21, 1976, San Francisco; Kluger, *Simple Justice*, pp. 272–74; Jackie Robinson, *I Never Had It Made*, (Greenwich, Conn.: Fawcett Publications, 1972), pp. 125–30. Robinson was elected to the National Board of Directors of the NAACP and knew Franklin Williams intimately. Gloster B. Current to Annie L. Barnett, April 30, 1951; Roy Wilkins to C. L. Dellums, March 15, 1951, both from the Dellums Papers; *Who's Who among Black Americans, 1980–81*, 3d ed. (Northbrook, Ill.: Who's Who among Black Americans Publishing, 1981), p. 859; Franklin Williams to Peter Straus, April 8, 1955, WCRF, NAACP Papers.

25. "Comparative Study of West Coast Branches," n.d.; memo, Everett P. Brandon to Executive Committee, San Francisco, NAACP, January 14, 1960; Thurgood Marshall to Franklin Williams, March 27, 1953, and February 24, 1955, all from WCRF, NAACP Papers.

26. Noah W. Griffin to Walter White, September 13, 1946; "NAACP Press Release, Infiltration," March 11, 1948, both from the WCRF, NAACP Papers. Bernice Cofer to Walter White, April 8, 1947; Gloster B. Current to Mrs. Anthony M. Hart, May 20, 1947; Wilkins to Griffin, April 14, 1947; Griffin to Wilkins, July 28, 1947; Buell Gallagher to Roy Wilkins, n.d.; Terresa Griffin to Roy Wilkins, January 12, 1949; Walter White to Gloster B. Current, January 21, 1947; Pauline Wood to Walter White, January 12, 1948; White to Wood, February 18, 1948, all from the SFBF, NAACP Papers. Noah Griffin was so concerned over Communist influence within the San Francisco branch that he recommended that the national office suspend the branch charter "pending a complete investigation." See Noah Griffin to Roy Wilkins, November 21, 1949, SFBF, NAACP Papers.

27. Walter White to Noah Griffin, November 8, 1946, WCRF, NAACP Papers.

28. "Communist Suspects"; "Don't Get Sucked In," n.d., both from WCRF, NAACP Papers.

29. "Minutes of the Sub-Committee of the Committee on Political Domination," November 22, 1950, WCRF, NAACP Papers.

30. Kluger, *Simple Justice*, passim; Robert H. Brisbane, *The Black Vanguard: Origins of the Negro Social Revolution, 1900–1960* (Valley Forge, Pa.: Judson Press, 1970), pp. 237–47; Wilson Record, *The Negro and the Communist Party* (Chapel Hill: University of North Carolina Press, 1951), pp. 265–72; Wilson Record, *Race and Radicalism: The NAACP and the Communist Party in Conflict* (Ithaca, N.Y.: Cornell University Press, 1964), pp. 130–39, 141–46. See also Record, "Some Historical, Structural and Functional Differences between the NAACP and the Communist Party of the United States," August 1957, WCRF, NAACP Papers.

31. Walter White to members of the Board of Directors, December 20, 1950, WCRF, NAACP Papers.

32. "Excerpts from Resolutions Adopted by the NAACP Forty-Second Annual Convention, Anti-Communism," June 30, 1951; "Stalin's Greatest Defeat,"

American Magazine 152 (December 1951): 21, 107–110; "Forty-Fourth Annual Conference Resolutions," St. Louis, June 23–28, 1953, pp. 3, 10, all in the WCRF, NAACP Papers. Herbert Hill, "The Communist Party—Enemy of Negro Equality," *Crisis* 58 (June–July 1951): 365–71, 421–24.

33. "The NAACP and the Communists," *Crisis* 56 (March 1949): 72.

34. William H. Chafe, *The Unfinished Journey: America since World War II* (New York: Oxford University Press, 1986), pp. 97–101.

35. Roy Wilkins to William L. Patterson, November 23, 1949; Franklin Williams to Walter White, February 16, 1952; Franklin Williams to John Flowers, March 19, 1952, all in the WCRF, NAACP Papers. Record, *The Negro and the Communist Party*, pp. 265–66, 272.

36. Franklin Williams to Roy Wilkins, March 19, 1954, WCRF, NAACP Papers; *Chicago Defender*, February 16, 1952.

37. George Breitman to West Coast Regional Office, April 7, 1954; Franklin Williams to Henry Lee Moon, April 23, 1954; Williams to Wilkins, March 19, 1954; Tarea Pittman to Gloster B. Current, October 15, 1953, all in the WCRF, NAACP Papers.

38. Franklin Williams to editor, *People's World*, March 5, 1954; Al Richmond to Franklin Williams, March 29, 1954, both in the WCRF, NAACP Papers. Al Richmond, *A Long View from the Left: Memoirs of an American Revolutionary* (New York: Dell, 1972). For the start of the *Daily People's World*, consult Alexander Richmond, *Ten Years: The Story of a People's Newspaper* (San Francisco: Daily People's World, 1948).

39. Lester P. Bailey to Roy Wilkins, Gloster Current, and Franklin Williams, March 5, 1954; *Stewards News*, February 11, 1954; Williams to Henry Lee Moon, July 19, 1954; "NAACP News," November 1–2, 1951, all in the WCRF, NAACP Papers.

40. Franklin Williams to John Flowers, March 19, 1952; Helen Wheeler to Williams, December 20, 1951; Hugh Bryson to Williams, October 16, 1950, all in the WCRF, NAACP Papers.

41. Franklin Williams to Dr. May Edward Chinn, September 6, 1955, WCRF, NAACP Papers.

42. R. J. Reynolds, "The Negro and Crime in San Francisco, Final Report," September 1, 1947, WCRF, NAACP Papers. Biographical material on Reynolds can be found in "NAACP Press Release," April 29, 1947, WCRF, NAACP Papers.

43. Reynolds, "The Negro and Crime," pp. 4–7, 11–12. Charles Silberman arrived at a conclusion similar to Reynolds's in his study of American crime and violence, *Criminal Violence, Criminal Justice* (New York: Random House, 1978), pp. 163–65.

44. Reynolds, "The Negro and Crime," pp. 11–12.

45. *California Eagle*, November 20 and November 27, 1947. Gloster B. Current to Carlton Goodlet[t], November 28, 1947; Noah Griffin to Current, November 15, 1947, both in SFBF, NAACP Papers; *Sun-Reporter*, August 18, 1951, July 24, 1954, July 31, 1954, June 2, 1951.

46. *Sun-Reporter*, June 9, June 16, June 23, and October 2, 1951.

47. Ibid., June 9, June 16, and June 23, 1951.

48. Ibid., June 23, 1951.

49. Donn Rogosin, *Invisible Men: Life in Baseball's Negro Leagues* (New York: Atheneum, 1983); Jules Tygiel, *Baseball's Great Experiment: Jackie Robinson and His Legacy* (New York: Oxford University Press, 1983); Rob Ruck, *Sandlot Seasons: Sport in Black Pittsburgh* (Urbana: University of Illinois Press, 1987),

passim; Janet Bruce, *The Kansas City Monarchs: Champions of Black Baseball* (Lawrence: University Press of Kansas, 1985), p. 83; Joe Louis with Edna and Art Rust, Jr., *Joe Louis: My Life* (New York: Harcourt, Brace, Jovanovich, 1978); St. Clair Drake and Horace Cayton, *Black Metropolis: A Study of Negro Life in a Northern City*, vol. 2, rev. ed. (New York: Harcourt, Brace, and World, 1970), pp. 470–94; Donna Barnhill, "The Sun-Reporter: Its Role as a Negro Weekly in San Francisco Bay Area Negro Community," M.A. thesis, San Francisco State College, 1965, p. 25; James Borchert, *Alley Life in Washington: Family, Community, Religion, and Folklife in the City, 1850–1970* (Urbana: University of Illinois Press, 1980), pp. 182, 186.

50. *Sun-Reporter*, June 23, June 30, July 7, July 21, and August 11, 1951, February 23 and April 26, 1952, May 1, 1954.

51. *California Eagle*, April 16 and October 15, 1942, January 8, October 7, and November 4, 1943; "Walter Gordon, Athlete, Officer in Law Enforcement and Administration, Governor of the Virgin Islands," interview conducted by the Bancroft Regional Oral History Office, 1976–1979, Bancroft Library, University of California, Berkeley. For another view of Warren by a black, see Edgar James Patterson, "Governor's Mansion Aide to Prison Counselor," interview conducted by the Bancroft Regional Oral History Office, 1975.

52. *Sun-Reporter*, July 28, 1951.

53. Ibid., December 1, 1951, April 26, 1952.

54. *Chronicle*, February 26, 1950; *Sun-Reporter*, July 28 and August 4, 1951, June 21, 1952.

55. *Sun-Reporter*, January 10, 1953. For a discussion of the demise of segregation in the California National Guard, consult the *American Civil Liberties Union News*, October 1947 and July 1949; *Sun-Reporter*, April 26, 1952, June 21, 1952, August 15, 1953, February 27, 1954.

56. Earl Warren, *The Memoirs of Chief Justice Earl Warren* (Garden City, N.Y.: Doubleday, 1977), pp. 260–61; Harvard Sitkoff, *The Black Struggle for Equality, 1954–1980* (New York: Hill and Wang, 1981), pp. 22–25; Kluger, *Simple Justice*, pp. 840–43, 887–94.

57. *Sun-Reporter*, October 27, 1951, September 18, 1953, November 21, 1953.

58. Ibid., July 21, 1953; "NAACP Press Release," December 1949, WCRF, NAACP Papers. For information concerning Poole's later political appointments, see the *Chronicle*, December 16, 1958, July 7, 1961, October 9, 1964, December 20, 1965, June 19, 1976; *Examiner*, July 26, 1976.

59. *Sun-Reporter*, July 25 and March 14, 1943; *Who's Who in Colored America, 1950*, p. 490. See the undated [1961] biographical clipping of James Stratten naming his appointment to the San Francisco Board of Education in 1961, carton 39, WCRF, NAACP Papers.

60. *Sun-Reporter*, November 3 and November 10, 1951, January 12, January 19, June 7, October 18, and November 1, 1952, March 14 and August 1, 1953; Gloster B. Current, "Research Report for Hill for Council Committee," n.d., carton 12, WCRF, NAACP Papers; John B. McGloin, *San Francisco: The Story of a City* (San Rafael, Calif.: Presidio Press, 1978), pp. 330–31.

61. *Sun-Reporter*, June 5, 1954.

62. Ibid., February 13, May 1, May 29, and June 12, 1954; McGloin, *San Francisco: The Story of a City*, pp. 331–33.

63. *Sun-Reporter*, September 1, 1951; "Haynes Transcript," n.d., transcript of an interview of Reverend Haynes on radio station KYA, San Francisco; "Haynes Broadcast," transcript of interview of Reverend Haynes on radio station KSAN,

November 1 [1951], San Francisco, both from the Stewart-Flippin Papers; Martin Kilson, "Adam Clayton Powell, Jr.: The Militant as Politician," in John Hope Franklin and August Meier, eds., *Black Leaders of the Twentieth Century* (Urbana: University of Illinois Press, 1982), pp. 259–75.

64. "Haynes Broadcast," Stewart-Flippin Papers. For information on Haynes's church during the 1940s, consult the *California Eagle*, September 3, 1942, and August 12, 1943.

65. "Haynes Transcript" and "Haynes Broadcast," Stewart-Flippin Papers; *Sun-Reporter*, November 14, 1953.

66. Mary Melcher, "Blacks and Whites Together: Interracial Leadership in the Phoenix Civil Rights Movement," *Journal of Arizona History* 32 (Summer 1991): 195–216; Bradford Luckingham, *The Urban Southwest: A Profile History of Albuquerque, El Paso, Phoenix, and Tucson* (El Paso: Texas Western Press, 1982), pp. 124–25.

EPILOGUE: THE DREAM AND THE REALITY

1. *Sun-Reporter*, January 16, 1954.

2. Herb Caen, *Herb Caen's San Francisco* (New York: Doubleday, 1965), p. 17.

3. *Sun-Reporter*, January 16, 1954.

4. Ibid., May 1, 1954.

5. Statement by Franklin H. Williams to Cole, n.d. [1952–1953], carton 39, West Coast Regional Files, NAACP Papers, Bancroft Library, University of California, Berkeley (hereafter cited as WCRF, NAACP Papers).

6. Kenneth T. Jackson, "Race, Ethnicity, and Real Estate Appraisal: The Home Owners' Loan Corporation and the Federal Housing Administration," *Journal of Urban History* 6 (August 1980): p. 447; Kenneth T. Jackson, *Crabgrass Frontier: The Suburbanization of the United States* (New York: Oxford University Press, 1985), pp. 195–203.

7. *Sun-Reporter*, November 23, 1957; *San Francisco News*, November 14, 1957; Oakland, *California Voice*, November 22, 1957; Mayor George Christopher to Willie Mays, November 14, 1957, WCRF, NAACP Papers; Pittsburgh *Courier*, November 23, 1957; "Housing A Giant," *Council for Civic Unity Newsletter*, December 5, 1957, copy in my possession, a gift from Edward Howden; memo from Edward Howden on the "Willie Mays Incident," November 27, 1957, WCRF, NAACP Papers.

8. "Statement on Housing," Tarea H. Pittman, acting regional secretary, NAACP, to the United States Commission on Civil Rights, January 27–28, 1960, 17 p., WCRF, NAACP Papers.

9. Arnold R. Hirsch, *Making the Second Ghetto: Race and Housing in Chicago, 1940–1960* (New York: Cambridge University Press, 1983); Emory Tolbert and Lawrence B. de Graaf, "The Unseen Minority: Blacks in Orange County," *Journal of Orange County Studies* 3/4 (Fall 1989/Spring 1991): 54–61.

10. *Sun-Reporter*, August 2 and August 16, 1958; Irving Babow and Edward Howden, *A Civil Rights Inventory of San Francisco, Part 1, Employment* (San Francisco: Council for Civil Rights Inventory, 1958), pp. 304–306; *Sun-Reporter*, January 16, 1954.

11. *Sun-Reporter*, June 21, 1958; undated biographical clipping of James Stratten, WCRF, NAACP Papers; *San Francisco Examiner*, March 27, 1961, p. 32; Rudolph Lapp, *Afro-Americans in California* (San Francisco: Boyd and

Fraser Publishing, 1979), p. 55; *Examiner*, June 9, 1961; *Chronicle*, July 7, 1961; *San Francisco News Call*, August 24 and August 26, 1964; *Chronicle*, October 6, 1976; *Examiner*, July 26, 1976; *Chronicle*, October 12, 1979; *San Francisco Housing Authority, Twenty-Seventh Annual Report, 1964–65* (San Francisco: City and County of San Francisco, 1965) p. 1.

12. Arthur E. Hippler, *Hunter's Point: A Black Ghetto* (New York: Basic Books, 1974), pp. 203–14; McGloin, *San Francisco: The Story of a City* (San Raphael, Calif.: Presidio Press, 1978), pp. 334–35.

13. Taylor, "Blacks and Asians in a White City: Japanese Americans and African Americans in Seattle, 1890–1940," Western Historical Quarterly 22 (November 1991): 401–29.

14. On Richmond, California, see Shirley Ann Moore, "Getting There, Being There: African-American Migration to Richmond, California, 1910–1945," paper presented at the annual meeting of the Western Historical Association, 1990, Reno, Nevada.

15. Jacqueline Jones, *Labor of Love, Labor of Sorrow: Black Women, Work, and the Family from Slavery to the Present* (New York: Basic Books, 1985), p. 4.

16. Lawrence B. de Graaf, "From Virtual Exclusion to Limited Assimilation: Blacks in Orange County, 1940–1980," p. 17, paper presented at the annual meeting of the Western Historical Association, Reno, Nevada, 1990.

17. de Graaf, "From Virtual Exclusion to Limited Assimilation," p. 18.

18. Stephan Thernstrom, *The Other Bostonians: Poverty and Progress in the American Metropolis, 1880–1970* (Cambridge, Mass.: Harvard University Press, 1973), p. 199.

19. Ibid., p. 200.

20. Ibid., p. 202; U.S. Bureau of the Census, *1950 Census of Population: Detailed Characteristics of the Population, California* (Washington, D.C.: Government Printing Office, 1950), pp. 5-463, 5-466.

21. Alonzo Smith and Quintard Taylor, "Racial Discrimination in the Workplace: A Study of Two West Coast Cities during the 1940s," *Journal of Ethnic Studies* 8 (Spring 1980): 35–54.

22. Mary Melcher, "Blacks and Whites Together: Interracial Leadership in the Phoenix Civil Rights Movement," Journal of Arizona History 32 (Summer 1991): 195–216; Gerald D. Nash, *The American West Transformed: The Impact of the Second World War* (Bloomington: Indiana University Press, 1985), p. 106; George M. Fredrickson, *The Black Image in the White Mind: The Debate On Afro-American Character and Destiny, 1817–1914* (New York, 1971), pp. 320–21.

INDEX